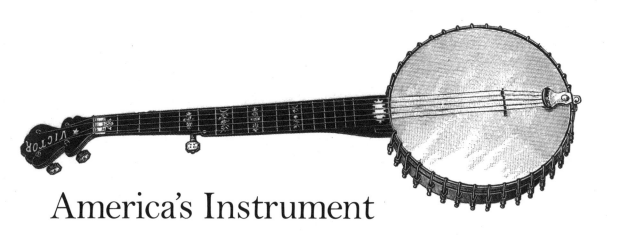

America's Instrument

The Banjo in the Nineteenth Century

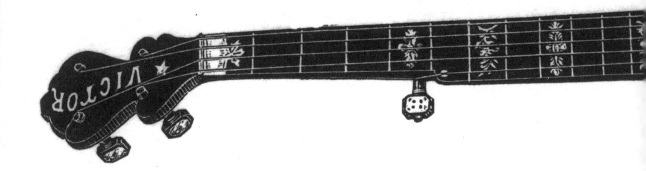

Philip F. Gura & James F. Bollman

America's Instrument

The University of North Carolina Press   Chapel Hill & London

© 1999
The University of North Carolina Press
All rights reserved
Designed by Richard Hendel
Set in Monotype Bell and Didot
by Eric M. Brooks
Manufactured in the United States of America
The paper in this book meets the guidelines for
permanence and durability of the Committee on
Production Guidelines for Book Longevity of the
Council on Library Resources.

Unless otherwise noted, all illustrations come from
the James F. Bollman Collection. We would like to
thank Fred Stipe for the black-and-white photography
and Donald F. Eaton and Peter Szego for the color.

Library of Congress Cataloging-in-Publication Data
Gura, Philip F., 1950–
America's instrument: the banjo in the nineteenth century /
Philip F. Gura and James F. Bollman.
     p.   cm.
Includes bibliographical references and index.
ISBN 0-8078-2484-4 (cloth: alk. paper)
1. Banjo—United States—History—19th century.
I. Bollman, James F.   II. Title.
ML1015.B3G87   1999
787.8'81973'09034—dc21   98-46164
                              CIP
                              MN

03 02 01 00 99   5 4 3 2 1

The piano may do for love-sick girls who lace themselves to skeletons, and lunch on chalk, pickles, and slate pencils. But give me the banjo. Gottschalk compared to Sam Pride or Charley Rhoades, is as a Dashaway Cocktail to a hot whisky punch. When you want genuine music—*music that will come right home to you like a bad quarter, suffuse your system like strychnine whisky, go right through you like Brandreth's pills, ramify your whole constitution like the measles, and break out on your hide like the pin-feather pimples on a pickled goose*—when you want all this, just smash your piano, and invoke the glory-beaming banjo!
— Mark Twain, 1865

The Banjo, as an instrument, has long needed a book of this kind; something that could be read with interest by those who know nothing about the Banjo; and at the same time, a book that gives valuable hints to those who are students. A work that is neatly gotten up, and as a volume is attractive for the centre-table or for the book-shelves.
— S. S. Stewart, 1888

During his latest appearance at Keith's Theatre . . . Mr. E. M. Hall, the famous banjoist and comedian, introduced an interesting novelty in illustrating the changes of style in playing the banjo, which the instrument has undergone during the past sixty years. . . . The audience places itself en rapport *with the speaker at once, for the history of the banjo is comparatively unknown to the general public, let alone the banjo fraternity.*
—Gatcomb's Musical Gazette, *1897*

The modern banjo is known throughout the world as the product of America, and as its National Musical Instrument.
—*American Guild of Banjoists, Mandolinists and Guitarists, 1900*

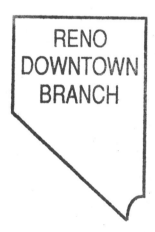

CONTENTS

Selections of color illustrations follow pages 48, 112, 176, and 240.

PREFACE

This book is unlike most coauthored works published by university presses, for it is not the result of the labors of two similarly trained individuals who in different ways or in different sections have done the same kinds of work. Rather, it is an unusual collaboration between a cultural historian and a world-renowned collector. From its inception five years ago, this project has been special. It began with my realization that the age of the connoisseur, epitomized by great nineteenth- and early-twentieth-century collectors who literally created whole fields of study in such areas as art history, bibliography, or the antique trades, had not ended. Among other things, this volume demonstrates the importance, even in the twenty-first century, of the single-minded assembly of a unique collection.

Over thirty years ago James F. Bollman began to assemble what has become this country's largest collection, in public or private hands, of rare nineteenth- and early-twentieth-century banjos and banjo-related materials. In addition to approximately three hundred instruments made between the 1840s and 1920s, he holds thousands of photographic images (including daguerreotypes, ambrotypes, and tintypes, as well as photographs in various paper formats), lithographed sheet-music covers, trade catalogs and other advertising ephemera, periodicals devoted to the banjo trade, decorative ceramics and statuary, paintings, toys, and, for lack of a better word, a seemingly endless assortment of Victorian bric-a-brac that has the banjo as a theme. His is quite simply a museum collection and he the master curator.

I first learned of Jim's collection as a budding musician who was pointed in his direction if I wanted to purchase a fine vintage instrument. As I got to know him better, I was impressed by both his unparalleled knowledge of the banjo's history and the generosity with which he shared his priceless collection. As an academic in the interdisciplinary field of American studies who had drifted into music history, first as a hobby and then as an outgrowth of an interest in nineteenth-century popular culture, I began to realize that the range and depth of his collection might form the basis for a detailed scholarly history of the development of the banjo, from its

African American folk roots in the colonial period through its golden age of popularity at the turn of the twentieth century.

For a traditional scholar like myself the remarkable thing to understand was that I could better write such a book in Jim's home, near Boston, Massachusetts, than I could in the university and public libraries of that area, institutions considered among the world's finest. Indeed, the only public collections that complement his are found at the New York Public Library and the Library of Congress, but in most cases his runs of periodicals and examples of advertising ephemera equal or exceed the holdings of these repositories.

Our relationship with regard to this invaluable collection began slowly and carefully, with my borrowing a selected item here or there to quell my curiosity on some subject. That trust was greatly increased when he consented to my transcribing and publishing an essay from a remarkable primary source he then owned, the manuscript account book of the Connecticut guitar and banjo maker James Ashborn. The positive reception that met this work boosted my confidence, and I decided to approach Jim with the idea to collaborate on a wide-ranging study of the banjo in nineteenth-century America. This volume is the result.

From the beginning, we knew that our respective contributions would differ. Jim provided the raw materials and the immense body of knowledge about banjos, particularly about extant instruments themselves, that he had built up over three decades. With my interest in music history and cultural history generally, I provided the organization, an interpretive narrative based in large measure on his collection of printed and graphic materials and augmented by our many conversations at his home, his business, or the many music festivals we have attended together over the past decade. After drafting a section of the manuscript, I would send it to Jim, who checked its accuracy and completeness. As one might expect, his commentary demonstrated a mastery of the subject in all its particulars. In good measure the utility of this book derives from his particular kinds of knowledge.

Along the way we have been assisted by a number of banjo enthusiasts who have shared their own collections and knowledge and thus have enabled us to make this a stronger volume. Prominent among these is Peter Szego, whose collection of minstrel-era banjos is the envy of many of us (including Jim himself). We thank Peter for sharing his riches and for consenting to our inclusion of photographs of his important collection. Michael Holmes, who has been studying banjos as long as Jim has, and in particular has researched nineteenth- and early-twentieth-century instrument makers throughout the United States, always was willing to answer our questions, as seemingly unimportant as they were. Ed Britt, a designer and engineer by profession, has favored us with consultations on many of the finer technological points in the development of the banjo. Jim's long-time business partner and friend, Stu Cohen, has generously shared the wealth of his own knowledge and collections, particularly of banjo catalogs. Bob Carlin, fine musician and historian of fretted instruments, has always been available to share his immense knowledge of all things related to the banjo and its players.

My own forays into music history have been greatly assisted by professionals in that field who have labored therein much longer than I. In particular, I would like to thank Laurence Libin, Frederick P. Rose Curator-in-Charge of the Department of Musical Instruments at the Metropolitan Museum of Art, for his quick attention to my many inquiries. He also provided a detailed and highly attentive reading of the entire manuscript in an earlier draft. Likewise, Robert Eliason has clarified many questions of music history for us, as have Eli Kaufman and Robert Winans, themselves historians of the banjo.

I would particularly like to thank Bob Winans for sharing a presentation on S. S. Stewart with me at the Library Company of Philadelphia and to thank that institution's librarian, James Green, and his able staff, who tracked down some important documentation. Also very helpful, and infallibly courteous, were Joanne Chaison and other members of the staff at the American Antiquarian Society, which in 1998 generously granted me a Kate B. and Hall J. Peterson Fellowship for work on this project. Annette Fern at the Harvard Theatre Collection and Scott Odell and Gary Sturm at the Smithsonian Institution expedited the use of those marvelous repositories. We thank Stuart Frank, director of the Kendall Whaling Museum, for allowing us to include photographs of the unique whale-bone banjo in its collection. We also acknowledge Nancy, Donald, and Spencer Nitchie for their unbridled enthusiasm in promoting interest in the banjo, particularly through their publication of the *Banjo Newsletter*. Finally, the University Research Council at the University of North Carolina at Chapel Hill generously provided grants for photographic services and manuscript preparation.

I would like to thank John Pringle for his remarkable restoration of my nineteenth-century instruments, L. Michael Bell and Donald Eaton for teaching me the relation between three chords and the truth, and Bob Cantwell for his constant support at the coffee bar and elsewhere. Jim wishes to thank Alan Green for his early guidance into the mysteries of old banjos, and restoration artists Doug Unger, John Gough, Tom Stapleton, Mark Simon, Edie Schroeder, and Emery Hutchins for their sensitive repairs to many of his instruments and banjo-related items. He also acknowledges fellow fretted-instrument historians, collectors, and purveyors Dr. Bill Michal, Jim White, Stan Werbin, Leonard Coulson, Tony Creamer, John Bernunzio, George Gibson, Joe Hornung, Bob Hutton, Keith Wilson, and Roddy Moore, who are always ready to share their knowledge and expertise. Finally, Jim thanks his partner, Peggy Conant, for her forbearance during this project and for her assistance in explaining some of the intricacies of cyberspace.

We were fortunate to test some of our ideas in public forums. As noted above, the Library Company of Philadelphia provided one such opportunity, and another came at the American Antiquarian Society, where I gave a seminar on "Documenting the Early Minstrel Banjo." Jim and I gave another version of this talk as a lecture at the University of Virginia's pioneering conference on the antebellum banjo in 1997. The Daguerreian Society generously made available a different sort of forum at its annual meeting in 1998, where I lectured on documenting musical instruments through early photographic processes.

Finally, this book is also the result of countless conversations over decades among enthusiasts who offered parts of what became the intricate historical narrative we have tried to relate. We thank them all for their information and support, and we hope that this volume goes some way toward satisfying their endless curiosity.

Philip F. Gura
November 1998

A NOTE ON EARLY PHOTOGRAPHY

For readers unfamiliar with the early photographic processes referred to in our captions, we offer the following brief guide. In many cases these images can be dated to within a few years either through evidence regarding the photographic processes themselves or by identification of the photographers.

Cased Images

Daguerreotypes, ambrotypes, and tintypes are often referred to as "cased images" because they were mounted inside handsome wooden cases covered with leather or paper or in cases made from a mixture of shellac and wood fibers pressed into various designs that were themselves works of art. Such images often were framed with attractive brass mats and most commonly came in these sizes: *full plate* (6½ × 8½ inches), *half plate* (4½ × 5½ inches), *quarter plate* (3⅛ × 4⅛ inches), *sixth plate* (2⅝ × 3¼ inches), and *ninth plate* (2 × 2½ inches).

Daguerreotype: ca. 1839–65 (very few after 1860). Named after its French inventor, Louis Jacques Mandé Daguerre, this earliest photographic process consists of an image produced on a silver-coated copper plate. Of unusual clarity because the silver is highly polished (its surface resembles a mirror), daguerreotypes differ from other early photographic images in the artist's use of iodine for a sensitizing agent and mercury for a developer.

Ambrotype: ca. 1854–65. From the Greek "amber" (eternal), an ambrotype is an image produced on a glass plate that has been sensitized with silver nitrate and is developed with pyrogallic acid. The image appears on the glass as a negative and is made positive by the addition of a black backing, usually a lacquer applied to the back of the plate.

Tintype: ca. 1856 to late 1860s as a cased image, but produced in other forms through the early twentieth century. Also known as a *ferrotype* or *melainotype*, the tintype is a negative image on a thin piece of iron (hence, "ferrotype"; "tintype" is really a misnomer) and is viewed positively because of a black backing. Sensitizing and developing agents are the same as for ambrotypes.

Paper Images

Although before 1860 there were various attempts to fix images in paper from negatives, most notably by W. H. Fox Talbot in England, such processes did not become widespread in the United States until after that date. Unlike the English *calotype*, which was printed from a negative itself made on salted paper, the early American paper image was most commonly produced from a glass negative on paper coated with albumen, or egg white.

Albumen print: ca. 1850–1910; most popular between 1860 and 1890. A positive print on paper covered with egg whites (albumen). Made from a glass negative sensitized by silver nitrate and developed with pyrogallic acid. The first common paper photographic process. Photographs were in various sizes.

Carte-de-visite: ca. 1854 to about 1900; most popular in the 1860s. A small albumen print ($2\frac{1}{2} \times 3\frac{1}{2}$ inches) usually mounted on a slightly larger card.

Cabinet card: ca. 1863 to early twentieth century. A photographic print, sometimes albumen but also on gelatin-coated paper, usually $4 \times 5\frac{1}{2}$ inches and mounted on a slightly larger card.

Real-photo postcard: ca. 1900–1915. An inexpensive postcard-sized photograph intended to be mailed.

Stereograph: ca. 1851 through the early twentieth century. A pair of identical paper photographs (most commonly, either albumen or by some other inexpensive process), taken with a special camera with two lenses, intended for viewing through a stereoscope for a three-dimensional effect.

Image Reversal

In the early years of photography, images often were reversed; that is, they appeared as mirror images. Thus, a right-handed banjo player would appear left-handed. To appear right-handed, the subject holds the instrument left-handed, but when this is done, the fifth-string peg points downward. Such images accurately depict the right-handed players but give an erroneous impression of the instruments.

By the mid-1850s, Americans were awash in popular music. With the spread of laborsaving technology and the concomitant extension of leisure time, they not only flocked to musical theater and the minstrel shows but also purchased hundreds of thousands of pieces of sheet music intended for performance on the stage or in the parlor, the center of the new domestic sphere. Familiarity with such folios, songs meant to be accompanied on piano, flute, guitar, or, with increasing frequency, the banjo, as well as purely instrumental music, marked those who aspired to middle-class respectability. The phenomena of such immensely popular performers as the Hutchinson Family singers and Jenny Lind, the "Swedish Nightingale," who toured the United States to packed houses, and of composers such as Stephen Foster, whose song sheets were eagerly purchased by his admirers, signaled the nation's infatuation with popular music.[1]

But while we recently have learned much about the cultural role of music, what we might term its varied consumption in antebellum America, we know little about the production and distribution of the instruments used to accompany it. Given the pervasive interest in music in nineteenth-century culture, it is important to understand who produced musical instruments and how.[2] Moreover, because the interest in popular music coincided with an expanding economy that both required and engendered new distribution and market systems, studies of musical instrument makers allow us to understand better the transition from artisanal to factory production in this crucial period of America's economic expansion.[3] In this book, we seek to provide such a history of the manufacture and marketing of one of these popular instruments, the five-string banjo, which, as the renowned banjo designer and manufacturer David L. Day put it in 1905, "lays claim to being our national instrument." For "what the mandolin is to Italy," he continued, "and the guitar is to Spain, the banjo is to America."[4]

Although the banjo as we know it derives from African ancestors, in the early nineteenth century people most often associated it with the United States, particularly with images of the South and African American slavery.

It had been brought to the New World by enslaved Africans as early as the seventeenth century, but by the 1840s the instrument and its music were transformed by white, working-class musicians who made the banjo integral to a new popular entertainment, the minstrel show. Surrounded by other blackface performers on violin, tambourine, and bones, the banjoist anchored the minstrel line.[5] Using a slightly more sophisticated instrument than those which African Americans had built from long-necked gourds, the banjo player provided the melodic line to the plantation songs and dances that urban audiences flocked to hear.

Important as it was, however, this appropriation marked only the first chapter in the history of the banjo in nineteenth-century America, for subsequently the instrument and its music insinuated themselves more deeply into the nation's culture. In the aftermath of the Civil War, for example, the banjo was heard as often in the Victorian parlor as on the minstrel stage, accompaniment to the popular songs that marked an engagement with genteel culture. Amateur musicians quickly accepted the banjo as a substitute for the bulky and expensive piano or the more fragile "Spanish" guitar and sought to perform the same kinds of music upon it as on the other two. In response, innovative makers modified their instruments so that they might be played more easily in a "guitar" style. Moreover, the increased demand for instruments by new devotees helped to move banjo manufacture out of the artisans' shops into small-scale factories.

Public interest only increased through the 1880s and 1890s as stage personalities, no longer in blackface but attired as elegantly as European virtuosos, sold their endorsements to large banjo "manufacturers" who competed for a share of the vast new market for the instrument. To win and keep the allegiance of this new class of performers, whose celebrity was gained through astonishing technical mastery of the instrument, and of the many amateurs who emulated them, banjo companies designed ever more sophisticated instruments and made them in varying grades so that they were accessible to virtually all social classes. Moreover, banjos from this period often had ingeniously constructed tone rings or sound chambers to allow the music to carry in large concert halls, as well as elaborately inlaid and engraved pearl decoration to impress audiences with the beauty of the instruments.

While in this period the banjo was designed specifically for the concert hall, it was present throughout popular culture: in advertisements for foodstuffs, hardware, and dry goods; as a prop in popular fiction and drama; and as an integral part of the Victorian gewgaws—ceramic troubadours, cast-iron penny banks or frog clocks, paper valentines and tin toys—that decorated every home. So too was its music, perhaps nowhere more memorably than in the ubiquitous municipal and college banjo clubs and orchestras that rivaled brass bands in popularity as they performed ever more demanding music—most of it now composed specifically for this instrument—to audiences whose appetite for the latest march or mazurka seemed insatiable.[6] Thus, by the 1890s the Philadelphia banjo manufacturer S. S. Stewart, one of the largest of the new entrepreneurs in musical goods, could claim (without too much exaggeration) that each year he manufactured tens of thousands of banjos and shipped them literally around the world, as testimonials from his Australian customers proved.

Virtually omnipresent in both popular and high culture at the turn of the century, the five-stringed banjo abruptly ended its reign as America's instrument with the rise of ragtime and jazz. Encouraged in part by the new popularity of the mandolin, banjo manufacturers developed four-stringed "tenor" banjos that were similarly tuned in fifths and allowed vastly more chording possibilities than their five-stringed progenitors. By the 1920s the new companies—Epiphone, Paramount, and Bacon, among others—and even older manufacturers like Vega, concentrated their research and design, and their advertising, on new and very different instruments for professional musicians who had to be heard in twenty-piece big-band orchestras. The result was predictable: in the period from 1915 to 1940, production of five-stringed models comprised a mere fraction of total banjo manufacture.

Despite the banjo's centrality to nineteenth-century American music and culture, there has been no detailed study of its transformation from African folk origins into a sophisticated parlor and orchestra instrument. Indeed, as the renowned banjoist George C. Dobson put it in 1880, "the early history of the banjo is wrapped in obscurity." "Little is known concerning it," he continued, "save that in its present shape it seems to be almost the only distinctively American musical instrument."[7] Although musicologists might quarrel with Dobson's claim for the banjo's preeminence, his view was widely shared among his contemporaries.[8] Further, while we recently have learned in what ways the *idea* of the banjo impinged on American self-consciousness over two centuries, no one has essayed a history of how changes in musical taste affected the technology and business of banjo making.[9] *America's Instrument* traces the banjo's evolution from primitive gourd instrument to sophisticated musical machine, with particular attention to the ways in which craftsmen and manufacturers championed, built, and marketed their products to an American public immersed in the production or consumption of popular music.[10]

Admittedly this reconstruction is difficult, for as one writer noted in the

1920s, "the studious person who endeavors to trace the early history of the banjo" confronts the problem that "the most authentic stories of the banjo's beginnings are more or less legendary."[11] To be sure, some doubtful assertions about the banjo's development long have been uncritically accepted, and, particularly for the period before the Civil War, documentary information about the banjo and its manufacture is sporadic at best. However, for this work we have had access to remarkable collections of banjos and banjo-related materials assembled in the past thirty years that hitherto have not been systematically studied.

Thus, in addition to extant nineteenth-century instruments, we have examined hundreds of graphics, not only lithographed sheet-music covers that often depicted the instrument but also rare contemporary photographic images; large archives of advertising and other promotional material from nineteenth-century banjo makers and musical instrument dealers; and the various trade periodicals that serve as invaluable repositories of information about the instrument, its makers, and its consumers. From these and other sources we have assembled an interpretive history of the instrument that by 1880 was described as "having won its way to the hearts of the people of all classes alike" and whose "sweet, tender and idyllic music" was heard everywhere—"on the public stage," in "the home circle," and among "refined and fashionable society."[12]

We first review briefly the current state of knowledge about the origins of the banjo among families of sub-Saharan instruments, its early appearance in the Caribbean islands, and its presence among slaves in the plantation culture in the American South as well as among free blacks in the North. We then synthesize information concerning the emergence of minstrelsy in the 1840s, paying particular attention to how white banjo players involved in the minstrel theater discovered and learned to play the banjo. Because such individuals were primarily responsible for bringing the instrument from its obscure, rural roots to a much larger, urban audience, their reminiscences, along with contemporary evidence from minstrel broadsides and sheet-music covers, provide the means to reexamine the emergence of the banjo in the hands of white players. More important, such professional musicians' needs for sturdier and more dependable instruments prompted urban craftsmen to begin to produce banjos specifically for the minstrel stage, thus initiating the transition from folk instrument to marketable commodity, a passage also hastened by the appearance of the first tutors published specifically for the banjo.

We also present and interpret available information about the design, construction, and sale of banjos in the early minstrel period (1843–60), paying particular attention to initial attempts at refinement and standardization of the instrument's constituent parts. For example, the banjos that the first white players (usually members of circus troupes who performed with a "Negro" dancer) took on stage in the 1830s often had gourd bodies and just three or four strings, presumably as did the instruments used by plantation slaves.[13] But extant minstrel-era banjos, as well as contemporary daguerreotypes and ambrotypes of banjo players, indicate that by the late 1840s the banjo had become much more sophisticated. By then, most instruments had three-to-four-inch-deep rims (twelve to fourteen inches across) and five gut strings, one decidedly shorter than the others.[14] The wooden rim created a sturdier sound chamber than was found on gourd instruments, and metal brackets and hooks often replaced tacks for stretching the animal-skin "head" over the rim, allowing for easy adjustment of it when changes in humidity loosened the tension. Further, although there was considerable variation in the shape of the neck and peg head, the neck's length was usually long, in part because of the low tunings associated with the instrument in this period.[15]

In addition to generalizing about the physical form of banjos from this period, we emphasize how innovative craftsmen began to market themselves specifically as banjo makers. Although in most cases these individuals were engaged in the construction of other instruments as well—most commonly drums or guitars—by the 1850s such entrepreneurs as William Boucher of Baltimore, Maryland, and James Ashborn of Wolcottville, Connecticut, began to build banjos whose design makes clear their makers' serious reconsideration of the nature and function of the instruments, a fact not lost on those who sought to purchase them. Ashborn, for example, experimented with different tuning mechanisms as well as with a unique bracket band for attaching the head to the rim. Significantly, by the end of this period, as the manufacture of banjos grew more sophisticated, and potentially lucrative, he patented some of his innovations, an action that signaled the increased professionalization of the music industry.

We illustrate such changes by examining the financial records for Ashborn's guitar factory, where from the late 1840s through the early 1860s he turned out thousands of instruments for the New York City music market.[16] Although records of his banjo making are not extant, study of the ways in which he built, transported, and sold his guitars opens a window on the manufacture of antebellum stringed instruments in general. From Ashborn's accounting journal we learn, for example, about antebellum water-powered woodworking equipment, typical expenses for supplies and labor in a small mechanized factory, and the nature of financial arrangements with the New York musical world. These detailed financial accounts also suggest how Ashborn's modification of a traditional craft workshop through standardized and simplified construction methods might have applied as well to contemporary banjo manufacture.

Next we focus on the wide variety of improvements made to the banjo in the 1860s and 1870s by a growing number of urban craftsmen who responded to increased demand for the instrument. In this period the evolution of the banjo was accelerated by the introduction of and proselytizing for an entirely new way of playing the instrument: by plucking up on the strings with three or four fingers (as one then would have played the guitar) rather than stroking downward and hitting the strings with one's index finger and hooked thumb, as was the common practice in minstrelsy.[17] This shift in playing style from striking to picking, codified in a banjo tutor published in 1865, meant, among other things, that different kinds of music, of the sort also intended for guitar, now could be played on the banjo. It also meant that more and more frequently the banjo could be heard in the Victorian parlor as well as on the minstrel or variety stage.

By the 1860s the natural playing key of the banjo had been firmly established as A major rather than the earlier-used keys of F or G, and the length of the banjo neck now was often shortened to allow the strings to be tightened to the higher pitch without breaking.[18] Similarly, because much of the music to accompany popular song often demanded notes above those in "first" position (which could be made without shifting the hand higher on the fingerboard), either standard guitar frets or ones that were inlaid flush to the fingerboard became more common on the instruments. Finally, whether to simulate more closely the sound of the guitar—in which, some banjo aficionados claimed, there was renewed interest because of "the improved banjo"—or to project the banjo's sound better, because guitar-style playing was not so percussive as stroke style, many banjo manufacturers began to experiment radically with the sound chambers of their instruments.[19]

Some developed different sorts of metal tone rings, across which the head was stretched, and thus improved the instrument's "brightness." Others fully enclosed the backs of their instruments to project the sound forward through holes in the tops. In England, for example, which also had been swept by the banjo mania, the American maker Alfred Cammeyer's "zither-banjo," a closed-back instrument designed specifically to be played with wire as well as gut strings, quickly caught on.[20] Such constant invention led to more varied and sophisticated banjos than those found in the antebellum era, but at the same time it mitigated against the establishment of standard specifications for the instrument.

Of particular interest here are two of the five brothers in the remarkable Dobson family, Henry Clay Dobson (1832–1908) and George Clifton

Dobson (1842–90), each of whom held several patents for banjo design and who over two decades constantly redesigned the banjo the better to suit its new music, players, and audience. In addition, George composed music for the banjo and, as an extension of his work as one of the nation's most well-known music instructors, wrote or compiled half a dozen tutors in which he championed a novel, "simplified" tablature through which to learn the instrument. Among those whom George introduced to the banjo, for example, was the later instrument maker S. S. Stewart. The Dobson family's engagement with the banjo as designers, builders, musicians, composers, and teachers—at one point or another all five were involved with the instrument in some way—demonstrates how by 1880 the banjo had begun to engender an entire culture around itself—a fascinating world defined by instruments, music, performers, venues, and audiences—a fact that set the stage for the efforts to "elevate" the instrument even more in the next two decades.[21]

We move on to assess the remarkable career of Samuel Swaim Stewart (1855–98), the self-proclaimed first banjo manufacturer, whose Philadelphia banjo factory was reputedly the largest in the country and who tirelessly championed the instrument as America's most distinguished contribution to the development of music. Even more than the Dobsons, Stewart immersed himself in the emergent culture of the banjo. By the 1870s, for example, still in his teens, he performed on and taught the instrument, and in 1879 he started the business for which he became best known.

In addition to his attempts to standardize banjo design and manufacture, Stewart also wrote extensively about the instrument and pioneered advertising techniques, including *S. S. Stewart's Banjo and Guitar Journal* (1882–1902), that indelibly imprinted the instrument in the minds of nineteenth-century Americans—indeed, of people in Europe and on other continents as well. Early in his career he began systematically and indefatigably to promote, first, the instrument itself and, second, *his* instruments to a public increasingly eager to participate in banjo culture. Among other things, Stewart popularized the use of metal rims, and he also produced banjos in many different sizes, which were played in banjo orchestras, and in many grades, from very plain, inexpensive models to ornately carved and inlaid "presentation" models that were truly works of art, all to capture the widest possible market for the instrument. He also effected the full transfer of instrument construction to a factory setting in which strict division of labor became the rule. As banjo manufacturer, composer, publisher and wholesaler of banjo music, and tireless publicist, Stewart provides a case study of how the business of American music moved from the artisan to the entrepreneur.

We also briefly discuss several of Stewart's competitors, particularly J. H. Buckbee, a New York City business that contracted with other, smaller firms to produce thousands of low-grade banjos, and the Lyon and Healy Company of Chicago, whose stringed instruments flowed in great numbers through the nation's new mail-order houses. Though not contributing significantly to the banjo's design, in the 1880s and 1890s these companies became successful because they shared Stewart's shrewd assessment of the marketplace. While never as eagerly sought as Stewart's products, these companies' banjos undeniably contributed to the increased popularity of the instrument and its music in the late nineteenth century.

In our final section we focus on the achievements in the 1880s and 1890s of the "Boston school" of banjo craftsmen, particularly Albert Conant Fairbanks (1852–1914) and William A. Cole (1853–1909), whose various patents and refinements came to set the standards for the industry.[22] Always in direct competition with Stewart, the firm of Fairbanks and Cole—and, after the partnership dissolved about 1890, the companies run by Fairbanks and Cole, respectively—never capitulated fully to the factory system that characterized the activities of Buckbee, Lyon and Healy, and other competitors, but rather maintained the high level of workmanship and artistry earlier associated with artisanal production. Particularly because of their commitment to detail, most readily observable in their sophisticated inlay and engraving work, as well as in their various innovative tone ring and rim designs, the Boston makers produced instruments whose beauty and utility were unsurpassed.

Thus, if Stewart's was the story of entrepreneurship at a time when American industry was increasingly defined by mass production and cheap imitation, theirs was about the continuing significance of hand-craftsmanship as it could be improved by attention to scientific or technological experiment.[23] In the final decade of the century, Boston's banjo makers concentrated on perfecting the instrument's tonal qualities for the various orchestral music now regularly played on it. The result was a successful marriage of art and technology: a handmade work of art that was a highly sophisticated acoustical machine as well. In this regard, the A. C. Fairbanks Company was particularly significant, for it developed not only a revolutionary scalloped tone ring (installed on a model of banjo called the Electric) in the 1890s but also, on its Whyte Laydie banjo, an ingenious bracket band around the rim to obviate the need to drill through it to accommodate the brackets for tension hooks and, on the Tubaphone, a sophisticated tubular steel tone ring that greatly amplified the banjo's tone.

To compete with Fairbanks, his one-time partner William Cole offered the Eclipse, which featured its own improved tone ring as well as the same remarkable attention to the details of its appearance. Advertising their instruments in *The Cadenza* and other popular trade journals, these and other companies (particularly the one which, under John C. Haynes, made Bay State instruments) sought to impress upon the public both the craft and invention of their musical wares. Now, even an amateur club musician could own an instrument that was at once a work of art and also a sophisticated musical machine—the perfect banjo, in other words, upon which to play the ever more complex music that was written for it. These and other makers, who at the turn of the century signaled their professionalization through the formation of the American Guild of Banjoists, Guitarists and Mandolinists, a national organization (based in Boston) to further the cause of these instruments, provide a fitting conclusion to our study, for with their work the construction of the open-back, five-string banjo reached its greatest sophistication. The music of the Jazz Age would demand very different kinds of instruments.

As this overview suggests, in this study we are not primarily interested in the history of music for the banjo, for in a variety of ways that topic already has been seriously addressed.[24] Rather, we emphasize the impact of different styles of banjo playing, dictated by changing tastes in music, on the design, manufacture, and marketing of the banjo. Nor do we wish to revisit at any length such topics as the cultural meaning of blackface minstrelsy or the significance of the image of the banjo in Victorian culture, for these, too, are topics that recently have garnered much scholarly attention.[25]

The strength and novelty of this book resides instead in our attention to such hitherto neglected or understudied primary sources as the instruments themselves; daguerreotypes, ambrotypes, tintypes, and other contemporary photographic mediums; minstrel-era broadsides, sheet-music covers, and other graphic materials; banjo tutors and tune books; and trade periodicals that provide information relevant to an understanding of the development and manufacture of the banjo. No previous study has made such extensive use of such ephemeral materials. The result, we believe, is a contribution not only to the history of nineteenth-century American music but to cultural history and the history of technology as well.

1

From the Plantation to the Stage

Bringing the Banjo to Market

    Long before the banjo appeared on the minstrel stage, Africans and African Americans had been making music with similar long-necked, stringed instruments. As early as 1880, the well-known banjo instructor George C. Dobson recognized the transatlantic heritage of the instrument when he observed that "the natives of Africa have musical instruments which, though differing in minor particulars, possess essentially the same basic peculiarities as the banjo." Displaying for his time a sophisticated understanding of African instruments, Dobson wrote that the "Nubians" have "the *kissar*, very much like the banjo," and "the negroes of Eastern Africa, the *nanaa*, a five-stringed instrument with head of wood and skin." More significantly, in "Western Africa" natives have "the *omlic* with eight strings, the *boulou* with ten strings, and in Senegambia the *bania*, which it is sometimes claimed was imported to the United States by the negro slaves, and became the banjo."[1]

Although twentieth-century musicologists still debate the precise nature of the instrument's origins, they agree with Dobson that what became the American banjo most likely originated from West African instruments that found their way to America through the slave trade. In particular, the various long-necked plucked lutes used by griots today in such countries as Mauritania, Senegal, and Mali, as well as other similar, nongriot instruments from Niger, Chad, and other sub-Saharan areas, are regarded as its most likely prototypes. Most of these are picked both upward (guitar style) and downward with the thumb and first or other fingers, a variation of what was called striking or banjo style; many have a rounded fingerboard rather than the flat one that characterizes banjos and sometimes lack a shorter, high-pitched string on the thumb side (plate 1-1).[2]

From the seventeenth century on, virtually contemporaneous reports from the West African coast, where the traders loaded their human cargo, and the Caribbean islands, to whose sugar plantations they brought it, indicate the presence of such folk instruments. Seventeenth- and eighteenth-century European visitors to both areas report gourd-bodied instruments (but not hollowed-out wooden ones like the *xalam* or *molo*) resembling what we know as banjos.[3] Traveling in Africa in 1620 and 1621, for example, the author of *The Golden Trade; or, A Discovery of the River Gambra* (1623) noted that the instrument most commonly found among the "Aethiopians" was "made out of a great gourd, and a necke thereunto fastnd, resembling in some sort our Bandora," and having "not above sixe strings." Unlike the European instrument, however, this one had "no manner of fret."[4] In 1684, on Africa's Gold Coast, Johan Nieman noted that one tribe, the Akan, had "a sort of Guitar, which they can play fairly well and sing pleasantly to."[5] In 1689, across the Atlantic, Sir Hans Sloane, a physician who extensively documented Jamaica's music, noted that the island's Africans have "strum-strums," that is, "several sorts of Instruments in imitation of Lutes, made of small Gourds fitted with Necks, strung with Horse hairs, or the peeled stalks of climbing Plants or Withs." These, he went on, "are sometimes made of hollow'd Timber covered with Parchment or other Skin wetted, having a bow for its neck, the Strings ty'd longer or shorter, as they would alter their sounds."[6] Such a "strum-strum" no doubt was the same as what Adrien Dessalles, in his *Histoire Générale des Antilles* (1678), called a "banza," to which slaves on Martinique danced "in their own style."[7]

Dessalles invoked the term that, with slight linguistic variants and along with "merry-wang," was most frequently used throughout the Caribbean to describe such instruments. In his history of the *British Empire in America* (1708), for example, John Oldmixon observed that among other instruments slaves on Barbados had the "*Bangil* not much unlike our Lute in any thing, but the Musick."[8] A few years later, in a promotional tract called *The Importance of Jamaica to Great Britain Consider'd* (1740?), the unknown author reported that on Jamaica hundreds of slaves gathered together on Sunday evenings "according to the Customs of their Country (which many of they retain) with Strum-Strums and Calibashes, which they beat and make a horrid Noise with."[9] In *The Sugar-Cane* (ca. 1763), a long narrative poem celebrating sugar's place in England's mercantile empire, Thomas Grainger, who had lived on St. Kitts, wrote of a "banshaw," which he described as "a sort of rude guitar, invented by the Negroes"; and Edward Long, Jamaica's historian, noted that the "merry-wang" was a "favorite instrument" and resembled "a rustic guitar, of four strings," made from a "calabash" that had been sliced and covered with "a dried bladder, or skin," spread across it.[10] By the late eighteenth century these terms were so common that upon visiting Sierra Leone Thomas Winterbottom described a native instrument as like "the banja or merrywang, as it is called in the West Indies."[11]

By the mid-eighteenth century the instrument was noted in the mainland North American colonies. In 1749, for example, the South Carolina Council, investigating an alleged slave conspiracy, examined a young slave named Tony. When asked about his attendance at a meeting of slaves on a neighboring plantation, he explained that "as he was a Young fellow he kept out in the Yard where they were playing on the Bangio for the most part," while the older men met in one of the slave quarters.[12] Also in 1749, the *Pennsylvania Gazette* carried a notice for a "Negroe man, named Scipio," who several months earlier had run off from Prince Georges County, Maryland, and supposedly headed for the Philadelphia area where he had friends. He "plays on the banjo," the advertiser noted, "and can sing." Four months later this same man, now held by a Philadelphia baker, was again on the run. He "wears a blue broad cloth coat, or a black ditto," the report noted, "old shoes, and stockings, [is] of a short stature," and "plays on the banjou, and sings with it," though he could speak but "indifferent English." Eight years later this same recalcitrant slave, now living with yet another master in "Chester Town," Kent County, Maryland, still was causing problems. The advertiser, Joseph Nicholson, suspected that Scipio was headed to Philadelphia yet again and noted that he "speaks broken English, pretends to be a hatter by trade," and "plays well on the banjoe."[13]

In 1766 a notice in a Charleston, South Carolina, newspaper asking for the return of a wallet stolen by a pickpocket provides important information about the presence and use of the banjo by African Americans in urban areas. The theft of the wallet, the advertiser noted, was "strongly suspected to be effected by a Negro wench, who rubbed herself close to the sufferer as he passed through a crowd of Negroes assembled at the lower end of Elliot-street, with a banjer playing," presumably at some entertainment.[14] Such performance by African American musicians was widespread through both the upper and lower South. In the 1770s James Barclay, an overseer on a Low Country plantation, noted other social occasions at which the banjo was played. The slave's favorite instrument, he reported, "is called a Bangier, made of a Calabash [gourd]," and to its music the slaves danced "pair and pair in their own way, hollowing, shrieking, and making an intolerable noise."[15] At the century's end one visitor to the Chesapeake observed that the slaves would "walk five or six miles after a hard day's work to enjoy the pleasures of flinging their hands, heads, and legs to the music of the banjo."[16]

Later in the eighteenth century runaway slave ads continued to note the escapee's skill on the instrument. In 1778, for example, John McPherson's advertisement in a Maryland newspaper asked for the return of "one of the Piccawaxon glebe slaves" who had run off from "Richard Gambra's, near Port Tobacco." He was "a tall stout young fellow with prominent jaws, and bends somewhat forward in his walk, and is much addicted to gambling, and plays upon the banjo." Four years later the same paper reported the theft of two horses and a "new Negro man, named Jack, about thirty years old, 5 feet 4 or 5 inches high, with a flat nose," who "plays well on a Negro banjor."[17] Indeed, in Maryland the instrument was so well known that it even inspired the literati who gathered around the publisher and poet Joseph Green. A poem published in an Annapolis journal in the late 1760s, addressed "To the Author of the Verses in your last [issue]," ends by noting that "He flatters too long in so delicate a manner: / What a pity his talents so long lay hid! / You shall be Poet Laureat: A new Birth-Day Ode every year," and observes that this work should be "set for the Banjour."[18]

A final tantalizing eighteenth-century reference comes from New York, where on Long Island a freed black named "Billy Banjo" served the family of Adam Mott. Born about 1738 to enslaved parents and marrying "Aunt Jinny," who had come from Africa and was sold in New York City in 1744,

Billy was "a famous banjo player." And "not on the fanciful instrument of today, handled by cork-blacked counterfeits," one of Mott's descendants recalled, "but the genuine banjo of the negro." Further, Billy "not only *played*, but he *made* banjos, having a large dried gourd for the sounding board." He died in 1826, well before the rise of minstrelsy.[19]

Beyond such verbal descriptions, however, there is very little evidence concerning the banjo in this early period. Few extant banjos, for example, can be positively dated from before the turn of the nineteenth century, and even contemporary graphic depiction is scarce. Virtually unique is an engraving in Sloane's *Voyage to the Islands*, which shows instruments he found in Jamaica, one of which, a long-necked, gourd-bodied instrument akin to a central African lute, he placed near an Indian *tanpura*, presumably for comparison.[20] Of even greater significance because of its provenance from the region around Charleston, South Carolina, is a remarkable watercolor, *The Old Plantation*, which illustrates no fewer than ten slaves outside their quarters, some of them dancing to music being played on a gourd instrument that one musicologist likens to the African *molo*. Attributed to the late eighteenth century, this image is particularly important because the banjo-like instrument has a shorter string on the side of the fingerboard, as most later banjos did (plate 1-2).[21]

Epstein's exhaustive canvass yields three more images from before 1830, two from the United States and the other from Jamaica, all of which are reproduced in her study of African American folk music. Most significant is the banjo-like gourd instrument that the Philadelphia artist Samuel Jennings (active ca. 1787–92) depicted in the hands of an African American in his large mural, *Liberty Displaying the Arts and Sciences*.[22] Benjamin Latrobe's sketch (ca. 1819) of gourd instruments that he saw played by slaves in "Congo Square" in New Orleans shows a carved human figure at the top of one of the instruments, which also has both a bridge and an ornamented sound hole.[23] Finally, an engraving, "The Interior of a Negro House," in Cynric R. Williams's *A Tour through the Island of Jamaica . . . in the Year 1823* (1826) contains a gourd "bonja" on the wall with other household implements.[24] Because of this dearth of graphic evidence from before the 1830s, however, up to that point we must document the banjo in the Western Hemisphere almost wholly through verbal descriptions.

The most important fact established by such accounts is that, through the emergence of blackface minstrelsy in the early 1840s, the African American banjo continued to be made, as "Billy Banjo" made his, primarily with a gourd, not a wooden, sound chamber, even though a century earlier in the West Indies Sloane had indeed seen an instrument with the latter. In 1774, for example, Nicholas Creswell of Maryland reported going to a

"Negro ball" where slaves danced to the banjo. The instrument was "made of a Gourd something in the imitation of a Guitar," he wrote, "with only four strings and played with the fingers in the same manner."[25] His contemporary Jonathan Boucher recalled that in Virginia the "bandore" (which he said was pronounced "banjor") was "the favorite and almost only instrument in use among the slaves." Its body "was a large hollow gourd," he continued, "with a long handle attached to it, strung with catgut, and played on with the fingers."[26]

Equally important, the folk banjo kept this predictable form through the 1830s and into the era of early minstrelsy. When the caricaturist David Claypoole Johnston, for example, turned his hand to Frances Trollope, whose highly critical book about the United States had just appeared, in one sketch he showed "Trollop at Home in De Fust Color'd Circles." Prominent in the drawing was an African American playing a gourd banjo. In 1855 Peter Randolph, an emancipated slave, recalled (as had Creswell) large African American gatherings where the slaves danced "to the music of a banjo, made out of a large gourd."[27] And Alfred Mercier, in his novel *L'Habitation Saint-Ybars; ou, Maîtres et Esclaves en Louisiane*, set in Louisiana in 1851, had one of his slave characters, an old man born in Africa, play a "banza," "une espèce de guitare à quatre cordes" [a type of guitar with four strings].

> Pour cela il prend une grosse calebasse dont il enlève une calotte; il tend dessus une peau de serpent, c'est sa table d'harmonie. Il fait son manche avec du cypre, parceque c'est un bois très droit et qui ne travaille pas sensiblement. Il fabrique ses cordes avec des crins de cheval.

> [For this he takes a large gourd from which he removes the top; he covers it with snakeskin for its sound board. He makes its neck from cypress because this wood is very straight and does not bend. He makes the strings from horsehair.][28]

Epstein's evidence thus suggests that white musicians who later reported having learned to play the banjo from African Americans in the South very likely used such instruments made from gourds. It was not until the 1850s, for example, that we have reports of African Americans making their sound chambers in other ways. John Allan Wyeth of Alabama recalled that "the banjo was the real instrument of the Southern Negroes," but at first it was "a very crude device" made from "a large gourd with a long straight neck or handle, shaped like those of smaller growth, used commonly then for drinking-dippers." The bowl of this gourd was "cut away on a plane level with the surface of the neck, the seed and contents removed, and over this, like a drumhead, a freshly tanned coon-skin was stretched, fastened, and allowed to dry."

But by the mid-1850s, in the heyday of minstrelsy, the African American who taught Wyeth to play the banjo had fashioned an instrument whose rim consisted of "the circle of a cheese box." He tacked a wet calfskin, which had been "soaked in lime solution" to remove the hair, "over one surface of this, while the stem [i.e., the neck] was carved from a suitable piece of soft poplar."[29] At about the same time in Virginia, and just before he escaped to freedom, Isaac D. Williams recalled, his fellow slaves had made a banjo by stretching a groundhog hide "over a piece of timber fashioned like a cheese box." "You couldn't tell the difference between that homely affair and a store bought one," he observed (fig. 1-1).[30]

As this brief overview indicates, the banjo's long background as a folk instrument among non-European peoples raises problems different from those encountered by someone who writes about, say, the history of the violin. By the nineteenth century the design and manufacture of that instrument were well established through strong family groups who, with trained apprentices, could turn out great numbers of similarly constructed instruments, while banjos, in America as in Africa, continued to be crafted in a variety of forms by folk artisans who in their lifetimes probably never produced more than a few instruments. Beginning in the early 1840s, however, the rage for minstrelsy created a demand for sturdier and more reliable banjos that was met by skilled urban woodworkers who transformed a folk artifact into a manufactured commodity.

The emergence and rise of the minstrel phenomenon has been well described, and we need not revisit it in detail.[31] It is important to remind ourselves, however, that such musical and dramatic entertainment (which originated in the urban Northeast) was very ideologically charged, for, as one historian of the phenomenon has noted, through minstrelsy's window "appeared cultural identifications and hostilities, ethnic satire, and social and political commentary of a wide-ranging and sometimes radical character." Drawing their audiences primarily from immigrant and working class males, these early minstrel shows were a "kind of underground theater in which black-face convention rendered permissible topics that were difficult to handle explicitly on the Victorian stage or in print" (fig. 1-2). Within a few years the infatuation with such caricatured representation of African Americans — explicable in terms of the audience's simultaneous attraction to and repulsion from the black's liminal social and psychological condition — spread throughout the United States and to England as well (fig. 1-3). One result was that the instruments associated with the performances—particularly the banjo—became iconic of minstrelsy in general (fig. 1-4).[32]

The late-eighteenth-century humorous stage and circus acts from which the minstrel show derived consisted of blackface dancers and banjo or violin players who provided the music, thus providing the germ for the kinds of elaborate stagecraft that soon enough emerged (fig. 1-5).[33] Hans Nathan, for example, cites the billing for one such act: "Mr. [Billy] Whitlock, the King of the Banjo Players, and the Emperor of Extravaganza Singers. Second night of the engagement of the little 'Wirginny Nigger,' only twelve years old [the equally well-known John Diamond], who can outdance the nation" (plate 1-3).[34] Another historian reports that during this period there were "many 'nigger dancers,' banjoists, and Ethiopian celebrities" performing "individually, in the saloons and concert halls, [and] with circuses and elephant shows, while the newspapers carried numerous references to the battles between rival banjoists and singers."

Uncle Tom's Cabin.   Onkel Toms Hütte.

Figure 1-1. Chromolithograph from *Comic Sketches of American Life* (Philadelphia, [ca. 1855]), purporting to represent a scene in the slave quarters from Harriet Beecher Stowe's immensely popular *Uncle Tom's Cabin* (1852). Note that this banjo player is left-handed, and that the publisher of this volume of twelve beautiful chromolithographs offers his descriptions in German as well as in English, no doubt for the still-large number of German-speakers in the mid-Atlantic region.

At the Bowery Theater in 1841, for example, "Joe Sweeney" was advertised as the "Virginia Melodist," who would "introduce those never-to-be-forgotten JIGS, REELS, and BREAKDOWNS . . . only done by *the real niggers of the old Dominion*," except for Sweeney, who "can give the 'scientific touches to perfection on a *Southern Banjo*.'"[35] Although present on the stage at least since the late eighteenth century, however, such blackface entertainers themselves did not constitute a "minstrel show" (fig. 1-6). Rather, it

Figure 1-2. Sixth-plate ambrotype, late 1850s. This disturbing image depicts the caricatured African American central to the minstrel stage. Throughout early minstrelsy (1843–70), the banjo was iconic of this entertainment. Note the vertical fifth-string tuning peg, large neck, and the small number of brackets, all characteristic of early banjos. Also note that in this image, as in several others we reproduce, the fifth string of the banjo points down. In the early years of photography, images often were reversed; that is, they appeared as mirror images. Thus, a right-handed banjo player would appear left-handed. To appear right-handed, the subject holds the instrument left-handed, but when this is done, the fifth-string peg points downward. Such images accurately depict the right-handed players but give an erroneous impression of the instruments.

Figure 1-3. "Dixey's Land Galop." Lithographed sheet-music cover (London, [ca. 1870]). Here R. Bishop Buckley, a member of the famed Buckley family of minstrels, is dressed in "inimitable Plantation Character." Many lithographed sheet-music covers were produced in England, indicative of minstrelsy's popularity outside the United States.

opposite
Figure 1-4. Carte-de-visite by R. A. Lord, 158 Chatham Street, New York, ca. 1860s, of minstrel in clown outfit, with his banjo. Such exaggerated clothing and overall appearance characterized minstrel shows on both sides of the Atlantic and presumably allowed working-class whites to think of themselves as superior to the African Americans against whom they often competed for jobs, particularly in the urban Northeast. Note the vertical fifth-string tuning peg on this instrument, as well as the relatively large number of brackets.

was the powerful combination of banjo, violin, tambourine, and bones in the hands of those who in part constituted and catered to the nation's first bohemia that caught the public's imagination and came to define the genre.

Toward the end of January 1843, Dan Emmett, Billy Whitlock, Frank Brower, and Dick Pelham, all veterans of blackface circus and stage acts, serendipitously came together on these instruments to practice a few tunes in a New York City boardinghouse. When shortly thereafter they performed publicly as the Virginia Minstrels, minstrelsy was born (fig. 1-7, plate 1-4). As Wittke describes it, "The nation soon was in the grip of a minstrel craze"; and while the audiences themselves consisted, as we have noted, primarily of the white working class, the tunes and songs "made an amazing appeal to all classes of the American people" (fig. 1-8). "New melodies for the minstrels, which appeared almost as rapidly as they could be printed and copyrighted," Wittke continues, "were quickly seized upon by the eager public, tried on the piano and other available instruments, and whistled in the streets."[36] Within weeks the Virginia Minstrels and other newly formed troupes were crisscrossing the eastern states, and by May Emmett and his crew took their show to Liverpool and other English cities, where they were just as enthusiastically received.[37]

Figure 1-5. Half-plate ambrotype, ca. 1855. A banjoist and bones player in blackface. The latter has his legs akimbo, in the style of contemporary jig dancers often associated with circus and other popular entertainment in the decades prior to the emergence of the minstrel show. Also see figure 1-18 and plate 1-3.

opposite
Figure 1-6. Carte-de-visite, ca. 1860s, of minstrel banjoist. Even after the Virginia Minstrels' first performances in 1843, banjoists like this one still might play unaccompanied by other instruments. Note the horizontal fifth-string peg on this instrument, as well as the scooped out area where the neck meets the head. This is characteristic of many banjos after 1860, but there is no consensus as to its purpose.

Figure 1-7. Sixth-plate daguerreotype, ca. 1855. Three young white musicians, probably stage performers, with some of the instruments that defined the minstrel ensemble: violin, banjo, and bones. Like these, many of the early minstrels were in their teens and twenties; they often were recent Irish immigrants who melded the music of their home with the music of the plantation South. Note the narrow neck of this banjo and its large head.

While minstrel groups eventually used a variety of instrumentation, in the first five years of the phenomenon, as Robert Winans notes, the banjo, along with the tambourine, was "indispensable." It was "at the heart of the sound of the minstrel ensemble," he concludes, and the banjo's was the "most common solo" to be heard (fig. 1-9).[38] Guitars, accordions, flutes, and other instruments later were added to the blackface acts, but for early audiences nothing defined the minstrel show so much as the sound of the banjo (figs. 1-10, 1-11). But where did such performers as Whitlock, Joel W. Sweeney, and other very early white banjoists acquire their instruments and learn to play?

What little evidence we have suggests that initially they got their instruments and lessons primarily in the plantation South, from enslaved African Americans or those who lived in close proximity to them. In 1897,

Figure 1-8. Half-plate ambrotype, ca. 1850s. These young urban men, probably telegraphers (two hold telegraphic apparatuses), pose jauntily with a banjo, indicative of their interest in the rage of minstrelsy. Historians agree that in minstrelsy's early years its audience was comprised largely of such young working-class males.

for example, the veteran minstrel Ben Cotton recalled that when he had worked on riverboats on the Mississippi River as a youth, he used to visit with slaves "in front of their cabins" in order to hear them "start the banjo twanging," their voices ringing out "in the quiet night air in their weird melodies." "They did not quite understand me," Cotton continued, for "I was the first white man they had seen who sang as they did."[39] Tom Briggs acquired his tunes in the same way. The preface to his banjo tutor, one of the earliest such compilations, relates that the work "contains many choice plantation melodies which the author learned when at the south from negroes, which have never been published before."[40]

Joel Sweeney, one of the greatest of the early stage banjoists, grew up on a plantation near Appomattox, Virginia, where he similarly acquired his introduction to the instrument (fig. 1-12, plate 1-5). One of his neighbors later recalled that as a boy Sweeney "would hang around the negroes at all times learning some of their rude songs and playing an accompaniment on a gourd banjo."[41] Billy Whitlock, the banjo player for the original

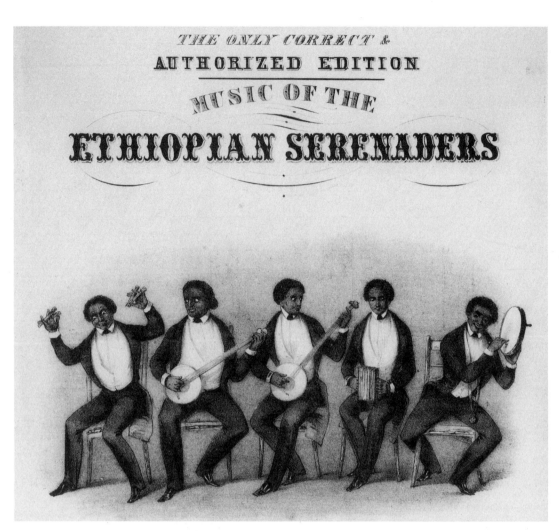

Figure 1-9. "Ethiopian Serenaders." Lithographed sheet-music cover (New York, [ca. late 1840s]). This highly caricatured depiction of the minstrel line shows the centrality of the banjo to this kind of performance. The second player from the right holds a small accordion, or "flutina," sometimes used in minstrel performances. Collection of Philip F. Gura.

Virginia Minstrels, then learned directly from Sweeney. In 1837 Whitlock had left his job as a typesetter for the *New York Herald* and joined a circus that played as far south as Savannah. On their return north the troupe stopped for four days in Lynchburg, Virginia, where Sweeney showed Whitlock his first banjo. "Up to that time" he "had never seen a banjo," we learn from a correspondent of the *New York Clipper* who had access to his now-missing manuscript autobiography, but during his stay in Lynchburg "Sweeney had one made for him and taught him a tune." Thus began Whitlock's lifelong interest in the instrument, which by 1843 had brought him to the New York stage.[42]

Such cultural exchange was greatly facilitated by the Civil War, when thousands of northern soldiers were introduced firsthand to the music of

Figure 1-10. Sixth-plate daguerreotype, ca. late 1840s. A rare image illustrating a full minstrel group—bones, banjo, violin, triangle, and tambourine—ready to play, but not in blackface. It is very likely that these musicians blackened up to play on the same stage after this daguerreotype was taken. Particularly in daguerreotypy's early years, it was difficult for the artist to take images outside of the studio, where the light, often from windows or skylights, could be carefully controlled. Note how in this image the light raking across from some source on the left of the stage is indeed a problem.

African Americans (fig. 1-13). Writing in the 1890s, for example, the great stage banjoist Albert Baur gives credence to some historians' conjectures about the close relation between minstrelsy and behavior that was socially or psychologically illicit.[43] He recalled that while in the army he was "always watching for darkey banjo players on the different plantations in the vicinity of camps" where he happened to be. When his corps was assigned to the region around Murfreesboro, Tennessee, "as usual" Baur inquired "of every negro [he] could see as to the whereabouts of any banjo players among the plantation negroes in that vicinity." One day "a contraband" told him that there was to be a dance at a house in town "where the musicians would be principally banjo players"; though restricted by orders to camp, he and two fellow soldiers found their way to the event. Entering the shut-up cabin, Baur found seventy to eighty people dancing to two banjo players and a fiddler, a scene so remarkable to him that "the most exaggerated minstrel representation of plantation life could not equal it." "Here was a scene," he reminisced, "that I had often wished to witness, a regular plantation frolic."[44]

One also could find white banjoists in the South before the Civil War. Manly Reece (1830–69), a native of Rockingham County, North Carolina, could play the banjo by the time he was in his teens, and after moving to southwestern Virginia he became well known for his musical skill. Letters to him from family members and friends after he joined the Confederate army speak to the importance of his banjo playing to their community. "Listen," wrote Elizabeth Kegley in 1861, "when you can, come home and sing and pick the banjo." "I have often thought of past times," she contin-

Figure 1-11. Sixth-plate ambrotype, ca. 1860, of minstrel troupe. This rare outdoor image shows a large minstrel group, with cello, two violins, accordion, triangle, tambourine, and bones, outside a public building, in all likelihood the hall in which they later would perform. Although this group is unusual because it lacks a banjoist, the other instruments leave little doubt as to what sort of music they would play. Collection of Philip F. Gura.

ued, "and wish that times was like they were." A couple of years later Reece's sister Louisa echoed these sentiments. "Amos Ballard wrote you had been to see them," she noted, "and said to tell me you was well and could pick the banjo yet." "I wish you could pick my favorite tune for me," she added, "and just imagine I was listening."[45]

Equally revealing of the banjo's presence among lower-class whites in the South is the reminiscence of C. J. Rogers, the circus manager for whom Dan Emmett (soon to be one of the most famous minstrels) worked. Rogers recalled that in the spring of 1840 his Cincinnati Circus Company played throughout Ohio, Indiana, Kentucky, and Virginia. While they were traveling through "Western Virginia," Emmett "found a banjo player named 'Ferguson,' who was a very ignorant person and 'nigger all over' except in color." Emmett urged his employer to hire the man. "'Ferguson'

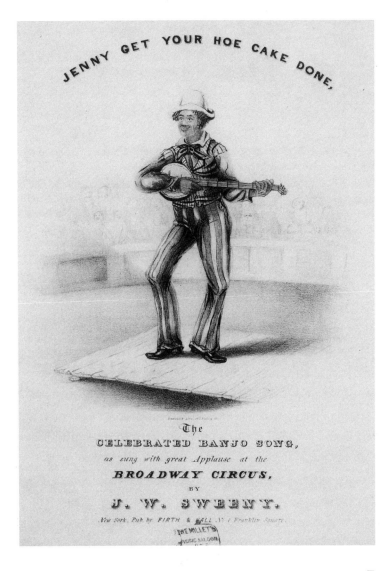

Figure 1-12. "Jenny Get Your Hoe Cake Done." Lithographed sheet-music cover (New York, [ca. early 1840s]). This image depicts the renowned Joel Sweeney, who learned to play the banjo from enslaved African Americans on the plantations adjoining the one on which he grew up near Appomattox, Virginia. Sweeney was instrumental in popularizing the banjo on the minstrel stage.

Figure 1-13. Carte-de-visite, ca. 1861–64, of members of the 99th Regiment, Ohio Volunteer Infantry. This rare image shows the soldiers, whose regiment saw much service in Tennessee and Georgia during the Civil War, in the field with their instruments. Beginning second from the left we find tambourine, banjo, guitar, fiddle, triangle, and bones. The war introduced many northern soldiers to the banjo, but the ensemble of these instruments suggests that these men already were intimately acquainted with the minstrel stage. The inscription on the back reads: "Bro. Harrison Your discharge papers are at my hose Your brother Hen." This "Hen." is the guitar player, Henry Shuey, who is speaking of his brother, Captain Harrison Shuey.

was the greatest card we ever had," Rogers wrote, and it was during this musician's stay that Emmett learned to play the banjo. The next season, when Frank Brower joined the troupe, Emmett, "after a good deal of persuasion," agreed "to play in the orchestra and assist Frank in the ring with the banjo." This, Rogers concluded, was "the beginning of that popularity which continued so many years"—and which secured Brower and Emmett's subsequent fame.[46]

Once minstrel acts proliferated, budding amateurs as well as seasoned performers sought to acquire instruments in the cities in which they worked. They most often brought their requests to "turners" (that is, woodworkers), or to craftsmen who produced other stringed or percussion instruments but did not necessarily have any experience with the banjo, and who themselves often found their way to the musicians' shows. One old minstrel, for example, who claimed to have been Dan Emmett's "Sunday School mate" and to have played with the great early banjoist Tom Briggs, recalled that in 1839 in Hartford, Connecticut, he had seen "Mr. Williams' Olio Company," in which one Peter Jenkins had sung "several good old songs and accompanied his singing with the banjo." Infatuated by the instrument, the young man decided to have a banjo made for himself and for that purpose went to "Ed. Atherton, a carpenter" in that city. For $7 he acquired an instrument whose "neck was made of pine, the hoop was made of oak." "The head was sheep skin," he recalled, "and tacked on with nails" (fig. 1-14). Oddly, he did not see another banjo until the fall of 1847, in the hands of "W. W. Newcomb," a minstrel playing in Boston.[47] A few years later, in New York State, Frank B. Converse (1837–1903), later a renowned banjoist and instructor, also had an instrument made by a carpenter. This banjo, his second, had a cherry neck, a rim cut down from a peck measure, and six brackets to tighten a "dog-skin" head. His first instrument had been even cruder: a pine neck, a rim from a flour sieve, and a tacked-on animal-skin head.[48]

Some early banjo enthusiasts even tried to make their own instruments. Such was the case with the young Henry C. Dobson, for example, who went on to become an important maker after the Civil War. In 1908, upon his death, his son recalled that "the first banjo his father made, in 1851," still hung in the son's music school on Broadway.[49] Often the results of such home manufacture, however, were humorous. After hearing his first banjo, George H. Coes of Providence, Rhode Island, decided to make his own. "Early in the forties," he wrote, he heard "the banjo played by Mr. Earl Pierce, the famous comedian who was then connected with E. P. Christy's Minstrels in New York City" (fig. 1-15). Coes worked with Pierce's brother, "a great friend," and when the minstrel visited his relative, he evidently had played some tunes at his brother's home, where Coes had been visiting. "I became infatuated with the instrument," Coes reported, and "watched him closely and took the first opportunity to examine its construction." Coes "secretly determined" to make one for himself but "simply guessed" at the dimensions, "being ashamed to ask him for them outright." Accomplishing his task before Pierce left Providence, Coes proudly showed his banjo to the musician. "Imagine my chagrin," Coes wrote, "when he smilingly said: 'Are you left-handed?,'" for Coes had put the thumb string on the wrong side of the neck. Embarrassed but undaunted, he made another neck the proper way and began to learn the instrument, particularly after hearing another banjoist, the renowned Tom Briggs. "I went every night

Figure 1-14. Sixth-plate ambrotype, ca. late 1850s. This working-class youth, identified as William J. Anderson, is dressed up in his finest clothes for the photographer. He plays an unsophisticated tack-head banjo that probably resembled the kind Joel Sweeney took to England in the early 1840s. Collection of Philip F. Gura.

opposite
Figure 1-15. "Hoop De Doodem Doo." Lithographed sheet-music cover (London, 1858) of the well-known minstrel E. H. Pierce, who for a time was connected with E. P. Christy's Minstrels. George H. Coes of Providence, Rhode Island, was inspired to build his own banjo after hearing Pierce play at a friend's home.

M & N. HANHART, LITH.

"HOOP DE DOODEM DOO"

THE POPULAR COMIC SCENE

AS PERFORMED BY E. H. PIERCE, MEMBER OF THE

CHRISTY MINSTRELS

to hear him and watched his right hand very close," Coes noted. "I obtained the motion of the thumb and finger and became familiar with the sound of the notes which were fairly fixed in my memory" (fig. 1-16).[50]

More intriguing was the experience of Joseph Cave (1823–1912), an Englishman who became one of that country's leading minstrels and general stage performers (fig. 1-17). In his lengthy reminiscences he recalled that in 1843 he had seen "Sand's Great American Circus Company," in

Figure 1-16. Sixth-plate ambrotype, late 1850s. This young musician holds a crude instrument that he might have made himself or had built for him by a "turner," or woodworker, a common source for early banjos. Note the reversed image, with the fifth-string peg pointing downward.

between whose equestrian acts were "sandwiched excellent biped recreations, musical, terpsichorean, acrobatic" (fig. 1-18). But the greatest attraction in the musical segment of the show, Cave recalled, was "Joseph [*sic*] Sweeney, [the] Negro Vocalist and Banjo Player" who "was credited with [the banjo's] invention." This was the "first time the instrument was brought to the attention of the English public," Cave observed, and "it 'froze' over at once."

Cave himself was among those "frozen" by the new sound. "I was present in the theatre," he wrote,

> on the evening of his second performance, and I shall never forget how my ears tingled and my mouth watered when I heard the tum, tum, tum of that blessed banjo. I thought to myself, if I could get one, there would be nothing between me and absolute affluence but the learning to play it. I knew it would be hopeless to think of getting a banjo in England— I might as well have cried for the moon. I fancied it would be equally impossible to obtain one in America, as I had heard Mr. Sweeney had the only example in existence, which he had made himself.

Besides revealing how Sweeney sought to cast an aura of mystery around his instrument, presumably to make the public more interested in his performances, Cave reminds us that in the early 1840s the banjo was still so novel that one could not simply walk around Liverpool or London— or Boston and New York, for that matter—and acquire one. Sweeney himself, for example, had only recently begun appearing with the banjo and kept it "a secret for fear anyone should copy it," Cave wrote. Indeed, at every performance he had a man "at the prompt entrance with the case," and as soon as Sweeney came off stage he put the banjo "in that case and lock[ed] it."

Cave's prayers for his own banjo were answered in a remarkable way. At Sweeney's performance he encountered a boyhood friend who had been working for Sand's Circus. This "Charley" confided to Cave that before the troupe had left New York their "property man" had "seen quite enough of the construction" of Sweeney's instrument "to enable him to make copies of it," one of which he offered the young man. Charley bought it on the spot, intending "only to use it as an amusement at home, and not in any way professionally." Indeed, on this English trip Sweeney had become so protective of his act that he had declared to his coworkers that if he learned of anybody "in the company having one of the copies of his invention, that party should quit or he would leave himself." Exacting a promise from Cave that he would not reveal where he had gotten it, his old friend Charley sold him his first banjo, and Cave, assuring his own man-

Figure 1-17. Engraving of Joseph Cave, from *Duncombe's Ethiopian Songster and Mississippi Screamer* (London, 1854). In the early 1840s, when banjos were still unusual across the Atlantic, this English performer secured a copy of Joel Sweeney's banjo from a stagehand who had had the instrument made without Sweeney's knowledge. Cave became one of England's most famous minstrels. Note that this illustration of the guitar-like banjo, with sound hole and a stationary, pin-style bridge, may have been done by an artist unfamiliar with actual banjo construction.

Figure 1-18. Sixth-plate daguerreotype, ca. 1850s, illustrating a banjoist and bones player in circus or acrobat attire. Before the advent of minstrelsy, such musicians often were part of the entertainment of antebellum circuses like that at which the Englishman Joseph Cave first heard Joel Sweeney play the banjo. Also see figure 1-5 and plate 1-3. Courtesy of Matthew Isenberg.

ager that he had in his possession "an instrument from America," there-upon began a lengthy and successful minstrel career.[51]

Before we turn from minstrelsy to the business of banjo making itself, we should emphasize what these reminiscences suggest: by the 1850s there had emerged a group of performers on the minstrel circuit whose fame resided quite specifically in their expertise on the banjo and who thus needed dependable sources for the instrument. In addition to Sweeney and Whitlock, for example, the early 1840s saw the rise of the above-mentioned Tom Briggs (1824–54), "one of the earliest and greatest banjo performers in minstrelsy," who unfortunately died at a young age while on a voyage to California, but whose virtuosity was enshrined in a banjo tutor under his name. Another of this cohort was George Swayne Buckley (1829–79), the banjoist for Buckley's Serenaders, who was billed for a time as the "Young Sweeney," the great man himself having taken "an interest" in his career. Other important players in this early period included Hy Rumsey (1828–71), Frank Converse, Jasper Ross (1826–89), Matt Peel (1830–59), and James Wambold (1834–1901) (figs. 1-19, 1-20).[52] On the ubiquitous play-bills that announced different minstrel acts and contests, the appearance of these and other players marked the banjo's arrival as a solo instrument whose best practitioners won national renown (fig. 1-21, plate 1-6).[53] Soon enough, particularly in the large cities of the eastern seaboard, craftsmen now called banjo makers began to transform the instrument from folk artifact to market commodity.

If the earliest minstrel banjoists acquired their instruments and learned to play wherever they could, by the late 1840s not only the banjo's manufacture but its instruction were becoming more and more professionalized. In 1848, for example, Elias Howe issued his *Complete Preceptor for the Banjo* under the pseudonym (which he used for other of his musical publications between 1847 and 1851) "Gumbo Chaff, First Banjo Player to the King of the Congo."[54] As music historians have pointed out, however, nothing in this compilation of tunes and songs suggests familiarity with minstrel-style banjo playing; in effect, Howe merely had published popular music in arrangements derived from those for violin or flute.[55]

Much more significant was the publication in 1855 of *Briggs' Banjo Instructor*, issued shortly after Thomas F. Briggs's death (fig. 1-22). Ads from the publisher of this book indicate that he was solicited by Briggs's friends to issue the book because Briggs had "acquired a great reputation as a performer" and had given the world "a scientific and practical method for an instrument which has ever been considered a mystery unlearnable, and for which music had never been written." Whoever compiled it, which is unclear, this tutor is indeed important for its detailed directions for playing the instrument in the stroke style.[56] By 1860 Briggs's sophisticated tutor had been joined by three more: another from Howe's hand (this one continuing instruction specifically for the banjo), one by Phil Rice (d. 1857), and another by James Buckley (1803–72).[57] No longer did the aspiring

Figure 1-19. Sixth-plate daguerreotype, ca. 1850s, of banjoist Matt Peel and Luke West. Peel began to perform on stage in New York in 1840; in 1850 he joined with West, a renowned whistler as well as a banjoist himself, to form Murphy, West, and Peel's Minstrels. We know of very few daguerreotypes of identified players, hence the significance of this and the following image. Notice the tack-head banjo and that the image is reversed. Courtesy of the Harvard Theatre Collection, the Houghton Library.

Figure 1-20. Sixth-plate daguerreotype, ca. 1850s, of Dave Wambold, considered minstrelsy's "greatest balladist." His brother James was also a renowned banjo player, and in the 1850s both men were popular on the minstrel stage. This image is part of a remarkable grouping of nine minstrel portraits housed in one large frame. Courtesy of the Harvard Theatre Collection, the Houghton Library.

opposite
Figure 1-21. Broadside announcing the appearance of an American minstrel troupe in London in 1848. Notice that various of the songs or routines are associated with specific performers. Of particular significance here is the presence of "Briggs," that is, Tom Briggs, one of the most acclaimed of the early banjoists, who unfortunately died in the 1850s when his fame was at its height. Collection of Bob Carlin.

BOZ'S JUBA,

WITH

C. W. PELL'S ETHIOPIAN SERENADERS,

FROM THE ROYAL GARDENS, VAUXHALL,

WILL GIVE A

MORNING

CONCERT

AT THE THEATRE,

This Day, Saturday, October 7,

Commencing at TWO o'Clock.—Doors open at Half-past One. *1848*

The Lessee begs to inform the Nobility, Gentry, and the Public in general, that she has secured the services of a Corps of **ETHIOPIAN SERENADERS,** the most talented that have ever appeared in this Country, under the direction of Mr. G. W. PELL, the Celebrated Bone Player (late of the St. James's Theatre), including **Juba, the Inimitable Juba,** a genuine Son of the Southern Clime, who is immortalised by Boz in his humourous Sketches of American Life and Character.

JUBA is a perfect Phenomenon ; and, among other Terpsichorean Feats, accomplishes with most perfect ease the extraordinary number of TWO HUNDRED DIFFERENT STEPS !

PROGRAMME.

PART FIRST.

Overture	Band.
Song (New) "Carry me back to old Virginny."	Ludlow.
Chaunt (New) "I seen her at de Window."	Pell.
Ballad (New) "Ladies wont you Marry?"	Valentine.
Song, "Rosa Lee."	Irwen.
Solo and Chorus, "Stop dat Knockin."	Valentine.

"Miss Lucy Long," - (in Character) Original - **BOZ'S JUBA.**

PART SECOND.

Slow Movement	Band.
Quintette, "Coloured Fancy Ball."	Company.
Chaunt (New) "Old King Crow."	Pell.
Trio (New) "The spot that we were born on."	Valentine, Irwen, & Ludlow
Refrain (New) "Railroad Travelling."	Pell.
Chaunt "Dan Tucker."	Briggs.

PART THIRD.

Overture	Band.
Solo and Chorus, "Come with a Darky Band."	Valentine and Company.
Chaunt (New) "Way down South."	Juba.
Ballad (New) "Rosa Mae."	Valentine.
Chaunt, "Old Joe."	Pell.
Refrain (New) "Jenny put the Kittle on."	Juba.
Solo (on the Banjo)	BRIGGS.

"Festival, or Plantation Dances," Original, **BOZ's JUBA.**

Tickets and Places for the Boxes to be taken of Mr. BROWNELL, at the Theatre.
DRESS BOXES, 4s.   UPPER BOXES, 2s. 6d.   PIT, 2s.   GALLERY, 1s.

This Evening, Saturday, a Variety of Performances, for the Benefit of Boz's Juba, and Last Night of the Engagement.
On Tuesday next, Mr. WRIGHT, from the Adelphi, will appear.

JOHN AND JAMES KEENE PRINTERS, KINGSMEAD STREET, BATH

banjoist have to go to the South, or even to another banjo player, to learn the repertoire. Instruction was available as near as one of the nation's large music emporiums.

Just as the method of banjo playing now could be transmitted "with or without a master" through such tutors, so, too, did the instrument become easier to acquire as some urban craftsmen became known specifically as makers or suppliers of banjos. The earliest we have documented is John Stevens of New York City, who, after four years of advertising himself as a cabinetmaker, in 1844 listed himself in a city directory as a "Banjo Maker," even though he continued in the woodworking trade as well. Thereafter more and more craftsmen better known for producing other goods also began to make banjos. The New York cabinetmaker Charles Kyes, for example, was awarded a diploma for the best banjo at the American Institute Fair in 1848, and J. S. Ray (occupation unknown) placed second. As early as 1849 Silas P. Hinds advertised banjos for sale at his Newark, New Jersey, address, though we do not know who manufactured them. The exhibition of manufactures at the Franklin Institute in Philadelphia allows us to add a few more names to this group of pre-1850 makers. In 1848 both John Zeair and A. Meyer entered instruments to be judged, and the following year there were two new participants, J. Wesley Watt and M. Mathews; Watt exhibited as well in 1850.[58]

Surprisingly, as early as 1848 in rural Massachusetts, Horatio N. Corbett entered a banjo in the first exhibition of the Worcester County Mechanics Association, and the association received another banjo entry the following year but unfortunately did not name the maker. But in a comment as revelatory of antebellum racism as of the public's unfamiliarity with this novel instrument, the prize committee of 1849 noted that, though this banjo "was well made and neatly finished," the superintendent of the fair had "failed to place upon the Committee any gentleman of the *proper complexion* to judge rightly of the merits of the Banjo, in respect to power and quality of tone." "Under this disadvantage," the committee still ventured the opinion that "this instrument might make glad the fingers of a Christy [a member of the Christy's Minstrels, a popular troupe], and impart new vigor and vivacity to the anterior extremities of Miss Lucy Long [the title of a popular minstrel song]."[59]

By the 1850s more makers had appeared in New York City, the center of the nation's musical life (plates 1-7, 1-8). In 1851 David Jacobs announced banjos for sale with his other musical instruments, which included tambourines for the minstrel trade, and in the same year he was awarded a diploma at the American Institute Fair. By 1850 Jacob Cohen, who had begun as a watchmaker, listed himself as an instrument maker, and a banjo of his took second prize at the 1852 American Institute exhibit. The next year Nathaniel W. Gould entered both a guitar and a banjo in the city's Crystal Palace Exhibition, as did F. G. Resch, from Brooklyn, and Jacobs. William H. Ross won first prize for his instrument at the American Institute fair of 1856, and the drum maker Charles Kell (who later moved to Brooklyn and became a cabinetmaker) was runner-up. In 1858 another cabinetmaker, Frederick Lohr, began to specialize in banjos, establishing with George Unruh a short-lived partnership for the manufacture of instruments. At the end of the decade one W. H. Senior, of 544 Broome Street, was awarded a diploma by the American Institute for a "beautiful specimen of work." New Jersey, too, added its share of opportunities for musicians who sought banjos. In Newark in 1856 George O. Duncklee sold them along with tambourines, and William Pearson of Trenton (1854) and Samuel B. Field of Patterson (1858) also offered the instrument. As with their neighbor Samuel Hinds, however, it is not clear whether these individuals manufactured the instruments they sold or secured them from other individuals.[60]

In the 1850s craftsmen began to appear in other regions: James Ashborn (1852) in Wolcottville, Connecticut; C. M. Zimmerman (1858) in Philadelphia; and George Kilbourne (1859) in Albany, New York. At the first annual exhibition of the Metropolitan Mechanics' Institute in Washington, D.C., in 1853, George Hilbus exhibited a case of instruments that included violins, guitars, harps, and a banjo, and, remarkably, one Edmund W. Woodruff, "aged 12 years," also showed a banjo. The judges noted that the instrument "deserve[d] credit as the work of a youth" and awarded him a book (figs. 1-23, 1-24, 1-25, plates 1-9, 1-10, 1-11). Farther north, in Worcester, Massachusetts, in 1851, George B. Farley entered an instrument in the local mechanics' fair, but the prize committee, like that of a

Figure 1-23. Sixth-plate daguerreotype by A. A. Fish, Boston, Massachusetts, ca. 1855. This well-dressed musician holds a scroll peg head banjo of the sort that by this time could be found in music emporia in cities and larger towns. Note, however, that this banjo still has tack-head construction.

opposite
Figure 1-24. Carte-de-visite by E. P. Fowler, Hartford, Connecticut, ca. 1860s. This player has a six-bracket, swelled-neck banjo. Note the wear to the top of the fingerboard visible on this instrument. Also see figure 1-31 and plate 1-14.

previous year (see above), "were unable to draw out the merry music of this pet aid to minstrelsy." They noted, however, that the instrument was "a gem to look at and had a perfection of finish provokingly attractive to their unskilled hands."[61]

As early as 1853 a banjo "with two strings, and an ornamented perime-

Figure 1-25. Sixth-plate daguerreotype by Cooper and Demarest, 222 Canal Street, New York, ca. 1853–54. This image illustrates a well-made banjo of the sort that by this period was available through professional banjo makers. Note the very unusual scoop to the neck where it joins the rim.

ter," unfortunately not attributed, was displayed at the Massachusetts Mechanic Association exhibition in Boston. Seven years later, Isaiah F. Arey of Boscawen, New Hampshire, who also made violins and guitars, won a diploma for a "banjo of exquisite workmanship," and another was awarded to H. Westerman of East Boston for an instrument "of great beauty and elegance of workmanship." By 1850 Baltimore, like New York, had become an important area for banjo making. At that year's exhibition of the Maryland Institute for the Promotion of the Mechanic Arts, William Hyman entered a banjo "with wooden heads," and the next year no fewer than three makers competed. William E. Boucher Jr. won the first diploma, and James Mayo and T. Fieldhouse were runners-up (fig. 1-26). Of particular interest that year was E. W. Boucher, probably William's father, who exhibited a banjo but chose not to compete. The catalog for the 1856 exhibition adds Levi Brown, a music store owner, to this list of Baltimore makers, and in 1859 both Brown and George Rosenberger entered banjos. In a comment echoing that of the Worcester County Mechanics Association, and indicating how infrequently the instruments were displayed at such

---

Class No. 42.—Musical Instruments.

3.—A large Church Organ, made and dep'd by Henry Erben, Baltimore.

368.—1 Banjo, made and deposited by James Mayo.

869.—1 case Musical Instruments, made and deposited by T. Fieldhouse, 8 E. Baltimore street.

1072.—2 Banjos, by Wm. Boucher, Jr., 32 E. Baltimore street, and deposited by him.

1240.—1 Bell, weighing 700 lbs., made and deposited by Clampitt & Register, 53 Holliday street.

1265.—2 7-Octave Square Pianos, made and deposited by James E. Boswell, Holliday street.

1280.—1 7-Octave Rosewood Piano, (Round) made and deposited by Niel & Duross, 77 Baltimore street.

1331.—2 Violins, made and deposited by Joseph Neff, Philadelphia.

1351.—A case of Musical Instruments, made and deposited by C. H. Eisenbrant, 78 Baltimore street.

Figure 1-26. Page from the *Fourth Annual Exhibition of the Maryland Institute* (Baltimore, 1852). This indicates entries by banjo makers in the "Musical Instruments" category. Such mechanics' exhibitions in the larger cities were an important venue at which banjo makers presented their instruments to the public. Note that William E. Boucher Jr., one of the period's best-known makers, exhibited in this year.

mechanics' fairs, in both of these years the judges apologized for not being qualified to evaluate the banjos because they were "wholly unacquainted with the general quality and requirements" of them. In 1859, however, they observed that "if beauty and workmanship is any test of excellence in other respects," Brown had "succeeded admirably" with his instrument. Interestingly, in these same years the younger Boucher, who today is considered a very important maker, submitted military drums and violins, but no banjos.[62]

By this decade banjos had made their way to the Pacific Coast as well, for they had been available in California at least since 1854, when two different music houses had listed them among their imported stock. In 1857 the firm of Atwill and Company advertised in a New York City trade paper that "among the many interesting manufactures carried out in San Francisco" was that of "Making Guitars, Violins, Banjos, and Stringed Instruments generally," going on to note that these were made by "Mr. Charles Stumcke, an old gentleman of Bremen, who learned his trade 35 years ago in Verona, Italy." Stumcke had worked in New York and had gone to California in 1853. By 1859 the same Charles Morrell who earlier in the decade had made banjos in New York City relocated in San Francisco and was listed as a "Musical Instrument Manufacturer." Interestingly, given minstrelsy's association with the beer halls, he boarded with a brewer.[63]

Overall, however, it is surprising how few craftsmen before the Civil War advertised themselves specifically as banjo makers. In 1861, for example, George Teed, well known for his instruments and holder of two post–Civil War patents for banjos, still listed himself in city directories as a "turner," while Morrell, who reportedly opened his workshop to other New York City banjoists and specialized in the making of "prize banjos" and the repair of banjo heads, operated a bookbinding shop. James Clarke, another person frequently mentioned as an early maker, was a professional dancer on the minstrel stage and appears in city directories only as a commercial "agent." Thus, he might only have been a middleman for those in and outside the city who produced instruments for the New York music trade.[64] The relatively small number of antebellum makers about whom even the slightest information is available suggests that during this period the market for the instruments may still have been fairly limited.

On the other hand, from extant instruments and contemporary photographic evidence, it is clear that by the late 1850s banjo makers had begun to refine the instrument significantly, even if they were nowhere near effecting any sort of standardization of its constituent parts. For a striking example, consider what one of Sweeney's neighbors recalled about the

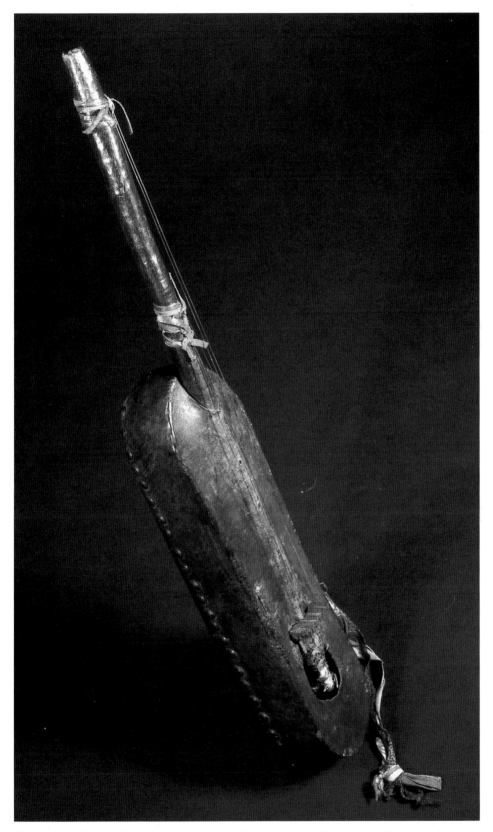

Plate 1-1. African *xalam*, nineteenth century. Many ethnomusicologists believe that the American banjo derived from instruments like this, found in the West African regions from which many enslaved Africans were taken to America. These instruments, however, lack the shortened string on the top of the fingerboard that is characteristic of later banjos. Collection of Peter Szego.

Plate 1-2. *The Old Plantation*. Watercolor, eighteenth century, found in the vicinity of Charleston, South Carolina. This painting illustrates one musician playing a gourd-bodied instrument that resembles a banjo. Most important, although it only has four strings, one of them is clearly shorter than the others and is tightened by a peg on the top side of the neck, like later banjos. Courtesy of Abby Aldrich Rockefeller Folk Art Center, Williamsburg, Virginia.

THEATRE ROYAL, DUBLIN.

THE

VIRGINIA MINSTRELS

(FROM AMERICA,)

Messrs. F. M. BROWER, R. W. PELHAM, D. D. EMMIT, in conjunction with Mr. J. W. SWEENY, (Leader) the *Original Banjo Player,*

BEG RESPECTFULLY TO ANNOUNCE THAT THEIR

BENEFIT

And LAST APPEARANCE in Dublin will take place
This present Tuesday, May 7, 1844,

On which occasion they will be assisted by the valuable services of

MR. COLLINS.

The Performances will commence with the Comedy, in Two Acts, of the

Irish Ambassador.

Sir Patrick O'Plenipo, A.D.C. .... Mr. COLLINS
The Grand Duke, Mr. H. COOKE
Prince Rodolph, Mr. CHUTE   Count Morenos, the Spanish Ambassador, Mr. BARRETT
Baron Lowincraft, the Saxon Ambassador, Mr. J. PENSON   Olmutz, Mr. F. COOKE.   Hermann, Mr. HERON
Isabella, Miss CHALMERS.   Lady Emily de Launcy, Mrs. BARRETT

AFTER WHICH THE

VIRGINIA MINSTRELS

WILL PORTRAY, THROUGH THE MEDIUM OF

Songs, Dances, Lectures, Sayings & Doings,

THE ODDITIES, PECULIARITIES, ECCENTRICITIES AND COMICALITIES, OF THAT

SABLE GENUS OF HUMANITY!!

Each Performer plays on an Instrument such as the Slaves use in the
Southern parts of the United States.

PELHAM, Tamborine.   EMMIT, Violin.
SWEENY, Banjo.   BROWER, Bone Castanets.

☞ Not a trace or shadow of *vulgarity* is mixed up with this truly original attempt at introducing a NEW AND BETTER SCHOOL OF NEGROISM. There is nothing offered either in *word, look,* or *action,* that can in the least degree offend the most fastidious taste.

After which the Comic Piece of the

Nervous Man

AND THE

MAN OF NERVE.

M'Shane, the Man of Nerve ....Mr. COLLINS
IN WHICH HE WILL SING "THE SPRIG OF SHILLELACH."
Mr. Aspen, the Nervous Man, Mr. BAKER
Vivian, Mr. BARRETT.   Captain Burnish, Mr. HOUGHTON.   Lord Lounge, Mr. SALA
Merton, Mr. CHUTE, jun.   Dr. Oxyde, Mr. J. PENSON.   Brown, Mr. HERON
Biggs, Mr. F. COOKE.   Topknot, Mr. SAKER
Lady Leach, Miss PELHAM.   Emily Vivian, Miss HUDDART.   Mrs. Clackit, Mrs. T. HILL
Betty, Mrs. BARRETT.   Mary, Miss PENSON

To be followed by the New Fashionable Dance of

THE POLKA, IN CHARACTER,

By Miss Massall, Miss Cooke, Mr. F. Cooke & Mr. Chute, jun.
UNDER THE INSTRUCTION OF MONSIEUR BARNET.

To conclude with the SECOND PART of the Performances of the

VIRGINIA MINSTRELS,

IN WHICH

Plate 1-4. Broadside, ca. 1840s, announcing the appearance of the famed Virginia Minstrels in Dublin, Ireland. This group, comprised of Dan Emmett, Billy Whitlock, Frank Brower, and Dick Pelham, is acknowledged as the first professional minstrel troupe. Shortly after their successful debut in New York, they crossed the Atlantic, bringing the craze for minstrelsy to the British Isles. Collection of Peter Szego.

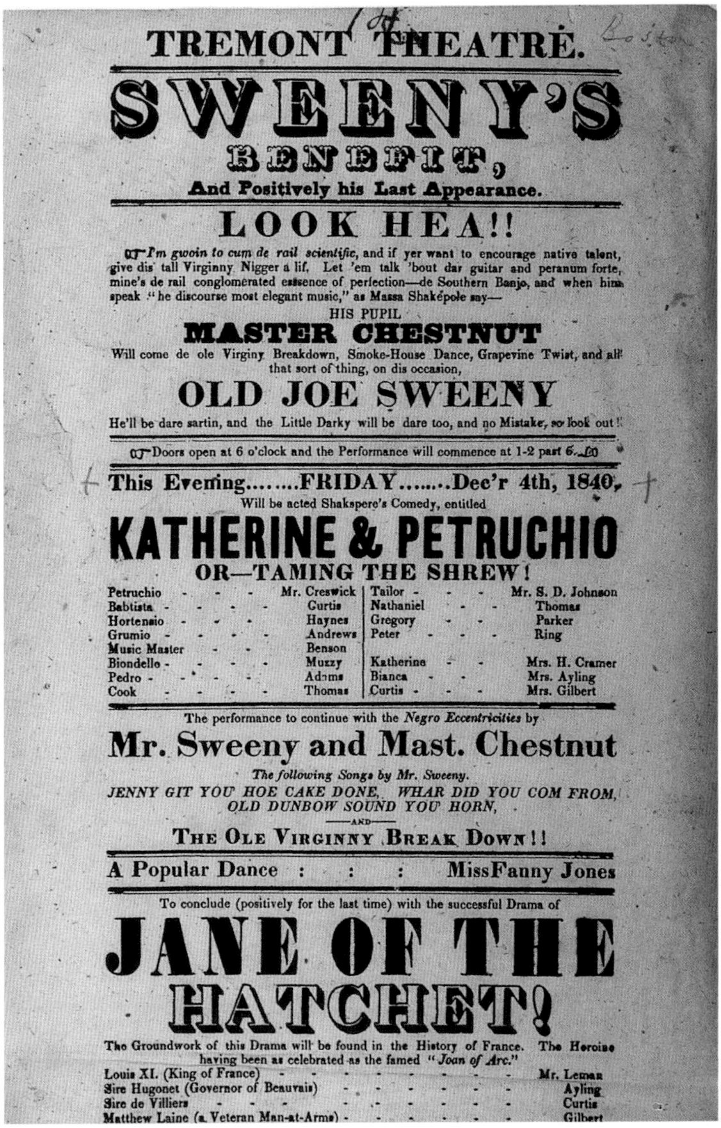

Plate 1-5. Broadside, ca. 1840s, announcing the performance of the great minstrel banjoist Joel Sweeney at the Tremont Theater in Boston. Collection of Peter Szego.

Plate 1-6. Broadside, 19 October 1857, announcing a banjo contest in New York. This is the earliest known advertisement for such an event, at which well-known minstrel performers showed off in front of large and appreciative audiences. Such contests became much more common after the Civil War as banjo makers sought to prove the superiority of their instruments. Collection of Peter Szego.

Plate 1-7. Minstrel banjo, ca. late 1840s or 1850s. This unusual instrument has two fifth-string tuning pegs, on the top and bottom of the neck, perhaps so that the banjo could be played right- or left-handed. Its unusual peg head closely resembles the one on a banjo made in the 1850s by Henry Stichter that is in the Bollman collection. Collection of Peter Szego.

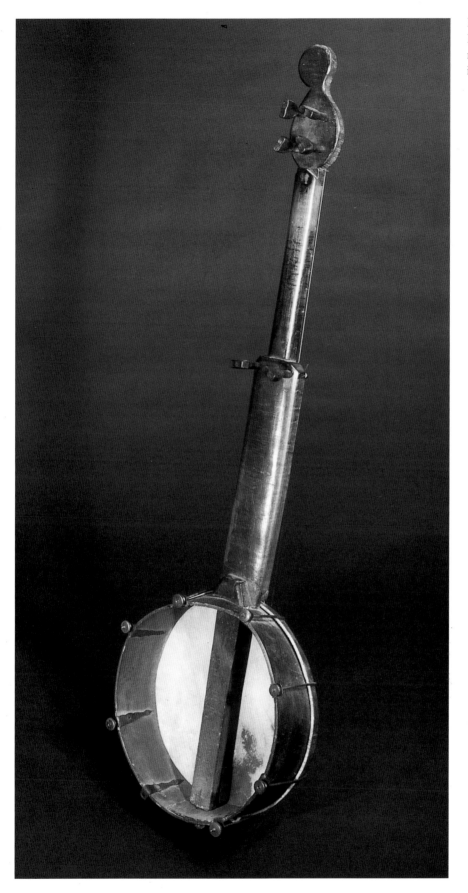

Plate 1-8.
Rear view of the
minstrel banjo
in plate 1-7.

Plate 1-9. Minstrel-era banjo, ca. 1850. This banjo features an unusual exaggerated scroll peg head and a neck that is made of tight-grained "gun stock" maple. For such an early instrument, it also is unusual because of its enclosed back, with stunning marquetry decoration characteristic of the finest cabinetmaking of that period. Note the low position of the fifth-string tuning peg. Collection of Peter Szego.

Plate 1-10. Rear view of the minstrel-era banjo in plate 1-9.

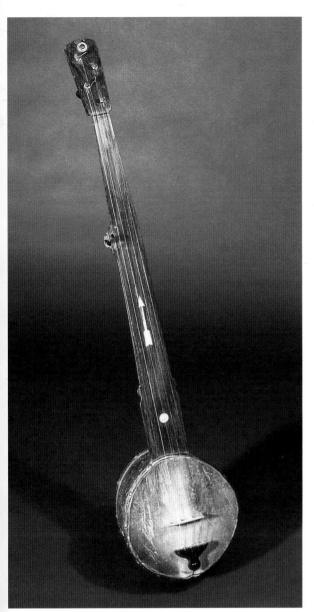

top left
Plate 1-12. Tack-head banjo, double-headed, that is, with skin on the bottom as well as the top of the rim, ca. 1850s. The dowel stick reads "Made by D. P. Diuguid, Lynchburg, Virginia." In addition to being double-headed, reminiscent of a drum, this banjo has an unusual neck, turned like a furniture leg, a design that would come naturally to a cabinet-maker, the trade Diuguid followed. Collection of Peter Szego.

top right
Plate 1-13. Rear view of the tack-head banjo in plate 1-12.

opposite
Plate 1-11. Detail of the minstrel-era banjo in plate 1-9, showing the back of the rim with its elaborate marquetry.

Plate 1-14. Minstrel-era banjo, ca. 1850. This instrument has an unusual scroll and also a swell in the neck close to the rim (also see figures 1-24 and 1-31). Note the unusual brass inlay on the peg head and fingerboard. Banjos of this design would have been seen on the New York stage in the early years of minstrelsy and probably were built in that city. They were depicted in some of the early broadside advertisements for minstrels but are known today in only a very few examples. Collection of Peter Szego.

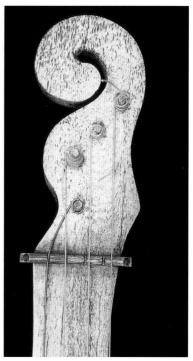

left
Plate 1-15. Minstrel-era banjo, ca. 1850s, with neck, tailpiece, tuners, and rim made from whalebone. This highly unusual instrument, probably made by a sailor in the course of a lengthy whaling voyage, has a scroll peg head characteristic of early banjos, and other unusual appointments that indicate that its maker was a master at scrimshaw. Although the banjo came from a collection in England, its general shape strongly suggests an American instrument. Courtesy of the Kendall Whaling Museum, Randolph, Massachusetts.

top
Plate 1-16. Detail of the peg head of the scrimshaw banjo (plate 1-15), showing the fine scrimshaw carving.

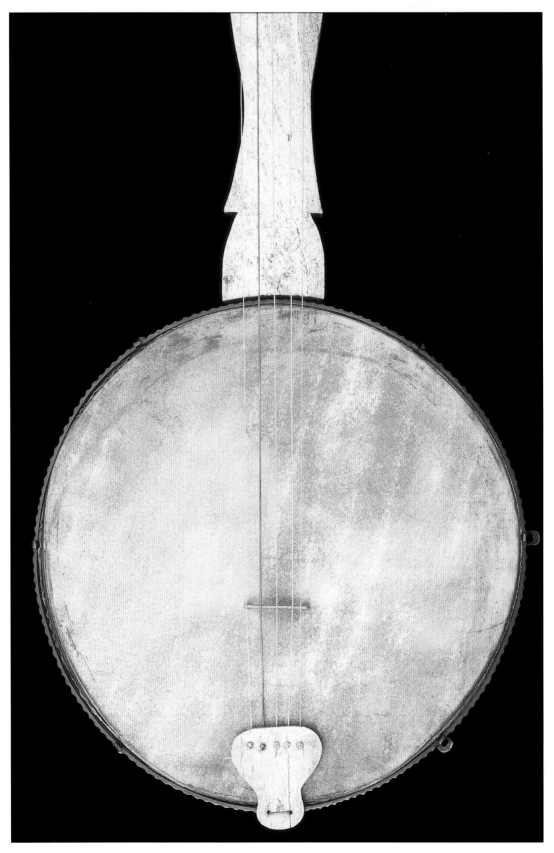

Plate 1-17. Detail of the scrimshaw banjo (plate 1-15), showing an unusual carved neck where it joins the rim.

Plate 1-18. Detail of the scrimshaw banjo (plate 1-15), showing the back of the rim, with reinforcements at the top and bottom of the rim and a whalebone dowel. The rim is made from "pan" bone, that is, a heavier piece of the whale skeleton.

Plate 1-19. Banjo made by William Esperance Boucher Jr., Baltimore, Maryland, ca. 1850s. This instrument features this maker's distinctive peg head and scalloped fingerboard, as well as beautiful faux-rosewood graining on its rim. On this instrument Boucher also scalloped the bottom of the rim where the nuts for tightening the head are located, presumably so that they would not protrude beyond the bottom of the rim and catch on clothing (also see plate 1-23). Collection of Peter Szego.

Plate 1-20. Banjo made by William Esperance Boucher Jr., ca. late 1840s or 1850s. This is a typical six-bracket, scalloped-rim Boucher. The roman numerals "XIII" are found on top of the dowel and on the end block through which the dowel fits. Since two banjos have been seen with identical numerals, these may represent batch or model numbers rather than serial numbers.

Plate 1-21. Banjo made by William Esperance Boucher Jr., ca. late 1840s–early 1850s. This instrument is unusual because of its rectangular peg head, but it still shows Boucher's characteristic double-ogee scallop on the fingerboard. Having a much longer string length than the banjo in plate 1-20, this instrument may have been made earlier, a fact supported as well by the unusual rim design (see plate 1-22). Collection of Philip F. Gura.

Plate 1-22. Detail of the Boucher banjo in plate 1-21, showing holes cut through the rim to allow easier tightening of the wing nuts that secure the skin head.

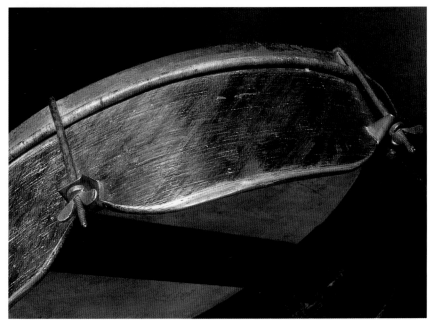

Plate 1-23. Detail of the scalloped rim on the Boucher banjo in plate 1-19, illustrating how a nut is tightened within each scallop, thus keeping the ends of the hooks and nuts from protruding beyond the rim (also see plate 1-19). Note the beautiful faux graining to make the rim look as if it were rosewood.

Plate 1-24. Detail of the Boucher banjo in plate 1-19, showing the neck and dowel, the latter passing through an end block for reinforcement before going through the rim to serve as an attachment for the tailpiece.

Plate 1-25. Guitar made by James Ashborn, Wolcottville, Connecticut, 1854. This beautiful guitar, made for William Hall and Son, New York musical dealers, is a No. 6, the highest grade that Ashborn produced. In addition to having Brazilian rosewood sides and back and an ebony fingerboard, it features elaborate marquetry around the top and end pin. It sold for $25. Collection of Philip F. Gura.

Plate 1-26. Banjo made by James Ashborn, ca. 1855–60. Stamped on the back of the peg head, "J. Ashborn/ Patented 1852," this fretless instrument has Ashborn's patented tuners (see figure 1-38) but lacks the bracket band found on most of his other extant instruments. Note the fretless ebony fingerboard and the guitar-style peg head. Collection of Peter Szego.

top
Plate 1-28. Detail of the Ashborn banjo in plate 1-26. Note the flat heel, thick round dowel, and the unusual arrangement of hooks, which allow tightening of the rim without the necessity of drilling through it to install shoes. In his later models Ashborn solved this same problem by having the hooks go through a bracket band glued around the rim.

bottom
Plate 1-29. Detail of a banjo made by James Ashborn, ca. late 1850s. This instrument (also shown in plate 1-30) has Ashborn's unique external bracket band that allows the hooks to be tightened without shoes, which require drilling through the rim. In this novel manner Ashborn preserved the physical and acoustical integrity of the rim. Collection of Peter Szego.

opposite
Plate 1-27. Rear view of the Ashborn banjo in plate 1-26. Note the diamond joint with which the peg head is attached to the neck, typical of Ashborn's and other mid-nineteenth-century guitars.

Plate 1-30. Banjo made by James Ashborn, ca. late 1850s. Ashborn made this instrument (seen in detail in plate 1-29) with a slotted, guitar-style peg head and geared brass tuners. It also is fretted, and while such instruments were known in the late 1850s, it usually is difficult to tell precisely when frets were added to an instrument. They were added to many older banjos in the 1870s, for example, as frets became more fashionable. Collection of Peter Szego.

kind of instruments the young Sweeney saw on his Virginia plantation. "The negro slaves used to take large gourds," George Inge wrote, "and put on four strings made of horse hair, using a crooked handle gourd and putting in a stick for a staff [that is, a neck]." By the time Sweeney was eighteen (in the late 1820s), however, he had made, another friend remembered, a five-string banjo, which probably resembled the one that Joseph Cave subsequently acquired in England.[65] This banjo was "rather crudely constructed, consisting of nothing more than a hoop about four inches wide, with a piece of vellum fastened on with brass-headed nails, and a light shaft of wood running through the tambourine-like body forming the fingerboard. There were four larger strings and a smaller one, always tuned to the octave of the key the instrument was tuned in."[66]

But given that other banjoists had performed on stage for at least a decade, what was it about this kind of banjo that Sweeney might have wished to hide from others? Clearly it was not a novel way of attaching the head to the rim, for tacking was the most obvious way of stretching the membrane across the top of the instrument. Was it the shorter fifth string, which, as *The Old Plantation* watercolor indicates, did not originate with him but still might have been unusual? Unfortunately, nothing in Cave's anecdote provides an answer. But we know that the tack-headed instrument Cave acquired in 1843 bore only the slightest resemblance to, say, the sophisticated Ashborn banjo with which James Buckley posed for the cover illustration of his *New Banjo Book* in 1860 (see figure 1-39).

Even with such limited information, however, in this period we are able to document the emergence of banjo making as a separate and distinct craft as the instrument was "improved" in various ways, establishing the foundation for more extensive innovation in the postbellum period. The description of Cave's banjo provides a good starting point, for perhaps the most conspicuous aspect of its construction, the way the membrane was stretched over the rim by tacks, early on was modified by makers who sought a more reliable tone. However well this method of stretching the membrane over the sound chamber worked for players in the folk tradition, for example, it was unsatisfactory if one used the instrument regularly in front of large audiences or wished to play in tune with instruments like the violin, for the skin head sags in humid atmospheric conditions, making difficult both the banjo's tuning and the maintenance of a strong sound. The great classical banjoist Albert Baur, for example, recalled that in the antebellum period stage performers often had to warm up "the old tack head banjo" before they could go on stage, sometimes utilizing "a gaslight or flame from a burning newspaper" for the task (fig. 1-27).[67]

Very quickly, "nearly every banjo player" tried to "get up" an "improved

Figure 1-27. Quarter-plate daguerreotype, ca. 1850. One of the most technologically
and artistically striking images that we have found, this portrait of an obviously well-to-do
banjoist seated in a painted chair shows him with a large tack-head banjo typical of the
earliest years of banjo manufacture. Note as well the scroll peg head, the unusual scallop
below the fifth-string tuning peg, and the large tailpiece, identical in shape to the one
found on the Boucher banjo in plate 1-19.

Banjo." At the turn of the twentieth century, for example, the banjoist Thomas J. Armstrong recalled that such "a mania" existed among banjoists that "making a banjo appeared to be a rather tempting and easy proposition on account of the extreme simplicity of the instrument."[68] The principal challenge from the mechanic's viewpoint, though, was the way to attach and adjust the animal-skin head (fig. 1-28). Baur remembered seeing a few banjos "with holes drilled through the top hoop and corresponding ones in the rim," with "cords drawn through these holes, and on the cords . . . ears similar to drum tighteners."[69] Soon enough, though, banjo makers adopted various kinds of hooks, wing nuts, and tension hoops for this purpose, in some cases preserving the form of a drum by mounting a skin across the bottom of the rim as well as the top, and cutting holes in it to let out the sound (plates 1-12, 1-13). Eventually square or hexagonal nuts replaced the more awkward, protruding wings, and because most banjos were constructed with a single membrane on top of the instrument, shoes through which the hooks passed were mounted on the rim with a rivet or small nut and bolt (fig. 1-29). Other makers were more inventive. On his elegant banjos of the 1850s, Ashborn mounted an ingenious wooden bracket band (surprisingly unpatented, given that this maker took that step to protect other of his innovations) around the rim, with hooks tightened by a key into hex nuts countersunk in the band.

We still know very little about rim size and construction in this period; in particular, there is little documentation of gourd-bodied banjos of the kind described in folk tradition still being used on stage.[70] Although at the Maryland Institute in 1852 James Mayo exhibited a "Brass Banjo," steam-bent wooden hoops of the sort used by drum manufacturers quickly became the rule, bringing to banjo making an element of standardization not possible in gourd-bodied instruments.[71] Further, contemporary photographic evidence, as well as extant instruments, bears out Phil Rice's description, in 1858, of an ideal banjo's having a "drum twelve inches across inside, three and a half inches deep."[72] Such large dimensions produced the deeper tone characteristic of the keys of F or G in which the minstrel banjo usually was played prior to the 1860s (fig. 1-30). Finally, although a dependable supply of calfskin or sheepskin was essential to the construction of these instruments, we know virtually nothing about where the skins were acquired, though one banjoist called for "good lime-cured calf skin . . . not too thick, or too thin," and another for "premature calf-skin . . . extremely thin and transparent." One suspects that the cities' numerous slaughterhouses and tanneries provided all that were needed.[73]

Necks (or "handles" or "arms," as they were called in the contemporary literature) varied greatly, particularly in their length and, to a lesser ex-

Figure 1-28. Sixth-plate ambrotype, ca. late 1850s. This young player has a well-made instrument with a fairly large number of brackets tightening the skin head. In the early period of banjo making, the sophistication of the instrument's tightening mechanism often distinguished a professional's work from an amateur's.

Figure 1-29. Sixth-plate ambrotype, ca. late 1850s. This well-dressed musician has a
banjo on which one can easily see the six large metal bracket shoes through which hooks
were fastened to tighten the skin head of the instrument. Such improvements were
increasingly common by the 1850s, with a larger number of hooks providing a stronger
tension to the head.

Figure 1-30. Half-plate ambrotype, late 1850s. Large heads like the one on this banjo—
at least twelve inches in diameter—were typical of banjos before the 1870s and gave them
their characteristically deep sound. This image also illustrates the fifth-string "bump"
through which the peg was inserted vertically. Collection of Philip F. Gura.

tent, in the number of strings stretched over them. Minstrel sheet-music covers, for example, though not always fully reliable as documentation, often show a very long neck, ending in a flat scroll and having a swelled part high up, around the modern-day fourteenth-fret position, though very few such banjos are extant (figs. 1-31, 1-32, 1-33, plates 1-14, 1-15, 1-16, 1-17, 1-18).[74] On the other hand, most instruments made by Boucher have a scroll peg head, probably derived from those found on early guitars such as the ones made in New York and, later, Nazareth, Pennsylvania, by C. F. Martin, even as the neck length varies considerably. Again we might take Rice's measurement, in this case of a twenty-eight-inch scale from the nut to the bridge, as typical of the instruments. Rice's *Method* also establishes another important fact: by the late 1850s some makers placed either raised frets or marks (presumably inlaid or flush in the fingerboard) on their instruments to indicate finger positions. Rice, for example, both illustrates them in his drawings of the banjo's neck and describes them matter-of-factly in his written directions for tuning the banjo and learning music.[75]

Finally, by the 1850s most makers settled on five strings—not the four reported by the old banjo players with whom Albert Baur had spoken in the 1850s, nor the six that George Teed, beginning in the 1860s, regularly put on his instruments—as the most common number, one of which (the "buzz" string, Baur called it) tuned part way up the neck, usually between the modern-day fifth- to seventh-fret positions.[76] Tuning mechanisms for these strings varied. Violin-style tuners were most common, but in an attempt to improve them Ashborn developed two variations of these wooden friction tuners, which he used on both guitars and banjos, and which he took the trouble to patent (as we shall see below). From at least the 1850s some makers used guitar-style metal-geared tuning machines (usually termed "patent" tuners), even adapting them for the fifth string. Through the 1850s the fifth-string tuner was either put through the neck vertically, as on Bouchers, or horizontally, as on Ashborns (fig. 1-34).

The aim of antebellum banjo making, then, was to produce instruments whose sound quality was more dependable but whose overall dimensions were only minimally standardized. Two antebellum makers about whom more information is available provide the opportunity to examine in more detail both the nature of such experimentation and attempted standardization as well as the business arrangements through which such instruments were marketed in and through urban centers.

Based on the number of his extant instruments, one of the most prominent antebellum banjo makers was William Esperance Boucher Jr. (1822–

99) of Baltimore, whose firm also made drums, violins, and guitars.[77] The precise date at which he began to make instruments is unclear because his father, also named William, was an instrument maker, too, with at least one banjo to his credit; 1849 marks the first year in which city directories distinguished the two men. To complicate matters, advertisements in directories as well as other documentary evidence indicate that neither Boucher was known primarily for his banjos.[78] In Baltimore's mechanics' fairs, for example, the younger man was most likely to exhibit "military

Figure 1-31. Sixth-plate ambrotype, ca. late 1850s. The swelled neck on this instrument indicates that it probably was constructed before 1860 (also see figure 1-24 and plate 1-14). Lithographed sheet-music covers often show such instruments in the hands of stage banjoists. Note that this particular banjo was made for a left-handed player.

drums," which one jury declared "very beautiful specimens" that "fully en-
title him to continued public confidence and encouragement in this department" (fig. 1-35). He was also praised for violins that were "home productions, the back and sides of Maryland curly maple, the top of Albany
pine," and whose "form and finish," one panel of judges concluded, were
"highly creditable to the maker, and their musical qualities as good as
those for which much higher prices are frequently paid."[79]

Boucher's renown as a banjo maker derives in part from three instru-

Figure 1-32. Sixth-plate tintype, ca. 1860s. The scroll of the S-shaped peg head found on
this banjo was popular on minstrel-era instruments. Also note the vertical fifth-string tuner,
here situated fairly close to the peg head, and the image reversal.

Figure 1-33. Sixth-plate ambrotype, ca. late 1850s. This banjoist plays a very long-necked instrument of the sort often found before the 1860s. The rim size also is large and, coupled with the long neck, points to the low keys to which such instruments were tuned in the minstrel period. Note the image reversal.

opposite
Figure 1-34. Carte-de-visite by L. C. Laudy, Peekskill, New York, ca. 1860s. This early banjo, with a very large head, has its fifth-string tuning peg mounted horizontally into the neck rather than vertically as on many antebellum banjos.

ments that he bequeathed to the Smithsonian Institution in 1890, which were thus acknowledged: "Three Banjos, of the styles made in the years 1845–6–7, by Mr. Boucher, the inventor of tightening banjo-heads by screw fixtures, showing the first method, and two subsequent improvements."[80] All extant Boucher banjos save one have heads that are tightened by hooks and nuts that are inserted through shoes, but if he was indeed the first to improve the banjo in such a way, he never bothered to patent his method, perhaps because it was quickly and widely copied.[81] While it is impossible to say for sure whether Boucher's instruments were the first to have hook-and-nut assemblies that offered an advance over tack-head banjos, by the late 1840s and 1850s his banjos still had become quite distinctive.

Their most striking feature is a flat scroll peg head, which usually has a small "beehive" finial at its top (plate 1-19). Some Boucher banjos have only a simple rectangular peg head, while one of the Smithsonian's instruments has very unusual "rabbit-ears"; most of the other twenty-odd extant minstrel-era instruments have a characteristic, graceful S-shaped design (figs. 1-36, 1-37). Moreover, Boucher's minstrel-era necks always have a scallop or curvature on the top or fifth-string side, with the first bump where the fifth-string peg protrudes (usually vertically), following in a graceful double-ogee pattern to the seventh-, ninth-, and twelfth-fret positions on some long-scaled instruments, but only to the seventh (a single ogee) on other, shorter-scale examples (plates 1-20, 1-21).[82] Other characteristics of Boucher necks, which are usually made from three pieces of wood, are their rather flattened, wide fingerboards, up to an inch-and-a-half wide at the nut and two-and-three-quarters inches where the neck joins the rim, and a squared "perchpole," or dowel, with a rounded, off-

---

Class No. 45—Musical Instruments.

1—Banjo, made and deposited by George Rosenberger, Vine street.
2—Banjo, made and deposited by Levi Brown, 568 W. Baltimore street.
3—Pyramid of Drums, one with improvements, made and deposited by W. Boucher, 38 E. Baltimore street.
4—Church Bell, made and deposited by Regester & Webb, Holliday-st.

Figure 1-35. *Twelfth Annual Report of the . . . Maryland Institute* (Baltimore, 1860). This page lists William E. Boucher's drums, for which he was very well known, as well as two other makers' banjos.

centered end where it protrudes through the rim so that the tailpiece can be secured to it.

Just as Boucher's neck is distinctive for its scalloped side and scroll peg head, his rims, despite their variations, indicate his attempts to standardize the instrument's construction. Rim size on extant instruments, for example, is large, from eleven-and-three-quarters to twelve-and-a-half inches in diameter, and from three to three-and-a-quarter inches deep, from a sin-

Figure 1-36. Half-plate tintype, ca. 1860s. The man in the middle holds over his shoulder a Boucher banjo, its distinctive scroll clearly visible.

gle piece of bent wood, usually split oak. The novelty appears in the various ways in which Boucher tightened the skin head over the rim, borrowed from contemporary drum making, usually with six hooks and wing nuts pulling on a tension hoop.[83] On the simplest (and perhaps the oldest) models, he cut holes in the middle of the rim where a wing nut was tightened, thus allowing one to adjust the head's tension easily without the need for a longer hook that would protrude beyond the bottom of the rim (plate 1-22). On other banjos, he scalloped the bottom of the rim in such a way that the nut was tightened in the space where the curvature was most pronounced, again so that the hook's end would not protrude beyond the rim (plate 1-23). On some double-headed instruments (that is, with skin stretched across the top and bottom of the rim, like a narrow drum), he welded a bracket shoe to the lower tension hoop, so that the long hook's end would protrude through it and thus enable one to tighten both heads at once. Finally, particularly on his earlier banjos, his brackets were not cast metal but were cut rather simply from sheet metal and were riveted, not bolted, to the rim.

Boucher's banjos have little ornamentation but are elegantly proportioned, the beehive finial prominent and distinctive. He also attractively faux-grained some of his rims, usually to simulate rosewood; his necks have no separate fingerboard and are usually finished in a brown, reddish-brown, or dark red that complements the rim (plate 1-24). One extant banjo, double-headed, has a beautiful bird's-eye maple neck and the same wood veneered over an oak rim. With the exception of the hooks and brackets, on most extant instruments few other appointments survive: his tuning pegs resemble wooden violin friction tuners, and the remains of an original tailpiece indicate a large (five-inch) size, appropriate to the diameter of the rim. Finally, he usually stamped his banjos "W. Boucher, Jr./ Baltimore" at the base of the neck on the heel, and his instruments often have numerals (usually roman, but occasionally arabic) stamped on the dowel and/or the tail block through which the end of the dowel passes. Numbered to about forty, these might be serial numbers, but since one duplication of number has been found, they more likely are woodworkers' marks to indicate which sections fit with each other, or perhaps batch numbers that identify instruments made around the same time, often on the basis of advance orders.

opposite
Figure 1-37. Tintype of Mattie Vernon of Beverly Centre, Ohio, ca. 1860s. Vernon plays a very long-necked Boucher with a double ogee rather than the more common single ogee (see plates 1-19, 1-20, and 1-21).

The overall impression of Boucher's instruments is of subtle hand-craftsmanship, and in the late 1840s and 1850s they obviously offered significant improvement over the cruder instruments made by amateurs or the specialty items produced by other kinds of craftsmen. Boucher took the trouble to display his banjos at the famous Crystal Palace Exhibition in New York City in 1853, where he also showed a guitar. He frequently exhibited at the Maryland Institute for the Promotion of the Mechanic Arts and at the Franklin Institute in Philadelphia; but, as we have noted, at these venues he was as likely to show violins, guitars, and drums, which he probably learned to make in his father's workshop and for which he also won awards.[84]

Given the construction of his instruments, which throughout his career suggest handcraftsmanship rather than factory production, Boucher is perhaps best understood in a tradition of European musical instrument making epitomized by the careers of the noted American guitar maker Christian Frederick Martin (1796–1873) in New York City and Nazareth, Pennsylvania, and Heinrich Christian Eisenbrandt (1790–1860) in Boucher's own Baltimore.[85] Martin, the son of Johann Georg Martin, a cabinetmaker and sometime guitar maker in the region around Markneukirchen in Saxony, had been apprenticed to the noted maker Johann Stauffer in Vienna, rising to become a foreman in his shop. In 1826 he returned to Markneukirchen to make guitars, but by the end of 1833 he had followed his friend Henry Schatz, another guitar maker, to New York City to open a music store (he sold the same variety of goods that Boucher later would) and continue his guitar making. In 1839, after corresponding with other Germans, including Schatz, who had moved to the Lehigh Valley of Pennsylvania and found the area to their liking, Martin took his family and guitar works to that region. But he continued to market his instruments through New York, forming various partnerships—one with his fellow countryman Charles A. Zoebisch—for the distribution of his instruments.

Eisenbrandt, whose father was a well-known maker of woodwinds in Göttingen, also followed the family trade and emigrated to the United States in 1808 to avoid conscription in the Napoleonic Wars. After working briefly in Philadelphia (as a flute instructor) and in New York City, Eisenbrandt married the daughter of family friends in Baltimore. By 1815, however, he returned to Germany and through his parents' considerable influence became a court instrument maker in Hanover. But, unsympathetic to the autocratic German state, in 1819 he returned to Baltimore and went into business as a woodwind maker and musical instrument importer, starting a dynasty that lasted into the twentieth century.[86]

For our purposes, the important parts of these congruent biographies are Martin's and Eisenbrandt's European apprenticeships and their cultivation and maintenance of business contacts with other family and friends in Europe or America. For, as Laurence Libin has pointed out, it is likely that a similar extended network of musical instrument makers, centered on the Eisenbrandt family, was established by these emigrants in Baltimore, and that the Bouchers may have been in their orbit. Some of the accordions, organs, "clarionettes," and flutes that the Bouchers carried in their shops, for example, very likely were made or imported by the Eisenbrandt circle. And Eisenbrandt, who like the elder Boucher had emigrated to the United States from Germany, and who frequently returned to Europe to maintain contacts among suppliers of musical instruments, may initially have encouraged Boucher to move to Baltimore.[87] Upon reaching that city, in any case, Boucher established his own music business in the shop once used by Eisenbrandt and eventually located his operation at 84½ Baltimore Street, in the heart of the city's music district and a few doors up from Eisenbrandt's shop.

Extended family and business arrangements like those of Schatz, Martin, Eisenbrandt, and Boucher are best understood in the tradition of European guilds. We know, for example, that C. F. Martin emigrated to New York in part because of an extended conflict in Markneukirchen between the powerful violin makers' guild and that of the cabinetmakers, which included guitar makers, the former claiming that the latter did not have the right to make musical instruments.[88] In Europe such craftsmen—violin makers and guitar makers both—would have acquired their skills over several years (as Martin had) as apprentices working meticulously with hand tools. Like Martin and Eisenbrandt, the elder Boucher had been raised in this tradition; he did not establish his own music business (near his parents) until he was in his mid-twenties, obviously long enough to have had such an apprenticeship, though we have no concrete proof of it.

These observations and speculations assume more weight if we juxtapose them to the very different career of the English guitar and banjo maker James Ashborn, who in the late 1840s established a mechanized guitar factory in rural Connecticut that became one of the nation's chief sources for parlor guitars and banjos for the minstrel stage. Despite a lack of documentation specifically for Ashborn's banjos, his accounting journal for the guitar works, covering the period from April 1851 to January 1856 and recording his expenses for supplies and labor, the numbers and types of guitars he produced, and his financial arrangements with the music trade in New York City, where all his instruments were sold, opens a remarkable window on little-known aspects of the early American music trade.[89] In particular, the Ashborn materials allow us to compare the transition from specialized workshop production of the sort typified by Martin and Boucher to early factory production, marked as much by the division of labor as by the use of new machinery, that soon transformed American manufacturing.

Born in England in 1816, Ashborn emigrated to New York in the 1830s and a decade later established his residence in the area around Wolcottville, now part of Torrington, Connecticut, perhaps to join the forty-odd English men and women recruited by the principal manager of a projected brass works in Wolcottville.[90] In any event, unlike Boucher and other contemporary instrument makers, after Ashborn had begun to make guitars he continued for several years to designate himself as a "mechanic," a term usually denoting someone who made mechanical devices or was somehow involved in the mechanized labor that characterized the industrial revolution.[91]

Departing from traditional stringed-instrument making, Ashborn produced his guitars in a mechanized workshop in which he utilized water-powered machinery to manufacture instruments more productively.[92] After identifying a large and dependable market—New York City's music emporia—he had sought local investment from those already engaged in, and thus knowledgeable about, the ways in which manufactured goods could be distributed; he then set about modifying a traditional craft (hitherto practiced, as we have seen, primarily by luthiers) to produce instruments in greater numbers and at a good profit.[93] He accomplished this through standardized and simplified construction of his instruments, consolidation of hitherto segregated segments of instrument manufacture in one factory, and the assembly of a workforce whose labor was divided to expedite the assembly of guitars and their accessories.

In this setting Ashborn and his workmen manufactured a remarkable number of instruments. Between April 1851 and December 1855, for example, the years covered in the accounting journal, he produced 3,152 guitars, shipping on average fifty-four per month to William Hall and Son and to Firth, Pond and Company, the sole firms through which the guitars were distributed. In contrast, during this same period C. F. Martin produced only about thirty instruments per year.[94] No doubt because the factory helped Ashborn and his partner increase production without incurring significantly greater labor costs, they were able to keep their prices constant throughout this five-year period, from $8.50 for a No. 1, the lowest grade, to $25 for a No. 6, the top-of-the-line model (plate 1-25).

To meet the ever-increasing demands of the New York market, Ashborn simplified production by making his guitars all the same size and shape, eliminating the need for different sized molds and jigs for shaping the instruments' ribs or for different scales for marking frets. Most important, he also adapted traditional design to more rapid factory production.[95] For example, he attached the neck to the body of the instrument with the use of a dovetailed joint and the addition of a short collar glued to the back, a more expeditious manner of assembly than that which used the traditional "Spanish" heel, for which a maker had to slot the sides of the body into the neck (which then continues a short way into the body), a method that requires tedious adjustment and thus allows for more variation among instruments. Finally, Ashborn spliced the peg head to the top of the neck with a distinctive diamond joint that permitted a large gluing surface and thus a strong bond, a method he used on his banjo work as well.

Equally significant was Ashborn's division of labor within the factory among his ten or so workers, a phenomenon that historians have identified as one of the distinguishing characteristics of the industrial revolution, especially in rural areas.[96] One employee, for example, was retained primarily as a "Polisher," who was paid extra for "bridging" guitars, that is, for properly setting the height of the bridges and gluing them in place. Another machined brass for Ashborn's distinctive metal tuners. Others worked in sawing and shaping the wood, and still others in more menial labor—the winding of strings that Ashborn also manufactured or the assembly of wooden cases for the instruments. With a pay scale that ranged from $.50 to $1.50 per day, Ashborn paid on the average about $290 per month for labor, from as little as $212 just before construction began for a new factory to $388 the month before he sent his largest shipment ever to the city.

Although Ashborn worked almost a hundred miles from New York City, his livelihood depended on the metropolis, for he marketed all his instruments there, shipping them directly by rail from the station in Torrington to William Hall and Son, with whom he did 85 percent of his business, and Firth, Pond and Company, who accounted for the other 15 percent. Each month Ashborn meticulously recorded transactions with these companies, listing as debits the cost of the different grades of guitars shipped (also noting the instruments' serial numbers) and of the numbers of strings (in dozens) and other items provided, as well as the salaries for the work his employees performed—sawing lumber for the companies' piano manufactories in the city, for example. He also indicated the days on which the factory shipped the items or performed the work, for in any given month Ashborn sent goods to the same firm in several different shipments.

The companies paid Ashborn in one of two ways, either in cash, in the form of bank drafts payable in ten, twenty, thirty, sixty, ninety, or occasionally up to 120 days, or in goods, usually materials he needed for his instrument work but had difficulty obtaining locally—tropical woods like mahogany, rosewood, and ebony, for example, or the silver wire and silk needed for string manufacture. Further, when the New York companies wrote bank drafts to Ashborn, they often issued a series of them on one day, payable at different times over the next few months, standard practice in the contemporary business world, and they usually did so only once or twice in a given month, even if the factory shipped items in several different batches. In addition to depositing drafts from New York in their local bank in Winsted, Ashborn and his partner also issued their own notes to local people in payment for purchases for the factory, and they frequently drew substantial amounts of cash—sometimes $100 or more—for themselves, presumably as salary as well as reimbursement for goods procured for work carried out at the factory.

Until more such records come to light, the accounts from Ashborn's guitar works provide our most detailed look at the business of stringed instrument making in the antebellum period and thus illuminate his banjo production as well. Virtually all his extant banjos, for example, prominently display (as do his guitars) the stamp of one of the New York companies—William Hall and Son, Firth, Pond and Company, or, in the 1860s, William A. Pond and Company, which, with Firth, Son and Company, succeeded the latter—to whom he sold his instruments. There is no reason to believe that his arrangements for the sale and distribution of these instruments was any different than that for his guitars. Moreover, the sophistication of, as well as the innovation displayed in, his banjos—the product of an engineer or "mechanic" used to thinking about technology and innovation rather than a craftsman settled comfortably in a guild tradition— point the direction for the development of banjo manufacture in a post– Civil War world of ever-growing industry and enterprise.

Ashborn's banjos show refined craftsmanship, as befits the work of a guitar maker. For example, both necks and rims are typically made of attractive maple, with a standard rim size of about twelve-and-a-half inches and a scale ranging from twenty-six to twenty-eight inches. As we have noted, the peg head is spliced to the neck with an attractive diamond joint, in the manner of his guitar head stocks (plates 1-26, 1-27). Overt decoration is minimal, although there is usually rosewood veneer on the fingerboard and the front of the peg head and, on some instruments, ebony on both the front and back of the latter. One extant instrument has curly maple veneer over a straight-grained rim, as well as herringbone marquetry on the its wooden bracket band. Finally, on Ashborn's instruments the dowel is nicely turned and goes into an end block before passing through the rim to form an attachment for the tailpiece. Near the flat heel the dowel is secured against the rim by a wooden wedge (plate 1-28).

The most remarkable thing about Ashborn's banjos, however, is the novel system for tightening the head (plate 1-29). On all extant instruments save one (which has conventional metal shoes secured to the rim by screws), Ashborn used a wooden bracket band that he glued to the side of the rim, toward its bottom, with brackets (usually twelve, but on one example, eighteen) tightened into it by a key that turned small hex-nut assemblies flush inside the band. Thus, he did not have to drill holes through the rim, as in more conventional assemblies, to hold the shoes through which the hooks fit, and no hook ends protruded to catch on clothing. This innovative design kept down the overall weight of a banjo by eliminating the shoes and larger nuts and also preserved the integrity of the rim for better acoustics.

Ashborn was particularly interested in the tuning mechanisms on both his guitars and banjos, and a brief discussion of his innovations in this regard provides insight into his general concerns as an instrument manufacturer.[97] On some banjos, for example, he installed simple violin-style wooden pegs, and on others (even on the fifth string), a variation of the elegant geared brass tuning machines found on some of his guitars. But in 1850 and again in 1852 he registered with the U.S. Patent Office drawings for "Guitar-Heads" that demonstrate his attempts to improve his instruments.[98]

The first patent was for a peg-and-spindle mechanism to enable one to tune more easily and precisely than with the violin-style pegs or the metal geared tuners, which Ashborn found undesirable not only because of the "great cost of a guitar head thus constructed" but also because "the weight of all these pieces of metal injuriously affects the vibrations of the instrument" (no doubt his same concern in his refinement for tightening the banjo's head). His solution was to make a larger-sized spindle to attach to the head of the instrument but not protrude on the back side, connected by catgut to a regular-shafted violin tuner passing all the way through the peg head, slightly behind the spindle for that string. When the violin-style tuner was turned, the resulting action was like that of a windlass—easier, more accurate adjustment, Ashborn claimed, without the cost or weight of brass tuning machines.

This design seems unwieldy. Indeed, no extant instrument has such tuners, and few if any may have been made. In his second patent Ashborn simplified the concept (fig. 1-38). Like his other tuner, the new design was made wholly of wood in a shape easily produced on a lathe. Here he patented what we now essentially would call a multi-ratio tuning peg. Cit-

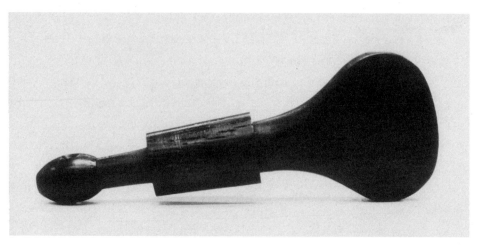

Figure 1-38. Close-up of tuning peg patented by James Ashborn in 1852. The peg fit into a hole considerably larger than the end diameter of the peg. Thus, a smaller degree of turning would eventuate in greater movement, and more precise tuning, at the thinner end of the peg through which the string passed. Collection of Edmund Britt.

ing the same defects in tuning mechanisms that he noted in his previous patent, Ashborn described a tuner with "that part of the wooden peg which is fitted to and turns in the handle of the instrument, and which may be called the journal, of much greater diameter than the barrel or part on which the string is coiled or wound up, and thereby giving such leverage to the surface of which makes friction and which resists the tension of the string as effectual to hold the string without the necessity of wedging or driving the peg too hard." The result was a larger hole in the peg head into which the "journal" was fitted, but Ashborn obviously thought that the ease with which such pegs could be made and the efficiency and accuracy gained in tuning were significant.

The larger point is Ashborn's attempt, visible on his guitars as well as his banjos, to refine his instruments so that they could be efficiently produced in a water-powered factory by workers of various proficiencies. By standardizing the features of his instruments and reducing his dependence on other suppliers—brass tuning machines, for example, had to be made elsewhere, whereas his patented wooden tuners could be produced in-house—Ashborn was able to manufacture high quality instruments quickly and inexpensively enough to be competitive in the burgeoning New York market (plate 1-30). On the eve of the Civil War, his were among the most sophisticated banjos being made, a fact signaled by James Buckley's *New Banjo Book* (1860), which on its lithographed cover portrayed the author playing an Ashborn banjo (fig. 1-39).

Figure 1-39. Printed cover for *Buckley's New Banjo Book* (Boston, 1860). This picture shows James Buckley, the leader of Buckley's Serenaders, playing a fretted Ashborn banjo, its unique bracket band clearly visible. In this instruction book, Buckley urged the use of frets on banjos. Courtesy of the John Carter Brown Library, Brown University.

Boucher and Ashborn, the antebellum makers from whom we have more extant banjos than from any others, took very different approaches to instrument making. Boucher's productions, with their beautiful faux-grained rims and delicately turned beehive finials, which survive in a great variety of sizes and rim design, are the work of a traditionally trained craftsman, someone for whom each instrument was a careful and unique project. On the other hand, Ashborn found his niche in the industrial revolution and produced large numbers of high quality instruments in a factory run by operatives who performed set tasks in a division of labor established by a master "mechanic," Ashborn himself.

By the 1860s more and more banjo makers followed in Ashborn's footsteps, for, as we shall see, most often inventive banjo design, that which might indeed lead to true innovation, originated with those makers who wholeheartedly embraced the possibilities of mechanized production. Most

Figure 1-40. Albumen photograph, ca. 1860s. This rare image shows four African American musicians in the minstrel line, sitting in front of a painted backdrop that prominently features the American flag. The banjoist holds a scroll-headed Boucher banjo.

violin makers, for example, as well as guitar makers such as Martin, continued to build instruments by traditional methods, patiently training apprentices in the various steps necessary to produce an entire instrument by themselves. But by the 1860s the banjo had become anything but traditional, with a score of patents filed in which its design was changed, often quite radically, as various banjo makers capitalized on the nation's growing infatuation with the instrument. Its basic form—a five-string neck and a circular sounding chamber—established, the banjo began to appear in a bewildering number of variations as makers sought to adapt the instrument to the new kinds of music people wished to play on it. In 1840 the banjo had been a symbol of the American South in general and the slave plantation in particular. But after its initial popularization on the minstrel stage led to its wholesale embrace by Victorian America, it came to represent the aspirations of a burgeoning mechanic class who brought to its design and manufacture the same invention through which they had transformed other areas of American industry. It truly was becoming America's instrument (fig. 1-40).

2 An Expanding Market

The Dobson Brothers and the
Rise of Banjo Culture

By 1850 Elias Howe, an astute observer of the antebellum American music scene, had become so successful a purveyor of musical goods that he sold his entire list of titles to the Oliver Ditson Company of Boston at considerable profit.[1] With his usual good sense of the market, in a new banjo tutor that he published in 1857 with another music house he noted that "until recently" the use of the banjo had been "almost entirely confined to the negroes of the South and their imitators, the members of various negro minstrels," and as such "often [had been] made in a very rough and clumsy manner, totally devoid of scientific principles such as guide the makers of Guitars and Violins." But within the past few years, "improvements" in its manufacture had been "truly wonderful," so much so that instead of its being considered "among the third and fourth class instruments, it is now ranked in the first class." Moreover, Howe believed that the banjo had not yet reached its full potential and was poised for new and very different kinds of cultural work. It was "destined to perform," he concluded, a very important role "as an accompaniment to vocal music" and would assume as well "a prominent position in the performance of instrumental music."[2] This trajectory of the banjo, from the minstrel stage to the Victorian parlor and concert hall, that Howe so accurately predicted greatly influenced the physical development of the instrument (fig. 2-1, plates 2-1, 2-2).

By the late 1850s there was good reason to think that new constituencies were ready to adopt the banjo. On the minstrel stage, for example, one found ever more sophisticated banjo players whose considerable talents allowed them not only to embellish original "plantation melodies" but also to compose their own music (figs. 2-2, 2-3). Equally significant, some of these virtuosos began to include art songs and other compositions from the European tradition in their performances. Howe himself contributed significantly to this expansion of musical culture through his banjo tutors, which, along with those of Tom Briggs, Phil Rice, and James Buckley, codified and extended the banjo repertoire. Indeed, the banjo so permeated contemporary musical culture that even well-known composers—Louis Moreau Gottschalk, most famously—wrote compositions in imitation of the instrument (fig. 2-4). Even the poet Walt Whitman connected the banjo to higher forms of music. Speaking of how one might compose an American opera, he noted, "American opera—put three banjos (or more?) in the orchestra—and let them accompany (at times exclusively) the songs of the baritone or tenor."[3]

Concomitantly, as the public heard more and different kinds of music on the banjo, general interest in the instrument increased, spawning not only new venues for the music's performance but also a new class of professional musicians, epitomized by the five remarkable Dobson brothers of New York, who offered private instruction on the banjo and worked as well in various ways to improve its design and accessibility. As often as not their students were not training for the minstrel stage but were those who, once they had learned of the banjo's suitability for parlor music, wished to play it themselves in the home. This interest led in turn to an increased number of craftsmen who produced the instruments for both am-

Figure 2-1. Whole-plate ambrotype, ca. 1860s. As tutors for the banjo became more
widely disseminated, more people began to play the instrument. Here a musician poses
in an elaborately appointed photographer's studio with an instrument customized with
tiny photographs (probably tintypes) of other people, perhaps his family or a minstrel
troupe of which he was a member, inlaid in the neck. Also see plates 2-1 and 2-2.

Figure 2-2. Lithographed poster, ca. 1860. This poster depicts the famed minstrel Dan Bryant (1833–75) in a variety of his stage roles (one of which, the left figure in the center vignette, derives from the carte-de-visite illustrated in figure 2-3) as well as in a formal portrait. Renowned for his "Essence of Old Virginny Dance" and other compositions, Bryant also appeared on stage as an actor in nonminstrel productions. Courtesy of the Harvard Theatre Collection, the Houghton Library.

opposite
Figure 2-3. Carte-de-visite, ca. 1860s, of Dan Bryant, by A. A. Turner, New York. Through the 1870s Bryant was one of the most popular blackface comedians. Note that this particular pose was borrowed by a lithographer for use in the poster illustrated in figure 2-2. Courtesy of the Harvard Theatre Collection, the Houghton Library.

ateurs and professionals, and who modified their instruments the better to meet the needs of these new players (plates 2-3, 2-4, 2-5). By 1880 the competition among banjo makers who vied for the attention and patronage of growing numbers of musicians marked an extensive commodification of the banjo in Victorian America. There now existed a veritable banjo culture, fueled not only by widespread audience interest, as antebellum minstrelsy had been, but also by the public's ever-increasing urge to participate actively in it.

Figure 2-4. Lithographed sheet-music cover for Louis Moreau Gottschalk's "The Banjo, An American Sketch" (New York, 1855). Internationally renowned as a composer and pianist, Gottschalk was so moved by the banjo that he devoted this entire "Grotesque Fantasie" to it. Note how the title of the piece is spelled out with banjos and a tambourine.

Within this inclusive culture of the banjo one can trace the physical evolution of the instrument by paying particular attention to the relation of changes in banjo repertoire (and thus, by extension, in musical taste) to technological invention. For this purpose contemporary instruction books like Howe's are invaluable, for they frequently include not only tunes and song lyrics but detailed descriptions of right- and left-hand technique, as well as indications of precisely how certain kinds of music was to be played. Most significant in this regard, beginning in the mid-1860s banjo instruction manuals popularized a very different right-hand method than hitherto had been used on the minstrel stage.

The style codified in all tutors prior to the publication of Frank Converse's *New and Complete Method for the Banjo with or without a Master* (1865) was down-stroking or "striking."[4] In the basic movement in this method, one strikes an individual string with a downward motion of the index finger (that is, by hitting the string with the fingernail) and then hooks another string (most commonly the fifth, or shortest) with the thumb. This style is directly related to how African griots still play the *xalam* and *molo* and very probably was how early white performers learned the banjo from enslaved African Americans with whom they came into contact. All the banjo tutors published before the 1860s (except for Howe's pioneering effort in 1848, which contained virtually no information about playing technique) taught this method.

In this codification of the down-picking or stroke style, the tutors of Phil Rice and James Buckley were particularly important. The former offered for the first time in such detail, as one historian puts it, "the application of classic European methodology" (i.e., musical notation) to the rhythmic complexities of African American music; the latter adapted the banjo, in the stroke natural to the instrument, to what Buckley clearly regarded as the more refined and elegant music of the European tradition.[5] Within a few years, however, some players realized that such music was more easily performed in a guitar or finger-picking style, and this had important ramifications for banjo design. But one cannot overestimate the importance of Rice's and Buckley's initial attempts to elevate the banjo by demonstrating its capabilities for other sorts of music than that found on the minstrel stage.

In this regard, Buckley's efforts are worth detailing. An Englishman who had come to America in 1839 with three equally talented sons, musicians who like their father got caught up in the minstrelsy craze, Buckley had begun teaching the banjo in New York in the early 1840s.[6] By the mid-1850s he was taken with the banjo's still-untapped potential for playing music from the European concert tradition. Thus, in addition to the requisite minstrel tunes and American parlor songs, and a considerable number of challenging jigs and hornpipes, his own tutor included European waltzes, schottisches, and marches "arranged" by him for the banjo. In addition, *Buckley's New Banjo Book* (1860) carried a testimonial from the eminent Austrian concert pianist and composer Sigismond Thalberg, who claimed that "when in this country [ca. 1856–58]," he gave both the banjo and "Buckley's method of instruction, a considerable portion of his time and practice."[7] As Joseph Ayers has noted, through his tutor and probable editing of Briggs's and Rice's works (Rice, for example, similarly invoked Thalberg, noting that he had "produc[ed]" his "method of instruction" with Thalberg's and Buckley's aid), Buckley was the prime mover in bringing to public attention the banjo's worth and versatility, equal, he believed, to those of any instrument in the European tradition. The very production of such banjo tutors, in standard notation and encompassing an expanded repertoire, clearly demonstrated the banjo's adaptability to the type of music played on such instruments as the violin, guitar, and piano.

Once Buckley, Thalberg, and others had expedited the banjo's crossover into such new musical territory, the guitar became, if not quite its casualty, the instrument most frequently compared to it. As early as 1855, for example, Tom Briggs had been praised for "elevat[ing] the banjo to the rank of the guitar," and the comparison remained common. A decade later, John S. Adams, the compiler of a dictionary of musical terms, defined the banjo as "a rude imitation of the guitar, united with the tambourine."[8] Indeed, the novelty of hearing complex music formerly reserved for the guitar on this very different sounding instrument prompted the first patent (no. 25,872) specifically for a banjo, Stephen F. Van Hagen's of 18 October 1859, for his "Dolce Campana Guitar-Banjo" (fig. 2-5).

As the name for his instrument suggests, Van Hagen (who came from Albany, New York, and in the same patent assigned his rights to his invention to George Kilbourne of the same city) sought to "combine the best points of these two instruments."[9] After praising the banjo's "highly resonant sound," which he attributed to the instrument's unique sound chamber, he observed that in its present construction it remained "a feeble instrument, its music forming a trifling accompaniment to other instruments, or to the voice, and capable of being used to the extent of only one, or at most two scales of music." But the guitar, too, had its drawbacks. With its small sound hole, it had "scarcely any resonance at all" and thus "was much less effective, so as to be scarcely of any worth excepting as an accompaniment to the human voice." The guitar's chief recommendation thus lay in its greater number of strings and its frets, which in combina-

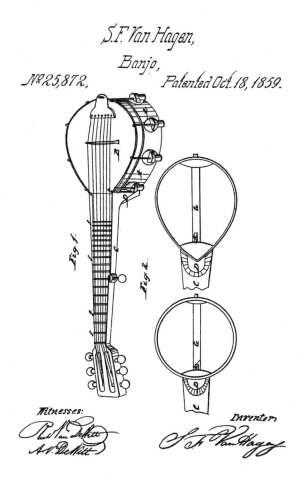

S.F. Van Hagen,

Banjo,

N°25,872,   *Patented Oct. 18, 1859.*

Fig. 1.

Fig. 2.

Witnesses:

Inventor:

Figure 2-5. Patent drawing for Stephen F. Van Hagen's guitar-banjo, 18 October 1859. As its name suggests, this instrument incorporated features of both guitar and banjo, presumably to attract players of one or the other instrument who wished to master both. Note that this instrument is fretted like a guitar and has a head stock characteristic of that instrument. However, it also has a short string on the side of the neck and a movable bridge, characteristic of banjos.

tion afforded "the means of adapting its sounds to all the scales within the compass of music."

Van Hagen's solution was an instrument that indeed looked like a cross between the two. His patent drawing shows a guitar-style neck, to make accessible a greater range of notes (including a shorter, seventh string to give the instrument "the banjo character and tone when wanted"), and a wooden-rimmed body covered on its top side with stretched parchment for a sounding board. But Van Hagen made the thin wooden body more oval than round, so that it would not be pulled out of shape by the higher-pitched strings necessary in the guitar tuning, and developed an improved way of joining the neck to the rim (not with the common dowel but "vertically" with a "knee formed terminus" that fit downward into a "bar" that passed through the instrument), more insurance against the pressure produced by greater string tension. True to his hybrid design, his patent drawing also shows a slotted guitar-style peg head with geared tuners, and eight brackets and hooks, typical of contemporary banjos, to tighten the head.

Although George Kilbourne's brother William continued to offer the instrument as his patent banjo through the 1870s, there is no evidence that the guitar-banjo stirred the music world (fig. 2-6). But through the late 1850s and early 1860s the evolving banjo repertoire resulted in an increase in guitar-style playing, which in turn encouraged banjo makers to refigure the acoustic design of their instruments. We can date this decisive shift in playing styles very accurately, with the publication in 1865 of two banjo tutors by Frank Converse, considered by some to be the banjo's "paternal ancestor."

Born in Westfield, Massachusetts, in 1837, Converse first heard the banjo as a boy in Elmira, New York, "in the hands of a colored man—a bright mulatto," who frequently visited the vicinity "playing and singing and passing his hat for collections" (fig. 2-7). In 1851, when Converse heard G. Swaine Buckley, one of James Buckley's sons, perform on the in-

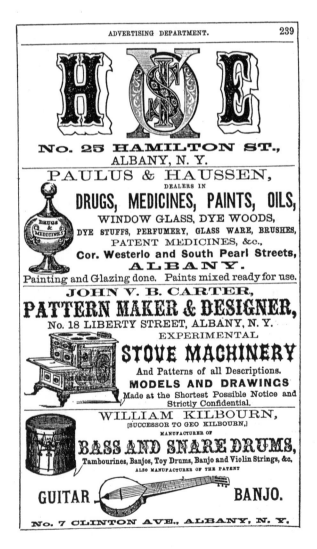

Figure 2-6. Advertisement from *The Albany Directory for 1866* (Albany, 1866) for Van Hagen's guitar-banjo, now offered by William Kilbourne, brother of George, to whom Van Hagen had assigned the patent.

Figure 2-7. Engraved portrait of Frank B. Converse from *Frank B. Converse's Analytical Method* (New York, 1887). In 1865 Converse published the first tutor that illustrated the new guitar style of playing the banjo. One of the most well-known players and instructors, he remained active through the end of the century.

strument, he was so taken that he decided to drop his piano studies to pursue it. As he recalled at the turn of the century, his switch from the piano to the banjo was "strenuously opposed by his parents," who thought "the banjo an instrument of but trifling consideration, not susceptible to any improvement and upon which labor and time would be foolishly thrown away."[10] He persisted, however, and soon found his way to the minstrel stage (fig. 2-8). By the late 1850s Converse was well enough known to have his name over some of the arrangements in Rice's tutor and to publish, in 1863, his own *"Old Cremona" Songster*, a compilation of popular and comic songs.[11] Like James Buckley, however, he also was interested in, as he himself phrased it, "elevating the instrument" and thus set about writing his own method books, seeking to apply to the banjo "the theoretical musical principles . . . acquired from his piano studies."[12]

As a consequence, in 1865 Converse published two important tutors (with confusingly similar titles), *Frank B. Converse's Banjo Instructor without a Master* and *Frank B. Converse's New and Complete Method for the Banjo with or without a Master* (fig. 2-9).[13] He intended the first for those students without "the slightest knowledge of even the simple rudiments of music," noting on the title page that it contained "A Choice Collection of Banjo Solos, Jigs, Songs, Reels, Walk Arounds, etc., Progressively Arranged, and Plainly Explained; Enabling the Learner to Become a Proficient Banjoist without the Aid of a Teacher." Much like Rice, Converse led the student

Figure 2-8. Cabinet card by Elmer Chickering, Boston (probably copied from an earlier carte-de-visite) of a young Frank Converse with Tommy Peel (1841–69), who was considered one of the "world's great jig dancers." When Converse first appeared on the minstrel stage he may well have played solo for dancers like Peel. Courtesy of the Harvard Theatre Collection, the Houghton Library.

through the tunes measure by measure and did not emphasize independently reading the music itself.

Converse's second publication was musically much more sophisticated and included polkas, marches, gallops, and even operatic selections, thus (like Buckley's tutor) expanding the repertoire of the instrument signifi-

Figure 2-9. Cover of *Frank B. Converse's Banjo Instructor without a Master* (New York, 1865), one of two tutors he published in 1865. In this one Converse introduced guitar-style playing for the banjo.

cantly. Most important, to allow such complex music to be played comfortably, Converse also introduced for the first time in printed form a style of banjo playing in which more of the fingers were used, with three or four of them picking *upward* on the strings and the thumb moving downward, similar to what today we call finger-picking guitar style. In a departure from the technique of the percussive down-stroke style, the player was encouraged to "pull the strings with the points of the fingers and particularly avoid touching them with the nails." In a further directive indicating the tone one sought to achieve, Converse suggested that "to soften the sound" one should "move the hand forward [that is, farther from the bridge], touching the strings almost directly over the rim."[14]

There is no way of knowing whether Converse himself introduced such playing on the banjo. More likely than not, other musicians already familiar with the guitar had experimented with such a technique when they tried their hands at the banjo. Whatever the case, from 1865 on, banjo tutors consistently provided instruction in both methods of playing, and as the century progressed, while not totally eclipsing stroke style, guitar style became increasingly prominent, associated with that elevation of the instrument that Converse and others sought (fig. 2-10). Further, just as this shift in technique enabled players continually to expand the kinds of music they played on the banjo, their notions of the musical qualities they sought from their instruments influenced banjo design, making the period from 1860 to 1885 one of great technological experimentation and innovation.[15]

In the 1860s, for example, some makers followed Van Hagen's path and produced unusual hybrid instruments. This was the case with Levi Brown of Baltimore, whose banjos had been singled out for praise at the Maryland Institute exhibition in 1859. In the fall of 1865 he took out U.S. patent no. 50,444 for a "Guitar-Banjo," "so constructed as to produce with a smaller drum a tone superior to the finest guitar" (fig. 2-11). But Brown not only sought the sustaining tone of a guitar from his banjo; he took the added step of constructing it so that (presumably) it could be played as either instrument! Thus, in addition to constructing it in such as a way as to eliminate "the annoyance of a sheep-skin or calf-skin head, which invariably slackens in damp weather and injures the tone of the instrument," he reinforced its sound chamber so that one could tune it to "concert" pitch and use it "either as a guitar or a banjo." Interestingly, he also implied that by this time both men and women played the banjo. In addition to being "convenient and beautiful," he noted, with its novel construction his instrument prevented the "tearing and soiling [of] dresses by the numerous iron or brass screws, brackets, bands, &c." usually attached to the side of the banjo "drum" to tighten the skin. Nor was his banjo "objectionable" (again, presumably to women) on account of "extreme length and great weight."

What did this instrument look like? Most striking, instead of covering the sound chamber with skin, Brown used "very thin wood" strengthened by two bars on the underside, "running across the grain of the face board"—in other words, he braced the top like a guitar—in whose ends notches were cut to allow the top to fit snugly on the side of the rim. Similarly, "in order to add to the sweetness of the tone," he placed a comparable, though more convex, board on the bottom of the hoop, to strengthen the piece and "throw the sound forward." The sound escaped through holes in the side of the hoop that were "sufficiently large and numerous to allow the full tone of the instrument to pass through."

This description accounts for Brown's claims for an instrument more dependable and less ungainly than the usual banjo, but what of his claim that it could be played either as a banjo or a guitar? He accomplished this with a movable bridge, which he placed "precisely at the center of the sounding-board" (at about "twenty-four and one-half inches from the nut")

Figure 2-10. Cover of Frank B. Converse's *The Banjo and How to Play It* (New York, 1872), another of the important tutors in which Converse continued to popularize the new way of picking the banjo. Note that the young man has his right foot elevated on a stool to assume a playing position like that used by many guitarists.

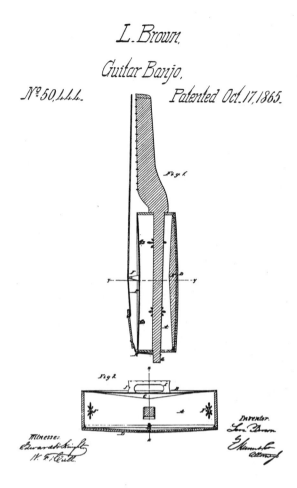

L. Brown,

Guitar Banjo,

N⁰ 50,444. *Patented Oct. 17, 1865.*

Figure 2-11. Patent drawing for Levi Brown's banjo, 17 October 1865. Another hybrid instrument, Brown's banjo could be strung either as a six-string guitar or a five-string banjo. The bottom sketch shows a bridge with a notch on its side so that the shorter string of the banjo could be moved out of the way for guitar playing. This instrument also had its sound chamber covered with thin wood rather than skin.

and to which he added a notch, "on the outside of the left foot," to hold the thumb string out of the way "while the instrument is being used as a guitar." Because (as is indicated by the bridge in the patent illustration) this instrument had seven strings and presumably was not fretted, one could tune the strings into either guitar or banjo configuration to accomplish Brown's aim. Finally, emphasizing yet again the conflation of guitar and banjo in the inventor's mind, he noted that his bridge placement allowed "sufficient pressure against the sounding board to cause a much louder sound than that of any guitar."

Of all the banjo patents of the 1860s, Brown's most clearly indicates how strongly the guitar influenced banjo making, but like those of Van Hagen and many other makers in this early period of banjo construction, his design had no lasting effect on the development of the instrument.[16] Much more influential was George Teed's patent of 1862 (no. 34,913) for a closed-back banjo, for here invention finally led to true innovation (fig. 2-12). Rather than seeking, as Brown did, to reproduce the guitar's musical range, Teed, a New York "turner," or woodworker, simply wanted

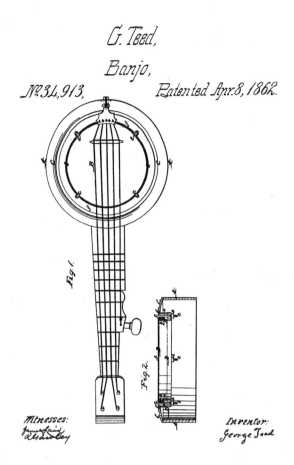

G. Teed,

Banjo,

№34,913,

Patented Apr.8, 1862.

Fig.1.

Fig.2.

Witnesses:
James Laird
Alfred Hay

Inventor:
George Teed

Figure 2-12. Patent drawing for George Teed's banjo, 8 April 1862. Teed was one of the first to fit a back to the banjo, to project the sound forward through holes or a space between the top rim and the bottom. This design was refined over the next thirty years and then resurfaced in new forms in the elaborately resonated instruments of the Jazz Age.

to improve the banjo's sound. To accomplish this he enclosed the back of his instrument but left an opening between that assembly and the head so that the sound would project forward. This provided a "more powerful and finer tone to the instrument" and proved to be an innovation that could be refined by a number of important makers over the next two decades who similarly sought to manufacture a banjo whose tone was more appropriate to the new kinds of music being played on it.

Teed accomplished his purpose by having a "deep ring of wood connecting the head . . . with the sound board" into which the head with its tightening hooks fit snugly. The outer edge of this wooden ring was attached "by gluing or other means" to the inner edge of the "sound-board" (what we call the resonator), and the skin head was "strained over the outer edge of the inner portion" of this rim with a wire ring and hooks, tightened below by nuts. Simply put, the banjo was composed of a head and rim assembly that fit down into another, larger, enclosed wooden rim, or pot, so that sound from the instrument projected forward.

Like Brown, Teed also did away with protruding external hooks, a project of interest to many other makers in the 1860s not just because, as Brown had implied, more banjos were being played by women attired in elegant Victorian fashions, but also, as banjo maker Christopher Burrowes put it in 1880, "because of the liability of the projecting pieces to catch in the clothing of the operator . . . especially when a trick is being performed, as is customary with banjo players" (fig. 2-13).[17]

Thus, in 1865 William Harlass of New York City, in U.S. patent no. 49,401, offered an open-back banjo that placed "the straining screws entirely within the cylindrical body out of the way." Like Brown, Harlass explained the need for his invention very practically, noting that in the more normal construction of the banjo, "the screws" were "likely to injure the person or clothing in handling the instrument rapidly." Through the 1860s he advertised accordingly, calling himself an "Inventor and Manufacturer of Patent American Ladies' & Parlor Banjos."[18] In 1866 William Tilton, another New York City maker, attacked the same problem and solved it similarly (U.S. patent no. 54,264), with an internal wooden ring in the banjo into which screws fit to put pressure on another ring, thus forcing it against the skin head to tighten it (fig. 2-14). Other than for their novel tensioning devices, however, these makers' banjos had little to distinguish them from other open-back instruments of the period.

Teed's most innovative contribution to banjo design, though, lay not in his solution to the problem of torn dresses but rather in his reconfiguration of the instrument's sound chamber to redirect the sound outward, toward those who were listening to the banjo. In another patent of 1866 (no. 57,540), for example, George Mein of Williamsburg, New York, described a similar instrument, which had "the combination of an interior rim with the exterior rim and with the head," with a tensioning system constructed so that the head could be easily adjusted by turning screws at its top (fig. 2-15). Mein also patented a different way of attaching the "stem" (that is, the neck) to the rim, by a dovetailed joint that eliminated the dowel. He claimed that this improvement allowed him to extend the fingerboard over the rim "so that the strings may be fingered farther down," an indication that many banjoists now sought to master more octaves on their instruments.

Jerome Mayberger, another New York maker, offered an even more

opposite

Figure 2-13. Carte-de-visite by W. Dyer, ca. 1860s, the earliest image we have found of a woman banjoist. In the 1860s makers like Levi Brown and George Teed modified the banjo's tensioning system so that its hooks would not catch on women's clothing. Note the scooped neck and horizontal fifth-string tuner, both characteristic of many banjos in this decade.

92 } *An Expanding Market*

complex improvement of Teed's basic design (fig. 2-16). Late in 1867 (U.S. patent no. 72,517) he entered an instrument that he thought would better channel the air through the banjo's "sound-board," or resonator. Thus, his "sound-board" consisted of "an annular drum or box" covered on the top "with a board having S-shaped holes, similar to those in the sound-boards of violins," and solid on the bottom. He attached the "parchment head" to a ring "which is fitted upon the sound-board enough above the same to permit the escape of the vibrating air between the said head and drum," a notion very similar to Teed's. More unusual was Mayberger's annular construction of the resonator. "The circular open space in the center of the drum," he claimed, would serve as "a channel for a new supply of air."

Mayberger more fully explained the acoustic principles (admittedly having no basis in science) that he had in mind with his design. When one played the instrument, he claimed, the bridge prevented "the central part of the head from vibrating, while the under part of the same will vibrate." "The air under the center of the head," he continued, "is thus at rest, and

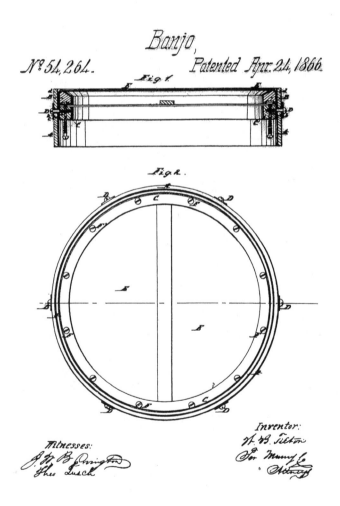

Figure 2-14. Patent drawing for William B. Tilton's banjo, 24 April 1866. Tilton's novel tensioning system for the head did away with external hooks and nuts. His banjos were popular in the late 1860s and 1870s.

will therefore be allowed to come up through the hole in the centre of the drum to supply the air which is driven out by the vibrations of the drum." Constantly replenishing its sound waves, Mayberger's banjo thus would produce a "very clear and harmonious" tone much "more powerful than on any of the banjos" then in use.

The sheer complexity of such an instrument worked against its popularity, for simple, open-back banjos like those made by William Tilton and John J. Bogan, and the less idiosyncratic closed-back models of Henry Clay Dobson, in fact dominated the market in the late 1860s and 1870s. An award at the American Institute Fair for "improvements on the Guitar and Violin" indicates that as early as 1853 Tilton was making other stringed instruments as well. By the early 1870s he had won an important endorsement for his "Tilton Patent" banjos from the large wholesale dealer Bruno and Son.[19] These banjos, the firm noted in a full-page advertisement

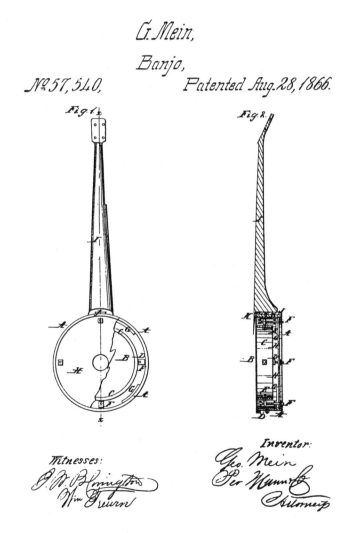

Figure 2-15. Patent drawing for George Mein's banjo, 28 April 1866. Like Teed's, Mein's instrument had an enclosed back, presumably the better to direct the banjo's sound.

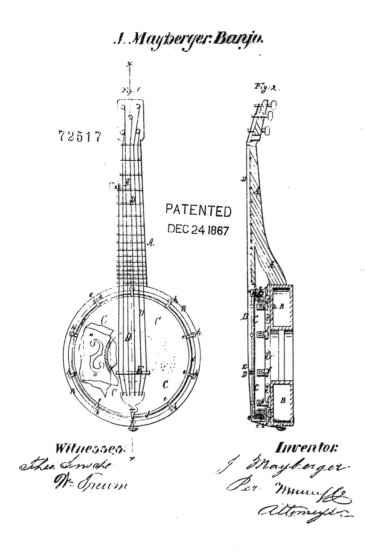

J. Mayberger. Banjo.

72517

PATENTED
DEC 24 1867

Witnesses:

Inventor:
J. Mayberger.
Per. [...]
Attorney

Figure 2-16. Patent drawing for Jerome Mayberger's banjo, 24 December 1867. Mayberger offered a more complex version of Teed's resonated instrument, but it is unlikely that many such banjos were ever produced. In the right-hand illustration note the cut-out portion of the neck where it joins the rim, a stylistic detail common on banjos in the late 1860s and 1870s.

opposite
Figure 2-17. Chromo-lithograph illustration of Tilton's patented banjo, from Bruno and Son's *Descriptive Price List* (New York, 1874). Note the brass rosettes around the rim, through which screws attach to its inner portion. The only other chromolithographs in this catalog are of harmonicas.

in its *Descriptive Price List* (1874), "are, without any question, the best, neatest, cheapest, and most saleable Banjos in the market." By this date, Tilton offered his instruments with metal rims as well as in wood, and the wholesalers duly noted that already "the several numbers with *Brass Rims*" were "favorite styles." "Notwithstanding the competition of various '*Patent Banjos*,'" they concluded, "the sale of the '*Tilton*' steadily increases," with the "Solid Brass Rim" model offered at $8 and a rosewood-grained wooden-rim instrument for $11 (figs. 2-17, 2-18, plate 2-6).

Advertisements in the 1870s in the *New York Clipper*, a popular weekly paper of turf and field sports and the stage, suggest that John J. Bogan's instruments, though tensioned with hooks and nuts, also were popular. Known primarily as a banjo maker and music instructor, Bogan first appeared in the New York directories in 1862 and manufactured instruments through the 1880s, also offering his own banjo instruction "manual." In the early 1870s he had for sale "silver rim, stage and parlor banjos" cele-

Figure 2-18. Price list for Tilton banjos from Bruno and Son's *Descriptive Price List* (New York, 1874). Note that by this period one could order an instrument with a metal (brass) rim.

16   **PRICE LIST.**

BANJOS—CONTINUED.

TILTON'S PATENT.

We beg to recommend these Banjos to those Dealers who do not keep them. They are, without any question, the best, neatest, cheapest, and most saleable Banjos in the market.

In tone and neatness, far superior to the old style. The several numbers with *Brass Rims* are favorite styles. Notwithstanding the competition of various "*Patent Banjos*," the sale of the "*Tilton*" steadily increases.

WILLIAM B. TILTON'S IMPROVEMENT,

PATENTED APRIL 24th, 1866.

ALL WITH CALFSKIN HEADS.

No. 201	Screws, (best Banjo made at the price)	Each $ 6 00
202¼	" SOLID BRASS RIM	" 8 00
202½	" Imitation Mahogany	" 8 00
202	Small Size, etc., Imitation Mahogany	" 7 50
203¼	" SOLID BRASS RIM	" 8 00
203	Screws, etc., Rosewood, Brass Trimmings	" 11 00
204¼	" SOLID BRASS RIM, Polished finely	" 16 00
204	" Rosewood, Silver Plated Trimmings	" 15 00
204	Small Size, etc., Rosewood, Silver Plated Trimmings	" 14 00
205	Screws, Rosewood, Silver Plated Trimmings, Fancy Inlaid	" 18 00
206	Machine Head, Rosewood, Brass Trimmings	" 16 00
206½	" SOLID BRASS RIM, Polished finely	" 22 00
207	" Silver Plated Trimmings	" 20 00
208	" " " Fancy Inlaid	" 25 00
209	Rosewood, " " Frets	" 18 00
210	" " " " and Machine Head	" 22 00
211	Very Fancy Inlaid	" 24 00
212	" "	" 28 00
213	" "	" 32 00
214	Solid German Silver, fine Polished, etc	" 24 00

FANCY BANJOS FOR PRESENTATION MADE TO ORDER.

CONSTANTLY ENLARGING OUR ASSORTMENT WITH NOVELTIES.

brated "for their loud and brilliant tone," priced anywhere from $10 to $75. In addition, he offered lessons in banjo and in "Irish Jig or Reel Dancing." Fourteen banjo lessons, in which he "guarantee[d]" to teach the pupil "14 perfect tunes," were $10, and "14 steps" in dancing were the same price (fig. 2-19).[20]

Alongside Bogan's advertisements in the *New York Clipper*, one finds the announcements of Henry C. Dobson for his "great patent stage and parlor banjos," whose "champion tone" had "no equal in the country." Dobson had

98 } *An Expanding Market*

Figure 2-19. Cover of four-page advertising brochure for John J. Bogan's banjos. Along with Tilton and Henry C. Dobson, Bogan was one of the more successful makers in the 1870s. His instruments showed no novel technological innovations but were simply and sturdily made.

first developed this banjo in 1867, when he took out a patent (no. 66,810) for "a novel manner of securing the parchment-head to and between two annular rings" (fig. 2-20). These, he explained in the patent description, were attached to the rim of the banjo "as to leave an opening or space between them and the banjo-rim for the escape of sounds produced by the vibrations of the sound-board which is upon the back side of the instrument." Its tension adjusted by screws on the top of the instrument, Dobson's "Patent" banjo became a popular and well-regarded instrument, "pronounced," as the maker baldly put it, "the master banjo of the age" and, as even Dobson's competitor S. S. Stewart admitted, "for a time" having "a large sale."[21] Starting at a price of $20 for a polished rosewood model, with "20 silver screws, 20 silver side pieces, silver tail piece, Italian [gut] strings, and ebony pegs," this banjo, "with very fancy inlay work," could cost as much as $100. "In general appearance," one New York cor-

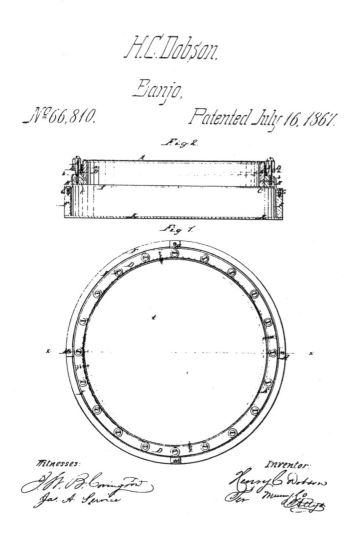

Figure 2-20. Patent drawing for Henry C. Dobson's banjo, 16 July 1867. This closed-back instrument, refined in another patent of 1873, assured Dobson a place in the emergent banjo market of the late 1860s. His design features a large wooden ring into which the head of the banjo fits, with the sound projecting forward from the space between the two.

respondent wrote, "it is even handsomer than the guitar" (fig. 2-21, plates 2-7, 2-8).[22]

Through the 1870s and 1880s Henry Dobson and his four talented brothers continued to refine both open- and closed-back banjos as they centered themselves in the constantly expanding banjo market. Before turning to their story, however, we should characterize some other developments in banjo manufacture through the early 1880s. First, aside from the Dobsons' experiments in rim design, the few patents entered in the 1870s primarily addressed the matter of tension hooks, or "strainers" as they often were called. In 1879, for example, Robert McManus of Brooklyn developed a novel way (U.S. patent no. 245,647) to tighten the head with external hooks that did not require drilling holes through the rim to mount the shoes through which the hooks pass. Instead, he offered a "bracket or plate provided with a hook for engagement with the [bottom] edge of the rim"; it had another lip with a hole drilled through it, through which one inserted the hook. By tightening the nut on this hook, the bottom of the rim and the tension hoop were pulled toward each other and the head tightened. Upon securing his patent, McManus immediately assigned it to Herman and Willy Sonntag, large-scale New York musical wholesalers who competed with Bruno and Son, and who presumably thought it potentially lucrative.

Unlike James Ashborn's banjos in the 1850s, however, with their unusual bracket band to maintain the acoustic integrity of the banjo's wooden rim, McManus's design pointed to important new considerations in the banjo trade as the instrument grew more popular and thus was manufactured in larger numbers. The object of his invention, McManus noted, was "to cheapen the production of the device itself, to save time and labor in the application, [and to] render the same more efficient." He observed as well that his way of setting the hooks on the banjo, engaging "the extremes [i.e., the top and bottom of the rim] of the respective parts in line with the movement of the same upon each other," also lessened the tendency of the rim to "spring, warp, or split."

McManus's manifest concern with low cost and efficiency as well as with the instrument's structural integrity marks an important transition in the history of the nineteenth-century banjo, for the kind of manufacture that Ashborn had begun in the 1850s in his Connecticut guitar and banjo works now began to bear different fruit. As steam-powered factory production came to rule the economy, entrepreneurs alert to the widespread interest in music—and in the banjo in particular—sought ever more inexpensive ways to build instruments. In this new industrial world McManus thus concerned himself with so seemingly small a matter as the "economy"

effected "by dispensing with a bolt and nut for securing [the hook] to the rim, and also in avoiding the necessity of perforating the rim to receive such bolt, particularly when a metallic rim is employed." To be sure, in consolidating different tasks in banjo making under one roof (making his own tuners, strings, and cases), Ashborn had sought independence from other craftsmen and manufacturers—and thus better control over the cost of his materials—as well as efficiency from skilled workmen.[23] The difference was that Ashborn's instruments, both guitars and banjos, remained of high quality, unlike many of the cheaply produced instruments of the 1870s and 1880s whose makers valued profit over craftsmanship.

McManus's offhand mention of a "metallic rim" further suggests the invisible hand of the market, for by the early 1870s some banjo manufacturers tried to cut costs by offering instruments with metal rather than wooden hoops. As we have noted, by 1874 Tilton banjos could be bought with either metal or wooden rims. A year earlier in Springfield, Vermont, John S. Stiles registered another "improvement" (U.S. patent no. 141,182): he made not just the rim, but the entire instrument, "face, back, and rim," of "thin sheet metal," perforating the rim to let out the sound (fig. 2-22). Anticipating McManus's pragmatic arguments for his new tensioning assembly, Stiles observed that, in addition to giving the instrument "a clear, metallic sound," his new rim was "far more durable, and very much cheaper than the wooden body, with a sheep-skin head." This instrument, its joints soldered together, was, he reiterated, "much cheaper in construction, and more durable in use" than other banjos, "since all liability of fracture of the body is avoided" and there was "no occasion for replacing the face or head of the body with sheep-skin."[24]

Although Stiles's "improvement" went the way of Van Hagen's and others' curiosities, by the 1880s (for acoustic, not economic, reasons) the use of a metal rim or, more precisely, a wooden one that was metal-clad, marked most banjos of any quality. The more important point here, though, is that by the 1870s the constant emphasis in banjo manufacture on attempts to cut costs even as production was increased eventuated not only in a shift, as one historian describes it, from "batch" to "bulk" production, but also, as might be expected, in a decline in overall workmanship in the instruments.[25] In New York City (still the center of the American

opposite
Figure 2-21. Carte-de-visite by M. K. Tripp, Attica, New York, ca. 1870. This banjoist plays an example of the instrument Henry C. Dobson patented in 1867. The screws visible on the top of the head are used to tighten it into the larger, resonator-like bottom of the instrument.

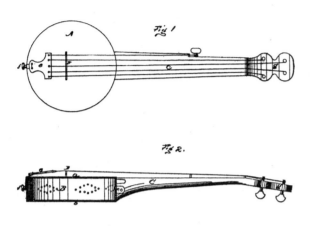

J. S. STILES.
Banjos.
No. 141,182.
Patented July 22, 1873.

Witnesses:
H.C. Hollenberg
M. Lovell

Inventor:
John S. Stiles
per Immelmeta
Atty.

Figure 2-22. Patent drawing for John S. Stiles's banjo, 22 July 1873. In the 1870s makers experimented with metal or metal-covered wooden rims. In this radical example, Stiles constructed his entire instrument, including the neck, from sheet metal, to give the banjo a "clear, metallic sound."

music trade), several large factories each year turned out thousands of low-grade banjos for music wholesalers, who marketed these relatively inexpensive commodities to an ever-receptive public. The same Bruno and Son catalog, for example, which sang the virtues of the Tilton patent instrument gave an equal amount of space to less expensive banjos (priced as low as $2 for a "Tack Head" banjo with a ten-inch rim) whose makers were not even identified.[26] Similarly, in a catalog issued by Herman Sonntag in the late 1870s, Henry Dobson's patent banjo was offered at prices from $9.65 to $16.50, opposite a page of banjos that could be purchased for as little as $3 each.[27] The ubiquity of such low-priced items challenged the Dobsons, Tilton, and other makers to expend considerable energy to distinguish what they considered their finer, "legitimate" instruments from "store tubs" aimed at the wholesale houses.[28]

The most extensive of these factories was operated by James H. Buckbee, who first appeared in the city directories in 1881 as a "Musical Instrument

Manufacturer" who specialized in making drums as well as banjos, "many of which were stenciled and sold through other firms" (fig. 2-23).[29] The well-known banjoist Albert Baur, in one of a valuable series of "Reminiscences" written in the late 1880s for *S. S. Stewart's Banjo and Guitar Journal*, described Buckbee's operation at length, noting that this was "probably the largest banjo factory in the world" and that it turned out "the best of that class of work," unlike, say, instruments from Henry Benary's operation, which "of all cheap and vile factory banjos" were "the cheapest and vilest."[30] But in his description of Buckbee's works (which, along with S. S. Stewart's similarly derogatory account of such factories in general in his lecture *The Banjo Philosophically* [1886], provides the most detailed account we have of steam-powered banjo manufacture), Baur also made clear that, given a choice, anyone serious about the banjo would purchase a more "legitimate" instrument, particularly since (as he may have been aware) Buckbee did not even make some of the key constituent parts, thus eroding the instruments' overall quality even more.[31]

In his criticism of factory-made instruments Baur singled out precisely what makers like McManus and Stiles had praised: shortcuts that maximized profit. For one thing, unlike the mechanized workshops such as Ashborn's, where the division of labor meant that sophisticated craftsmen made a higher salary than, say, those who assembled the instruments' cases, the new banjo factories had "no use for high-priced or skilled" workers. Rather, the necks, rims, and hardware were produced in such ways that "any cheap man or boy can fit the parts together," and workmen (often termed "boys") were not valued for any special skills but "according to their ability to put together a great number of banjos in a day."

In such factories each part of the banjo was made "in its own particular department," and everything was "rushed through." For example, Baur saw "handles [that is, necks] sawed out by the hundred and thousand, and piled up like cord wood." Stewart, who used some steam-powered machinery in his Philadelphia works but insisted that each banjo still be hand-finished by skilled craftsmen, similarly reported "large quantities" of necks made "by special machines, in a manner somewhat similar to which gun-stocks and ax-handles are turned out," which were then "sand-papered on 'buffs' run upon steam lathes." Indeed, steam-driven machinery was everywhere, with even the holes for the brackets, Stewart reported, bored with a drill, "the lathe of which runs by steam."

More insidious, such manufacturers often doctored their instruments to pass them off as being of higher quality. "Some of the cheaper factories," Baur observed, "have rims by the hundred, covered with metal and then dipped in a galvanizing solution," a coating so thin that "it wears off in a

Figure 2-23. Letterhead of J. H. Buckbee, New York, ca. 1890. One of the largest banjo factories in the country, beginning in the 1870s the Buckbee Company turned out thousands of lower-grade instruments as well as fairly good quality banjos, mostly as a "ghost" maker for stores or performers such as Converse, Herschel Fenton, and perhaps some of the Dobson brothers, who stamped them with their own names.

short time." When this solution discolored the inside of the rim, he continued, "a coat of black varnish" was put on "to hide it." Some manufacturers even "fasten[ed] a piece of bamboo on the inside of the rim on the upper side next to the head" and painted it with "bronze paint" so that "when the head is put on it looks as if the metal rim extended under the head." Faux graining also was utilized to make instruments appear to be of higher grade. In the Bruno catalog, for example, an "imitation Rosewood, 'Stage Banjo'" could be had for $4.50, while one constructed of real rosewood cost $7 more.

Here, then, the industrial revolution's emphasis on profit reached its logical conclusion: "No waste of time or material," Baur caustically observed; "no inspection; and no thought or care as to what becomes of [the instruments], so long as they are sold and paid for." "The more banjos in a day, the cheaper the material and the more saved," he continued, "the greater will be the manufacturer's profit." The result was a very inferior, if inexpensive, instrument. According to Baur, who knew "whereof he spoke," by 1880 such instruments permeated the market, sold "to the store through wholesale jobbing houses, who import and wholesale musical goods," and by "drummers or selling agents constantly on the road with samples." The factory owners knew, Stewart observed, that "nearly all beginners will buy a cheap banjo to learn on," and consequently they "[got] up" the instrument "cheaply enough so as to insure enough profit, first for the factory, next for the wholesale dealer, and still another for the retailer."

Moreover, the lure of quick profit attracted even prominent "teachers and dealers," who purchased necks, rims, and hardware from these factories and, after "inlaying a pearl or silver ornament here and there," stamped the banjos "with their own trade mark" and sold them "as their own manufacture." Baur was not afraid to name names. The Frank B. Converse banjos extensively advertised by J. F. Stratton were "all made by J. H. Buckbee" at the very factory Baur had been describing, he reported, as were the Victor banjos of George C. Dobson as well as Bruno and Son's instruments, subsequently stamped with their own name.[32]

Even allowing for some exaggeration—after all, Baur did endorse Stewart's banjos and was writing in that firm's house journal—these accounts reveal a market in which banjos had become so common that they could be assembled from constituent parts bought at different music emporia or purchased already assembled for a couple of dollars apiece, "suit[ing] the pockets better than expensive instruments" (fig. 2-24). Further, such trade was not restricted to the East Coast. As early as the 1850s wholesalers had commonly filled orders for musical instruments or parts by rail and steamer throughout the United States. In 1853, for example, the firm of Bourne and Torrey of Sandusky, Ohio, sold banjos as well as guitars, tambourines, and other instruments, and in the 1870s the music dealers Root and Cady of Chicago offered not only Tilton's patent banjos (at prices from $12 to $40) but also a range of other, less finely produced models for as low as $2.[33] Besides accounting for the fact that by 1880 no part of the nation seemed immune to the rage for banjos, such merchandising explains the presence during this period, in regions like the upland South, of interesting hybrid instruments whose hooks, nuts, and shoes were obviously factory-made, but whose rims and necks were handmade by folk artisans.[34] Even if Baur and Stewart were correct about the poor quality of many of the mass-produced instruments, large-scale factories such as Buckbee's nonetheless played a central role in the further popularization of the instrument.

In naming those who claimed to make their own instruments but in fact had them produced in one of New York's factories, Baur went out of his way to indict virtually the entire Dobson family. He named not only George C. Dobson but also his brother Charles Edgar (known as C. Edgar), whose Egyptian banjos had "rims, necks, and materials" purchased "in quantities from other dealers" and were assembled by a "cheap workman." Brother Edward, whom Baur thought should have known better, purportedly took "about 200 Buckbee banjos, costing from four to nine dollars each" to London, where he sold them "from four to ten pounds" apiece.

Nor did the oldest sibling, Henry, whose closed-back banjo was one of the most popular instruments of the late 1860s and 1870s, escape Baur's pen. Although "H. C. Dobson claims to have a factory of his own," Baur insisted that he never could find it and was "almost positive" that Dobson got his parts from "some factory."[35]

In wagging his finger at these individuals, Baur singled out the first family of American banjoists, for between the Civil War and the turn of the century these Dobsons (and one other sibling, who escaped Baur's censure) were intimately connected to the banjo culture. As stage players, well-known teachers, authors of method books, composers, inventors, and craftsmen, the Dobsons were central to the development, and the popularization among all classes, of this instrument. Raised in "needy circumstances," they had grown up in a New York abuzz over minstrelsy and early on became immersed in it. One patron of the minstrel shows, for example, recalled that during the 1840s the five brothers were "among the constant gallery patrons" of the Ethiopian Opera House in the Bowery.[36] And while some contemporaries argued that Frank Converse was the banjo's true paternal ancestor, the Dobson name, as one New York writer put it, was "synonymous with that of the banjo."[37] Henry Clay (1832–

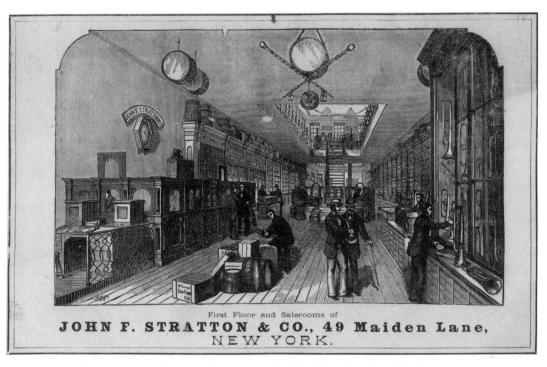

Figure 2-24. Back cover of *Catalogue of Holiday Goods Issued by John F. Stratton and Co.* (New York, 1882), illustrating the main showroom of this large New York musical instrument wholesaler. Firms like this sold instruments in a wide price range, including the cheap, factory-made banjos so many makers inveighed against.

1908), Charles Edgar (1839–1910), George Clifton (1842–90), Frank Prescott, and Edward Clarendon Dobson (1858–1919) demonstrated how inextricably the banjo and its music had become enmeshed in Victorian culture and economy.[38]

Henry and C. Edgar, for example, first made their mark as teachers, both beginning to give banjo instruction by the late 1850s.[39] Evidently they were not shy about their talents. "For the past eight years," one writer reported in 1866, "the newspapers have contained advertisements for the 'Dobson Brothers Banjo Instructors'"; he recalled as well that "huge posters" of the two, "presenting several square feet of mustache, digit, and banjo, have stared into the eyes of visitors and residents from every dead wall."[40]

Unlike many of the first generation of banjoists, however—but like their contemporary Converse—the Dobsons learned to play the instrument in the North, not on the southern plantation. Like Baur, a runaway teenager working in a bookbinding shop who learned to play from minstrels who met in an upstairs room on Fulton Street in New York City, Henry reportedly acquired his initial lessons from African American coworkers in the cloakroom of the Astor House in New York, where he was employed.[41] As he himself described his early infatuation with the banjo, he "went to bed nights, and found it almost impossible to sleep, for the mellow notes of the banjo were continually ringing" in his ears (fig. 2-25). "If I dreamed," Henry continued, "it was of the old *chremonia*"; all his "thoughts and impulses seemed tinged with its rich music." From that time on, all of his energies "were bent toward the ownership of such an in-

Figure 2-25. Engraving of Henry C. Dobson, from four-page advertising brochure, ca. 1880. Henry was the oldest of the five Dobson brothers, all of whom made their mark in the emergent banjo culture of the 1870s and 1880s.

strument," and when he finally acquired one, "the first touch of its strings" thrilled him "like the inspiration of a prophet."

In a few hours, noted the reporter for a Boston newspaper who provides the fullest account of the Dobsons' activities, Henry had "mastered a juba," and in two months more "his knowledge of the instrument surpassed that of all ordinary players." Realizing the musical possibilities of the banjo, Henry "disdain[ed] the common negro jigs" and "invaded the mystic realms of operatic music," building a repertoire "as varied as those of the most accomplished violinists and pianists." He was, as the correspondent put it, "far in advance of the age."

C. Edgar, who had been engaged similarly at the St. Nicholas Hotel, never was far behind his older brother and "soon became a champion player." From such inauspicious beginnings these two brothers—and eventually their younger siblings—went on to become the city's most prominent instructors, tutoring (as had Buckley) the great Thalberg and having as pupils such socialites as Lady Randolph Churchill, the famed actress Lotta, and members of the Vanderbilt and Belmont families. As one observer of New York's music scene put it, "These brothers have raised the instrument . . . to the pedestal of fashionable notoriety."[42]

As Henry shifted (as did many of his fellow banjoists) from stroke- to guitar-style playing, he also began to "improve" the banjo to make it more suitable for the different kinds of music he wished to play on it. One journalist made much of Henry's "invention" of a seven-stringed banjo, which "opened" a "new world of melody" to him. As we have noted, however, the first banjo that he patented was a closed-back instrument, whose production and distribution he tightly controlled. Advertisements in the *New York Clipper*, for example, indicate that these banjos were "not for sale in any store in the United States" but had to be acquired directly from him.[43] Not fully satisfied with that instrument's design, however, he followed it with several refinements that kept him at the center of the banjo's evolution through the 1870s.

In 1873 Henry patented (U.S. patent no. 136,491) "an improvement in the means employed for stretching and holding the parchment head of a banjo over the frame or hoop" (fig. 2-26, plates 2-9, 2-10, 2-11). A variation on the "top-tension" device he had entered in 1867, his invention consisted of a grooved clamp that fit over the tension hoop and had a hole through it on the opposite side for a screw. This last was tightened into "an outwardly-projecting part of the frame or hoop" inside the sound chamber of the banjo. Henry noted that one could use "metallic nuts" rather than a shoulder or blocks of wood to tighten down the head inside the sounding board, but he preferred wood because "the screws may be forced directly

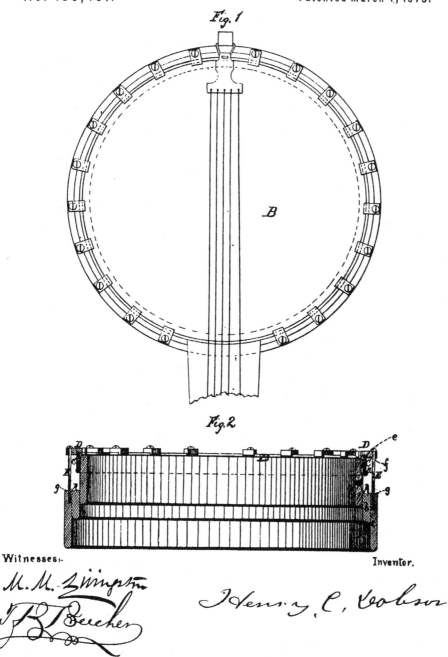

H. C. DOBSON.
Banjos.

No. 136,491.

Patented March 4, 1873.

Fig. 1

B

Fig. 2

Witnesses:-

M. M. Zimpton

J. B. Beecher

Inventor.

Henry C. Dobson

Figure 2-26. Patent drawing for Henry C. Dobson's banjo, 4 March 1873. In the 1870s Henry continued to refine the closed-back instrument he first developed in 1867. On this model, the screws for tightening the head fit into an outwardly projecting lip of the back.

into the wood and be sufficiently secure," a method which "saved the expense of tapping the metal with the necessary screw-threads." By this "simple, durable, and efficient clamping device," he concluded, "I materially decrease the cost of manufacture so that I am able to furnish the market first-class banjos at a considerably lower price than heretofore."

In 1878 Henry followed this patent with another that essentially refined and made more durable the banjo he first had developed in 1867 (fig. 2-27). The major change on the new model concerned the "straining ring" that was pressed over the head to tighten it. He made this of metal rather than wood, presumably to prevent its cracking. Further, this instrument had a neck partially cut away where it abutted the rim, with the top part of the fingerboard fitting under the lip of this metal ring. When the strings were "keyed up," the neck resisted "the strain of the strings in a direct line with their strain." This arrangement, Dobson wrote, prevented the neck from "springing, which would alter the tone of the instrument," and imparted "greater rigidity and strength" to the banjo.

As should be apparent from these descriptions (and is even more so upon examination of extant instruments), Baur's claim that these banjos were carelessly produced seems questionable, but it is possible that Buckbee or some other maker may have produced them on commission. On the one hand, the instruments' elaborate wood- and metalwork and their unusually configured hardware strongly suggest that if Henry did not actually manufacture the banjos himself, he closely supervised both the acquisition of their constituent parts (presumably from local foundries and woodworkers' shops) and their assembly, perhaps at the "Factory" whose address, 1368 Broadway, he distinguished from his business location, 1270 Broadway, in an illustrated brochure he issued around 1884.[44] On the other hand, some extant, marked Buckbee instruments bear striking resemblance—in peg-head design, for example—to some of the kinds of banjos Henry sold under his name, particularly his open-back models of the 1880s. But the majority of the Buckbee instruments, made with inexpensive hardware and lacking technological sophistication, appear just as Baur described them, produced for the bottom end of the market. A professional musician himself, Henry Dobson designed and made banjos of an entirely different quality.

This is particularly evident in the banjo that he patented (U.S. patent no. 249,321) in 1881 (fig. 2-28). With this instrument he returned to an open-back banjo with traditional (that is, external) hooks and shoes and focused on its tonal qualities. He redesigned the rim as a flanged, dome-shaped ring made from sheet metal (what we now call a tone ring) that when viewed from the inside indeed resembled the inside of a bell. The calfskin

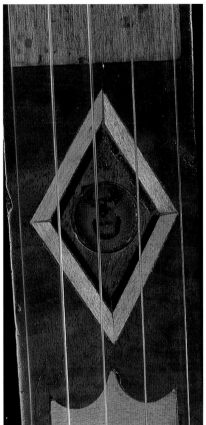

left

Plate 2-1. Unsigned fretless banjo, ca. 1860s. This Civil War–era instrument contains a tintype, probably of the original owner, inlaid in the fingerboard, similar to the presentation in a banjo depicted in a contemporary ambrotype (see figure 2-1). After the Civil War, as more people began to play the instrument, makers began to offer more elaborate decoration.

top

Plate 2-2. Detail of the tintype inlaid in the neck of a Civil War–era banjo (plate 2-1).

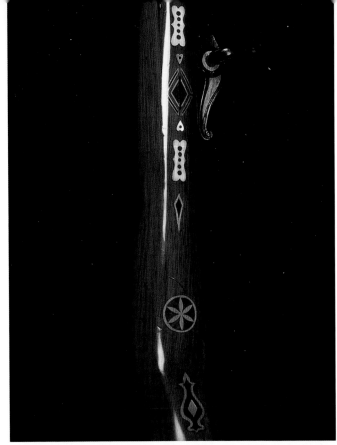

left
Plate 2-4. Detail of the neck of the fretless banjo in plate 2-3, showing the inlaid bone and wood designs.

bottom
Plate 2-5. Detail of the rim of the fretless banjo in plate 2-3, showing inlaid designs on dowel.

opposite
Plate 2-3. Unsigned fretless banjo, ca. 1870. Of unknown origin, this elegant banjo sports a pierced peg head, inlaid Masonic devices on the fingerboard, and bone and wood designs inlaid on the back of the neck and the dowel, all characteristic of banjos in this period. The bulge at the end of the neck is found on only a few extant minstrel banjos. Its purpose is unknown, but some historians think that it aided performers who were spinning or juggling their instruments as part of their acts.

Plate 2-6. Fretless banjo, ca. 1870s. Note the elaborate marquetry on the finger-board and rim, and the slotted, guitar-style peg head. Although this instrument is unsigned, it has an unusual tensioning design similar to that found on contemporary Tilton banjos. This instrument was originally purchased by Benjamin K. G. Butterfield of Jamestown, California; an extant photograph (unfortunately of poor quality) dated 1877 shows him holding the instrument.

Plate 2-7.
Banjo made by
Henry C. Dobson,
1867 patent.
Dobson's first
design featured
a top-tension
tightening
system and an
enclosed back.
These models, as
in the example
here, were usually
made from hand-
somely figured
rosewood.
Collection of
Peter Szego.

Plate 2-8.
Banjo made by
Henry C. Dobson,
1867 patent,
ca. 1870. Dobson
banjos from this
period show a
wide variety of
rim designs—
top-tension as
in this example,
and with a
closed-back, all-
metal rim, for
example—show-
ing the rapid
evolution of the
instrument.
Dobson evidently
sold the rights
to this particular
design to the
Martin Brothers
(no relation to
C. F. Martin) of
New York, whose
stamp is on
the instrument.
Note the intricate
marquetry the
whole length of
the fingerboard.

left

Plate 2-9. Banjo by Henry C. Dobson, 1873 patent. This beautiful example of one of Dobson's banjos features the top-tension design he developed in the early 1870s, with most of the tensioning parts made from metal rather than from wood, as on his 1867 patent. In addition, this banjo features striking marquetry on the fingerboard and on the back and sides of the sound chamber. Collection of Peter Szego.

top

Plate 2-10. Detail of the fingerboard on the Dobson banjo in plate 2-9.

Plate 2-11. Banjo by Henry C. Dobson, 1873 patent. A great variety of store-bought marquetry, some of it made specifically for the banjo trade, was available in the 1870s and 1880s. By the 1890s marquetry decoration was still used as trim on banjo necks, but for the most part it had been supplanted by mother-of-pearl or metal designs on the banjo fingerboards.

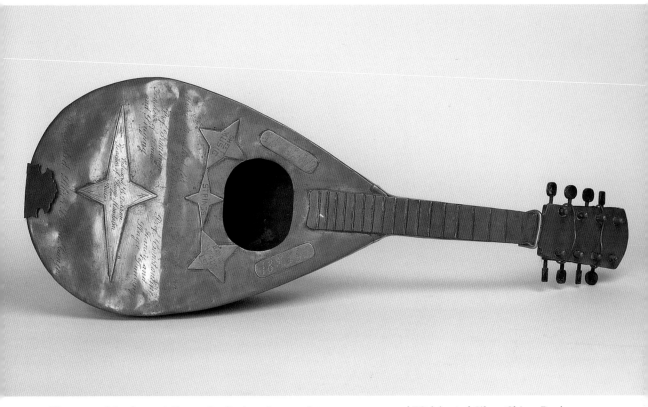

Plate 2-12. Metal mandolin studio display piece, ca. late 1890s, engraved "Celebrated Silver Chime Banjos, Edward C. Dobson, Teacher of Banjo, Mandolin, and Guitar." The mandolin bears the dates 1876 and 1897. Like his four brothers, Edward was well known as an instructor. The fact that he lists guitar and mandolin on this display suggests the increased popularity of these instruments in the late 1890s.

Plate 2-14. Crank-operated wooden litho toy, "The Lime Kiln Club, Old Kentucky Home," ca. 1880s, manufactured by W. S. Reed, Leominster, Massachusetts. Such references to the era of minstrelsy, with the concomitant caricature of African Americans, continued through the 1890s, and by the early years of the new century they had become even more virulent.

opposite

Plate 2-13. These sand-activated toys, with minstrel show themes, were popular in the United States in the 1870s and 1880s. Working like an hourglass, the box must be rotated in a counterclockwise direction, catching the sand in the upper reservoir. As the sand trickles down, it strikes various paddles that activate the musicians, dancers, and animals. The double-figure toy (bottom right) is labeled "C. F. Martine, Milton, Ma 1874)." The one on the top in the middle is signed "Robert Link, 44 Vesey Street, N. Y." The rest of these are unlabeled, but others in the Bollman collection bear the label of Gerard Camagni (one of which has instructions printed in French, German, and English, suggesting the international popularity of such novelties).

Plate 2-15. American clockwork toy, "Old Black Joe, The Minstrel Show," patented 29 January 1884 by the Courier Litho Company, Buffalo, New York. The patent pertains to the mechanism for sound production: a series of thin wire rods that are struck by an eccentric crank with attached wooden cams. Patent dates are often the only clues to the age of such ephemeral objects. On either side are two panorama toys, ca. 1880s, made by McLoughlin. These rare toys have twelve different African American scenes, through which one scrolls by means of the knobs on top. In front are some miniature banjo novelties.

Plate 2-16. An assortment of bisque and other china banjo figurines, German, Austrian, and English, ca. 1880–1915. The widespread presence of the banjo even on such expensive decorative objects suggests how deeply it suffused American, indeed Western, culture by the late nineteenth century.

Plate 2-17. A grouping of Staffordshire and other English pottery, decorated with minstrel themes, ca. 1850–1919. Even common household objects like cups, platters, and pitchers reflected the age's infatuation with minstrelsy in general and the banjo in particular.

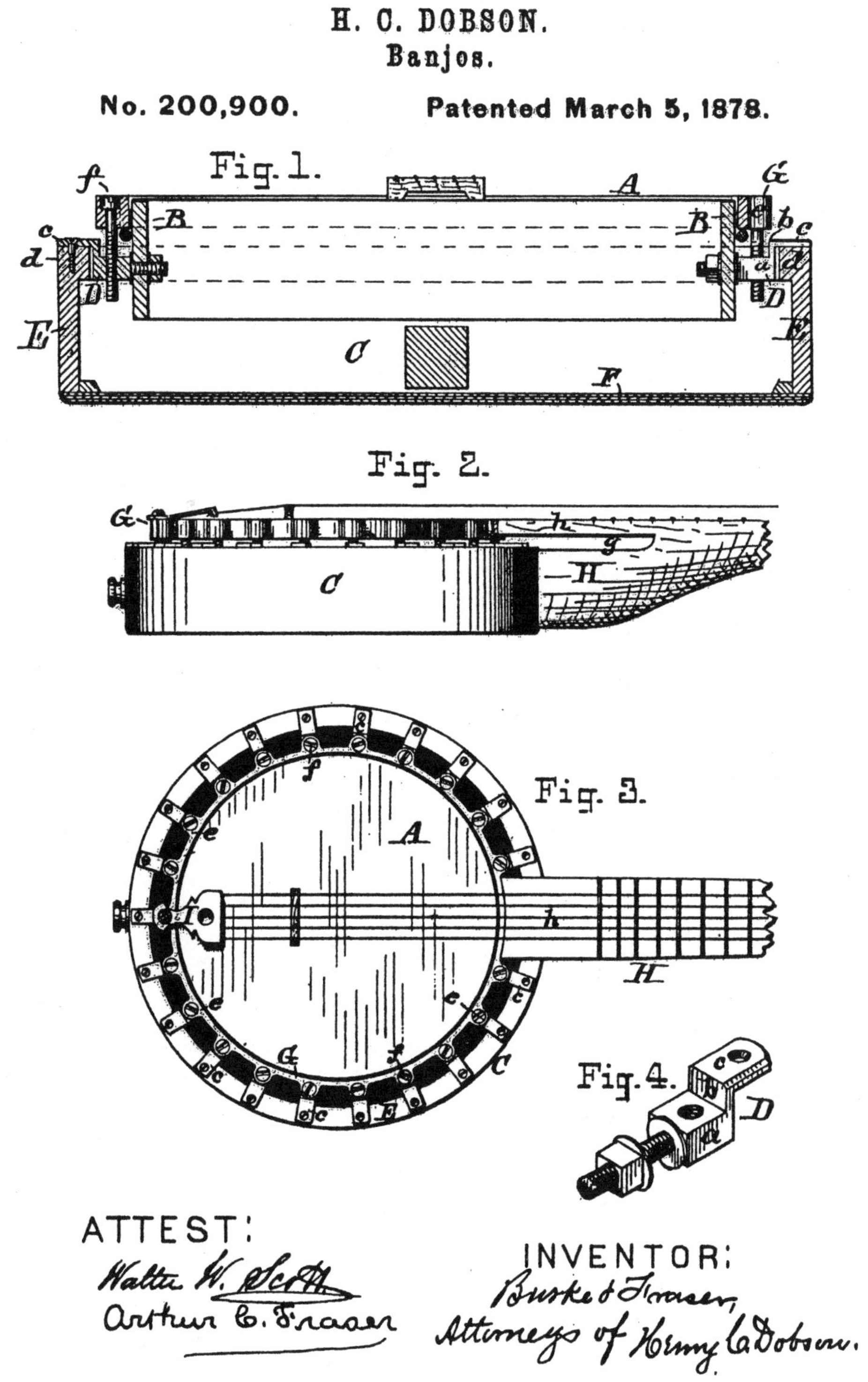

H. C. DOBSON.
Banjos.

No. 200,900.   Patented March 5, 1878.

Fig. 1.

Fig. 2.

Fig. 3.

Fig. 4.

ATTEST:
Walter W. Scott
Arthur C. Fraser

INVENTOR:
Burke & Fraser,
Attorneys of Henry C. Dobson.

Figure 2-27. Patent drawing for Henry C. Dobson's banjo, 5 March 1878. Henry's last closed-back patent, this refinement used a metal rather than a wooden restraining ring, which fit over the head to tighten it. As a result the banjo was heavier and sturdier.

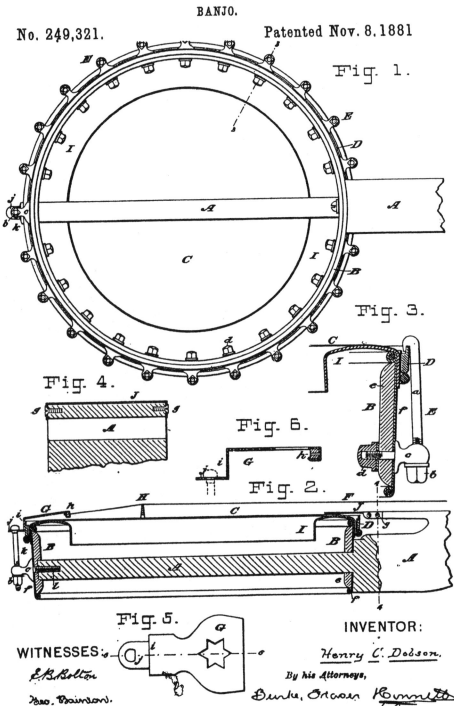

Figure 2-28. Patent drawing for Henry C. Dobson's banjo, 8 November 1881. Rejecting his earlier designs, Henry now built an open-back model that had a large ring under the skin head that gave the instrument, so he claimed, a bell-like tone. It proved to be one of his most successful models.

head rested on this "dome shaped bell, instead of the wood, as in the old style," and this imparted to the instrument "a tone as sweet as silver bells," yet one which would "flood the largest theatre in the world with its exquisite and powerful notes, without extra exertion from the artist." In this patent Henry included other slight improvements—notching the tension hoop in such a way, for example, that the hooks did not touch the stretched membrane and so would not cut it, and extending the fingerboard over the rim, the better to sound high notes—but his primary contribution was his radical idea for altering the tone of the banjo, which he aptly called his Silver Bell (fig. 2-29). He offered the instrument in eight grades, priced from $20 to $100, and noted that he made the banjos "in small sizes for ladies, prices same."[45]

A notice of Henry Dobson in the *New York Clipper* in 1881 suggests the importance of his various improvements in banjo design. "Away back in the long ago—full twenty years—," the editor wrote, "we find our columns advertising the well known banjo player, teacher, and maker, Henry C. Dobson." Today, the writer continued, "his card still notifies the profession and amateurs that his banjos have been improved with the years and are offered as a desideratum for players."[46] Simply put, for twenty years his patents defined the state of the art of the instrument and set the terms for its improvement through the final decades of the century.

Figure 2-29. Envelope from Henry C. Dobson, ca. 1885, illustrating his Silver Bell banjo, first patented in 1881. Note the metal plate at the base of the neck, a distinctive appointment on Dobson's banjos from this period.

Equally significant, however, were the contributions of his brother George, who, after beginning his career as a performer (one observer commented that, except for his brother C. Edgar, he was "the finest living banjoist") and instructor in New York City, moved to Boston in 1869, where he became "one of the most noted teachers of banjos" in the United States (fig. 2-30).[47] Although not known primarily as an inventor, in the same year that he moved north he entered a patent (U.S. patent no. 90,530) with one William McDonnell for a new way of "securing and stretching" the head of a banjo over the rim, "whereby the tone of the instrument is softened, and rendered more harmonious," because the skin came into contact only with wooden parts rather than metal. But this patent never caught the public's attention. Although he took out one more patent, in 1895 (U.S. patent no. 550,951), for a tone ring that sat on ball bearings (presumably to allow more free vibration of the ring itself), George achieved his stature in banjo culture primarily through the publication of a series of important banjo tutors in which he popularized a "simplified method" for learning to play the instrument, and then, after the mid-1880s, through the manufacture of his trademarked (but not patented) Victor banjo (fig. 2-31).[48]

As Dobson explained in his *Simplified Method and Thorough School for the Banjo* (1874), he had developed his new manner of instruction around 1861 to assist one of his pupils ("a lady") who did not have enough time to master reading the standard musical notation in which banjo tutors hitherto had been composed (fig. 2-32).[49] "I then and there," he continued, "received the idea of the simplified method for the Banjo, written on five lines," with the tones represented by "two kinds of notes," a closed (black) ring for "a tone required to be stopped by a finger of the left hand" and an open ring to represent the tone made on an unstopped (open) string. Although he had taught this method for years, Dobson noted, he had never "attached so great an importance" to it as to publish it. Now "seeing the pleasure the many have experienced by its simplicity," particularly those "who have other duties that would preclude the possibility of their making a study of music," he finally decided to publish it in a tutor, so "that all lovers of the Banjo may be benefitted by it."

Like the earlier banjo methods, Dobson's is significant for what it suggests about both the instrument and its music. Before detailing his special method, for example, he addressed the question of what strings a banjoist should use and also explained the importance of having one's instrument fretted, by which he meant with position markers "inlaid, level with the surface of the finger-board, an eight of an inch in width."[50] Moreover, in explaining how to "handle" the instrument Dobson suggested that the

Figure 2-30. Engraving of George C. Dobson in the *New York Clipper*, 20 December 1884. George, a highly regarded banjo instructor, developed a "Simplified Method," a tablature for learning to play the banjo, but he was roundly attacked by those who thought that to help "elevate" the banjo in the public's estimation one should learn to read standard musical notation.

prospective banjoist bring the right hand "directly in front of the bridge" and "rest the little finger on the parchment to steady the hand"—in other words, in the guitar style (fig. 2-33).

A few pages later he explained both "guitar style or picking" and "stroke or banjo style," but the examples in his method and in the "Thorough School" that comprised the second part of the book lend themselves most readily to the former. Indeed, Dobson did not hide his prejudice in the matter. Stroke style "is characteristic of the instrument," he explained, "and much admired by all lovers of the banjo," a polite way of saying that it was old-fashioned and simplistic, while guitar style "admits of expression, feeling, a display of taste, &c." A good banjoist, he added, learns both styles, enabling one to produce "the rich music of the guitar in soft, silver strains" as well as "the genuine banjo music made by the stroke."[51]

Dobson's method, essentially what we call tablature, is as simple as he suggested. The five lines represent the strings of the banjo, and a number underneath one of the closed notes indicates at what position (fret) a tone is played. He also explained "snapping the string" (pulling off to get two rapid notes) and barre chords, added some scale exercises, and then provided thirty pages of tunes written in his method. He prepared the second half of the tutor in standard notation, for "those desiring to advance to higher stages in the art," and included a number of pieces identified with "G.C.D." after the titles—the "Williams Polka," for example, and "Dobson's Clog Hornpipe"—tunes presumably written by him and testament to his musical knowledge.

Dobson's *Simplified Method* went through several editions, some of which had other tunes added to them, and, to judge from the consternation of its detractors, it enjoyed much popularity.[52] It seems genuinely to have popularized the instrument, allowing those whose "duties," as Dobson put it, precluded their taking more formal music lessons to learn to play fairly sophisticated music with some dispatch (figs. 2-34, 2-35). Further, in an advertisement on the inside cover of the tutor Dobson indicated how he imagined some of his customers might use the instrument: "While most brilliant when played as a solo," he noted, the banjo also was "an ex-

Figure 2-31. Cover of advertising pamphlet, *Geo. C. Dobson's Victor Banjos* (Boston, 1886). The most prominent banjo teacher in Boston, like many other instructors George Dobson developed his own line of instruments. It is likely, however, that he had them manufactured by others.

cellent accompaniment for the Voice" and as such could be used in "HOME AMUSEMENTS." "A little investment in music," Dobson counseled, "yields far more satisfactory returns than any other, and he or she who can perform upon any instrument need never be at a *loss for company*: a congenial friend is ever at hand" (fig. 2-36).

Dobson's attempt to popularize the instrument among amateurs was highly important for its subsequent development. One can see, for example, the relationship between a simplified method like his and the instruments produced in the banjo factories that so infuriated Baur and Stewart. Indeed, in the 1880s Stewart expended considerable energy to claim just this linkage and lambasted Dobson for what he considered to be his misguided efforts to teach music in any way but through standard notation, a folly supposedly fraught with disastrous results for any students who truly sought to master the instrument.

Stewart was virtually apoplectic on this topic. In reviewing the banjo's progress from African folk instrument to its pinnacle of development (obviously, as it came from his own factory), for example, he remarked that in

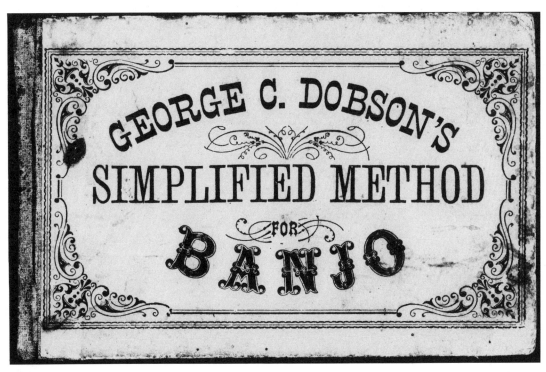

Figure 2-32. Cover of *George C. Dobson's Simplified Method for Banjo* (Boston, 1874). Issued in various editions, Dobson's method went through several revisions and remained popular into the 1890s. Essentially a kind of tablature for those who could not read standard musical notation, Dobson's simplified method brought the banjo within the compass of many new players. Collection of Philip F. Gura.

Figure 2-33. Albumen photograph of Orrin S. Riddout, "Taken on the 23d of April, 1866, Age 21 Years." This unusual full-length photograph of a banjoist shows his right hand in position to play the instrument in guitar style, what we now call finger-picking. This was the primary method taught by George C. Dobson and others in the 1870s, but they also offered rudimentary instruction in the older down-picking style because it was most appropriate for the "characteristic" music of the banjo, that is, the older repertoire from antebellum minstrelsy. Formerly in the collection of Philip F. Gura.

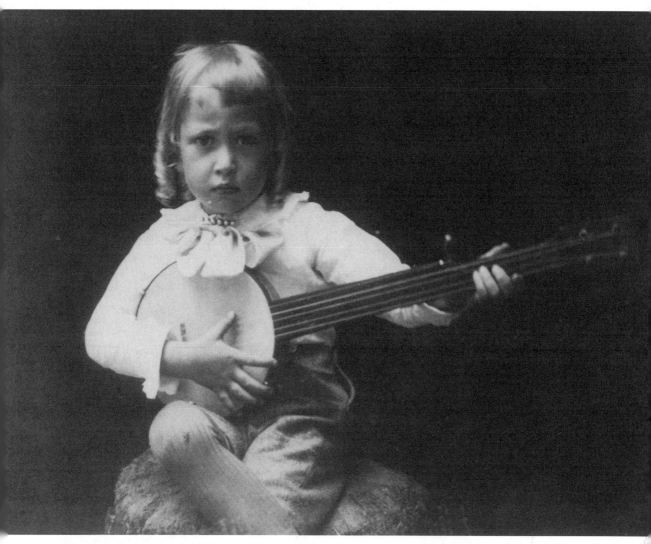

Figure 2-34. Albumen photograph, "Robert Lane, 1886, Weston, [Massachusetts]." The boy is playing a child's-size fretless instrument. As simplified methods for learning the banjo such as George Dobson's became popular, even children were encouraged to play.

the 1860s the reputation of the banjo had been on the rise, "attracting admirers and among a large class of people gaining adherents," particularly through its sponsorship by such eminent musicians as Thalberg. "But then suddenly," he continued dramatically, "a dark cloud seemed to hover over it, shadowing its very existence." Like Edgar Allan Poe's "great, black-winged creature, the Raven," this "thing" seemed to say to the banjo that it would "'haunt you until I blacken your very existence'" and would "'not leave you until I have so shaken you that you will never—no, never, recover from the effects of my presence.'" What was this remarkable "polluted creature"? Nothing less than the "'catch-penny' system of learning to play the banjo, called by its projectors the 'simplified method.'"

Stewart variously termed this system the "Idiot's Delight," "Ham's De-

Figure 2-36. Stereoview, ca. 1890, showing an elaborately furnished Victorian parlor, the new venue for playing the banjo. Two instruments, one of them an 1867-patent Henry C. Dobson, grace the room.

opposite
Figure 2-35. Albumen photograph, "Uncle Sam Tout—blind," by Wright's, 421½ Main Street, Terre Haute, Indiana, ca. 1870s. The banjoist is playing in the guitar style. Note the inlaid metal star near the bottom of the neck, a common form of decoration in this period. His banjo has only eight brackets and is reminiscent of those made for the minstrel stage, but this did not prevent him from adopting the new style of playing.

light" (after the nickname for a minstrel performer), "Open and Shut," and "Simpleton's Method." But no matter how he named it, he always viewed it (and, by implication, its designer) with utter contempt. Chafing at the method's popularity—in 1883, for example, Stewart admitted that "some five years ago" it had "held full sway"—he saw it only as adding "greatly to ignorance, by closing the door to knowledge." "Like opium smokers,"

Figure 2-37. Mounted paper photograph, ca. 1890s, of five homesteaders outside a primitive log hut on the western prairie. No doubt S. S. Stewart had such musicians in mind when he inveighed against those who never bothered to read music but learned to play their instruments by some simplified method. The image speaks to the great popularity of the banjo, which by this time was played with guitars as well as fiddles.

he wrote, "aspiring banjoists" found the method "hard to give up," even though "no man ever gained or cultivated a taste for music, or a musical ear," by devotion to it (figs. 2-37, 2-38). Indeed, "it was so easy and simple" that a person could learn to pick out, Stewart wrote sarcastically, "with perhaps one finger and thumb," such "soul-inspiring tunes as 'Sho-fly, don't bodder me.'" But Dobson's students rarely got further and "had taken the express train for Banjo Botchtown." A year later Stewart's lament was the same. "*Simple Method*," he wrote, is "the cow-catcher which catches sleepy gawks too lazy to get out of its tracks."[53]

Of more immediate interest than Stewart's invective (partially explicable, as we shall see, by his own peculiar investment in wishing to elevate the banjo and its music to a new level of sophistication) was his linkage of the method to Dobson's supposed cupidity, the same vice that possessed manufacturers of the "factory tubs" who peddled their wares to Dobson's students. The "'Open and Shut' notes," Stewart wrote in 1883, "were doubtless originally put on the public by some ingenious Yankee, who thought that by pampering to depraved tastes he could fill his pockets."

Figure 2-38. Half-plate ambrotype, ca. 1860s. This banjoist, like the older man in figure 2-35, plays a large minstrel-era banjo, but in the popular guitar style (perhaps learned from Converse's tutor), his right hand plucking up on the strings near the bridge. Also note the style of violin playing. In this period many violinists played without chin rests, steadying the fiddle against their shoulders or chests (see figure 5-4).

Five years later he sang the same tune, only more stridently. The simplified method, Stewart told readers of his book on the banjo, was the brainchild of "a set of unscrupulous individuals, possessing a very limited knowledge of music and very little love for the science and art—and therefore being ignorant and also disinclined to labor or effort—[who] did not feel inclined to spend their valuable time in teaching pupils to play the Banjo properly" (fig. 2-39). What Dobson wanted "most and only," Stewart concluded, "was to secure a good fee for a quarter's lessons" in advance and then to "let the pupils come in, when he was out," or, what was nearly as bad, "come in and sit down to a beer drinking bout[,] picking on the Banjo at the same time, or between whiles."[54]

Painting George C. Dobson as a sharp and greedy Yankee, condemning his purported lack of musical ability and laziness as a teacher, and suggesting that he was a toper more at home in an immigrant's beer hall than a music studio, Stewart signals how large Dobson and his brothers loomed in the banjo culture of the 1870s and early 1880s and how deeply Stewart was troubled by what he considered to be the instrument's trivialization at their hands. Ironically, however, his own eventual success in supplanting Dobson as the nation's premier exponent of the banjo had as much to do with the continuing democratization of the instrument, which the Dobsons had pioneered, as it did with his efforts to raise the banjo's musical stock. Stewart may have disliked the Dobsons' methods, but his own compulsive embrace of the market smelled of the same greed he attributed to them.

Despite Stewart's vicious attacks, through the mid-1880s George Dobson continued to enjoy much renown, both as an instructor and as a banjo "manufacturer" who "carefully superintend[ed]" the production of his Victor banjo, whose trademark he registered in 1884 and which he termed the "crowning effect of years devoted to the study of the banjo, as a player, teacher, and manufacturer."[55] He also was particularly proud of his "Banjo Headquarters" (as he called it in one of his catalogs) at 280 Shawmut Street, Boston, which had "every facility for the accommodation" of his patrons (fig. 2-40). In addition to private "Instruction Parlors" for each student, "free from the distractions and annoyances of a single office, such as used by many teachers," there one found his "Business Rooms," filled with "the largest stock of first-class instruments anywhere to be seen." Offering two private, half-hour lessons a week for ten weeks at a cost of $25, Dobson maintained his position as one of the country's most respected teachers. Despite Stewart's ridicule of the simplified method, Dobson offered new versions of it through 1879 and kept it in print at least through

Figure 2-39. Advertising broadsheet for the Dime Music Company, ca. 1880. Once other "unscrupulous" entrepreneurs realized the popularity of George C. Dobson's "open-and-shut," simplified method for learning the banjo, they shamelessly copied it, as did the Dime Music Company here. Collection of Philip F. Gura.

GEO. C. DOBSON'S

RATES FOR PRIVATE LESSONS

Ten Weeks (20) Lessons, two lessons each week, - $25.00

Ten Weeks (10) Lessons, one lesson each week, - $15.00

Four Weeks (8) Lessons, two lessons each week, - $12.00

The payment for either course strictly in advance when arrangements are made.

HOURS FOR LESSONS, 9 A. M. TO 1 P. M., AND 5 TO 8 P. M.

✳ Special Notice. ✳

The duration of each lesson is half an hour. Pupils are requested to arrive at least five minutes before the appointed time, so that the lesson may be promptly begun.

The time at which any term of lessons ends is specified on the receipt given for the same when arrangements are made.

No lesson can be given at any other than the appointed time, save by the mutual consent of teacher and pupil, and any lesson thus omitted must be made up before the course ends or not at all. *Special rates for any lessons given other than as above described.*

GEO. C. DOBSON.

Sept. 21, 1885.

Figure 2-40. From advertising pamphlet, *Geo. C. Dobson's Victor Banjos* (Boston, 1886). This page provides the rates for Dobson's tutorials as well as instructions for the proper deportment expected of his pupils. Dobson was particularly proud of the furnishings of his studio, which suggests that by this period the banjo had become deeply entangled with matters of class.

the mid-1880s, even as he issued "new, fresh, comprehensive, and complete" tutors in standard notation.[56]

Clearly, Stewart believed that if he were to claim preeminence as a banjo maker he had to close the space that the Dobsons occupied. As we have suggested, Henry and George were more on his mind than their three brothers, yet all five contributed to their family's prominence in the world of American music. As one writer noted in the 1860s, banjoists like "Rumsey, Converse, Ross, Wambold and others have obtained a reputation among the jig-dancing and lower classes of the community," but it was "reserved" for the Dobsons "to raise the instrument from its depth of popular degradation, and make it a peculiar favorite with all classes of society." Often performing together, playing "five banjos in concert at the same time, each executing a different part," the family was a musical sensation. "They were then preeminently recognized as the fathers of the banjo," one observer noted, and "the bare announcement of their appearance in public will fill the largest musical halls to overflowing."[57]

But in addition to performing, the other Dobsons also were deeply involved in production and sale of musical instruments. As early as 1861 Frank had joined with his brother Charles in the firm Dobson and Brother, banjo makers and music retailers, and though this firm was short-lived, through 1868 they continued to be listed—with separate entries but at the same address—as music dealers or banjo makers.[58] In 1869 Frank was involved enough in banjo making to enter a patent (U.S. patent no. 88,555) for an unusual double-headed banjo, with a "reversible handle, so adapted and arranged that it may be quickly adjusted, so as to face either head" of the instrument. Each of the banjo's two heads was tightened by screws inserted into the rim, which itself was drilled with "apertures" to let out the sound, and the neck was made in such a way that it could easily be turned from one head to the other. The manner in which this was done was not as important to Dobson as the idea: he considered his invention "comprehensive enough to cover, broadly, the combination with a double-headed banjo, of a handle, so arranged as to be reversible." And what was the point? This invention, Frank explained, enabled him to combine "two banjos in one," two heads that gave out "different tones." He had thus produced a "simple and cheap instrument, adapted for playing all manner of tunes."

Frank's patent was another response to the ongoing debate between advocates of stroke- versus guitar-style playing, for by keeping one of the heads looser than the other a musician could achieve the more hollow sound desired for minstrel tunes, while the other, tighter side was more appropriate for brighter, finger-picked music. As far-fetched as it might seem, stage banjoists evidently did perform upon various instruments. Even in the antebellum period, for example, Tom Briggs had kept two banjos, "a light one and a heavy one for different kinds of work." And thirty years later the musician William A. Huntley, proprietor of Huntley's Concert Company and an endorser of Stewart's banjos, remarked that he was "now the possessor of eight banjos of [Stewart's] manufacture." "I introduce the entire number nightly in my performance," he added.[59]

Frank's brother C. Edgar was equally well known as a musician and banjo dealer and joined him in business for a number of years (fig. 2-41). In 1865, however, he and his older brother Henry became partners under the same name, Dobson and Brother. Indeed, financial arrangements in this first family of music often were very complex, for during part of the same period (1863–66) C. Edgar also was in partnership with George as Dobson Brothers, when the two actually manufactured instruments or had them custom made.

The urge to patent designs swept C. Edgar, too. In 1878 (U.S. patent no. 203,604) he entered a banjo with an "arc or dome shaped ring" over which the head was stretched, which he thought caused "less wear upon the head than the more angular corner or edge now in use, and contributes materially to increase the tone or resonance" (fig. 2-42). Not meeting with much success with this instrument (although, as we have seen, ideas like his soon were everywhere in the air), through the decade of the 1880s C. Edgar settled into life as a musician, venturing into banjo "improvement" only two more times. In 1886 he filed a patent (U.S. patent no. 338,142) for another version of what by then was known as a spun-over rim, which he immediately assigned to Henry Benary, providing some grounding to Baur's hostile comments on Benary's banjo factory and the various Dobsons' involvement with it.[60] In 1894 (U.S. patent no. 514,311), he again experimented with a tone ring, this time registering an instrument with a tubular ring at both the top and bottom of the rim. This, he explained, served to strengthen the rim and also added to the tone of the instrument.

Of this remarkable family, brother Edward was the only one who over the course of a lengthy career as a teacher and a musician—from 1868 through the 1890s—did not enter his own banjo patent, although in 1885 the *American Musical Directory* listed him as both the proprietor of a "Banjo College" and a "Manufacturer" (fig. 2-43, plate 2-12).[61] Like his siblings, though, through his work with students and on stage as a performer he marketed banjos, most likely those developed and manufactured by his brothers, along with other musical merchandise. And, no less than the others, his life was defined by engagement with this instrument, reason

Figure 2-41. Cabinet card of C. Edgar Dobson by Gurney, New York, late 1870s. Here
one of the Dobsons holds a closed-back banjo similar to instruments made by George Teed.
Although C. Edgar also tinkered with banjo improvement, he was known primarily as a
teacher and player. Courtesy of the Harvard Theatre Collection, the Houghton Library.

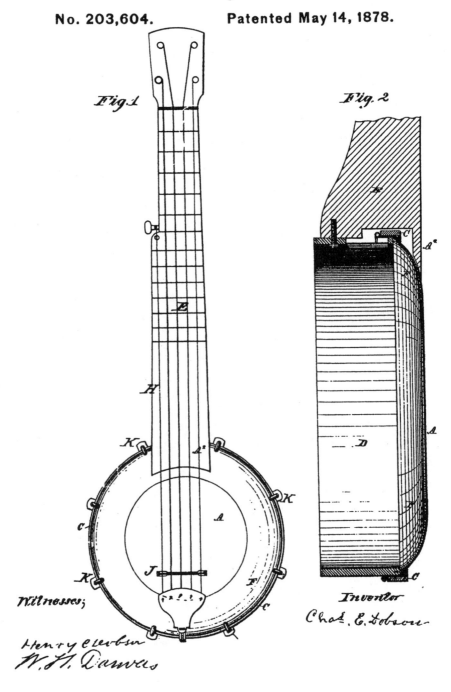

Figure 2-42. Patent drawing for C. Edgar Dobson's banjo, 14 May 1878. The domed or
arched head on this banjo presumably increased its resonance, but this model never was
widely distributed.

opposite
Figure 2-43. Cabinet card of Edward C. Dobson, ca. 1880, by Eisenmann, New York.
On the photograph Dobson is noted as "Sole Proprietor of the Stage and Orchestra Banjo.
Author, Teacher, Concert Performer and Dealer," a description that might fit any of his four
brothers as well. Courtesy of the Harvard Theatre Collection, the Houghton Library.

EDWARD C. DOBSON.
SOLE PROPRIETOR OF THE STAGE & ORCHESTRA
BANJO.
AUTHOR, TEACHER, CONCERT PERFORMER & DEALER.

Figure 2-44. Albumen photograph, ca. 1880. The banjo eventually became so popular in Victorian America that it was widely used to advertise all sorts of goods. Here three men pose in a wagon in front of Niagara Falls, their photograph used to peddle Bassett's Native Herbs.

enough to include him in this discussion of the Dobsons' extensive contributions to banjo culture. Indeed, to summarize this family's achievement we can do no better than cite an admiring New Yorker who, writing in particular about Henry's and C. Edgar's achievements, observed that early on they had "recognized the crudeness of the instrument, studied it in all its chords and octaves, discovered its musical defects, invented notes and published a note book, and made surprising improvements in its mechanical construction."[62] By the 1880s these words described the entire family.

The development of the banjo between the end of the Civil War and the early 1880s was epitomized by the various Dobsons, who dominated its culture and market in a period marked by an immense growth of interest in the instrument. Manufacturers of all sorts of goods quickly capitalized on the public's raging "banjo fever" (fig. 2-44, plates 2-13, 2-14, 2-15, 2-16, 2-17). Indeed, we cannot overestimate the magnitude of this change. As one writer put it in the mid-1860s, "In 1844 there were not half a dozen banjos" in New York City, "and they were only to be met with in grog-shops or bagnios." But he estimated that by 1866 there were "over 10,000 instruments" in use in that city alone, "and the rich melody of its five strings" reached "from the marble fronts of Fifth Avenue down to the slums of Baxter Street."[63]

In this climate banjo makers proliferated, and some of their "improvements" were central to the further technological development of the instrument. But to catalog, as we attempted for the antebellum period, virtually all known makers would entail years of research in city directories and other archival sources and would swell considerably the bulk of this study without greatly altering its general narrative. For many of these new "manufacturers" did precisely what Baur accused the New York companies of doing—they purchased the instrument's constituent parts wholesale and then assembled banjos that may have been distinctive through the shape of their peg heads or the beauty of their ornamentation but offered little change in the instrument's basic acoustic design. Thus, despite the centrality of these many individuals to the spread of public interest in the banjo, unlike the Dobsons and others who filed important patents or otherwise contributed to the banjo's physical evolution, they occupy no significant technological niche.

By 1880, however, the stage was set for the entrance of yet another entrepreneur, one who eventually superseded the Dobsons as the nation's chief purveyor of the banjo. With interest in the instrument now clearly on the rise, the young Samuel Swaim Stewart stepped forward to define more completely the banjo's place in American music and culture. Before his premature death in 1898 he had built an empire of musical goods that was the envy of his competitors. In addition, Stewart offers a vivid example of what an enterprising businessman could accomplish in a nation whose myriad consumers, most likely introduced to the banjo by one of the Dobsons, now sought to buy culture as well as dependability.

3

Selling the Banjo
to All America

Philadelphia's S. S. Stewart

In 1872 George Dobson found himself in Philadelphia, tutoring a seventeen-year-old student whose "passion for music" had manifested itself "at an extremely early age."[1] The boy had studied violin with "Professor" Carl Gaertner, a "music master" in that city, and the young student seemed destined to excel on that instrument. He also loved to tinker, so much so that his parents "provided him with a work-shop and with suitable tools" where "he was wont," one biographer noted, "to occupy himself for several hours daily in the construction of toy fiddles, guitars, mechanical figures, and various other contrivances." The boy's veritable "mania for musical instruments" only increased as he grew older. In addition to taking apart "old and broken violins" and studying and repairing them, he eagerly searched the public libraries and secondhand bookstores for books about musical instruments and their construction.

But Samuel Swaim Stewart's life had changed irrevocably when he attended a minstrel show at the Eleventh Street Opera House and heard the renowned banjoist Lew Simmons.[2] Stewart put aside the violin and devoted himself to the new instrument. He took several lessons from Dobson, already renowned as one of the nation's foremost performers and instructors, and soon began to perform in public, billing himself as "banjoist, Teacher and Vocalist." In addition, he transferred his interest in the history and construction of instruments to his new hobby and labored to understand how the banjo might be constructed to conform to the same standards set for instruments in the European classical tradition.

Although Dobson could not then have known it, his young student would immerse himself in the culture of the banjo so completely that within a decade his name supplanted his instructor's as synonymous with the instrument, his highly successful self-promotion the envy of all other manufacturers. Indeed, the Dobson brothers could only dream of such commercial success, for until his premature death on 6 April 1898 Stewart oversaw an extensive mercantile empire—he sold great quantities of banjos, instrument parts, strings, instruction books, sheet music, and advertising—centered on what in a mere twenty years he had enshrined as America's instrument.

By the late 1870s the banjo already was widely known in American popular culture, with some performers, instructors, and manufacturers enjoying comfortable careers through their association with it. But Stewart's success was of a different order. It depended first on his identification and manipulation of a market for the instrument among middle-class Americans now eager to purchase consumer goods, and then on his refinement of its manufacture so that he could produce it in a variety of grades and thus offer it at a range of prices, without sacrifice of quality.[3]

Moreover, with him the banjo was not so much a business as a passion. Thus, his success derived from his wish to elevate the banjo from associations with blackface minstrelsy and the variety shows to the genteel world of Victorian parlors and concert halls.[4] To make the banjo as popular and respectable as the piano or violin, Stewart aimed his advertising at those who, despite their newly acquired economic success, still needed guidance in how they might mark and display their cultural sophistication. Toward this end, Stewart built a large manufactory where he oversaw the production of thousands of quality instruments that satisfied his customers' desires for goods that signaled their newly acquired wealth and leisure. He also developed an extensive publishing empire through which he tirelessly proselytized for the banjo in general and his instruments in particular, assuring his readers (and would-be customers) that to own and play a Stewart banjo marked them as tasteful, sophisticated consumers.

Stewart's adoption of what we might term the "cause" of the banjo— nothing short of everything about it—set him apart from other makers. By the 1890s other firms (most notably, those of Lyon and Healy in Chicago and Fairbanks, Cole, and Gatcomb in Boston) challenged his preeminence by building high-grade instruments and promoting their goods through similar marketing strategies, but until his death Stewart remained the commercial and public relations giant. His multifaceted career illustrates how an instrument once marginalized because of its associations with the lower classes became iconic of American culture at all levels, and in particular of middle-class pretensions to gentility. Equally important, in the face of burgeoning production of all manner of consumer goods, he insisted that his own banjos were the finest because they still were produced by skilled craftsmen rather than by untutored laborers. This desire to continue to associate the instrument with artisanal rather than factory production, even as he boasted of the size and sophistication of his "manufactory," centers Stewart squarely in the midst of the late-nineteenth-century debates over the authenticity of goods that erupted in the wake of the nation's industrial transformation. He allows us to understand further the emergence and development of modern consumer culture.

Unlike the Dobsons, who left a lengthy list of patents, Stewart was not a technological innovator but, rather, a master salesman whose forte was advertising.[5] As the *New York Clipper* put it in 1889 in an approving notice of his frequent use of their pages for advertising, Stewart "is evidently a believer in printer's ink and is never afraid to use plenty of it."[6] Thus, in addition to his instruments, he left a remarkable paper trail of writings on the banjo: promotional broadsides and brochures, catalogs of his goods, instruction books, treatises on banjo construction, dissertations on the instrument's history, and, perhaps most significant, *S. S. Stewart's Banjo and Guitar Journal* (1882–1902), a bimonthly publication supposedly dedicated to both those instruments but in fact given over almost wholly to the former.[7]

Stewart needed to look no further than his own family for his first lessons in such salesmanship. Born in Philadelphia on 8 January 1855, he was the son of Dr. Franklin Stewart, a purveyor of the patent medicine called Swaim's Panacea, developed in the 1820s by his father-in-law, William Swaim, and reputedly good for every ailment including cancer. Like many of his contemporaries, Swaim had unabashedly used the medium of print to peddle his goods, never shying away from controversy that promoted his sales, and in particular made much use (as would his grandson) of "testimonials" from satisfied customers all over the country. At some point after his daughter's marriage to Franklin Stewart, William arranged to have his son-in-law operate the patent medicine business for him, an arrangement that continued after the death of his own son, James, in 1870.[8]

But however lucrative the family business (at mid-century Swaim's estate reputedly was valued at half a million dollars), the Stewarts wanted something different for young Samuel, and when he was twelve they pointed him toward the career of a musician. Although in one sense Samuel did not disappoint them—in his first publications in the late 1870s and early 1880s, for example, when he was still performing regularly, he billed himself as the "Artistic Banjoist"—they most likely were not thinking of the banjo, for in the public mind this instrument still was linked to lower-class entertainment like minstrel shows or dance halls. Stewart's subsequent attempts to elevate the instrument thus may have derived from his need to justify to himself (as well as to his parents) the relevance of his early musical training to his new career as banjoist and, eventually, instrument maker (fig. 3-1).[9]

Moreover, Stewart's early tutorial in music of the European tradition probably accounts for his insistence virtually from the beginning of his career that one learn the banjo through standard musical notation, typified in his popular *Complete American Banjo School* (1883), and not through any of the contemporary short-cuts (most notably George Dobson's simplified method).[10] As we have seen, on this topic Stewart could hardly be restrained, and it figured along with other concerns in his campaigns to make the banjo more popular and respectable.

In a promotional brochure issued in 1880 Stewart commenced the attack (aimed primarily at the Dobsons) that he carried on for years in his *Banjo and Guitar Journal*, urging those who wished to play the instrument to learn to read music by note. Aligning himself with the belief in progress that drove late-nineteenth-century America, he asked aspiring banjo players if they were "advancing with the times" or had "fallen into the ditch of the 'Simplified Method'?" "The Banjoist who cannot read music today," he noted, "is like the man who is unable to read a sign-post or a newspaper."[11]

But it was not only how one learned to play the banjo that mattered, but

Figure 3-1. Carte-de-visite of
S. S. Stewart, dated on the verso
8 September 1875, a few years
after he had studied the banjo
with George C. Dobson.

what one played on it, and by 1880 Stewart frequently linked the skill of
note-reading to what he considered the proper repertoire for the instrument. Here Stewart's cultivation of the middle class and its cultural aspirations is readily apparent, for he particularly condemned the "vulgar"
uses of the banjo. Not missing the chance to tar Dobson yet again, Stewart observed that the most likely devotee of the simplified method was uncouth: "a chap with a cigar stump in the corner of his mouth, hat one side
of his head, blue shirt, spring-bottom pants, and Banjo in a bag under his
arm" (fig. 3-2). When this person talked, Stewart continued, his boorish-
ness became even more evident. "He talks loud, using many slang words,
and does not know one note of music from another, but he is able to 'sling'
a glass of beer with anybody."[12] The lesson was clear: prospective players
should not "go around among variety halls or drinking saloons to hear
some negro or mountebank attempt to play the instrument" but instead
ought to go "into [the] parlor or drawing room, and among gentlemen
and ladies," where they might find more refined music played on it.[13]

Stewart, however, was nothing if not a shrewd businessman, and when

Figure 3-2. Sixth-plate daguerreotype, ca. 1850s, of a young banjo player, probably a laborer. Although dating from a slightly earlier period, this image accurately portrays the kind of uncouth player Stewart thought particularly susceptible to Dobson's simplified method of instruction: "a chap with a cigar stump in the corner of his mouth" dressed in workingman's clothes. Note that this individual plays a tack-head banjo; tacks are clearly visible holding down the skin where the neck meets the rim.

he opened his studio in August 1878 he realized that for the time being, to guarantee his financial success as an instructor, he had to cater to all sorts of students, including precisely those who had heard the banjo in the city's music halls (fig. 3-3).[14] He issued one of his early tutors, for example, "for those who desire to learn the Banjo for the Minstrel stage" and therein addressed, among other topics, how to organize a minstrel troupe, how to

Figure 3-3. Quarter-plate tintype, ca. 1860s. This striking image, with a large-headed banjo as the focal point, portrays three working-class men (perhaps a father and his sons), who may have been introduced to the banjo through the minstrel shows or music halls and obviously wished to be associated with the instrument. Note the "bump" in the neck of the banjo for the vertical fifth-string tuner, as well as the primitive photographer's studio, with both backdrop and floor covering made from heavy cloth. Collection of Philip F. Gura.

"Black Up," and with what jokes and gags one could win over an audience.[15] Even though Stewart condemned those who went a step further than George Dobson and "profess[ed] to teach the Banjo by mail"—they only reminded him "of the numerous charlatans and quacks" who "profess to cure all sorts of diseases without ever seeing their patients" (was he thinking of his own father?)—in the early 1880s there still was enough interest in such methods for him to publish an edition of Edmund Clark's *Self-Instructing Music for the Banjo, with Figures* (fig. 3-4).[16] While Stewart observed that this selection of twenty tunes "for new beginners" should not be "confounded with the 'Open and Closed Note System,'" above the book's regular notation Clark included figures "showing the string and fret where each note is to be found on the banjo," surely a simplified method!

As Stewart gained confidence as an instructor and an interpreter of what he considered more refined music for the banjo, he broke more decisively with the minstrel and variety hall repertoire, adapting and arranging European music and insisting at every opportunity that the banjo ought to "tak[e] its place as a MUSICAL INSTRUMENT" equal to the violin, piano, guitar, or flute. "Our aim," he wrote in a typical passage, is "to invite the attention of musical minds to the capabilities of the instrument."[17] Through the 1880s he carried on this campaign in a variety of ways, most prominently through a series of pamphlets and books that mark him as the first serious historian of the banjo, as well as in his *Banjo and Guitar Journal*, which he published from 1882 until his death and which serves as his commercial autobiography (fig. 3-5).

To those familiar with the history of late-nineteenth-century advertising, Stewart's efforts as a publicist are not unusual, for during this period modern large-scale advertising was established.[18] Nor was his idea for a journal devoted to the banjo unique. In 1869, for example, Frank Converse and one Degroot had begun to issue an instruction book in serial form, "as a magazine," and in the late 1880s, when Stewart was deriding a new journal started by one of his competitors in Boston, he noted that it had been preceded by an issue or two of the *Banjo Herald*, which had "followed the path" of the similarly defunct "Dobson's Banjo Magazine."[19]

The scale of his efforts, however, distinguished Stewart's advertising campaign from those of Henry Dobson, John Bogan, and others who through 1870s had issued flyers and leaflets in which they sang the praises of their patents or methods: Stewart sought to draw truly national attention to the banjo generally and his company in particular. Early in 1882, therefore, he established his journal, publishing it monthly "in the interests of the Banjo and Guitar Player, Music and Minstrelsy," charging a subscription rate of fifty cents per year, and offering music teachers and

Figure 3-4. Printed cover for *Edmund Clark's Simplified Method for the Banjo* (Boston, 1879). Although Stewart condemned George Dobson's simplified method for teaching the banjo, in the early 1880s he published a version of Clark's tutor, probably because he realized that he might make some profit from it.

music dealers various premiums if they brought in new subscriptions. In an interview in 1886 he recalled that he "started out with the idea of making [the journal] simply an advertising medium" for his banjos and publications, but he eventually realized that a high enough volume of outside advertisements would bring in more revenue, though he never wished to make the journal dependent on such funding.[20] Thus, he accepted all sorts of business announcements, "including Professional and Teachers' Cards," at ten cents per line, with none shorter than ten lines; early issues of the journal (four pages in length) carried advertising for music instructors and music-related goods as well as for his own goods (fig. 3-6).

But the journal promised and delivered much more. Subscribers could expect at least two new pieces of music in each issue and in addition found notices of prominent musicians, essays on all manner of topics related to the banjo and its construction, and, very prominently, letters of endorsement for Stewart's banjos and music. Over the years, as the journal grew in size to as many as twenty-four pages, Stewart expanded his coverage of the music world to concerts and performances by banjo clubs and orches-

Figure 3-5. Carte-de-visite of S. S. Stewart, ca. 1882, at the start of his career as a music publisher and banjo maker. This evidently was the photograph from which a woodcut was made for use in his various advertisements; on the verso is written "make cut the same size."

S. S. STEWART'S BANJO AND GUITAR JOURNAL

VOL. I., NO. 9.   JANUARY 1, 1883.   PRICE, 5 CENTS.

S. S. STEWART'S, Banjo and Guitar Journal,

PUBLISHED EVERY MONTH.

S. S. STEWART, Proprietor,

Music Depot, No. 412 North Eighth Street,

PHILADELPHIA PA., U. S. A.

Price, 5 cents per copy, or 50 cents per year.

Select Advertisements inserted.

ENGLAND AGENT.

J. E. BREWSTER,

No. 20 OXFORD STREET, W.

LONDON, ENGLAND.

S. S. STEWART'S BANJOS ARE FOR SALE IN SAN FRANCISCO, CAL.,

By Messrs. KOHLER & CHASE,

Nos. 137 and 139 Post Street.

S. S. STEWART'S BANJO BOOKS.

A GOOD BANJO BOOK.— The Banjoist's Own Collection of Choice Music, by S. S. Stewart. Price, 50 cents per copy.

STEWART'S FAMOUS BANJO BOOK. Stewart's Thorough School for the Banjo. Price, $2.50 per copy by mail.

NOW WE HAVE IT.—The Banjo Player's Hand Book and Complete Instructor. Stewart's well known Banjo book. Price, 75 cents per copy, by mail.

DON'T FORGET THE GREAT FAVORITE Book, The Young Banjoist, by S. S. Stewart. Price, $1.00 per copy, by mail.

STEWART'S EVER POPULAR BOOK FOR young and old, The Minstrel Banjoist. Price, 50 cents per copy, by mail.

A BOOK FOR THE MILLION, The Universal Banjo Instructor, by S. S. Stewart. Price only 10 cents per copy.

THE ARTISTIC BANJOIST, a book of fine music for the Banjo; Stewart's celebrated publication. Sent on receipt of $1.00

THE BANJOIST'S COMPENDIUM, a choice collection of jigs and fancy tunes. Sent on receipt of 60 cents.

THE BANJOIST'S DELIGHT, a fine collection of music, by Horace Weston and others. Sent on receipt of $1.50

Our Editor's Annual Message.

I was about to shove this number upon you, my kind patrons, forgetting my manners, as the boy said who grabbed the last piece of cake. I forgot that this number enters upon a new year, and that some comments on the subject were in place. In shooting off the last ball of the '82 pop-gun, and loading up for '83, I will thank all my patrons with as much grace as though I had written a personal letter to each, which would be something of a job. I will state that never before has my business been as large and prosperous as at present, which shows that my friends do not forget me. Adieu, kind friends, I shall soon have a new book for you.

S. S. STEWART.

A "penny-wise and pound-foolish" genius wrote to us recently that if we would send him the Journal occasionally he would buy all his goods from us. We think that a man who is mean enough to ask a free subscription to a five cents a month paper cannot have much trade to dispose of.

Squibs.

Ed. H. Hulse, of Buffalo, is doing a fine banjo business.

Keating and Sands have been making great hits with Sam Hague's minstrels.

Read Professor Mansfield's letter in this issue—interesting to our California friends.

Lew Keyes, the "Classic Banjoist," has been "knocking things" through the East.

Our old friend, Horace McLeon, is traveling with Skiff & Gaylord's minstrels.

Gibbons & Stone, our Rochester agents, are "knocking things out."

New songs are advertised in this issue by A. Shattinger, St. Louis, Mo.

Guitarists should send to W. L. Hayden, 120 Tremont street, Boston, Mass., for his catalogue.

S. R. Schiedell, of Detroit, Mich., banjo teacher, says he is doing well and has made a good opening.

All letters are promptly attended to here, but no postal cards are answered "by return mail."

Mr. Emil Herbruger, Guitarist, of Egg Harbor, New Jersey, contributes to this number.

C. E. Latshaw, the popular banjo teacher, of St. Louis, reports favorable business, and swears by the Journal.

Those who are too poor to pay 50 cents a year for a paper like the Journal may have it sent free by stating the case to the publisher.

Mr. Charles H. Loag, of Lancaster, Pa., one of our valued contributors, is a fine banjo and guitar player and a popular teacher.

Recently a young man paid $50 for a "Tub banjo," but if he had paid 50 cents a year for the Journal he might have been "booked up" and saved his money.

Our readers should send to Messrs. Guenther & Co, Pittsburgh, Pa., for the "Lung healer" Racquet Galop, which they mail free. Mention this paper.

This Journal will contain new guitar music every month from this date, as well as banjo music. Please make your friend, the guitarist, acquainted with this fact.

Mr. Charles Gorton, the great bicycle rider, finds time to give some attention to the "Old Cremona." He appeared with Messrs. Stewart and Everest in several concerts last month.

Success is not made by "blowing." Real merit is sure to tell. If Stewart's banjos had not all the real merit claimed for them he could not have achieved his success. The new edition of the pamphlet, "The Banjo as a Musical Instrument," will give some of Stewart's testimonials. Read them and compare with those shown by his imitators. The pamphlet is sent free.

Subscribe for the Journal now. Don't be mean enough to think you are on the charity list. Send 50 cents (stamps or cash), for one year's subscription. Remember, new banjo and guitar music in every number.

Some people are so mean that they would rather be cheated three or four times in buying a banjo or guitar than spend the amount of 50 cents a year for the Journal which would give them facts.

Some banjo and guitar teachers would rather jog along in a little room, year in and year out, than advance themselves and become known by advertising in a good medium like the Journal.

Do not forget, friends on the Pacific Coast, that the large and well-known music house of Messrs. Kohler & Chase, Post street, San Francisco, are agents for the Stewart banjo. The foremost houses handle only the leading instruments.

Mr. J. E. Brewster, of London, England, has sold a great many of Stewart's best banjos to some of the highest class of English aristocracy. Mr. Patty, our worthy poetical contributor, puts in a poem, in this issue, worthy of his subject.

Mr. Nathan Francis has opened banjo instruction rooms at No. 564 Benson street, Camden, N. J., and is going to treat his friends to a dose of Jersey lightning. He will be pleased to exchange correspondence with all teachers.

No, sir! we do not run the Journal to puff up any one who choses to send in his article. We put no notices in the Journal except what are merited, neither do we insert advertisements for nothing; some of our friends should make note of this.

Send us the address of every guitar player you know of and we will present him with a specimen copy of the Journal. If he subscribes it will be much to his advantage, and if he does not subscribe it is only 50 cents difference to us, and it won't stop the publication of the paper.

The Chord-Hunters Fate.

He was a chord-hunter; one of those fellows who had studied harmony and double-bass. All day long he would twist his bony fingers around the finger-board, searching after the lost chord. Every time he struck a false position he had a new chord (in his mind), and rejoiced to think what a sensation he was about to create in the musical world. One night he struck the chord of ambition, and his hopes soared high, only to drop again as he lost his grip and modulated into the chord of despair. At last an idea struck him to diminish a seventh of his ambition and go for the discord, which was dominant to his mother-in-law's dog. He went to diminish the key of G at one, sharp, and then sat down to a dessert of suspended harmonies. For three long months he studied the minors and never struck one. Now you may see him any day at noon investigating the triads of lunch counters to be found on many of our minor streets—a disappointed chord fiend, descended to a lunch fiend, a wanderer on the face of the earth, lacking the sinews of war.

The Stewart Banjo.

Through this wide world will go,
And always be reckoned the "King."
For "picking" or "thimble"
When fingers are nimble,
It is noted for clear liquid ring.

The Stewart model is the darling of all,
And is by far the superior thing;
So be merry and wise and seize at a prize,
Or the beautiful bird may take wing.

It will last through your life,
And when you marry a wife,
If her tongue is the usual length,
You can strike a few chords and sing
a few words,
And her anger will lose all its strength.

When baby is weeping when it should be sleeping,
You can drown all its horrible shouts;
For tho' they say infants' voices are sweet,
my own choice is
That infant voices were out.

And now I'll conclude in a manner quite rude,
For which I should no doubt be slammed;
But if you won't be convinced that the Stewart is the Prince,
You can think as you like and go to the angels.

The complimentary testimonial to Arthur J. Fisk took place at Institute Hall, Broad and Spring Garden streets, on Friday evening, December 1st. The entertainment was a complete success both artistically and financially; a crowded house greeting the Howard & Wayne Combination, whose different specialties gave full satisfaction. The entertainment opened with Mr. Harry P. Wayne, the well-known comedian, in his own original version of "Modern School of Acting," supported by the veteran actor and vocalist, Mr. Paul Berger; both of these gentlemen kept the audience in roars of laughter for over twenty minutes, and kept them in good humor to receive Mrs. James Howard, who appeared to good advantage in operatic selections. Mr. Joseph Howard followed in his Dutch specialties, convulsing the audience with laughter, and being repeatedly encored. Leonas Wells, in feats of juggling and plate spinning, appeared and performed a number of difficult feats; he was followed by Dale and Adams in their break-neck song and dances George McCoy in pathetic ballads; Little Bob in his original Womans' Rights Oration. Mr. S. S. Stewart, the artistic banjoist, who kindly volunteered his services, then appeared, and, assisted by the talented artists, Messrs. C. N. Gorton and D. C. Everest, performed the Mocking Bird and Carnival of Venice (with variations), in admirable style, concluding with a display of "old-time" banjo playing and singing, which was heartily applauded. The old veteran, Paul Berger, then followed in his laughable imitations, which were very well received; the entertainment concluded with Jas. Howard's version of "Dodging for a Wife," in which Mr. Howard, as Jake, a Dutch servant, was seen to good advantage; he was ably supported by Mr. Lou Frazer (who kindly volunteered for this occasion), as the father; Harry P. Wayne, as the "love," and Mrs. Jas. Howard as "Lucy." The management deserve great credit for the manner in which the entertainment was conducted, and we hope soon to have the pleasure of witnessing another performance by the same combination.

See second and fourth pages for testimonials in reference to the "Stewart Banjo."

tras and, in a section called "Banjo World," provided space for news of banjo players of all levels of sophistication (fig. 3-7).

Stewart's venture into publishing met with immediate success. As early as September 1882, in his fifth number, he boasted that the journal was meeting "with unparalleled success" and claimed to have circulated 5,000 copies of the previous issue, doubling that number for the present one.[21] By 1884, as he began the bimonthly publication that characterized the journal through its remaining years and also issued it in a new eight-page magazine format rather than as a folded four-page newspaper, he reported that over the first twenty issues he could claim an actual circulation (not just publication) of from 3,000 to 11,000 copies per issue. He also took pains to point out that "it is the habit of many papers to claim a circulation about five times the actual number of copies printed and circulated in order to deceive advertisers." But because Stewart "asked no advertising of anyone" (so that he always had enough space for his own notices), he had "no possible need of speaking untruthfully of the number of copies printed and mailed."[22] Whether or not he inflated these figures, within a few years of its inception Stewart's paper was a fixture of banjo culture.

By the late 1880s other banjo manufacturers, most notably Lincoln B.

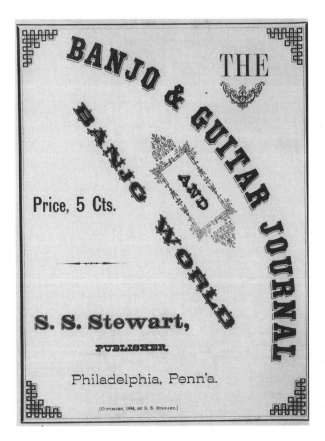

Figure 3-7. *S. S. Stewart's Banjo and Guitar Journal* 2, no. 9 (April/May 1884). Over the years Stewart's journal grew in size and changed in format. Here it is issued in magazine rather than newspaper format.

Gatcomb of Boston, began to issue comparable journals, but they lagged far behind Stewart in subscriptions. He sneeringly dismissed such competition. He informed his readers, for example, "that the little Rooster which flapped its featherless wings under the name of the 'Banjo Herald'" was now defunct, and he delighted in informing them that Gatcomb's comparable venture, into which the *Herald* had been "consolidated," was equally vapid and thus would be just as short-lived. "Our young professor [i.e., Gatcomb]," Stewart wrote, "has not brought to the public a single new idea in any shape or form, for all that he says is simply a rehash of various writings of S. S. Stewart."[23]

Even allowing for Stewart's immense ego, he probably was right, for *S. S. Stewart's Banjo and Guitar Journal* was as remarkable for the variety of its contents as for its longevity. A sampling of the journal's pages over twenty years yields articles on the origin and history of the banjo, the proper construction of instrument necks, stroke- versus guitar-style playing, the necessity of having frets on one's instruments, how a banjo factory is operated, how to replace a calfskin head—all this in addition to reminiscences by well-known banjoists; short stories, poetry, rebuses, and cartoons about the instrument; the obligatory music; notices of the "Banjo World"; and the ubiquitous advertising. Little wonder that Stewart felt that anyone who followed in his path had nothing new to offer!

Through this print medium Stewart linked and consolidated the thousands of individuals around the nation—and the world—who were interested in the banjo, creating a virtual community united every other month through their interest in his pages. He had other venues for his notices— most prominently the *New York Clipper*, the paper of record for New York's musical and theatrical trades—and he used them. By the late 1880s, for example, he was placing weekly ads in the *Clipper*, and in 1891 he so astonished its proprietors by his purchase of four full pages of advertising in one issue that they gave him and his banjos a lengthy, highly laudatory notice (fig. 3-8).[24] But throughout Stewart's career the *Banjo and Guitar Journal* remained his primary way of promulgating and maintaining interest in his own instruments and in the banjo generally. So convinced was he of the publication's importance—and that of the medium of print generally— that when he expanded his factory in 1886 he allotted an entire floor to his printing operations.[25]

As much as it spread camaraderie and sold instruments, however, a journal devoted to the interests of the banjo did not alone allow Stewart to realize his many goals, pragmatic and otherwise. To increase his business he had to speak not only to the converted—those who already owned banjos

Figure 3-8. Full-page advertisement for Stewart's business in the pages of the *New York Clipper*, 20 February 1884. Even with his own in-house periodical Stewart still widely advertised his banjos and other paraphernalia in the *Clipper*, the journal of record of the New York music and theater world. At one point Stewart bought four full pages in one issue.

and thus might want to subscribe to his journal—but also to the ever-expanding number of consumers who now had the money and leisure to consider incorporating the banjo and its music into their lives but did not know enough about either to do so. Stewart targeted this potential audience in various ways.

Beginning in the early 1880s, he made a concerted effort to bring more attention to his instruments, first through issuing in the *New York Clipper* a "Banjo Challenge" to other makers, and then by garnering endorsements for his instruments from prominent banjo "artists" who lent their names, and usually their photographs (thereupon suitably engraved), to his ubiquitous advertisements. In addition, Stewart published works about the banjo aimed at a more general audience in an attempt to educate them about the banjo's potential as a musical instrument. Of these the most significant were his "lecture," *The Banjo Philosophically* (1886), published in pamphlet form, and his clothbound book, *The Banjo! A Dissertation* (1888), the first attempt to provide a full-scale history of the instrument. By the late 1880s Stewart's gambles had paid off: his were the most widely known and respected banjos in the world.

One of Stewart's first advertising ploys was to use the well-known *New York Clipper* as a platform from which to bully his competitors by challenging them to test their instruments against his. Late in 1880, for example, Stewart announced an offer of $100 to any maker who could display a banjo "equal in tone" to his concert instrument, setting off a war of words between himself and the Boston firm of Fairbanks and Cole, which was emerging as his chief rival and in the next issue of the *Clipper* accepted his challenge.[26] Fairbanks and Cole were outraged that the only parties other than himself whom Stewart would accept as judges were the banjoists E. M. Hall, Horace Weston, or William A. Huntley, all of whom they regarded as Stewart's "personal friends." Fairbanks and Cole wanted a serious competition, with a board of judges "appointed by disinterested parties" and the instruments judged in a number of categories (e.g., "Variety of Designs," "Beauty and Finish of Workmanship," "Number of Improvements of Real Importance," and "General Excellence"). Stewart, however, continued to insist that the instruments be judged only on their tone and (though he agreed to hold the competition in New York) that the decision be made by "the WORLD-RENOWNED and WELL-KNOWN BANJO EXPERT HORACE WESTON." For two months the two parties exchanged insults in the *Clipper*, but the challenge never was held.

Stewart did not let the matter lie. Convinced that such controversy brought him the attention he wanted, he soon resurrected it in his new periodical. In one of the early issues he ran a large notice in which he lambasted "a firm in an Eastern city" for not accepting his challenge and yet having the "gall" to claim that theirs were the "champion" instruments. He appended a long list of names of those who used his banjos, noting a truly distinguished group including Horace Weston (1825–90), E. M. Hall (1845–1903), Billy Emerson (1846–1902), Sam Devere (1842?–1907), John H. Lee (d. 1890), and Albert Baur (1845–1910), among others, some of whom played in the stroke style and some in the new "artistic" guitar style.[27]

Stewart warned prospective banjo players not to be gulled by ambiguous or downright false advertising claims but instead to procure banjos of the kind used by "LEADING PROFESSIONAL PERFORMERS," an "immense number" of whom, he claimed, favored his goods. In contrast, he wrote, his competitors only hunted up "unknown amateurs, who had a spite against [him]," and then gave them banjos "at a nominal price" if they would "mention the Stewart Banjo in a slurring manner, and then publish their letters." But these, Stewart told his readership, were the opinions of "MERE PIGMIES" and amounted to "nothing whatever." Unlike his highly regarded endorsers, his competitors were "unknown to fame" and "likely to remain so until they shake off their Mortal Coil."[28]

By the 1880s some musicians evidently were well enough known even outside banjo circles to bring credit to Stewart's instruments, for from this point on he invariably used these and other performers for endorsements. These might consist, on the one hand, of brief letters that he printed in his periodical, but just as often they were quite elaborate, full-page advertisements centrally placed in his various catalogs and other publications or in the *New York Clipper*. The endorsement of William A. Huntley (1850–83), for example, "America's Classic Banjo Artist, Vocalist and Composer," in one of Stewart's catalogs featured a full-length woodcut of the banjoist with two Stewart instruments. Having had "TWENTY YEARS experience in the Banjo business," Huntley wrote, and having seen "about all different styles of Banjos, both in this country and in Europe, of any note," he did not hesitate to say that he considered Stewart's instruments "far superior to all others, both as regards style, tone and finish." "You are at liberty," he told the manufacturer, "to add my name to your long list of commendations in its favor." Stewart's use of E. M. Hall's endorsement in his sensational four-page ad in the *New York Clipper* in 1891 was even more elaborate, incorporating a lengthy biographical notice of this "Paganini of the banjo" and describing, among other things, his first encounter with a Stewart instrument.[29]

As the exchanges over Stewart's challenge make clear, Horace Weston was a particularly valuable (and, by Stewart's recollection, his very first) endorser. This well-known banjoist, whom Stewart cultivated throughout his career and who became a powerful weapon in the manufacturer's assault on the banjo's purportedly low and undistinguished past, was African American, and his remarkable expertise on the instrument offered the public undeniable proof that even in the hands of those among whom it had originated the banjo was destined for greater things than the minstrel stage or variety hall, where one still heard music that was "characteristic," that is, derived from plantation melodies (fig. 3-9). As Stewart put it in a notice after Weston's death in 1890, "though colored," he "was musically endowed to a high degree" and "through his masterly performances in all our principal cities . . . attracted universal attention to this instrument."[30] As Stewart sought to move the banjo from its status as a primitive folk instrument associated with southern plantation life into the world of high culture, Weston became invaluable. With his already wide acclaim he was a shining example of a black man who understood and accepted the banjo's newly elevated status.[31]

Ironically, though, like most other banjoists prior to the 1880s Weston had made his career with the minstrel troupes. After serving in the Union army during the Civil War, he had joined Buckley's Minstrels and then, in 1867, signed on with the Georgia Colored Minstrels. By the mid-1870s his stage talents had become widely acknowledged, and he came to national prominence in one of the many dramatic productions of *Uncle Tom's Cabin*. The troupe with which he was associated eventually toured Europe with great success, but after his return to the States, Weston again played in the variety halls, places that, as one person who saw him recalled, "were nothing more nor less than public drinking houses on a large scale."[32] At this point, in the early 1880s, Stewart enlisted Weston in his cause.

At first Weston's endorsements were almost perfunctory. In one of Stewart's first brochures, for example, this "Champion Banjoist of the World, who has had fifty years' experience," briefly recommended Stewart's music books as the "best published." By 1883, however, their relationship had deepened. In a letter to the *Banjo and Guitar Journal*, for example, Weston offered to let Stewart publish a work on the banjo using his name, because, Weston claimed, he had "imparted [his] ideas to no one but him," making Stewart the "only" man "perfectly familiar" with his "system of Banjo playing."[33] By the mid-1880s Stewart's adulation of Weston led to full-page illustrated ads—in one case he was depicted with his wife, "as they appeared with Uncle Tom's Cabin Company"—and reached a pinnacle in 1884 with Stewart's publication of a "dime" fiction, *The Black Hercules; or, The Adventures of a Banjo Player*, loosely based on Weston's life and offered for sale and as a premium (figs. 3-10, 3-11).[34]

Figure 3-9. Real-photo postcard, ca. 1905, of two African American musicians.
On the verso is written "Left Billy Smith—former slave, had whip scar on his back.
Right Billy Russell Played for Dances in houses in early 1900s. Great old men, especially
Billy Smith." It was this rural tradition of African American banjo playing from which
Stewart assiduously sought to elevate the instrument through his various publications.

Stewart's relation to Weston was admittedly complicated, for as the
banjo maker's fame grew, Weston probably derived as much benefit from
his association with Stewart as he gave to him (fig. 3-12). But the issue of
Weston's race was unavoidable, and there is evidence that, when it would
serve Stewart's purpose, he raised it head-on. In 1883, for example, he felt
that Weston had been slighted in a well-publicized banjo contest held at
Steinway Hall in New York City that was organized by Frank Dobson and
attended by about 1,500 people.[35] In a major review of the event entitled
"The Banjo Tournament in New York—A Complete Farce," which appeared in his *Banjo and Guitar Journal,* Stewart lit into this "grand carnival of banjo playing" as a "farce gotten up" by the Dobsons "solely for their
own personal gain and glorification."[36] He was particularly incensed that
even after a "grand contest" had been announced among C. Edgar Dobson,
Frank Eckland of Boston, and Weston, "for supremacy and a gold medal"

Mr. & Mrs.

HORACE WESTON,

As they appeared with

THE UNCLE TOM'S CABIN COMPANY.

Read " The Banjo Philosophically," by S. S. Stewart.

Figure 3-10. Woodcut illustration of the African American banjoist Horace Weston, in the 1880s one of Stewart's strongest endorsers. This image appeared in *S. S. Stewart's Price List of Parlor, Concert, and Orchestra Banjos* (Philadelphia, 1887) but was frequently reprinted in other of his publications. Although Weston had once played in the minstrel halls, Stewart believed that he demonstrated to the public that African Americans could also contribute to the banjo's elevation.

(and presumably to swell the crowd), Weston did not place in either this competition or in the other, general one. It did not help matters (and probably instigated Stewart's outburst) that C. Edgar Dobson was awarded one gold medal for "picking" and his brother Edward C. another for "stroking," while five other players walked away with prizes of Dobson's patent "Harp Banjos," valued at $100 each.

In his report on the proceedings Stewart emphasized that the crowded

Figure 3-11. Cover illustration of Stewart's dime novel, *The Black Hercules; or, The Adventures of a Banjo Player* (Philadelphia, 1884). Loosely based on Horace Weston's early life, this publication was used primarily as another venue in which Stewart touted his business. The woodcut illustration is of Weston and was used in other of Stewart's advertisements.

house expected some award to go to Weston (a sentiment reported as well in some of the New York papers, several of which covered this event), with some of the audience beginning to chant, "What does Weston get?," but the crowd was dismissed without any satisfaction. "Did not Horace Weston draw more money to the house than any player on the bill?" Stewart asked rhetorically. "Then why," he continued, "was he so coolly snubbed and ill-treated? Was it because he was black?" Here was Weston, "this genius, with his dark skin," who had performed "in almost every part of the civilized world" and had "been courted by the music-loving of all classes, honoured likewise here and in Europe; the peer of many with whiter skin," simply being used, Stewart concluded, "to draw money to the pockets of men who have not one grain of his talent" (fig. 3-13).

As in the brouhaha over the Fairbanks and Cole challenge, Stewart stoked this controversy for a few months, continuing to champion Weston's cause and presumably cementing his relationship to him, always aligning him with others in his stable of endorsers associated with the kind of elevation that Stewart sought for the banjo and its music (fig. 3-14). In the same article on the contest, for example, Stewart published approving opinions of Weston's sophistication by well-known banjoists who had

Figure 3-12. Pencil drawing, presumably by S. S. Stewart, ca. 1880s, for the heel carving of a banjo intended for Horace Weston. The script reads "Design for heel of Banjo neck— (Horace)." In this period banjo makers began to offer custom-grade "presentation" banjos to stage celebrities such as Weston who endorsed their products.

Figure 3-13. Mounted paper photograph, ca. 1890–1900, of African American banjo player outside his family's home. Through his sponsorship of Horace Weston, Stewart sought to replace such images of blacks with those of the well-dressed professional musician that Weston embodied.

been in the audience, and he invited his subscribers to write their own letters on the issue, which he published in the next number of the *Banjo and Guitar Journal.*[37] And a few years later in his book *The Banjo! A Dissertation*, Stewart emphasized that Weston was as outstanding in guitar style as in "thumping" the banjo; indeed, he had "heard him pick with so delicate . . . a touch that one would scarcely believe the instrument he was manipulating was a banjo."[38] While we cannot say for sure why Weston was snubbed—whether it was because he was black, or just that he was associated with Stewart in an event engineered to showcase the Dobsons—

Figure 3-14. Sixth-plate tintype, ca. 1885, of young African American musician in a photographer's studio. Although it is difficult to gauge Weston's influence on other blacks, in this period they continued to play the banjo in both rural and urban settings. Presumably, Stewart would have approved of the banjo playing of this well-dressed young man with his factory-made instrument.

Stewart understood, given Weston's general renown, how he might profit by defending and associating himself with him.

Stewart also found more productive ways to publicize the banjo among a wider audience. Particularly important were the pair of publications that he advertised and distributed widely in the later 1880s. In *The Banjo Philosophically* (1886) and *The Banjo! A Dissertation* (1888), in addition to providing his notion of the history of the instrument, at considerable length he explained its acoustical properties and thus laid the basis for his claims for the preeminence of his own instruments. Unique in the period for their length and sophistication, these publications document Stewart's understanding of his contributions to the art of banjo design and manufacture.

Internal evidence indicates that *The Banjo Philosophically* was in fact first given as a lecture—itself indicative of the lengths to which Stewart went to proselytize for his instrument—and then was published, as he put it, "just as it proceed[ed] from my pen—without elaboration—without any pretension to rhetorical style" (fig. 3-15). His subtitle reveals his larger purpose. He would speak about the banjo: "Its Construction. Its Capabilities. Its Evolution. Its place as a Musical Instrument. Its Possibilities and its Future."[39] The result was nothing if not thorough. Indeed, the lecture is a virtual primer to the instrument, including sections on how the neck scale of a banjo is calculated, whether frets are necessary, what to do about warped rims, what kinds of strings to use, and how to keep the instrument in good playing condition. But its main thrust was to establish the supremacy of the banjo as Stewart understood it, and as such it was, like virtually all that he wrote, a thinly veiled advertisement for himself. Selling the pamphlet for ten cents to any interested party, reprinting it in various of his large catalogs, and offering it as a premium when people purchased instruments or instruction or music books, by 1888 Stewart claimed to have circulated 9,000 copies, thus widely broadcasting the principles on which the excellence of his banjos was based.[40]

Admittedly, parts of Stewart's historical account are problematic. Among other things, for example, he claimed that the banjo was "not of negro origin" as others thought, but rather took its name from the Spanish "bandore." As we have seen, there is no doubt that the instrument is of African origin, and Stewart's effort to provide it with a lineage that ran through Europe rather than Africa is a distortion that may be explicable as part of his effort to legitimize it as a concert instrument. Indeed, two years later in his longer treatise, when he was more willing to allow the possibility of the banjo's African heritage, his basic prejudice was still intact. If it were the case that the instrument first developed among Africans, he wrote, we should recall that "Truth has often come into the world through lowly channels."[41]

Stewart also wrote that Joel Sweeney was "said to have added" two extra strings to the three-stringed gourd instruments common in the South and thus produced the five-string banjo as we know it (1). It is clear that the eighteenth-century African American banjo sometimes had a shorter fifth string, but Stewart's attribution of this "improvement" to Sweeney buttressed his claims that the instrument's significant development came at the hands of whites. In Stewart's account, the banjo as it was known on the minstrel stage marked an intermediate but still primitive stage of development, preliminary to the instrument's emergence in its most sophisticated form, whose manufacture he had perfected.

Stewart's main contribution in his historical overview lay in his genealogy of the "silver rim" banjo, which he considered the ultimate form of the instrument—a discussion grounded in what would then have been consid-

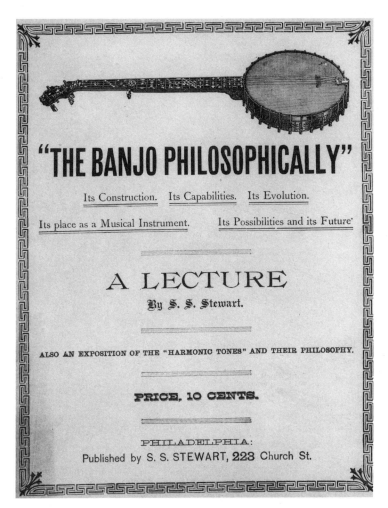

Figure 3-15. Cover of Stewart's pamphlet, *The Banjo Philosophically* (Philadelphia, 1886). Offered as a premium to subscribers to his journal and for sale independently in music stores that carried Stewart's instruments, this work offers the earliest detailed treatment of the banjo's history. Collection of Philip F. Gura.

ered a sophisticated theory of acoustics. As its name suggests, the silver rim banjo's uniqueness consisted in the construction of its sounding chamber: a maple hoop covered with a sheet of the alloy known as German or nickel silver, which was turned down over a wire ring on each side of the wooden rim. Stewart traced this design to the "old 'Troy' banjos" made by Albert Wilson, whom he termed "an eccentric genius," and William H. Farnham, both of whom lived in Troy, New York.[42] Of the two, Wilson probably originated the idea of covering the rim in metal, for before he disappeared from the city directories in 1865 he also was listed as a silversmith. But Farnham developed Wilson's notion into a business: between 1867 and 1875 he was listed as the "banjo manufacturer" in that city.[43] According to Stewart, these early Troy banjos were rather crude, with heads from 10½ to 11½ inches in diameter and necks that were bolted to the rims (i.e., without dowel sticks running through them).

So constructed, as Stewart observed, the instrument's neck had a tendency to pull or bow upwards from the tension of the strings, a problem remedied by the next maker whom he mentioned, James W. Clarke of New York City, who strengthened the neck by continuing the dowel across the diameter of the rim. Indeed, Stewart credited Clarke, widely known as a professional jig dancer before he made banjos, as the best maker before he himself came on the scene.[44] Clarke's instruments, he wrote, became "a standard among professional banjo players," both minstrels and "other stage performers," and were particularly prized for their "loud and sharp tone." It was a Clarke banjo, for example, that E. M. Hall was playing when Stewart asked him to compare one of his own make, built to the same large rim size and scale length that Hall favored, which the eminent banjoist subsequently acclaimed as the only banjo he had ever seen that "equalled" his Clarke.[45]

Stewart believed that he had brought the silver rim banjo to its pinnacle, a claim that may seem excessive but that was in character with his general understanding of himself as the father of the "modern" banjo. To his credit, however, because this instrument's construction was fairly straightforward, he was honest enough to admit that his banjos were not based on any unique, patented improvements but rather were designed after careful assessment of the acoustical properties of the banjo's constituent parts. His banjos were simply "improvements upon the same style of banjo manufactured by others before me." But, he continued, their excellence was "secured by new processes of manufacture, some of which remain secrets of my own, and which to attempt to protect by letters patent would merely place part of my knowledge in the hands of others." Without depending, then, on the kind of technological novelty that had characterized the development of the banjo to that point, Stewart tried to convince the public that, once the best design for the banjo was known (and that it was the silver rim instrument), further innovations were superfluous, only distractions from the true art of banjo making. "We have had," Stewart sarcastically noted, "patent closed-backs, patent hoops, patent hollow rims, patent bell rims, patent keys, patent bracket protectors, [and] patent tail pieces." But "none of these have added one jot nor tittle to the musical value of the banjo" (2).

How was an instrument improved, then, if not by technological progress? By close attention to the acoustical properties of its constituent parts, Stewart believed, and careful supervision of its construction. He had established his expertise in such matters by what he termed his wide reading in the history of instruments and their acoustical properties. He took pains to point out that his particular "skill in the construction of banjos" resulted not just from "a *natural musical gift*," but also from his "somewhat extended experience as a performer upon the instrument, and a student of the science of music." This preparation, "together with experimenting and constant observation," he continued, allowed him to make fine banjos, the construction of which, like that of all true musical instruments, "is a science only to a certain extent." More accurately, "it is an art . . . based on scientific principles" (4) and as such could not be streamlined beyond a certain point. Such instruments certainly could not be manufactured in factories like Buckbee's, where inferior materials were used and all the procedures were highly mechanized.

At this point, Stewart returned to an analogy of which he was fond, that of violin making, for to his mind geniuses like Stradivarius were successful precisely because they too had "worked upon perfectly scientific principles" (4). Like these master craftsmen, Stewart had studied his instrument in relation to its various components, particularly the effect on its sound of the "sonorousness" of different woods and the thickness of various metals. He also noted a list of the twelve "necessary constituents" that comprised a fine banjo, all the while speaking in generalities because, again, he did not wish to reveal the "secrets" of his business. He claimed that each instrument had its idiosyncrasies, which had to be recognized and compensated for by craftsmen who knew how to perform such fine-tuning—the kind of men, in other words, whom he employed in his factory. Attention to such matters, Stewart claimed, resulted in the world's finest banjos, a fact his less acoustically sophisticated competition was unable to accept. He ridiculed makers like the Dobsons who thought that a "bell-metal" rim would augment the tonal qualities of the banjo, and he had even less respect for those like Fairbanks and Cole who, in order to increase patronage, "resort[ed] to bogus challenges" and "advertisements flaunting un-attested assertions" (5).

Stewart followed this publication two years later with *The Banjo! A Dissertation*, at the instigation of, among others, banjoist John H. Lee, who wrote him that *The Banjo Philosophically* was "by far the best thing" that he had written and suggested that "a little more of the same class of Banjo literature would elevate its standing and force recognition from the few remaining bigots" who were prejudiced against its "establishment . . . as a legitimate instrument" (fig. 3-16).[46] Stewart had received other such accolades and encouragement, and he thereupon produced a work that was "neatly gotten up, and as a volume . . . attractive for the centre-table or for the book shelves."[47] The handsome, clothbound book included several portraits of prominent players, with one of Stewart as a frontispiece. Sold for fifty cents and distributed as widely as his lecture, it went through at least

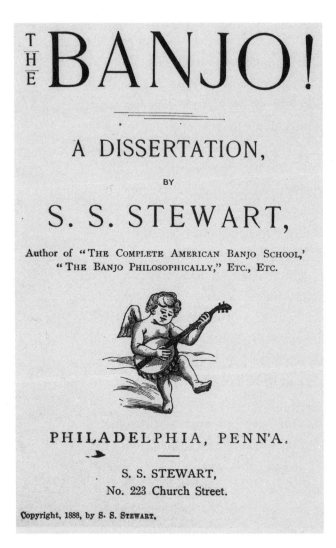

Figure 3-16. Title page of Stewart's *The Banjo! A Dissertation* (Philadelphia, 1888), the first book devoted to the instrument. A mixture of history as well as commentary about banjo playing by various of Stewart's contemporaries, this work represents the high water mark of his promotion of the instrument. Collection of Philip F. Gura.

two other editions, in 1891 and 1894. To these Stewart added supplementary material, primarily in the form of excerpts from newspapers or private letters, that augmented the thrust of his arguments.

In *The Banjo!* Stewart incorporated much of his earlier work but did not provide so much "scientific" detail about the banjo's acoustics. In his own words, it treated the banjo in such a way "as to make it of interest alike to the beginner, the more advanced pupil, the teacher and the player."[48] As Lee had urged, Stewart emphasized how the banjo recently had emerged as a much more versatile and popular instrument and reiterated the importance for beginning players to acquire the rudiments of music theory so that they could use the instrument as it had been intended, for sophisticated entertainment. *The Banjo!*, in other words, was Stewart's most blatant attempt to gain acceptance for the banjo among all classes of people.

This purpose is transparent in his section on the "Conditions Necessary to a Good Performance," in which Stewart noted that it had been his aim "for years, to bring the Banjo more into the parlor, and into the musical soiree," as the "variety theatre" and the "minstrel hall, with their associations, are not the proper places for any musically inclined person to listen to an effective performance." The clientele in such places, he continued, "go there to be amused—to have fun—and to laugh," not to be edified by music at its highest level of composition and performance. Underlining the associations with gentility that meant so much to him, Stewart reiterated that "the parlor, the drawing room, and the select musical entertainment" were the proper places for the instrument to be heard (69). Performances of "swinging solos," "trick playing," and "juggling" of the instrument would not "convert" people to an appreciation of the banjo. They had to hear the instrument played by "artists" (71).

Stewart also recurred to the topics of the overall quality of well-made musical instruments and the sophistication of those who knew how to judge it. "There are many persons," he wrote, "to whom a cheap chromo [lithograph] is as interesting as a fine painting," and there were "likewise those to whom a cheap fiddle is as good as a fine violin; and others who are just as pleased with a cheaply-made Banjo as with a finer instrument." But his "art," he explained, did not "depend, for its encouragement and support, upon persons of that character" (102), but rather on those with enough discernment to understand the difference between a factory "tub" and a Stewart banjo. To buy a Stewart, in other words, marked the individual who understood that some goods were more intrinsically valuable than others because they were made differently.[49] In a few more years such an attitude reached its apotheosis in the Arts and Crafts movement. As voiced by Stewart in the 1880s, however, it suggested his—and by extension his customers'—growing dissatisfaction with the general quality of factory-produced merchandise and a sense that social position was clearly indicated by one's taste in musical goods as much as in one's dress or home furnishings.[50] *The Banjo!* thus served as more than a primer to the instrument. It was one among many guidebooks that helped readers negotiate the shifting class boundaries of a society in rapid transition.

But what of the instruments that Stewart thought analogous to the masterpieces of the Italian violin makers? Where and how were they made, and by whom? What did they look like, and for how much were they sold? How did they compare to the instruments of other important makers, who, like Stewart, were taking advantage of an ever-expanding market to enlarge their operations and their sales, and who, despite Stewart's vocal skepticism of further "improvements" to the banjo, continued to patent technological innovations?

Stewart began his business in August 1878 "in one room" at 833 Race Street, and by late 1879 was at 429 North Eighth Street. He remained there until the fall of 1886, when he announced that he was buying a four-story building at 223 Church Street and acquiring as well the fourth floors of the two adjoining structures, numbers 219 and 221 (plate 3-1).[51] A year later, under the heading, "A Steady March Forward," he gave his *Banjo and Guitar Journal* readers a detailed description of his "Banjo Manufactory and Banjo Music Publishing House."[52]

"The entire building at No. 223 Church Street is occupied by the banjo business," he wrote (fig. 3-17). The first floor housed a salesroom for his banjos and music, while the second held the packing department and also had space for his office. The third floor was used "exclusively for music plate printing," and the fourth, which "extend[ed] over three buildings," was where the instruments were made. On the upper floor of the building at 223 Church Street his workers made the hoops and rims, and in the adjoining space at 221 Church there were "several benches where men [were] at work polishing and fitting banjo necks in rims." At the far end of this room one found the steam-powered machinery that ran the entire workshop. "Here is the main shaft," Stewart reported, "together with boiler and engine, carving and turning lathes, band saw, circular saw, grindstone, emery wheels, etc." In the next room, situated on an upper floor of the building at 219 Church, were "more benches with men putting on heads" and also "a large stock of sawed necks, sawed ebony," and other materials "in process of construction." Finally, Stewart noted, the basement of the main building served for storage of packing boxes and coal and held as well "a vault where all the music plates were stored."

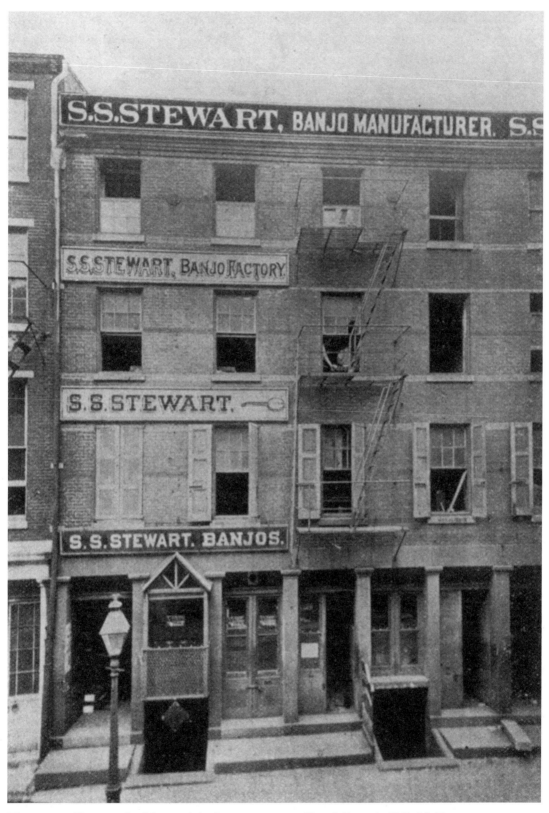

Figure 3-17. Photograph of Stewart's business at 221–223 Church Street in Philadelphia, ca. early 1890s, reproduced in *S. S. Stewart's Banjo and Guitar Journal* 11, no. 4 (October/ November 1894). During most of Stewart's career, this location served for both his factory and primary business office.

By 1888, though, Stewart's business was growing rapidly, and he needed more space. Thus, a year later he secured the entire building at 221 Church Street "from the Trustees of the Girard Estate" to annex to his operations.[53] This expanded physical plant served Stewart for most of his career, until January 1898 when he formed a partnership with the Philadelphia guitar and mandolin manufacturer George Bauer, who operated at 1410–12 North Sixth Street and to whose work force Stewart joined his own. At that point Stewart moved his banjo works to Bauer's address and retained his own buildings for his extensive music publishing business.[54]

There are no extant business records for Stewart's company, so it is difficult to ascertain much about his work force. From his four-page ad in the *New York Clipper* for 1891, though, we know that in that year he employed fifteen workers, who turned out about 250 banjos a month.[55] And a report on "A Great Instrument Factory" in *S. S. Stewart's Banjo, Guitar, and Mandolin Journal* (as his periodical was renamed after he merged with Bauer) notes that under their new arrangement Stewart and Bauer employed about forty men.[56]

Unfortunately, we have no information about who these workers were and how much they were paid, but from this article and its accompanying photographs, and from an earlier series of six woodcuts in the *Banjo and Guitar Journal* that illustrate different steps in the banjo making process, we can fairly accurately describe the division of labor in Stewart's factory.[57] In the first woodcut in the sequence from 1883, for example, a worker tacks together the ends of a wooden hoop, which he has bent around a large, long cylinder on which other finished hoops are also visible (fig. 3-18). To his left is a small stove and boiler, whose steam is directed by a pipe into a large chamber filled with wooden strips, indicating the way in which the wood was softened before being worked into circular form. The second cut shows a worker completing the "silver rim" by bending a piece of metal around a wooden hoop (fig. 3-19). He works at a table on which is mounted another large cylinder, connected to the factory's main power source by a thick leather belt, on which the wooden rim has been placed to ready it for turning or "spinning" the metal over it (hence our modern term for this kind of rim, "spun over").

In the following image an operative shapes or sands a banjo neck at another power-driven wheel, and in the next, two men work at inlaying and fretting necks (figs. 3-20, 3-21). The first uses a graver-like tool and has several more such tools in front of him; the second uses a handheld saw to cut slots in the neck for frets. Between them is a small glue pot over a burner, perhaps to hold hide glue for the inlay work. In the second-to-the-last image, a worker polishes the back of a banjo neck with a cloth, obvi-

Figure 3-18. Woodcut illustration, ca. 1883, of worker in Stewart's factory assembling wooden rims for banjos. On the left is a chamber in which wood is steamed so that it can more easily be bent into shape for such rims. This and the following woodcuts were used in various of Stewart's publications in the 1880s but first appeared in *S. S. Stewart's Banjo and Guitar Journal* 2, no. 6 (November 1883).

Figure 3-19. Woodcut illustration, ca. 1883. This worker completes one of Stewart's distinctive "silver" rims by bending a piece of nickel silver over a wooden hoop. Stewart believed that this combination of wood and metal produced a strong, resonant sound chamber.

ously doing finish work (fig. 3-22). In front of him is a pot of shellac or varnish, and another vessel with a spout. In the final cut, a worker stretches a skin head over a rim; in front are a bowl for wetting the skins, wrenches for tightening the nuts, other small pieces of hardware, and a completely assembled rim (fig. 3-23).

The series of photographs of the Stewart and Bauer works taken in 1898 is even more revealing, for in addition to recording the spatial

Figure 3-20. Woodcut illustration, ca. 1883. Here a banjo neck is sanded at a power-driven wheel.

Figure 3-21. Woodcut illustration, ca. 1883. One of these employees works with gravers on mother-of-pearl inlay for the banjo neck, while the other cuts slots for the instrument's frets. The pot in the middle, heated over a small alcohol burner, is for the hide glue for the inlay work.

Figure 3-22. Woodcut illustration, ca. 1883. A worker polishes a banjo neck with a cloth in what was called "finish" work. In front of him is a pot of shellac or varnish.

Figure 3-23. Woodcut illustration, ca. 1883. Stewart's employee stretches a piece of calfskin over the rim. Brackets and a bracket wrench lie in front of his work, indicating that he soon will complete the rim assembly.

arrangements in such work places and providing a rough idea of the numbers of workers in each space, its accompanying text explains in some detail the nature of the work performed therein. For one thing, the author of this tour of "A Great Instrument Factory" reminds the reader that even in such highly mechanized workplaces, much still depended on the individual craftsmen. "We hear so much about machinery these days," he notes, "that we are apt to imagine more is accomplished by machinery than is actually the case."[58] But, he explains, "highly systematized and scientific labor, mental and mechanical, is frequently alluded to as machinery," and it is in this sense—conjoining machines and men—that he uses the term in his article. This comment, intended to frame his subsequent praise of the Stewart and Bauer workforce, supports what scholars have noted of the late-nineteenth-century woodworking trades in general, that although certain procedures could be expedited by steam-powered machinery, the technology was such that the addition of more machines alone could not increase output or overall productivity. Skilled manual labor, in other words, remained essential to the overall preparation and assembly of, in this case, musical instruments.[59]

The author's "short tour" provides a remarkable picture of the Stewart and Bauer factory. The "Rough Woodworking Department," for example, is a profusion of circular saws, large emery wheels, and other tools used for sawing and planing the wood for the instruments, all powered from wide leather belts attached to an overhead shaft (fig. 3-24). Along with stacks of "the most carefully selected . . . seasoned timber," we also see "thousands of maple wood banjo rims, which have been undergoing a process of drying out for many years, thousands of necks likewise, and a drying chamber to still further insure the proper seasoning." Finally, in addition to "the saw, planing, &c., machine tools [of] the most accurate and expensive kinds made by leading American manufacturers," there are "numbers of labor-saving devices that were invented in the factory, the outcome of much serious study and experiments to facilitate and ensure the exact similarity of articles in any given quantity," another way of describing what we would term interchangeable parts. Unfortunately, our guide provides no detail of this special machinery.

In the "Fine Woodworking Department," wooden parts and sections of the banjos undergo "further shaping and fitting to permanent moulds and templates" (fig. 3-25). The assembly of the five-layer lamination that comprised the neck of Stewart's highly regarded Thoroughbred banjo, for example, was done here, as was the initial work of fretting the necks, with "each form of instrument" having "its own special measured fret board pattern." Equally exacting labor was carried out in the "Metal Spinning

Department," where the metal rims were made and spun over the wooden hoops, and other metal parts prepared and fitted. "None but the finest makes of metal working machine and hand tools" were used in this room, the author noted, but, as elsewhere, much work still depended on the skill of the operators. The joining of the metal rims, for example, was "accomplished by brazing with silver solder," and even the iron wire "flesh hoops" that fit over the skin head and rim had to be brazed by hand "with spelter, dipped in a pickle bath to make their surfaces rough," so that the skin will not slip, and then "copper plated."

Stewart's more expensive banjos often had attractive and intricate mother-of-pearl inlay in their fingerboards and ornately carved heels at the base of the necks, work carried out in the "Pearl, etc. Carving, and Inlaying Department." Here one found "numbers of varieties of sea shells . . . from different parts of the world," as well as the tiny jeweler's saws and gravers used in this painstaking work. Next, the instrument parts traveled to the "Banjo Finishing Department," where they were "built up"—that is, fully assembled (the skin heads were stretched over the hoops, for exam-

Figure 3-24. Photograph, ca. 1898, of the "Rough Woodworking Department" in Stewart and Bauer's factory. This and the following two images first appeared in *S. S. Stewart's Banjo, Guitar, and Mandolin Journal* 16, no. 3 (August/September 1899).

Figure 3-25. Photograph, ca. 1898, of the "Fine Woodworking Department" in Stewart and Bauer's factory, where neck lamination and fret work was carried out.

ple, and the necks joined to the rims)—and where the machinery used was "the scientific method of employing hand labor" (fig. 3-26). Finally, the banjos arrived at the "Polishing Department," where the finest polishing mediums were applied with the proverbial "'elbow grease.'" In all these departments, the author noted, "the work moves along in sections, one thing at a time for each instrument, so that numbers of instruments are reaching each stage of completion simultaneously."

In light of our discussion of Stewart's animus against lower-grade, factory-made instruments—the "tubs" against which he was always inveighing—it is worth noting that "A Great Instrument Factory" concludes with a reminder (certainly an exaggeration, if not an outright falsehood) that all of Stewart and Bauer's instruments were "made for professional use, and not as a matter of merchandise." As a result, he noted, work in the factory was obviously a matter of pride. "The reputation of the products," he wrote, "are [*sic*] guarded by every individual concerned, from the proprietor to the able foreman, and down to the apprentices," and as a result there was a noticeable "spirit of co-operation" among "all employees." Indeed, Stewart must have treated them well, for we learn that

Figure 3-26. Photograph, ca. 1898, of the "Banjo Finishing Department" in Stewart and Bauer's factory, where the skin heads were stretched over the assembled rims and then attached to the necks.

"most of the workmen have been at their present posts from ten to fifteen years, and some quite twenty"—that is, since he began to make banjos.[60]

The kinds of banjos Stewart produced in his factory were legion, and it would require a separate chapter to differentiate his various models and grades. Even from an early date, however, he was committed to the silver rim instrument. When he began business in the late 1870s, for example, he noted that, if the customer wished, he could make a "cheap nickel-rim" banjo for $9, but he touted as his best banjo his "large instrument for concert use," which had a "German silver rim" and was priced at $30. He also noted that for this banjo he had "made a new scale for fretting the instrument with twenty-one frets" (seventeen were usually found on banjos in this period) and that he had devised a new system for curing and putting on the heads that improved the tone of the banjos.[61] In a more detailed catalog from the same period he advertised "Improved Parlor and Concert Banjos, Possessing the Beauty of the Guitar, with Double the Power of Tone," in four models with German silver rims: an eleven-inch Universal Favorite at $20; another of the same size, "but more elaborate," for $25; the

Grand Concert, with a twelve-inch rim, at $30; and another instrument of the same size called the Daisy, at $35. For those who still did not get the message about the silver rim banjo, or for those looking for a less expensive instrument, he offered "all styles of Nickel-plated Rim Banjos" priced from $6 to $15. There is evidence, however, that he was not manufacturing the cheaper, nickel rim instruments himself but had them made for him, the same being true of the seven- and eight-inch piccolo banjos with plain maple rims, priced at $4.50 and $7 respectively, that he offered.[62]

By the 1880s Stewart had greatly expanded his line of instruments, so that one could buy them in a great number of sizes and with a great variety of ornamentation, the German silver and maple rim construction the one constant in all but his lowest-priced instruments. His *Price List of Parlor and Concert Banjos* (ca. 1887), for example, still featured his Orchestra banjo, now made in twelve- or thirteen-inch sizes, with a nineteen-inch neck.[63] The No. 1 featured a "Fine German silver rim, with maple inside, wire edges, Stewart's imp[ro]v[e]d heavy turned edge nickel-plated hoop (the best hoop in existence), neck made of fine well-seasoned wood with ebony face, white fancy pegs and tail piece, 30 nickel-plated brackets, etc., pearl position marks, etc.," for $35; the fancier No. 2 boasted a "neck that is constructed with several veneers, having double the strength and finer appearance than No. 1, and will withstand climatic changes," for $5 more. Stewart also noted that "other numbers with carved necks, pearl inlaid work, gold and silver plating, and fancy carved ivory trimmings" could be made "at short notice" at prices from $60 to $100 and higher.[64] Indeed, Stewart's banjos were distinctive for such fine inlay work, done "in [his] own factory inclusive of sawing and making [the] pearl inlayings." Crescents and stars, complex geometrical patterns with triangles and squares, and "tree of life" vines and flowers the full length of the fingerboard are just some of the mother-of-pearl and abalone shell decorations found on his instruments (plates 3-2, 3-3, 3-4, 3-5, 3-6). Stewart's attention to heel carving was equally extraordinary, with fanciful lion heads, cherubs, jesters, kings, queens, and nudes adorning his higher-priced models.

Stewart was nothing, however, if not democratic in what he offered the public.[65] For example, he still marketed for only $10 a banjo with an eleven-inch, nickel-plated (i.e., not German silver) rim and an eighteen-inch walnut neck with rosewood veneer. A ten-inch "Ladies' Banjo," with a seventeen-inch neck, twenty nickel brackets, a German silver rim, ebony pegs, and a "fancy white tail piece," could be had for as little as $20. His Universal Favorite, with an eleven-inch rim, a nineteen-inch neck ("the size more in use than any other"), and simple pearl position markers, could be bought for the same price, and, with different degrees of pearl decora-

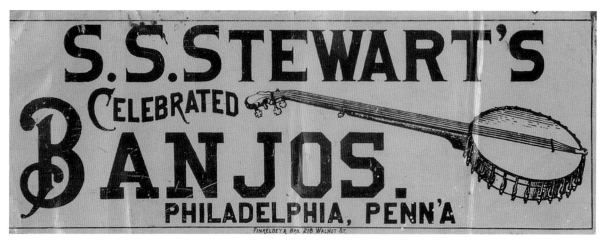

Plate 3-1. Rare metal trade sign for Stewart's Philadelphia banjo works.

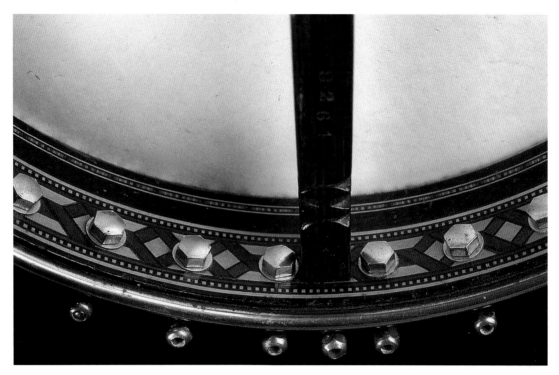

Plate 3-3. Detail of the marquetry inside the rim of Stewart banjo no. 54073 (plate 3-2).

Plate 3-4. Detail of the heel carving on Stewart banjo no. 54073 (plate 3-2).

opposite
Plate 3-2. S. S. Stewart banjo, serial no. 54073, ca. 1898. 11½ × 27¼ in. This is an interesting custom-grade banjo fitted with a Brazilian rosewood neck, unusual carving on the heel and the back of the peg head, and a rare, attractive butterfly motif in pearl on the fingerboard.

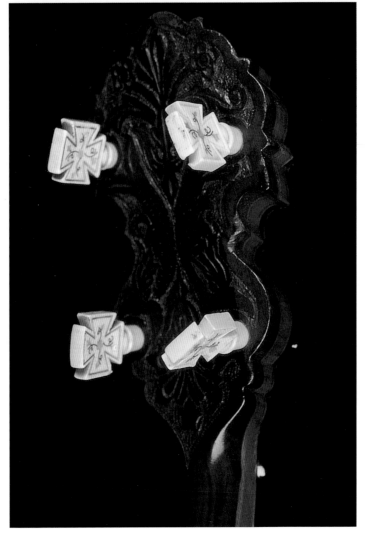

top
Plate 3-5.
Detail of the rim
engraving on
Stewart banjo no.
54073 (plate 3-2).

left
Plate 3-6.
Detail of the
carving on the
back of the peg
head and of the
ivory tuning
pegs on Stewart
banjo no. 54073
(plate 3-2).

Plate 3-7.
S. S. Stewart piccolo banjo, No. 2 grade, serial no. 16024, ca. 1892. 7 × 15 in. Stewart invented the piccolo banjo (designed to be tuned an octave above a regular banjo) for use in the banjo orchestras that were forming in the late 1880s. While Stewart's piccolos were made in quantity and many are still extant, the No. 2 grade and higher models are quite rare.

Plate 3-8. Terra cotta bust, 32 in. high, with banjo neck made from wood. Probably Austrian, ca. 1890s. This same figure also was made in spelter (pot metal) both in this size and as a miniature (9½ in.), mounted on a marble base. In addition, this figure was used as cover art on Victorian sheet music. That such decorations were popular in both Europe and the United States bespeaks the banjo's immense popularity.

Plate 3-9. Assorted tin wind-up toys, German (mostly by Gunterman, ca. 1890–1915), and a Gibson advertising string box from the early twentieth century. Many sophisticated mechanical toys for the American market were produced in Europe. Some figures are hand-painted; others show color lithography. The clown on the barrel (far right) is painted and lithographed; the other lithographed item is the seated minstrel figure in the top hat at the very center. This is a very rare steam-driven accessory toy.

Plate 3-10. The large (17 in.) automaton was made by Gustave Vichy of Paris, ca. 1900. It contains both a Swiss music box and a clockwork motor that, by means of cams and levers, causes head, arms, and legs to move in a lifelike manner. The smaller (10 in.) toy, ca. 1870s, is one of a set of clockwork minstrels manufactured by Jerome Secor, a sewing machine maker from Bridgeport, Connecticut. Such clockwork banjo figures, particularly the "Freedman" penny bank by Secor, are among the most elusive and rare of nineteenth-century toys.

Plate 3-11. These two large (16 in.) cast-iron blinking-eye "Sambo" clocks were produced by Bradley and Hubbard, with clockworks supplied by the Waterbury (Connecticut) Clock Company. These two variations of the standard clock—one with a "boater" hat and the other wearing a jockey cap—are extremely rare. The relatively common blinking-eye alarm clock (right) is German, ca. 1920. The other alarm clock was patented 15 May 1888 by the Waterbury Clock Company; only a few examples have been seen. The 18-inch brass thermometer in the form of a banjo is signed "Bailey Banks and Biddle, Phila." and has a patent date of 10 November 1885. It features working tuning pegs and other accurate banjo details.

Plate 3-12. Child's tambourine, ca. 1890, with hand-painted minstrel scene. Minstrel shows continued to be popular through the early twentieth century and in some parts of the United States persisted into the 1950s.

Plate 3-13. A lithographed cardboard apothecary shop display, ca. 1900, advertising throat lozenges from Hance Brothers and White, a Philadelphia firm. For some inexplicable reason, frogs and banjos were often pictured together in Victorian-era graphics.

Plate 3-14. Weeden penny bank (patented 7 August 1888) and related advertisement. Produced by the famous steam-toy maker of New Bedford, Massachusetts, these banks were not available to the public but were given away as premiums to children who sold subscriptions to various publications. The bank has an unusual mechanism: a key is used to wind a spring, which in turn activates the banjo player and clog dancer on the porch of their tin cabin after a penny or nickel is inserted into a slot in the roof.

Plantation Darkey Savings Bank.

This new Mechanical Bank is made of **sheet** metal in exact imitation of **A Plantation Shanty**, and contains Clock Work, Main Spring and Fan Regulator so arranged that when a penny or nickel is put in, the Banjo Player will **"Pick on de Ole Banjo,"** and the other Darkey will

DANCE A REAL BREAKDOWN

in perfect time, with a great variety of life-like comical steps. The Bank consists of 61 separate pieces, and over 600 distinct operations are required to make each Bank. Size is 3 1-2 inches square, height, 5 1-2 in front. **A Bank that will earn Money!** Because the bottom part is a Coin Safe into which the pennies drop after they have started the performers. It has a metal *door* with post office lock and key, so all money put in is in safe keeping for its owner. It is **NOT a** single quick motion like that of the common trick banks, but is a very comical performance lasting over a minute, during which time the dancer executes a great variety of "old plantation" steps to the picking of the old banjo. The spring is wound up from the back, and three jigs will be danced from once winding. It is excellent for use at fairs and other entertainments to catch pennies. It will

Make Money for your Boys and Girls.

Being artistically designed, made from metal, stamped in relief, and hand painted, is handsome enough for the parlor table, and will **be** sure to attract attention and gain pennies **for** its owner, as everyone wants to see the darkey dance and play on the banjo which they **will** not do unless they put money in the bank. It is **very useful** and **very funny,** and you cannot buy anything that will please the little folks as much as the **Plantation Darkey Bank.**

tion, for as much as $50. His Champion, another popular model, with an eleven-and-a-half-inch rim, a nineteen-inch neck, twenty-four brackets, white pegs and tailpiece, and ebony fingerboard, cost $30, with "more elaborate styles" from $50 up (fig. 3-27).

At the top of the line was the stunning $100 Presentation Champion, with an eleven-and-a-half-inch rim, gold-plated brackets and hooks, hexagonal nuts, a nineteen-inch fingerboard with several veneers, and elaborate carving at both the heel and the back of the peg head (fig. 3-28). In addition, there was elaborate pearl inlay, "with best Cut Shells," and carved ivory tuning pegs with ends of gold and inlaid with garnets. "Such Elaborately Inlaid Finger-boards," he noted, "are recommended as best made with Raised Frets" but could be ordered "in other styles of fretting."[66]

More important than the models or the great variety of ornamentation that marks Stewart banjos, however, is their variety of size. For Stewart made not only "regular" banjos in various rim diameters (usually ten to thirteen inches) and neck lengths (seventeen to nineteen inches, from the nut to the rim), but also banjos of very unusual sizes that originated in his experimentation with how the instruments might be played in an ensemble.

We have already mentioned, for example, his sale of tiny piccolo banjos,

Figure 3-27. Two-page advertisement for Stewart's Prince Imperial banjo from his *Price List of Parlor, Concert, and Orchestra Banjos* (Philadelphia, 1887). Various grades of the Champion were among his most popular banjos.

STEWART'S $100.00 PRESENTATION "CHAMPION"

These Cuts represent the $100.00 Banjo, Front and Back View.

DESCRIPTION.

German-silver Rim 11½ inches in diameter, 2¼ inches deep, Nickel-plated and Chased, Nickel-plated Band or Hoop with Turned Edge, 30 Gold-plated Brackets and Hooks, Hexagon Nuts, etc.

Neck, 19 inches in Length (Finger-board), with several Colored Veneers, and Ebony Top Strip for Finger-board. Neck Handsomely Carved at Base and at Scroll-head. Elaborately Pearl Inlaid with best Cut Shells, all work being done in my own factory inclusive of sawing and making pearl inlayings.

Pegs of Carved Ivory, or Inlaid Celluloid, as may be desired, Capped on Ends with Gold and Inlaid with Garnets. Handsomely Finished Carved Ivory Tail-piece, and all work of the best throughout.

Tone Warranted, Price. . $100.00.

A Fine Leather Case is included with this Banjo.

N. B.—Such Elaborately Inlaid Finger-boards are recommended as best made with RAISED FRETS, but will be furnished in other styles of fretting when so ordered, as this style Banjo is furnished only to order.

BACK VIEW.   FACE VIEW.

S. S. STEWART, Sole Manufacturer, Philad'a, Pa.

Figure 3-28. Advertisement for Stewart's presentation-grade Champion, which sold for $100 in his *Price List of Parlor, Concert, and Orchestra Banjos* (Philadelphia, 1887). Note the elaborate inlay the entire length of the fingerboard.

and by the mid-1880s he was manufacturing his own (plate 3-7). These were not at all intended as children's instruments but were designed, he explained, as "miniature" instruments, "tuned an octave higher than the concert banjo, and played with the same brilliant and striking effect." He made these with the same German silver rim as his larger banjos, and with a ten-inch fingerboard and fifteen raised frets. Although the Little Wonder Banjo is "very small in *size*," he explained, "it is not small in *tone*, and is not a toy, but a perfect musical instrument," made on the same principles as his larger models.[67]

Other makers had produced smaller rimmed banjos, usually ten inches in diameter, which they designated for boys or ladies, but Stewart intended the piccolo to be one of a series of banjos of different sizes and musical capabilities to be played in banjo orchestras.[68] These instruments ranged in size up to a bass (actually what we would call a cello-size) banjo with a sixteen-inch rim, and Stewart considered them counterparts to those sizes that comprised the violin family. As one might suspect, his design and production of this variety of banjos was another part of his plan to elevate the instrument to a level equal to that of others in the European musical tradition (fig. 3-29).

Stewart's "banjeaurine" was his most important contribution to this enlargement of the banjo's sphere. He developed this instrument in 1885 and first advertised it in February 1886.[69] Two years later, in a section of *The Banjo Philosophically* devoted to the banjeaurine, he described it as having a neck "shorter in length than the diameter of the rim" (which at first was quite large, usually twelve or thirteen inches in diameter) and a thick ebony fingerboard that extended over the rim, like that of a violin. With its short neck, it was tuned a fifth higher than an ordinary "concert" banjo; thus, as Stewart explained, the banjeaurine (usually tuned in C or F) "harmonizes beautifully with the ordinary banjo" and also with the "piano, organ, guitar, violin, mandoline, as well as the male or female voice." Finally, with its extended fingerboard, the instrument was meant to be played primarily in guitar style.[70]

The new instrument soon became very popular. Indeed, according to the contemporary banjoist Thomas J. Armstrong, Stewart's introduction of the banjeaurine in the mid-1880s essentially engendered the craze for banjo clubs and orchestras that erupted shortly thereafter, for it became "the *violin* of a banjo orchestra" (fig. 3-30). "Music for such organizations," he continued, could not "be properly rendered, unless the club contain[ed], at least, one of these instruments."[71] Indeed, the banjeaurine caught on so quickly and unexpectedly that Stewart evidently missed his chance to patent it. "Upon being apprised by certain artists who were using the instruments that other makers were preparing to copy" it, he wrote in 1886, he finally filed an application; but a patent was never granted, presumably because other makers already had adapted its design to their own instruments. Stewart's frustration in this regard was obvious in his invective at Gatcomb, for example, who by 1887 was using the same word to describe his own version of the instrument.[72] Other copies followed, so that by the late 1880s a banjeaurine could be bought from virtually any maker.

Figure 3-29. Photograph, ca. 1890, of banjo and guitar orchestra. In this image one sees examples of the various sizes in which Stewart made banjos to accommodate the interest of such clubs, immensely popular in the 1890s. Well-known teacher, composer, performer, and banjo club director Paul Eno is seated second row center, with his presentation-grade S. S. Stewart banjeaurine. In the back center is a bass or cello banjo.

Although it was shorter than a regular banjo, the banjeaurine was constructed similarly and thus was priced accordingly. In a catalog from the early 1890s Stewart listed the Imperial banjeaurine, "Invented and Manufactured by S. S. Stewart," at a base price of $30. In its standard version this instrument came with a twelve-and-a-half-inch nickel-plated, German silver rim and a ten-inch neck (from the nut to the rim, thus not counting the fingerboard extension) and was recommended with raised frets to insure a clearer sound. The instrument was advertised with one of Stewart's two patented items, a "neck adjuster" used to strengthen the banjeaurine's neck and adjust its angle to the rim (fig. 3-31). When he first introduced the instrument, he noted elsewhere, "there was some trouble with the fingerboard and neck," presumably warping caused by the high string ten-

Figure 3-30. Albumen photograph, ca. 1890, of women's banjo, mandolin, and guitar club. By this period the banjo was popular with clubs of both sexes, whose members played music elaborately arranged in different parts for the different sized instruments. The first and third women from the right, probably part of a college group, play Stewart banjos.

sion necessary to tune it to pitch. To obviate this problem, Stewart devised a finely wrought metallic strip "that ran from the heel to the opposite end of the rim" to reinforce the neck, and which had an "adjustable screw" where it attached to the rim under the tailpiece nut, "by which the pitch of the neck can be regulated at pleasure" (that is, so that one could adjust the height of the strings).[73] By 1896 he was offering the instrument in several models, including a "Banjo-Banjeaurine" that had a ten-inch rim, fourteen-inch neck, and twenty-two frets. As he described it, this was "a small banjo with the advantage of a full three octave compass upon the fingerboard," making it particularly suited to solo work out of the reach of the player with a "regular" banjeaurine. This version of the instrument was developed, Stewart explained, "to admit its being used with ease for the expression of the high order of music now being rendered by some of our own leading Banjo Clubs."[74]

The banjeaurine's popularity moved Stewart to manufacture as well a large "bass or cello" banjo, with a sixteen-inch head three inches deep, an eighteen-inch neck, and a slotted peg head with geared tuners, the better to adjust the heavy strings that were used on so large an instrument.[75] This behemoth was pitched in the key of C an octave below the ordinary

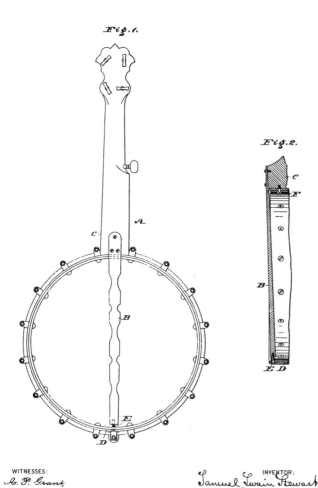

(No Model.)

S. S. STEWART.
BANJO.

No. 355 808.   Patented Jan. 11, 1887.

Fig.1.

Fig.2.

WITNESSES:
R. P. Grant,
Th. Rolle.

INVENTOR:
Samuel Swain Stewart
BY
John A. Niederstein
ATTORNEY

Figure 3-31. Patent drawing for S. S. Stewart's neck brace, 11 January 1887. He devised this nonadjustable brace specifically to reinforce the necks of his banjeaurines, which were prone to warping because of the high tension of the strings.

banjo and was intended to fill the position of a bass instrument in a banjo orchestra, examples of which by 1895 were everywhere. "Every college throughout the land has its little band," Armstrong wrote, and "nearly every community has its diminutive orchestra to make their social existence more attractive."[76]

By the early 1890s Stewart's *Banjo and Guitar Journal* (with growing competition from *Gatcomb's Banjo and Guitar Gazette*) was the periodical of record for all such groups—everything from the most sophisticated professional ensembles who filled large urban concert halls to the ubiquitous amateurs who played in town halls and college auditoriums. His business booming with sales of all manner and size of banjo, Stewart had achieved remarkable success in both spreading the instrument and its music throughout the United States and the Western world and, as he had hoped, convincing large segments of the public that the banjo could stand with the violin and piano as a virtuoso's instrument (fig. 3-32).[77] Thus, with Stewart's premature death shortly after his merger with Bauer in 1898, banjo culture lost its most effective advocate.

Although in the 1890s S. S. Stewart dominated the national market in banjos, he always had competition, particularly in cities or regions where other banjo makers were located. In the midwestern market, for example, he was challenged by the Lyon and Healy Company, which had begun in Chicago in 1864 as an arm of the Oliver Ditson Company of Boston (fig. 3-33). By the early 1880s Lyon and Healy had begun to manufacture or contract for its own stringed instruments, and at the start of the next decade the firm claimed to produce 100,000 musical instruments annually, a figure which included bugles, drums, tambourines, and other inexpensive items as well as mandolins, guitars, and banjos. Its high-quality instruments, sold under the George Washburn label, numbered significantly fewer, but the firm's aggressive marketing policy—in 1887 it had established a separate advertising department—quickly made it a national force in the music industry (fig. 3-34).[78]

In addition, there were literally hundreds of makers scattered in cities and towns throughout the United States, firms whose histories can be recovered only through the odd extant instrument, listings in city directories, and, for those makers who were more inventive, the patents that they filed for improvements in the instrument. The presence of these banjo makers indicates that not everyone was convinced that the banjo had reached its apogee in the silver rim instruments Stewart so widely advertised. Accurately terming his age that of the "Scientific Banjo Boom," Stewart eventually was left behind by more technologically sophisticated makers whose continuing experimentation in banjo design sometimes led to instruments whose tone and volume were far superior to those of his instruments.[79]

Many of the banjo patents from 1880 to 1895, for example, indicate other makers' attempts to refine the instrument's sound chamber. We have already discussed the constant tinkering of the Dobson brothers, who from 1867 through the turn of the century entered various patents for both open- and closed-back banjos and, in particular, tried to develop a banjo with a clearer and more bell-like tone. But other, smaller makers were equally inventive and offered instruments—some bizarre, others highly significant to the subsequent history of the instrument—that deserve our attention.

Figure 3-32. Cabinet card, ca. 1885, of Stewart and his son Fred. This photograph shows
the banjo maker at the height of his success, with one of the two sons who would take over
the firm after their father's premature death in 1898.

In 1882, for example, James Morrison, a New York maker, took out a
patent for an improved banjo with "a full, clear, and distinct sound." He
guaranteed this by attaching a series of "projections or pegs of any shape
or form, made of steel, brass, glass, or any other kind of metal or material
suitable for the purpose," to the wooden rim. On these projections he

Figure 3-33. Lithograph, Lyon and Healy Factory, Chicago, ca. 1898, frontispiece to *Catalogue of Musical Merchandise Imported and Manufactured by Lyon and Healy* (Chicago, 1898). This plant, which produced all sorts of musical instruments, dwarfed Stewart's operation during this same period (see figure 3-17).

Figure 3-34. Showrooms of Lyon and Healy, Chicago, 1898. This image, from the same catalog cited in figure 3-33, suggests the size of some musical instrument manufacturers at the turn of the century. Stewart may have been compelled to go into partnership with George Bauer, who made mandolins and guitars, in large measure because of his desire to keep pace with Lyon and Healy.

placed a hoop or ring "of round, square, or other section," again made of any kind of metal or material, which he attached to the rim by two screws. When the membrane was stretched over this in the usual way, Morrison claimed, the tone would be not only more powerful but also "prolongate[d]."[80] By claiming that the pegs and the second hoop could be made of virtually any material that conducted sound, he obviously tried to protect his improvement in the widest possible way. As we shall see, such a tubular tone ring (made of metal) eventually revolutionized the manufacture of the instrument.

In the same year Oliver R. Chase of Boston, also experimenting with rim design, went in a different direction. He developed a rim made entirely of one piece of metal, with its upper side curved over inwardly and over which the head was stretched. On this instrument, he claimed, "nothing whatever, either wood or metal, comes in contact with the rim that would be considered a disturbing element in the harmony of the instrument" (fig. 3-35). The skin, in other words, vibrated directly on the sound chamber

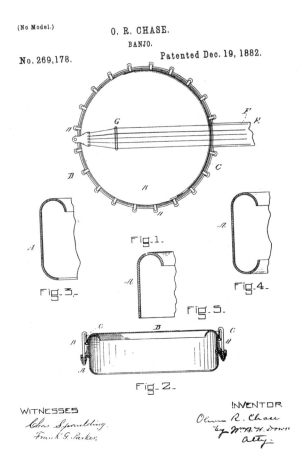

Figure 3-35. Patent drawing for O. R. Chase's banjo, 19 December 1882. Even though Stewart thought that his own banjos marked the apogee of design, other makers continued to experiment, particularly with rim construction. Chase made this part entirely from metal, presumably to get a brighter tone.

and, because the latter was made of a single piece of metal, thus increased the instrument's "sonorousness and resonance of tone."[81] Chase's focus on the integrity of the rim and a vibrating membrane whose sound was not absorbed by any extra metal or wood again points toward later innovations in banjo design.

In this period, however, probably Frederick J. Miller of Brooklyn explored most radically how one might increase the "sonorousness" of the banjo, even if his solution was bizarre. He suggested enclosing the top and sides of the regular wooden rim inside a "sheet-metal covering," leaving a bit of space between its top and the wooden rim, over which the head was stretched to create an air space that served as a sounding chamber. To amplify the sound as it issued from the banjo, he placed protruding "trumpet-shaped thimbles or tubes" inside holes around the side of the rim, and he suggested as well a disk of curved sheet metal (projecting "downwardly") attached inside the rim, off which the instrument's sound was deflected into these "trumpets." As if this did not promise enough amplification, Miller also built his instrument with a hollow neck, "sunken" frets to allow "the operator to run his hand more freely down the arm and to feel with more accuracy the points at which to press the strings," a hollow nut, and even a hollow dowel, which itself might be "perforated" to "increase the volume of sound" yet more![82]

Two other patents from the 1880s also deserve notice, in this case as indications of the ongoing debate over the banjo's basic shape, size, and utility even as Stewart declared the matter closed. In 1882, for example, Benjamin Bradbury of Brooklyn patented an instrument with "a softness and purity of tone resembling and approximating that of the violin," whose primary characteristic was a much shorter neck than a banjo, so that "the strings may be manipulated with the fingers of the left hand throughout the whole range of octaves usual in the instrument [i.e., the violin]." What made the instrument yet more unusual was Bradbury's suggestion that its strings be doubled, like a mandolin, because "the vibration of the two parts constitute, by their unity of tone, a single string producing a more melodious, stronger, and softer tone than when the string is composed of but one wire or catgut." Moreover, these strings need not number ten (double the number on a conventional banjo) but could be of "any suitable number"; the instrument in the patent drawing did not even have a shorter fifth string. It also had guitar-style, geared tuners in a slotted peg head, a seven-and-five-eighths-inch head, a fret scale of sixteen and three-sixteenths inches (that is, from the nut to the bridge). Essentially, it was what later would be called a banjo-mandolin.[83]

A few years later John Farris of Hartford, Connecticut, took the next

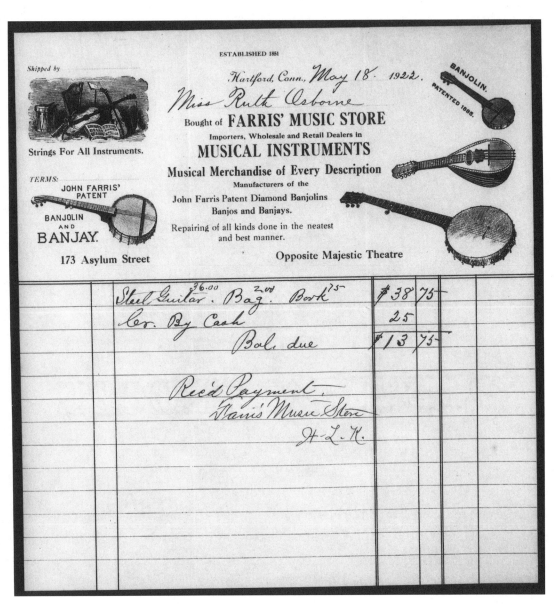

ESTABLISHED 1851

Shipped by _____

Strings For All Instruments.

TERMS:

JOHN FARRIS'
PATENT

BANJOLIN
AND
BANJAY.

173 Asylum Street

Hartford, Conn., *May 18. 1922.*

Miss Ruth Osborne

Bought of **FARRIS' MUSIC STORE**

Importers, Wholesale and Retail Dealers in

MUSICAL INSTRUMENTS

Musical Merchandise of Every Description

Manufacturers of the

John Farris Patent Diamond Banjolins

Banjos and Banjays.

Repairing of all kinds done in the neatest
and best manner.

Opposite Majestic Theatre

BANJOLIN.
PATENTED 1885.

		Steel Guitar. 36.00 Bag. 2nd Book 75	$38	75	
		Cr. By Cash	25		
		Bal. due	$13	75	
		Rec'd Payment.			
		Farris Music Store			
		H. L. K.			

Figure 3-36. Letterhead from John Farris's Store, 1922. The small banjo, upper right, now called a "banjolin," is the same instrument Farris patented in 1885.

opposite
Figure 3-37. Photograph of John Farris and his store in Hartford, Connecticut, ca. 1890. Note the signs for "banjays" and other of Farris's unusual instruments. Collection of Tony Creamer.

step and offered his "banjolin," with, logically enough, "some points of similarity to the banjo" and others "to the mandolin" (figs. 3-36, 3-37). The instrument was also distinctive for having a very long bridge, stretching all the way across the membrane, to lessen the sagging that would occur because of the great pressure necessary to tune the instrument to pitch (G-D-A-E), and it was reinforced as well from beneath the head by a

MUSIC STORE

DIAMOND
BANJOS

DIAMOND BANJOS,
BANJAYS, BANJOLINS.

Banjo Maker.

JNO. FARRIS.
PAT. BANJAYS,
PAT. BANJOLINS.

short pole that sat on the upper side of the dowel and supported the bridge.[84] Such "banjos" as Farris's and Bradbury's, as well as those of other contemporary makers, suggest, first of all, that we should not overemphasize Stewart's experimentation with and development of instruments of other sizes and acoustic capabilities, embodied most successfully in his banjeaurine. Such technological speculation was part of a general trend among makers as much to find ways to capitalize on novelty for its own sake in attracting customers as to expand the utility of banjo-like instruments as the public became more taken by the rage (plates 3-8, 3-9, 3-10, 3-11, 3-12, 3-13, 3-14).

More important, as unusual as such instruments appear, they marked a continuation of intense technological and acoustic experimentation that led to major changes in banjo manufacture, but which Stewart, because of his devotion to silver-rim banjos, finally resisted. As we shall see, the important innovations in banjo design that originated among the various banjo makers in the Boston area, particularly A. C. Fairbanks, flowed from their continual willingness to reinvent the instrument in light of their own scientific, technological, and commercial interests. Unfortunately, then, for all Stewart's care in the manufacture of his instruments, his scornful dismissal of such novelty—by then an indelible hallmark of the banjo trade—eventually relegated him to a lower rank of the country's banjo makers.

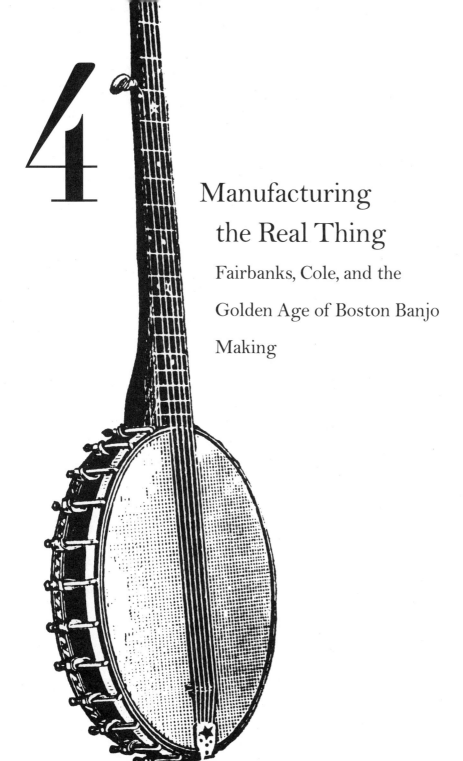

4

Manufacturing the Real Thing

Fairbanks, Cole, and the Golden Age of Boston Banjo Making

In 1869 the young woodworker Lincoln B. Gatcomb moved from Maine to Boston and found work in his specialty, stair making. Shortly after his arrival in the city he heard the popular banjoist Billy Carter play at the Howard Athenaeum and, already musically inclined, was transformed by this chance encounter.[1] Quickly infected by the "banjo mania" that had broken out "with a virulence that exceed[ed] anything known before," Gatcomb, like S. S. Stewart and so many others, began to play and tinker with the instrument. By 1875 he was so immersed in banjo culture that he devoted himself full-time to the instrument's manufacture. He fell in love with the banjo, he recalled a decade later, because it had become "the musical instrument of the people," found "in the homes of wealth" as well as "in the dwellings of poverty," where its "cheering notes enliven the gloom," and he was ready to do his part to increase its popularity even more.[2] By 1885, with the support of the renowned banjo teacher and performer George L. Lansing, Gatcomb established a guitar and banjo factory at 48 Hanover Street, and two years later, after buying out Boston music instructor Walter C. Bryant's short-lived *Banjo Herald*, he began to issue monthly numbers of *Gatcomb's Banjo and Guitar Gazette*, patterned on Stewart's widely circulated journal.[3]

As we have seen, Stewart dismissed this upstart publication—it was essentially a "rehash" of his own writings, he claimed—and predicted its rapid demise.[4] But for once he misread the market: Gatcomb's periodical lasted for more than a decade, its success proof that the public's infatuation with the banjo could support more than one national publication devoted to its cause.[5] More important, in no small measure Gatcomb traded on the public's awareness of the increasing number of Boston banjo makers whose wares he advertised and whose interests he represented—and who by the mid-1880s had begun to challenge Stewart's preeminence. By the 1890s, with Stewart preoccupied with the highly visible promotion of Lyon and Healy, the immense Chicago-based instrument manufacturers, Boston's makers—particularly Albert C. Fairbanks and William A. Cole—were beginning to design and build what became the acknowledged standards of the banjo world.

They accomplished this because of their instruments' widely recognized technological sophistication, for these makers had put the lie to Stewart's decade-long claims for the primacy of his silver rim construction—and thus to his self-serving contention that the banjo already had been brought to its ideal form. Continuing to refine the instrument's acoustical properties to suit players, both professional and amateur, who now performed primarily in guitar-style in a variety of venues, Fairbanks, Cole, and other Boston makers patented important "improvements" that increased the banjo's musical capabilities. Further, they resisted the trend toward large-scale manufacturing that so identified the New York makers, and with a highly skilled labor force in small mechanized workshops they brought the five-string banjo to a pinnacle of achievement, acoustically as well as aesthetically.[6] With Stewart essentially having won the battle for the instrument's elevation, Boston's banjo makers were free to concentrate on its design. If their own advertisements often rivaled the hyperbole of

Stewart's, there is no denying that their instruments were in fact better made.

The rise and continued success of these Boston firms, and the paths they opened for those in other of the nation's major cities, marked the decade of the 1890s as the one in which American stringed instrument manufacture became fully professionalized, a transformation that culminated in 1900 with the formation in Boston of the American Guild of Banjoists, Mandolinists and Guitarists, whose membership was open to stringed instrument makers, players, and teachers and whose foremost purpose was to "further advance the interests of the instruments in their literature, music, and manufacture." First proposed by Charles Morris of Philadelphia, the idea for such a national organization quickly caught fire, and the group's annual conventions, though attended by as many guitarists and mandolinists as banjoists, marked the final victory of the battle for respectability waged by advocates for the banjo from the 1850s on.[7] Although by 1900 fine banjos were being made in many cities throughout the United States, the accomplishments of the Boston makers allow us to see in detail the degree of professionalization that led to so important an organization as the American Guild.[8]

With the exception of the makers noted in Chapter 1, we know little about the craft or industry of banjo making in Boston before the late 1870s, when both Gatcomb and Fairbanks broke onto the field. Unlike New York City, for example, which had been the vital center of the early minstrel shows, Boston showed no makers in city directories before 1869, when George C. Dobson was listed at 687½ Washington Street. He was to appear regularly thereafter, though frequently at different addresses. In 1872 he was joined (only for a year) by another maker, Ebenezer B. Mansfield, at 103 Court Street, and in 1876 by O. A. Whitmore, at 282 Washington Street.[9] Presumably, then, before 1870 budding musicians got their instruments through New York or had them made by local woodworkers, like the "Old Timer" from Hartford, Connecticut, noted in Chapter 1, who had his first instrument made by a "carpenter."[10] Moreover, since in their first years of operation the output of both Gatcomb and Fairbanks appears to have been quite small, we can more properly date the rise of the industry in this city to the partnership that Fairbanks formed with Cole in 1880 (plate 4-1). During their decade of partnership, Fairbanks and Cole made banjos of increasing sophistication, and it was they who initially mounted the most serious challenge to the market supremacy of Stewart's instruments and those of the various Dobson brothers.

A. C. Fairbanks (1852–1919), the son of a butcher, was born in rural

Figure 4-1. Photograph of A. C. Fairbanks, ca. 1885. By this time Fairbanks, with his partner, William A. Cole, had begun to challenge S. S. Stewart's position as the nation's premier banjo maker.

Sterling, Massachusetts (fig. 4-1). His family moved to Sudbury in 1866, and two years later, to Boston. For the next year the boy worked in Quincy Market, presumably at his father's business; however, unlike his brother William, he evidently had no wish to remain in the family trade. In the 1870s he manufactured "fountain" syringes, but by 1880, bitten by the ubiquitous banjo "bug," he turned his attention full-time to that instrument. Unlike Stewart, however, he never became well known as a musician.[11]

Such was not the case with his soon-to-be partner, for as a young boy William A. Cole (1853–1909), who hailed from Methuen (north of Boston), had studied violin. By 1871 he, too, had discovered the banjo's magic and, like Stewart and so many others, had came under George Dobson's tutelage. Dobson trained the young musician well enough that Cole soon was playing professionally, assuming, for example, the role in blackface of "Kit, The Arkansas Traveler." By 1875 he was teaching the instrument, and in 1884, with Walter Vreeland, P. H. Foley, and Carlo Carciutto he formed the long-lived Imperial Quartet, also known in later years as the Mexican Serenaders, with whom he played into the early twentieth century (fig. 4-2).[12] We do not know what brought Fairbanks and Cole together, but by 1880 the new partners were in business at 121 Court Street, with Cole maintaining his teaching studio at 178 Tremont Street (plate 4-2).

Their business was fully launched in December of that year, when they accepted the prominent "Banjo Challenge" placed in the *New York Clipper* by the young Philadelphia banjo maker S. S. Stewart, who had just estab-

Figure 4-2. Promotional photograph, ca. 1890, for the Mexican Serenaders, one of the groups with which William A. Cole (second from right) was associated. Unlike his partner, A. C. Fairbanks, Cole was not as involved in the technological design of the firm's instruments.

lished himself in the same business (fig. 4-3). We have already noted the acrimonious paper war between the two firms carried on in the pages of the *Clipper*, but it is worthwhile to revisit the controversy from the standpoint of Fairbanks and Cole.[13] In the 4 December issue, we recall, Stewart had promised to pay $100 for a banjo equal in tone to his concert instrument. The next week's number carried Fairbanks and Cole's notice to the effect that, since for the "past three months" they too had "challenged the world of banjomakers on every point that makes a first-class banjo," they accepted Stewart's challenge "in the most friendly spirit possible," though not without feeling that in fact *he* should have accepted *their* challenge, because it had been "the first one in the field." They also asked Stewart to deposit with the *Clipper* a guaranty of the prize money and to appoint a time and place for the contest, "New York City being, perhaps, preferable to all parties." Finally, they offered $300 for a banjo that compared "in tone and general perfection" to their "BEAUTY," valued at $500, a piece so spectacular that they provided "an elegant stereoscopic view" of it to every purchaser of one of their banjos (fig. 4-4).

At this early point in banjo manufacture and promotion, both parties obviously thought that the stakes in such a contest, advertised in the country's premier newspaper devoted to the entertainment world, were large. Thus Stewart countered with a highly dismissive notice, observing, first, that his challenge was specifically for the "TONE" of the instrument and

A copy of our challenge to all Banjo makers, as it appeared in the New York Clipper, No. 40, dated December 25, 1880.

BANJO CHALLENGE.

Mr. Stewart's explanation of the meaning of his challenge may sound very well to his too susceptible ear; but the idea that a man can challenge all others in his particular line, and be his own JUDGE, REFEREE, STAKE-HOLDER, etc, must appear very ludicrous to any sensible person. We accepted his so-called challenge, knowing at the time that it was nothing of the kind, but simply a dose of braggadocio, and felt sure he would back out when he found any one who really meant BUSINESS. His acknowledgment that he never saw a Fairbanks' banjo simply proves that he has not traveled. If he had, he would never have issued his offer of $100, even in the weak manner shown. We cannot see how Mr. Fairbanks' Patent Syringes have anything to do with a Banjo Challenge. Perhaps Mr. Stewart can explain. It matters but very little to us whether Mr. Stewart ever heard of such firms as Fairbanks & Co. of Syringe renown, or Fairbanks & Cole of banjo celebrity, individually or collectively; but, when a man issues a challenge something is to be expected of him besides bluster, evasion, and their kindred smallness, Now, as Mr. Stewart refuses to bind himself to his offer or challenge, we give him another chance in the following

SWEEPING CHALLENGE,

showing that we at least mean business. The undersigned, in consideration of the vast amount of talk (in print and out) as to who makes the BEST BANJOS, and claiming as we do to make THE FINEST BANJOS in the UNITED STATES, at the LOWEST PRICES, do hereby issue the following Challenge: We do, therefore, challenge any one or more manufacturers of banjos to a full and fair exhibit of their product in this line. This exhibiton to take place in such city as may be decided upon by mutual agreement. Visiting parties to be allowed traveling expenses, etc. Said exhibition to be under the auspices of a board of judges to be appointed by disinterested parties, who shall appoint a referee, whose decision shall be final, in any sum from $50 to $500 a side. One-half of his stakes to be given by the winner to some charitable institution in his city. The following points of superiority to be competed for: 1st, QUALITY AND POWER OF TONE; 2nd, Variety of Designs; 3rd, Beauty and Finish of Workmanship; 4th, Number of Improvements of Real Importance; 5th, General Excellence. Immediately on appraisal of the acceptance of this challenge, we will deposit a forfeit of $50 with THE EDITOR OF THE CLIPPER. Now, if Mr. Stewart has the best-toned banjo in America he can have satisfaction, or retire from public view.

FAIRBANKS & COLE,

MANUFACTURERS AND TEACHERS OF THE IMPROVED MODERN BANJO,

121 COURT STREET, BOSTON, MASS., U. S. A.

Figure 4-3. Broadsheet of "Banjo Challenge," ca. 1880, issued by Fairbanks and Cole in response to Stewart's advertisements. This move initiated a long-standing feud between the two firms, the country's most prominent banjo makers through the 1880s.

nothing else. Fairbanks and Cole, he continued, seemed "MIXED UP in its ideas" of the criteria for the challenge. Moreover, Stewart added, he had "never [seen] a Fairbanks & Cole Banjo, and [had] never heard of Mr. Cole except as a teacher." As for "Mr. Fairbanks," Stewart declared that he only knew of him as "a very good maker of PATENT SYRINGES," adding, gratuitously, that "between the making of a Banjo and the making of a Syringe there is a wide difference."

Stewart then returned to the still-nebulous terms of this contest, for what he had in mind obviously differed significantly from Fairbanks and Cole's proposal. He had advertised, Stewart reiterated, for a banjo equal in *tone* to his concert model. Moreover, he resented the notion that he would have to put up a guaranty. If and when he found such an instrument, Stewart huffed, no one should doubt that his check would be honored. Finally, because, as he put it, "I want the Banjo for my own amusement, I reserve the right to be JUDGE OF THE TONE," though he capitulated to the extent that he also would accept the judgment of such well-known players as E. M. Hall, Horace Weston, or William A. Huntley, all of whom, as we have seen, already were sleeping in Stewart's tent.

The next issue of the *Clipper* contained Fairbanks and Cole's largest no-

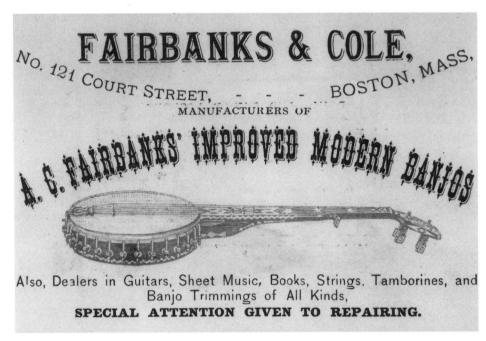

Figure 4-4. Trade card, ca. 1880, for Fairbanks and Cole banjos, illustrating a fancy instrument that may have been similar to the "Beauty" they mentioned in their challenge to Stewart. Note the marquetry around the base of the rim, on the heel, and on the fingerboard. In the 1880s many fancy banjos were still decorated with such wood inlay rather than with mother-of-pearl, which became immensely popular in the 1890s.

tice yet, criticizing their rival for assuming that a person could be "his own JUDGE, REFEREE, [and] STAKEHOLDER." Obviously, Stewart's challenge was "simply a dose of braggadocio," they wrote, and "his acknowledgment that he never saw a Fairbanks banjo simply proves that he has not traveled." It mattered very little to them, they continued, "whether Mr. Stewart ever heard of such a firm as Fairbanks & Co., of Syringe renown, or Fairbanks & Cole, of banjo celebrity." But when someone issues a challenge, they continued, something more is expected "besides bluster, evasion, and kindred smallness." They thereupon offered a *new* challenge to any and all makers, with judges to be appointed by disinterested parties, in which banjos would be evaluated by five different criteria: "QUALITY AND POWER OF TONE," "Variety of Designs," "Beauty and Finish of Workmanship," "Number of Improvements of Real Importance," and "General Excellence."

Obtusely, Stewart again accepted, saying he would meet the Boston makers in New York City no more than two months hence "for a public contest of Banjos" at a place that they might designate, with the banjos to be judged for "TONE." Moreover, he wanted the contest decided by the "WORLD-RENOWNED and WELL-KNOWN BANJO EXPERT" Horace Weston, or, if he declined, by any three other musicians well known to the public. Stewart evidently did not want to compete against Fairbanks and Cole on the other criteria they had set out (by which their instruments soon would be judged far superior to Stewart's).

The Boston partners "NAILED" Stewart in their next notice, pointing out that the public had just seen another "good example" of Stewart's ability "to avoid a square issue," the first of which had been "his ungentlemanly and slurring reply" to their initial acceptance of his challenge. By 22 January 1881 they had had enough: "NO PICAYUNE BUSINESS," their card exclaimed. They were sick and tired of Stewart's "braying": "We claim to make the best banjos in America for style, workmanship, finish, and tone." "No words of ours are needed," they concluded, "to answer such small language as that used by the man from Philadelphia, as any one who begins a controversy in such loud words as he has, and ends by calling names will, without any push from us, be accepted for what he is worth: A small man at a smaller occupation." "Calling names is not our line," they explained. "We have something else to do."

The rivalry thus established between these two firms only became more intense in the following decade. The two-month-long exchange in the *Clipper*, though no doubt amusing to the readership, had served as a highly publicized notice that, as much as Stewart assumed his supremacy in the banjo world, other makers did not accept it. Moreover, many rejected his claim that at his hands the instrument had reached its pinnacle of design in utility and beauty. Led by Fairbanks and Cole, Boston's banjo makers met Stewart head on, lining up their own endorsements from prominent musicians, advertising widely in the trade papers, sponsoring public concerts and contests for composers of banjo music, and, most important, constantly working to improve their banjos. With an ever-increasing number of manufacturers in the country as a whole, by the turn of the century Boston's makers would make their city at least equal in importance to New York and Philadelphia, with some of their instruments regarded as the ne plus ultra of the musical world.

Until Gatcomb founded his periodical in the late 1800s, Fairbanks and Cole led the charge on Stewart's reputation. One of their most highly visible promotions consisted of their sponsorship of contests for composers of banjo music, along with annual banjo concerts in Boston at which the winners' music was performed. Such events, and the sure signs that Fairbanks and Cole's banjos were meeting with more public acceptance, obviously got under Stewart's skin. Reviewing the "Fairbanks & Cole Fifth Annual Banjo Concert" in his journal, for example, he vented some of his jealousy at his competitors, caustically observing that Fairbanks had "worked very hard to build up a banjo trade, and worked by every means within his grasp to push his banjos to the front." "Only a few years ago," Stewart continued, Fairbanks "thought himself the 'coming' great gun of the banjo business" and was "chock full of conceit, and always frothing over like an uncorked bottle of beer." But "our esteemed co-patriot, Albert C.," Stewart concluded, "should open his eyes to the fact that neither himself nor his partner are makers of the banjo in any shape or form," a contention that was proved, he felt, by Fairbanks's "imitation of Stewart's banjeaurine, even to the spelling of the name." This appropriation, Stewart declared, "has given him a character by no means enviable."[14]

Their products garnering more and more popular acclaim, Fairbanks and Cole ignored such, by then, predictable diatribes from their competitor and concentrated on improving their instruments. In this regard, Fairbanks was clearly the technological innovator, for in the 1880s and early 1890s it was he and not Cole who was granted several banjo-related patents. The latter's contribution to the firm is less clear, but Cole does not appear to have been directly involved in its technological experimentation. Even after he left Fairbanks to establish his own company, he secured no patents. Throughout the 1880s, however, he remained one of the city's best-known music teachers and thus may have had a relationship to Fairbanks similar to that of Lansing to Gatcomb, his prominence as an instructor assuring an entree to musical venues where he touted the superiority of his firm's instruments.

What precisely did Fairbanks and Cole contribute to the development of the banjo? Fairbanks's first patent was for an end-opening leather banjo case, a useful but hardly revolutionary improvement for banjo players, and his second, for a supporting device to help stabilize the fifth-string peg on the instrument, was not the sort of thing that would make the banjo world beat a path to his door.[15] More promising, however, and indicative of where his future success would lie, was an unusual design for a "sounding device" for the instrument that he patented in 1885. With this design he set himself on a path that by decade's end would lead to his most significant contributions to the instrument's development (fig. 4-5).

The U.S. Patent Office description of Fairbanks's improvement indicates that he had filed an application for it as early as 1882, but we have no explanation for the three-year delay in the patent's approval.[16] The object of his invention, Fairbanks explained, was "to provide a cheap, simple, and efficient device whereby the musical tone or resonance of the banjo may be very much increased in volume or compass of sound." He accomplished this by the "construction, combination, and arrangement of a metallic cymbal or inverted dome-shaped sounder or bell" placed with "its concave surface or mouth in close proximity to or in contact with" the head of the banjo. The edge of this sounder sat on top of the wooden rim of the instrument, and the skin head was stretched over it. In addition, the sounder might have a series of sound holes drilled all around its perimeter, so that the whole assembly, when set in motion by the vibrations from the head, would be "capable of unrestrained vibrations, which in effect give out a clear and bell-ringing tone." Offering two other ways this sounding chamber might be mounted, Fairbanks was convinced that this device greatly improved the acoustical properties of the banjo.

As we have seen in the case of the Dobsons, such novel technological experimentation with tone rings constituted an important aspect of banjo manufacture in the 1880s, but very few such devices—a couple of the Dobsons' innovations were the exception that proves the rule—were manufactured for any length of time or in any significant numbers. In some cases a new "improvement" was not advertised widely enough to change public opinion, and in others, it was simply impractical, economically or technologically, to produce such an instrument.[17] Fairbanks's 1885 patent evidently fell into this latter category, for no instrument with such a sounding device is extant, nor was any model provided when he applied for the patent. It seems unlikely that he ever made such a banjo.

Equally important to the development of the banjo (and to Fairbanks's future success) were his and other makers' experiments toward finding better ways to stretch the skin head over the rim. Not convinced that the

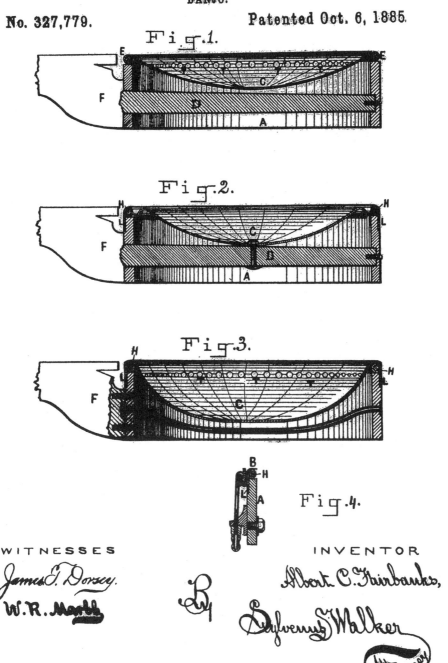

A. C. FAIRBANKS.
BANJO.

No. 327,779.   Patented Oct. 6, 1885.

Fig.1.

Fig.2.

Fig.3.

Fig.4.

WITNESSES
James G. Dorsey.
W. R. Mastt

INVENTOR
Albert C. Fairbanks,
By Sylvanus Walker
Attorney

Figure 4–5. Patent drawing for banjo designed by A. C. Fairbanks, 6 October 1885. Although this instrument was never commercially feasible, its unusual sounding chamber, with a dome-shaped metal "bell" under the skin, indicated Fairbanks's interest in augmenting the tone of his banjos.

simple hook-shoe-nut arrangement that still served so many makers was the most economical or practical way to secure the head, some makers developed highly unorthodox rim attachments. In 1883, for example, Hercules McCord of St. Louis, probably influenced by the development of novel tightening mechanisms for tympani, spun his entire rim from metal and then developed a way to pull the skin over it with a series of wires all connected to a bolt tightened into a central disk (fig. 4-6). In short, all one had to do to tighten the tension was to turn one bolt instead of thirty separate nuts. Obviously believing that he was on to something, a year later McCord offered a more refined version of the same idea.[18]

In 1885 Samuel Gibbs of Knox, Pennsylvania, offered his own version of such a device, "for adjusting the straining-hoop" in a way that possessed "superior advantages in point of simplicity, durability, and general efficiency, and in which all the brackets may be operated simultaneously for the purpose of adjusting the straining hoop by the action of a single thumb nut" (fig. 4-7).[19] His hooks were connected to metal strips arranged in a circle on the bottom of the rim, themselves attached to a central nut whose twist would simultaneously tighten all the hooks.

Such innovations—and between 1880 and 1900 there were others equally unusual—often revolved around the casting of an all-metal rim. Some makers, however, including Fairbanks and Cole, believed that the best-sounding banjos were those made with a solid wooden rim with some sort of tone ring mounted on top. Hence, their attempts at better tensioning of the head took a different approach, which eventually resulted in spectacular successes in banjo design. In an important patent awarded in 1887, for example, Fairbanks suggested an arrangement to tighten the hooks in the traditional manner without having to drill through the wooden rim to mount metal shoes. He accomplished this by spinning a piece of metal over the bottom of the rim, into which were cut small grooves to receive the bottom portion of a two-part hook, the top pulling over the tension hoop in the normal manner. The two hooks were then tightened by one turnbuckle that joined them together. Without holes drilled through the rim to mount the shoes for hooks, Fairbanks was able to preserve the structural and acoustical integrity of the rim (fig. 4-8).[20]

More remarkable, however, but then inexplicably shelved for almost twenty years, was another section of this patent. Fairbanks described a hollow, tubular tone ring that fit into a groove atop the tension hoop and was drilled with many small holes. These, he explained, were "to permit a free ingress and egress of air within and from the interior" of this tube, "so as to produce bell-like or ringing musical sound vibrations." Again, as with

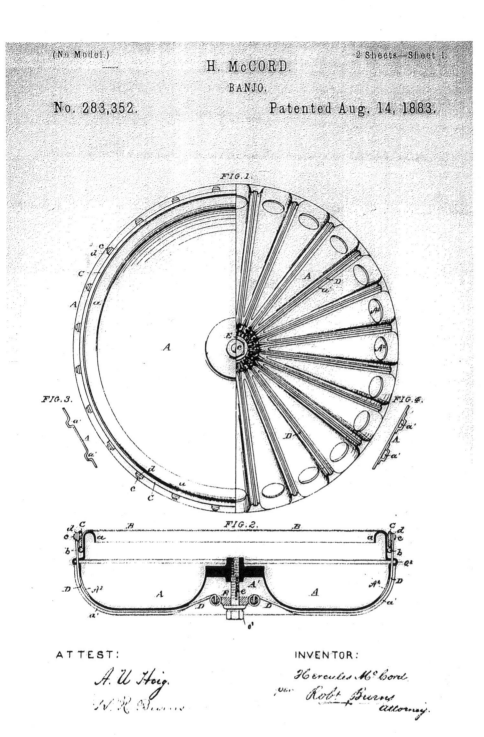

H. McCORD.

BANJO.

No. 283,352.

Patented Aug. 14, 1883.

FIG. 1.

FIG. 3.

FIG. 4.

FIG. 2.

ATTEST:

A. U. Hoig.

N. R. ......

INVENTOR:

Hercules McCord.

per Robt Burns

attorney.

Figure 4-6. Patent drawing for a banjo designed by Hercules McCord, 14 August 1883. McCord's device, probably derived from designs for tightening contemporary kettle drums, illustrates the lengths to which makers went to improve the tensioning mechanisms of their banjos. All edges of the skin were tightened by turning the single bolt in the center of the banjo.

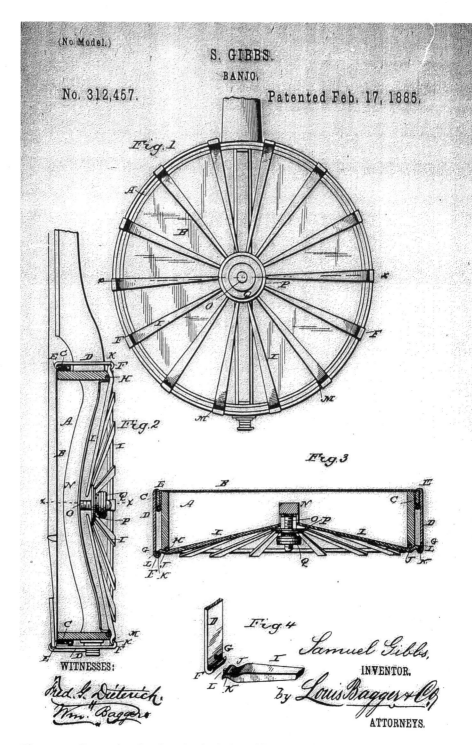

Figure 4–7. Patent drawing for a banjo designed by Samuel Gibbs, 17 February 1885. This invention, again probably derived from contemporary tympani design, indicates radical experimentation with the instrument's tensioning system.

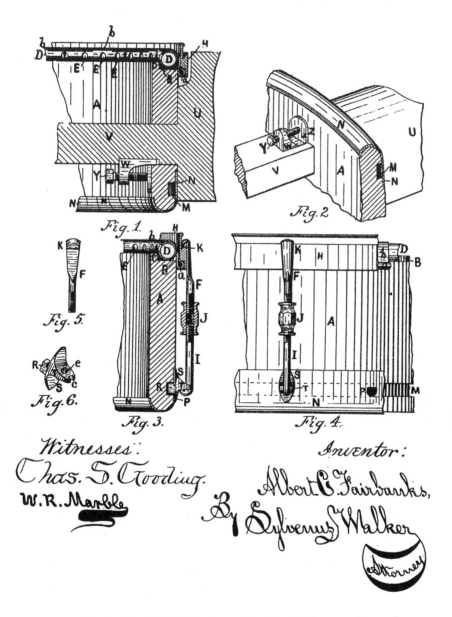

Figure 4–8. Patent drawing by A. C. Fairbanks, 29 March 1887, for a novel way of securing the tension hoop. In this design, no holes were drilled through the rim, thus preserving its structural and acoustical integrity. This drawing shows (upper left) a hollow, tubular tone ring that resembles the one that later would appear on the Vega Company's famous Tubaphone.

so many of the inventions patented in this period, we have no example of such a banjo, but the design of this tone ring essentially is the same as that which in 1909 appeared on the new banjo known as the Tubaphone, manufactured by the Vega Company, which early in the new century had bought out the A. C. Fairbanks Company. Why Fairbanks did not push this concept more vigorously in 1887 remains a mystery, but this patent, as well as the one of 1885, clearly illustrates his determination to find ways to increase "the musical tone" of the banjo and to render its volume of sound more "melodious" and its "resonance" more "mellifluous."

Other innovations were never patented but became singularly identified with the Fairbanks and Cole line. A catalog issued in 1889, just prior to the dissolution of the partnership, provides a detailed look at how the firm sought to set itself apart from other makers through such improvements. First, Fairbanks and Cole noted with dismay the prevalence of all kinds of hastily made factory goods in the marketplace. "The market is flooded with cheap goods of all kinds," they wrote, "and the banjo is a sufferer with the rest." "Competition among the class of banjo makers who wish to supply the world and cannot," they observed, "has forced poor goods upon the market." Thus, one found too many instruments made by "self-styled banjo makers" who cared "nothing for the artistic success of this beautiful instrument" and knew nothing "of its proper construction."[21]

Echoing Stewart's criticism of factory banjos, they observed that "nine-tenths of the banjos are gotten up to sell, the maker's name not appearing in any way," a situation that allowed manufacturers and music dealers to turn a pretty profit because so many of their customers "will not or cannot discriminate" among the goods they bought. "There never was a time in the history of the banjo," they concluded, "when so much judgment was required in [the banjo's] purchase." The truly judicious customer, however, would choose Fairbanks and Cole instruments because they were "the best possible article at the lowest possible price" and were produced by "skilled workmen" under the "personal supervision" of the owners. "The banjo," the catalog noted, like the violin and guitar, should only be made by those who are "especially educated to their labors, by artists true to their calling, [and] of material thoroughly seasoned atmospherically (not kiln-dried as usual)." Such care in workmanship and materials immediately set Fairbanks and Cole banjos apart from the factory "tubs."

Further, what distinguished their instruments from Stewart's (also supposedly made by skilled workmen under the owner's supervision) was the makers' attention to the banjo's "QUALITY AND POWER OF TONE," as well as the "Variety of Designs" they could offer, the "Beauty and Finish of [their] Workmanship," the "Number of Improvements of Real Importance" to the instrument, and the "General Excellence" of the final product, precisely the same criteria, in other words, on which the partners had challenged Stewart in 1880. Indeed, in this catalog—issued a decade after their challenge to the Philadelphia maker—they reprinted the whole of that challenge as it had appeared in the *New York Clipper*. This earlier notice, they claimed, had proved two things: *"that we thought we could make the best Banjo for the lowest price,"* and that *"all other makers were of the opinion that we really did."* Fairbanks and Cole's instruments, they concluded, now were unique because the partners were "not in competition with anyone" and only sought "to sell good goods every time."

And so they did. By producing instruments over whose every detail various craftsmen lavished much time and care, Fairbanks and Cole set a new standard in the industry for what we might term the "artistic" banjo. Along with close attention to the playability of their instruments (which had, Fairbanks and Cole claimed, "an absolutely correct scale" and "the easiest action of any make"), such detail as the French polish of the banjos' necks, the colorful marquetry on their rims, and, perhaps most striking, the elegance of the African snail and mother-of-pearl inlay in the ebony fingerboards of the higher-grade models distinctively marked Fairbanks and Cole's work.

This catalog also illustrated the firm's attempt, through the variety of their banjos' styles and models, to appeal to the same wide spectrum of the market at which Stewart aimed. Fairbanks and Cole regarded everyone from the rank beginner to the amateur banjo club musician to the professional stage performer as a potential customer. In 1889, for example, the bottom of their line was represented by their Class A models, selling from $10 to $30 and coming with an eleven-inch rim, in some cases veneered in rosewood and on other models, spun with German silver. They made these Class A models in any size rim from eight to fourteen inches, with necks from ten to twenty-one inches in length—everything from piccolo to cello banjo size, in other words. Finally, as raised frets became more accepted, they could be had (of ivory) for $3 extra on those models that sold for $25 or more.

Fairbanks and Cole also offered, in ascending order of sophistication, Acme, Standard, and Champion grades, which likewise could be customized in a variety of ways. They intended the Acme, for example, to meet "the growing demand for a medium-priced banjo made by a responsible house." They were most proud, however, of their Expert line, which had a novel rim laminated from five "heavy layers of selected old maple" and then spun with German silver, an improvement that they claimed kept such rims "perfectly round." These instruments, which cost from $28 to

$75 (and up to $90 for beautifully inlaid silver- or gold-plated models), embodied "all the needed improvements" to which these makers' experience "of many years devoted to the perfection of the banjo" had led. Indeed, Fairbanks and Cole added, "owing to the expense of producing this style of banjo," they reserved it for their "best retail trade" and so allowed "*no discount to any one under any circumstances.*"

When Fairbanks and Cole spoke of their "original improvements" to the banjo, they had in mind not only their laminated rim but also one that came to be called "half-spun," that is, with German silver extending over only one-half to two-thirds of the wood rim. They had introduced this design, they explained, three years earlier in some work done for their "fine custom trade" and now felt confident enough to offer the improvement to the general public in a line of instruments they called the Imperial. In addition to providing a contrast between the wood and metal that was "pleasing to the eye," this unusual rim, they claimed, greatly improved the tone of the instrument.

The Imperial also sported another innovation, a fingerboard that extended over the front of the rim, to allow "a clear and correct tone to the twenty-second fret," a full three octaves.[22] So confident were they in this banjo's potential appeal—they believed that the three-octave banjo was "destined to become very popular"—that they allowed customers to have it on a one-month trial. If the Imperial was not satisfactory, they promised, a customer could trade it for any instrument in their line of equal price. Slanting the Imperial's appeal to different segments of the trade, Fairbanks and Cole also offered a Lady Imperial size and a Professional grade, which could be had for $25 to $50. Finally, at the top of the line, for $75 a customer might choose Le Grande Imperial, with a twelve-and-a-half-inch rim and handsome decoration.

As Stewart had angrily noted, Fairbanks and Cole, building on the popularity of banjeaurines with the rapidly multiplying banjo clubs and orchestras, also made their own version of this specialty instrument (to distinguish it from Stewart's, they eventually termed it a "banjorine"), which they offered in several grades, from $20 upwards to $35 for an Imperial, noting as well that they would furnish any banjo in their catalog with a banjorine neck "at the same price" (fig. 4-9). In addition, they sold a large selection of rim hardware, skin heads, and other "extra fittings," including their "patent combination bar tail-piece," which they had registered in 1886, and their sewn leather cases, similarly protected.[23] Finally, they issued a limited amount of banjo music, some written and arranged by Cole and other compositions assembled from the entries in "prize" competitions that they had sponsored, which were judged anonymously by the eminent

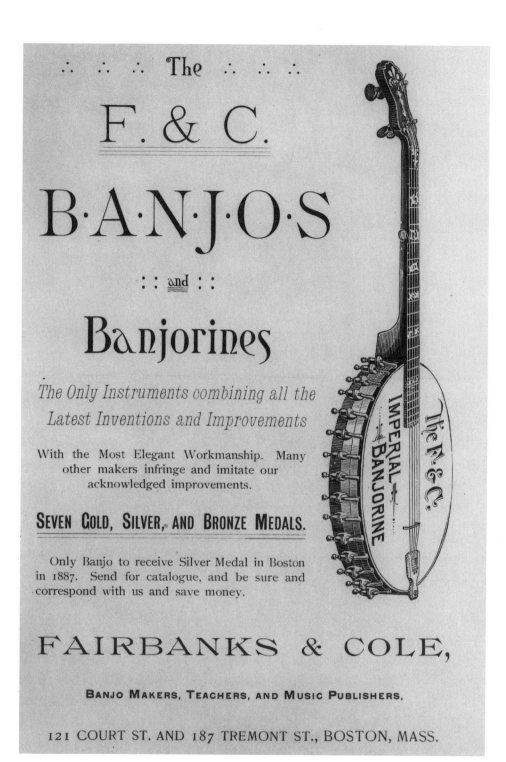

Figure 4-9. Advertisement for Fairbanks and Cole banjos, ca. 1888. Like Stewart, Fairbanks and Cole made their banjos in a variety of models and grades. This banjorine, as they spelled it to distinguish the instrument from Stewart's, features the half-spun metal and wood rim that marked their Imperial-grade instruments.

banjoists Albert Baur and John H. Lee.[24] Their sheet-music enterprise however, never rivaled Stewart's.

Fairbanks and Cole closed their catalog with two pages of "testimonials" to their instruments from players all over the country and another page of over a hundred names of those whose words they did not have room to include but who also endorsed their banjos. One of the testimonials, a reprint of a column in the *New York Clipper* for 12 May 1883, is particularly important as an indication of the popularity of their earlier banjos, which were described in some detail. "The Clipper Banjo," the editor reported, "the new instrument just put in the market" by Fairbanks and Cole, "carries the mark of eight patent applications" (some of which we have noted and others of which are contained in the same patent documents already reviewed):

> The hooks are oval on the face and have a flat surface on the back where they come in contact with the hoop. The hoop has a groove at the side to hold the hooks. The metallic bottom to the rim, which strengthens it and proves quite ornamental, is made of German silver, nickel-plated. They also direct special attention to the brace holding the neck and rim together; to the improved way of making holes in the tail-piece; and to the combination cap-nut and protector, in which there is no liability to twist the thread, and which, while it is ornamental, is also useful in protecting the clothes, and to the screw-attached bracket.

"In workmanship and finish," the *Clipper* concluded, "the banjo can certainly be admired, and to the ear it commends itself by its round, full tone." Building strongly on such praise, by the decade's end Fairbanks and Cole, even if they never approached Stewart's volume of instruments, clearly had established themselves as among the nation's most prominent makers.

For some reason, however, about 1890 Fairbanks and Cole dissolved their partnership and proceeded to manufacture banjos under their separate names (fig. 4-10). Earlier that year the two men had joined with Charles A. Sanborn, an organ builder, to manufacture bicycles, another of the period's popular new items, but in 1891 Cole left that partnership, too, probably as a result of his estrangement from Fairbanks. In any event, as the decade opened, customers of Fairbanks and Cole who went to the firm's address at 178 Tremont Street (originally the site of Cole's studio, but after 1887 the firm's headquarters) found only Fairbanks's sign—and were treated to the sight of Cole's across the street, at 179 Tremont.[25]

In the next decade Fairbanks actually left the company as he diversified his business interests. In 1894, for example, he founded the Fairbanks

Figure 4–10. Trade card for A. C. Fairbanks and Company, ca. 1893, after Fairbanks's separation from Cole. Fairbanks evidently was still using the Fairbanks and Cole label for its name recognition. Some of his banjos from the early 1890s are double-stamped on the dowel, with both "A. C. Fairbanks & Co." and "Fairbanks & Cole."

Wood Rim Company to make bicycle wheels. He moved to New York two years later, where he built another bicycle factory, and then to Pennsylvania, before returning to Boston about 1900. Throughout this period his banjo factory continued to prosper, however, in large measure because he had had the good sense to retain the services of David L. Day, who had been with him at Fairbanks and Cole since 1883 and became the chief technical designer at the new company (fig. 4-11). Incorporating in 1893 as the A. C. Fairbanks Company (after two years as A. C. Fairbanks), over the decade the firm became arguably the nation's premier banjo manufactory.

Its success was based in large measure on a new rim that Fairbanks patented in 1890, for this innovation defined the company's finest banjos for the next two decades.[26] He called the line of instruments fitted with this device the Electric.[27] In his patent description of the new design Fairbanks noted that the usual wood-and-metal construction of rims did not allow "sufficient vibration to enable the instrument to give out a clear bell-like tone." Thus, he designed his new banjo with a scalloped metal truss on top of the rim, and a smaller brass rod atop that, over which the skin head was then stretched. The open spaces between the "truss-bosses,"

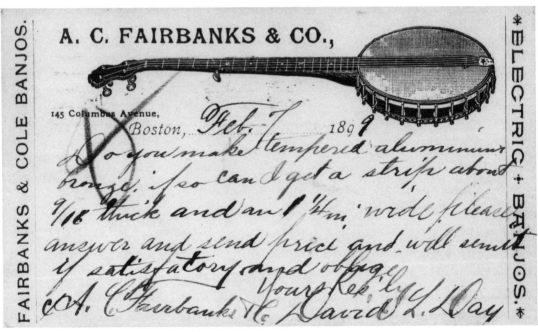

Figure 4-11. Postcard from A. C. Fairbanks and Company, 7 February 1899, to the Pittsburgh Reduction Company, signed by its chief designer, David L. Day, who was responsible for most of the firm's important technological innovations. Note that the card still lists "Fairbanks & Cole Banjos" at this late date. The addressee suggests how far afield the Fairbanks company had to go to secure the materials—in this case, "tempered aluminum bronze"—for its rims.

he observed, permit "vibration" of the rod, "increasing the sound much more than if a solid band of metal were combined with the wooden hoop" (fig. 4–12). In another version of the design described in the same patent, he suspended the brass rod over the wooden rim on metal studs for a similar effect, a design that became known as the Curtis Electric, named after Fairbanks's son, himself a prominent banjoist (fig. 4–13). Much more elegant and easier to construct than the banjo Fairbanks had patented five years earlier, the Electric soon was the talk of the banjo world, its tone as brilliant and resonant as its inventor claimed (figure 4–14). As Fairbanks put it in one of his early advertisements, the Electric possesses "great VOLUME and [the] sweetest QUALITY of TONE, especially in the higher register."[28]

This instrument spelled the end of Stewart's supremacy, for players at all levels could easily distinguish the differences in tone between these makers' banjos. Thus, by 1893, with business on the rise, Fairbanks again moved his operations, to numbers 25, 27, and 29 Beach Street, and there began to manufacture a wide range of banjos. His less expensive models ranged from the inexpensive Special (made in six grades, from 0 to 5) to the Senator and the Regent. In addition, to mark the World's Columbian Exhibition in 1892, he issued the Columbian. All of these models could be had in various grades, as could the Electrics, which ranged from 00 and 0 through 6, though there was inexplicably no Electric No. 4. Most instruments that carried the half-spun rim that Fairbanks and Cole had developed as well as the new scalloped tone ring were termed, aptly, Imperial Electrics. Another model, the Special Electric, sometimes carried the same half-spun rim but frequently had the tone ring installed upside down (fig. 4–15).[29]

All Fairbanks banjos from this decade, but most notably the higher grade Electrics, were characterized by remarkable elegance and attention to detail, particularly in the hardware and the pearl engraving. Without doubt the most spectacular of all the firm's instruments were custom-made "presentation" banjos, unique pieces made upon a customer's request. In addition to sometimes having the metal parts of the rim engraved in floral designs, for example, and fashioning the tuning pegs and tailpiece from ivory that itself was carved, Fairbanks's presentation-grade instruments exhibited extraordinary pearl inlay in the neck and peg head (plates 4–3, 4–4, 4–5, 4–6, 4–7). Fanciful animal-like inlays such as griffins, eagles, peacocks, lions, dolphins, and even a heron, standing in a marshy pond with a snake in its beak, were found on these instruments, the full length of the ebony fingerboard filled with pearl designs. The craftsmen who did such stunning work unfortunately remain unknown, but their artistry in this medium was matchless (plate 4–8).[30]

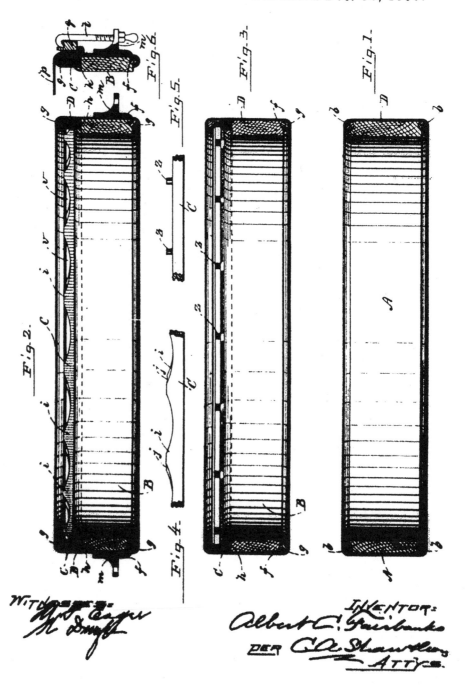

Figure 4-12. Patent drawing, 30 December 1890, by David L. Day for the Electric tone ring found on high-grade Fairbanks instruments. This device, which proved to be one of the most important developed by the firm, produced a tone that most contemporary players considered unrivaled, particularly when, after 1901, it was installed on Whyte Laydie models. Note the distinctive scallops to the tone ring. The name has nothing to do with electricity; it was probably used because of its association with one of the signal technologies of the period.

Figure 4-13. Photograph, ca. 1890s, of Curtis Fairbanks, after whom his father named one of the versions of the Electric banjo developed in 1890. Here, however, he holds a custom-grade Imperial Electric (serial no. 5244), which has a standard, not Curtis, Electric tone ring. The banjo features a carved heel and unusual inlays—a series of engraved stars and a mandolin crossed by something like a riding crop on the fingerboard and peg head.

right

Figure 4-14. Photograph, ca. 1895, of concert banjoist with a beautifully made Fairbanks Electric No. 5 or 6 banjo. During the 1890s this was the country's most highly regarded instrument.

The growing popularity of Fairbanks's banjos in this period is indicated by the fact that the firm frequently built instruments for other firms or individuals who in turn sold them to their own customers, presumably at some profit. In the early 1890s, for example, the well-known Boston instructor Gad Robinson, after having had a few instruments made for him by O. R. Chase, contracted with Gatcomb to make instruments that he then stamped with his own name, but he soon switched allegiance to Fairbanks. Around 1900 Fred Martin, another noted teacher who endorsed Fairbanks instruments, sold the firm's banjos from his music studio at 264 Tremont Street with his own name plate on them, even though these instruments carried Fairbanks's model designations and continued the firm's serial numbers sequentially (fig. 4-16). H. C. Barnes, owner of an-

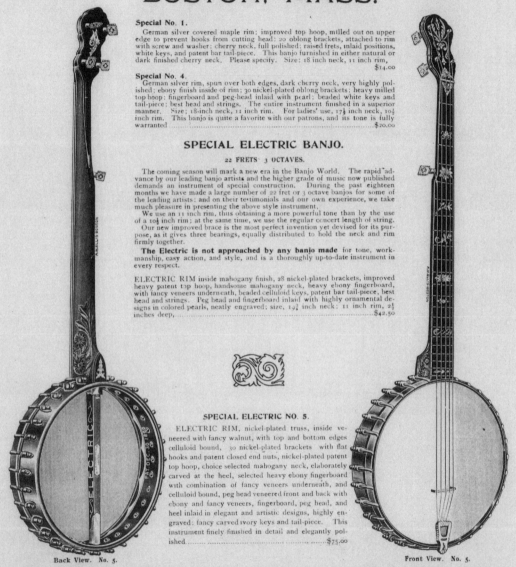

Figure 4-15. Advertisement, ca. 1897, for the Special Electric No. 5, the fanciest regularly cataloged model made by the firm. Note the beautifully carved heel, the German silver appointments on the dowel, and the elaborate peg head inlay.

other Boston music store, also contracted with Fairbanks to produce banjos under that store's name.

The reputation of Fairbanks's instruments spread to other cities as well (fig. 4-17). In Minneapolis and St. Paul, Minnesota, for example, the firm of J. W. Dyer and Brother stamped banjos built by the Boston maker with the name J. F. Stetson (presumably a music store owner or perhaps a prominent player). Made with an unusual rim—with spun metal sheathing inside as well as outside the thin wood—that also is found on some Fairbanks-marked banjos of the 1890s, these instruments frequently carried the same elaborately engraved pearl work found on Fairbanks's high grade models, although without the Electric tone ring they were acoustically inferior (plates 4-9, 4-10).[31] An 1896 catalog from J. W. Pepper of Philadelphia also shows about a dozen Fairbanks-made models, priced from $5 to $20, obviously intended to compete with Stewart's instruments at the lower end of the market. Unfortunately, we do not have any information about the financial arrangements between Fairbanks and such parties, but clearly they believed that what he was building, at the high or low end of the market, was worth selling to their own customers.[32]

Despite the popularity of Fairbanks's Electric, however, as well as the

STUDIO 38 SHAWMUT AV.

20 YEARS

TEACHING A SPECIALTY

INSTRUMENTS AT FACTORY PRICES

BANJO, MANDOLIN, GUITAR

ALL LESSONS PRIVATE

FIRST TEN LESSONS . . . $5.00
ADVANCED LESSONS . . . 7.50

TELEPHONE OXFORD

[OVER]

PROF. FRED MARTIN
LEADING TEACHER

Figure 4-16. Advertising card, ca. 1895, for the Boston banjo teacher Fred Martin, who contracted with A. C. Fairbanks and Company to have some of its banjos marked with his own name. Several other local instructors, as well as music dealers in Boston and other cities, had such arrangements with the firm.

Figure 4-17. Photograph of Teresa Vaughan, ca. 1895, playing a Fairbanks Electric No. 2 banjo. The beauty of such instruments made them popular throughout this country and in England.

interest other makers had in offering his line of instruments to supplement and boost their own, Fairbanks did not attain his greatest success until the new century, when in 1901 he introduced what proved to be his most popular model, the Whyte Laydie, so named because both neck and rim were of unstained maple, a light-colored wood. The technological hallmark of this banjo, made with a standard Electric tone ring, lay in its ingenious bracket band, which fitted around the rim of the banjo and eliminated the need for holes drilled through the rim to accommodate the shoe bolts (fig. 4-18). Oddly, despite the rapid and widespread popularity of this banjo, Day did not patent this improvement until 1909, when he was employed by the Vega Company, the successor to Fairbanks's firm.[33]

As the popularity of his bracket band attests, Day clearly was the mechanical genius of the firm.[34] In his patent description, for example, he explained that "the mode of restraining the head of a banjo" constituted "an important element in determining its tone efficiency." And the common manner of attaching the hooks, through shoes that were attached by bolts through the rim, was most "inexpedient" because every hole made in the banjo shell "detracts from its tone and value." Further, atmospheric changes that affected the wood of the rim, causing it to shrink or expand, created instability in the tensioning devices; when they were so loosened, he observed, the banjo sounded "a dry, metallic tone." Day addressed these problems by maintaining the rim's strength and integrity. Specifically, he attached the shoes to a metal hoop that was then fitted tightly over the rim and was prevented from moving by an annular groove cut in it. "A banjo fitted with the mode of fastening described," he concluded, "develops and maintains under all conditions tones not only of great brilliancy and ring but also tones that are resonant and sustaining, full of volume and of great carrying power."

And so it did, as the instant popularity of the Whyte Laydie attested. As Fairbanks put it in his ads for the new instrument, this banjo quickly became "the Sensation of the Banjo World." "The combination of wood and metal," one advertisement noted, "has been calculated so finely that the wonderful tone produced is a marvel to all." When one added to this "the eliminating of the boring of the holes through the rim for the brackets," the "benefit" for the "tone and artistic construction" was "very pronounced" and offered a "distinct advance in the development of the banjo."[35]

Fairbanks chose to sell the Whyte Laydie in three models: a fairly plain No. 2; a fancy No. 7, with a carved heel, elaborate inlays, multiple wood veneers under the ebony fingerboard, and fancy wooden rim marquetry; and a Deluxe, of which only a handful seem to have been built (fig. 4-19). The No. 7 model essentially replaced the No. 5 and No. 6 Electric models at the top of the catalog line. As with most of his other banjos, though, Fairbanks also offered the Whyte Laydie in a variety of rim sizes and scale lengths, and it was also produced as a banjeaurine, a piccolo banjo, and a contrabass. Boosted by frequent testimonials in *The Cadenza*, which had superseded Stewart's and Gatcomb's journals as the periodical of record for stringed instrument aficionados, the new banjo's popularity was assured on both sides of the Atlantic.[36] Even *The Cadenza*'s editor, C. L. Partee, publicly commented on the instrument's success. "Vess Ossman, the noted banjo artist," Partee wrote in August 1902, "is now using the 'Whyte Laydie' banjos," and "the same can truthfully be said concerning many of the most prominent artists and soloists."[37] Thus, in the early years of the twentieth century, with Stewart out of the picture and Fairbanks's new banjo acquiring new endorsements with each passing week, the A. C. Fairbanks Company proudly claimed that it made the finest instruments in America.

In the meantime, Fairbanks's one-time partner, William A. Cole, had established his own firm, superintended by his brother, Frank (1855–1922), a cabinetmaker. Through the 1890s Cole ran the business at 179 Tremont Street, but in the early twentieth century, presumably as the business expanded, he moved to 220 Tremont, and then to 788 Washington Street, still in the city's main business district, where he also turned out guitars and Imperial mandolins. Like Fairbanks, in addition to offering lower-grade instruments, Cole developed an important line of sophisticated banjos, marketed under the name Eclipse.[38]

Developed in the early 1890s, this design received a patent on 30 January 1894, with Frank Cole, now a junior partner in the concern, designated as the inventor.[39] Still attempting to draw better tones from the instrument, like so many contemporary banjo makers (and particularly like Fairbanks, his brother's erstwhile partner and now rival), Frank focused his attention on the rim. Beginning with the half-spun design that Fairbanks had popularized on many of his Imperial Electrics around the time of the partners' breakup, Cole "improved" the sound of his banjos by the

opposite
Figure 4-18. Photograph of renowned banjoist and banjo designer Fred Bacon, ca. 1904. He holds an early example of a Fairbanks Whyte Laydie No. 7 banjo, introduced a few years earlier. Note the carved ivory fifth-string peg and the distinctive fingerboard and peg head inlay, deeply and beautifully engraved. The banjo's most distinctive feature, not visible here, is a bracket band attached to the rim through which the tension hooks fit. Thus, there were no holes drilled through the rim, allowing a finer sound.

Figure 4-19. Photograph of a group of working men, ca. 1905, one of whom holds a Fairbanks Whyte Laydie No. 7 banjo, its distinctive inlays clearly visible. In the first decade of the twentieth century, this banjo was considered by many to be the finest instrument one could buy.

placement of approximately thirty thin metal rods atop a wire ring that sat where the wood was cut away from the rim for the metal to fit over it. On top of these rods was another ring, with the skin head pulled over it. As Frank Cole described his design, "The rods are held in contact with the rings at each end by the binding action of the sleeve," and the "contact of the wires and rings thus obtained materially improves the effectiveness of the banjo" (fig. 4-20).

This kind of rim did indeed improve the banjo's sound, and through the late 1890s and early twentieth century Cole widely advertised his innovation, touting the Eclipse as "the sweetest loud-toned banjo made."[40] One advertisement in particular spelled out what he believed to be the nature of his success. Reciting the "Evolution of the Banjo," Cole observed that at

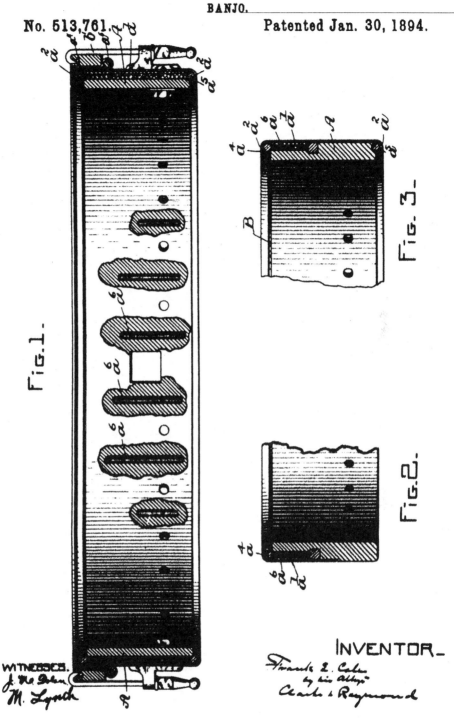

Figure 4-20. Patent drawing by Frank Cole for a banjo tone ring, 30 January 1894. Intended to compete with Fairbanks's Electric, this tone ring, found on William A. Cole's Eclipse banjos, made his firm competitive with his former partner's.

first instruments had been made with all wood rims, but such banjos never had been satisfactory because of their "dull, muffled tone." The next step was the improvement on which Stewart had capitalized, thin metal rims spun over wood, which were "somewhat more brilliant" in tone but finally, Cole wrote, "hard and lacking of a true tonal quality." Then followed all-metal rims, with their "disagreeable, tin-pan sound—metallic in quality." "The great desire," he concluded, "was to get a banjo with a strong, brilliant tone, yet with a musical resonant quality," and the Eclipse was the answer. "By combining wood and metal in such a manner," Cole wrote, "that the vibration from the head passes first to metal, then through wood, which takes off the rasping sound of the metal, and allows a strong, brilliant tone," he offered the public what he claimed was the best sounding banjo yet made.[41]

Cole's instruments did have more volume and richness of tone than, say, Stewart's, but they did not equal those of Fairbanks's Electric, the banjo Cole clearly viewed as his main competition. Nonetheless, during the 1890s, in large measure because of the Eclipse, Cole's company ran head-to-head with Fairbanks for the patronage of America's musical elite in Boston and around the country (plate 4-11). These banjos, which featured laminated maple half-spun rims that by the early twentieth century were treated by the company's "vibrant dryer" (a solution that gave the wood a uniform tonal value), also had a characteristic pointed heel design that looked like the prow and keel of a ship, as well as a device (into which the end of the dowel fit) for regulating the neck's angle relative to the rim.[42]

Cole's banjos came in a variety of grades to rival Fairbanks's and Stewart's various offerings. By the early twentieth century, for example, he manufactured five Eclipse models: the 2500, with an engraved star in the peg head, for $37.50; the 3000, with a distinctive man-in-the-moon inlay, at $46.25; the 3500, or Professional, with fancy peg head inlay and multiple veneers under the finger board, for $55; the 4000, with a beautiful butterfly inlaid at the fifth fret, for $63.75; and the 5000, with inlay like that on the 4000, but with a flat, carved heel and multiple veneers under the bound finger board, for $85.[43] In addition, Cole produced a few presentation models. These instruments, which featured wonderfully worked, long-toothed gargoyles carved into their heels, profusely inlaid peg heads, elaborate fingerboard inlays, carved peg head edges, and multiple rim inlays between the bracket shoes, equaled Fairbanks's own custom instruments for their striking beauty (plates 4-12, 4-13, 4-14).

Like Fairbanks, Cole soon found that other firms wanted him to build banjos for them, and thus we find both his Eclipses and his sub-Eclipse models, which had full-spun rims of German silver and a flat heel with a veneered cap, in the catalogs of other companies. Cole's work has appeared, for example, in an instrument offered by Charles Bobzin of Detroit (in the early 1890s), and in Elias Howe's advertisements as the Superbo line, as well as in instruments sold by W. E. Stratton, a longtime music teacher, and his business partner, J. A. Handley, who operated in Lowell, Massachusetts.[44]

The better grades of Cole banjos, and in particular the custom Eclipse models, were among the most beautiful and carefully constructed banjos ever made. Cole's carvings, inlay, and engraving, and his beautifully crafted rim hardware—most Eclipse models, for example, have elegant two-pointed bracket shoes, almost like teardrops—have never been surpassed by other makers. Fairbanks banjos of the same period, with their more sophisticated tone-ring designs, finally must be considered more satisfying acoustically, but certainly they were no lovelier than those crafted by Cole's workers. As C. L. Partee testified in 1902, W. A. Cole, the "manufacturer of the Eclipse Banjos, Imperial Mandolins and Boston Guitars," has "enjoyed a successful trade for a great many years and produces goods of the highest quality." "Thousands of professionals throughout America and Europe," he continued, use Cole instruments and are "enthusiastic concerning their merits" (fig. 4-21).[45]

By the turn of the century, though, William was devoting more time to his performances with the Imperial Quartet and Mexican Serenaders—and, after 1908, with the Boston Trio, which he formed with F. T. McGrath and Walter F. Vreeland—often traveling with them several months of the year. Consequently, Frank handled more and more of the company's daily concerns, and upon his brother's death on 2 July 1909 he assumed full control of the firm. The following year he relocated the factory (which had been at 67 Pitt Street at least since 1900) to 3 Appleton Street, on the corner of Tremont. Frank continued to oversee the business until early in 1922, when he was forced by poor health to sell it to Nokes and Nicolai, a drum making firm.[46]

When Frank Cole died on 19 July of that year at his summer home in Nova Scotia, one eulogist noted in particular his exceptional skill in adjusting fretted instruments and credited him with the idea for the company's unique neck-regulating device (never patented) and with the design of a five-footed bridge (rather than the more normal two-footed model), which increased the banjo's tone and volume significantly.[47] Although never attaining the popular success as a performer that his brother enjoyed, Frank also was remembered as a good musician, particularly in his younger years, and for having trained his three young sons (who eventually performed as the Cole Children) as very fine musicians. His greatest

legacy, however, was the Cole Eclipse and, more generally, his commitment to building instruments by consistently professional standards.

During the period when Fairbanks and Cole were sparring for supremacy in America's banjo culture, Lincoln Gatcomb continued his own important efforts to popularize and improve the instrument. Like Stewart, early on he had begun to publish banjo music, and at about the same time that he introduced his journal, he relocated from 48 to 30 Hanover Street, enlarging his facilities and putting in "extra machinery" to help him keep up with his burgeoning orders (fig. 4-22).[48] He also maintained a teaching studio at 58 Winter Street, a venue he shared with such prominent area musicians as H. W. Harris, Bert E. Shattuck, and George L. Lansing, who with A. D. Grover and L. H. Galeucia made up the renowned Boston Ideal Banjo, Mandolin and Guitar Club, and all of whom touted his banjos.[49] Gatcomb was particularly proud of this location, informing his readers that "the building is entirely new and furnished in the most luxurious manner, including electric lights, steam heat, an elegant elevator, and handsomely tinted walls and ceilings."[50] By the early 1890s, with Fairbanks and Cole parting ways to establish their own firms, Gatcomb's prospects improved, so much so that he opened a new plant at 15 Chardon Street and increased his workforce.

Although we have no detailed descriptions of the factory operations of either Fairbanks or Cole, on a couple of occasions in the late 1880s Gatcomb allowed "contributors" to speak of his own facilities (in this regard following Stewart's lead). In a piece called "What a Contributor Says of the Banjo," for example, one "H.W.P." described a "modern factory" (transparently Gatcomb's) and noted in particular how instruments there were produced by a combination of highly skilled handcraftsmanship and sophisticated machinery. The author did not have time, he wrote, to take the reader "through a tour of [the] ten or a dozen departments" of which the factory was comprised but rather "invite[d]" him into "an enormous room with ample accommodations in the way of the latest improvements in machinery, peculiarly adapted to this line of business, that the human mind can devise." Such inventions enabled Gatcomb to so "reduce the cost of time and labor" that he could produce "a beautiful instrument" at a price "which other concerns cannot rival."

opposite
Figure 4-21. Photograph of young girl, ca. 1894, holding an Eclipse model banjo made by William A. Cole. This instrument has a flying bird engraved in the peg head and is a particularly beautiful model that was produced for a few years around the time that Cole patented his Eclipse tone ring. Collection of Philip F. Gura.

VOL. I, No. I.   SEPTEMBER, 1887.   SINGLE COPY, 10 CENTS.

THE BANJO.

Probably no musical instrument has ever had to fight its way through such bitter antagonism as the BANJO, and the fact that it has become the most popular instrument in refined society should set at rest the mind of the most fastidious.

Foremost among those who have waged war against the BANJO, are the teachers of other instruments; the reason is obvious, recently however, we find not a few Pianists. Violinists, etc., looking into the rudiments of BANJO playing with a view to teaching.

It is now often heard in the most select concerts, always receiving the approval of the audience.

Banjo Orchestras are employed frequently to furnish music for Germans, Sociables, etc. So much for its popularity.

In regard to the merits of the BANJO, we would say in the first place, it is not difficult to learn to play. It is easily carried from place to place, and possesses two distinct characters; one, the soft plaintive tones of the Guitar and Zither, the other, those brilliant wide-awake strains which put life into a social gathering, and renewed vigor into the most sedate. In this respect it has no equal.

The BANJO is strictly an American instrument, and as its popularity is spreading in other countries, we may justly take great pride in our favorite instrument.

G. L. L.

THE GUITAR.

Who has not heard the soft rich tones of this beautiful instrument? Wherever or whenever it is played, it exerts a charm which is irresistible. The greatest writers of poetry and prose have accorded it their praises and gratitude. The minstrel of old has endorsed it to us by his serenades to his fair lady under her balcony, and hardly

any novelist would write of Spain without mentioning the "twang of the soft Guitar." As an accompaniment to the voice it is without an equal; its tone is beautiful and plaintive, and also full and strong when desired, while the deep resonance and power of the bass renders it the instrument above all others to use as an accompaniment to the Banjo or Mandolin.

The American Guitars have proved themselves superior to the foreign in the severest test, viz: resistance to climatic influence. A foreign instrument after being in this country a short time will crack and become nearly useless, it being made of beautiful woods indigenous to their own soft climate, but not adapted to the rigors of our winters.

THE MANDOLIN.

This instrument, according to the best authorities, belongs to the lute species, and the lute originated from the ancient lyre. Some think the lute was introduced into Spain by the Moors, where it was called "laoud," and from thence into Italy, where it was called "liuto." The "chelys" or "testudo" of the Romans was, probably, a similar instrument.

Thus, in the MANDOLIN, we are writing of a musical instrument which claims kindred with the first in use among humanity, before musical signs were known, a lineage to be proud of.

It has but recently been taken up in this country to any extent, but the constantly increasing interest and delight which it evokes is a sure indication that it is destined to become as popular here as in Italy or Spain.

Many persons have but a slight and imperfect knowledge of the MANDOLIN, and

the object of the writer will be accomplished if, in the following description, (which must necessarily be brief in a small article,) they may get a fair idea of it.

The body of the MANDOLIN is shaped like a shell or half a pear, formed of a number of pieces of wood, bent into the shape and glued together. On the open portion of the body is fixed the sounding board, and the neck or arm is fastened to the smaller end like a guitar.

The NEAPOLITAN MANDOLIN, which is the most perfect, has four double strings which are tuned like the violin, beginning with the lowest to G, D, A, E. The sound is produced by a plectrum which is generally a triangular shaped piece of tortoise shell, in the right hand, while the left hand produces the notes on the finger board.

It possesses all the range of the violin without the difficulties of the same. In fact the MANDOLIN is easier than the Banjo to acquire. The scale is very easy and the right hand work with the plectrum can be mastered in a very few lessons

The tone is beautiful and quivering, and totally unlike any other instrument. When played with a guitar or piano forte accompaniment, it makes delightful music.

The instrument aside from its tone is singularly beautiful, and together with the halo of old age and romance which surrounds it, is one which any person would do well to become acquainted with.

From time to time in the coming numbers of this Journal, we shall endeavor to acquaint our readers of all that is being published for the MANDOLIN, together with information concerning the best teachers, prices of instruments, etc.

L. H. G.

Figure 4–22. Cover of *Gatcomb's Banjo and Guitar Gazette* 1, no. 1 (September 1887), featuring a woodcut of the proprietor. Obviously patterned after Stewart's offering, in the late 1880s Gatcomb's periodical did for the Boston area what Stewart's did for Philadelphia.

But equally important, in such a modern factory "every person employed in his particular line is a master workman, and . . . nothing but the best work is recognized." Consequently, "this is a place," the writer continued, "where a specialty of order and fine work is accomplished" and where "every part of the banjo is made in their shop," making every part "interchangeable."[51] Indeed, despite all the machinery, "constructed at great expense" for the specific tasks at hand and not found "in any other factory," visitors would be most impressed by the degree of handwork still required in such manufacture. All the labor, another correspondent reported, is done "by men who throughout understand their work."

He noted, for example, how Gatcomb's workers painstakingly produced sectional wooden rims by veneering thin strips of maple, each with the grain running in the opposite direction from the one next to it, to increase the rim's strength. All the "handles" (that is, necks), too, were still shaped by hand, work that required "an experienced eye to get one [handle] down to a proper degree of fineness." Another worker then fit the neck to the rim, "perfectly true and tight," and passed on the assembly, first to a "polisher" and then to a worker who "strings it and fits the pegs." Finally, before the banjos were sold, they were "severely criticized by the foreman." If any instrument is "found lacking in any respect," it is "sold out to store trade or as a job lot."

Gatcomb's operation, with its combination of cost-efficient steam-powered machinery and fine handcraftsmanship, epitomized the ways in which the city's fine makers produced their instruments, and in the early 1890s he clearly built his banjos to compete with the likes of Fairbanks's and Cole's products. Gatcomb, for example, issued standard models priced from $10 to $100, including the Student, Amateur, Standard, Lansing, Special, and Peerless.[52] Moreover, his fanciest models displayed the same copious inlay work and the elegantly carved heels that identified the city's finest banjo work, although the pearl inlays were not generally engraved (plate 4-15). And although Gatcomb himself never secured any patents, he was not averse to technological innovation. On some of his models, for example, he offered the Little Gem arm adjuster, a cam-type device developed and patented by Bostonian Bert Shattuck that allowed for adjustment of the angle of the neck to the rim.[53]

Beginning in 1891, Gatcomb also made the Robinson banjo for the well-known teacher and performer Gad Robinson, a fixture in Boston's music scene. In that year Gatcomb told his subscribers that he had purchased the rights both to Robinson's banjo patent and to his name, and he offered three Robinson models, Nos. 30, 35, and 75.[54] These instruments, which

Gatcomb admitted were "of a different order" than his own, featured all-metal rims and Robinson's patented tone ring, which was scalloped and sat unattached on top of the rim, held in place by the downward pressure of the tension hoop. Robinson's association with Gatcomb was brief, however.[55] As we have noted, a few years later he contracted with Fairbanks to build his banjos, perhaps because by that time Fairbanks's reputation had clearly outdistanced his rivals'. In any event, Gatcomb continued to produce banjos at least through 1897, now at 171A Tremont Street, and advertised them prominently on the back cover of his journal.[56]

After that point, however, as Fairbanks's and Cole's products gained ever more recognition, he evidently ceased to manufacture instruments and listed himself in city directories as a music publisher. Thus, it is fair to say that, despite the beauty of some of his banjos and, particularly in the mid-1890s, the virtuoso George Lansing's strong support for them, it was through *Gatcomb's Banjo and Guitar Gazette* (later called *Gatcomb's Musical Gazette*) that Gatcomb exercised his greatest influence on the professionalization of Boston's stringed instrument trade. The city had needed such a journal to unite its many instrument makers, and his filled the task very well. As one national music journal put it, as "more attention is being paid to the study of the banjo, *Gatcomb's Musical Gazette* . . . has had a great deal to do with putting the banjo on a higher plane." And, despite what S. S. Stewart might have said about such presumption, another report, this time from the nation's capital, explicitly linked Boston and fine banjos in its praise of Gatcomb's periodical: "Naturally[,] coming from the 'Hub' it is the standard publication of its class."[57]

Fairbanks, Cole, and Gatcomb were unusual in establishing their reputations primarily as banjo makers: even though the first two boosted their revenues by tapping the new market for mandolins and guitars, most customers knew them through their finely wrought banjos (plates 4-16, 4-17). In the 1890s, however, the city was home to other important banjo makers whose careers had different trajectories. That is, from making or wholesaling guitars and other instruments and publishing music, they subsequently sought an entry to banjo culture, shrewdly betting that the fever for the instrument had not yet peaked. Most prominent of these firms were Thompson and Odell, who from the early 1880s imported instruments and published music and then began manufacturing banjos (later designed by the well-known performer John F. Luscomb), and the John C. Haynes Company, which, in addition to wholesaling instruments, began to build and market them under the Bay State label. Though several other firms in the city produced banjos, in the 1890s these two firms, along with

Fairbanks, Cole, and Gatcomb, most helped to cement the city's position in the first rank of American banjo making.

The history of Thompson and Odell began in 1872, when Ira Herbert Odell (1842–1928), a native of Randolph, Massachusetts, went into business in Boston importing music and instruments and publishing music. Two years later he was in partnership at 121 Court Street with C. W. Thompson (d. 1903) and one "Woods," listed as Woods, Thompson, and Odell, "musical instrument makers," but the following year Woods left the firm, which now appeared as Thompson and Odell, 86 Tremont Street, under the same heading.[58] By the early 1880s they were at 78 Tremont Street, known as the Tremont Temple of Music; as the firm grew, it continued to relocate—in 1886 to 180 Washington Street, and a year later to number 523 on the same thoroughfare. When Ira Odell retired from active involvement with the firm in 1892, his son Herbert Forrest Odell (1872–1926), later editor of *The Crescendo* and secretary and treasurer of the American Guild of Banjoists, Mandolinists and Guitarists, took his place. The family's connections to the American Guild were solidified when the elder Odell assumed its presidency early in the new century, an honor that speaks to the continued high respect he enjoyed among Boston's stringed instrument craftsmen.[59]

As instrument makers Thompson and Odell themselves were not great innovators, and through the 1880s they seemed content to job other makers' instruments, particularly those of the Washburn Company.[60] At least since 1882, however, they also had issued banjos under their own name, and through the early 1890s they continued to tout their Artist brand, sometimes sold with a tailpiece patented by G. E. Rogers.[61] Lacking the overall elegance of the Fairbanks and Cole banjos, though, and not marked by any technological innovation, before the late 1880s their banjos remained undistinguished.

This changed, however, when they began to manufacture the Luscomb, named after John F. Luscomb, a highly regarded banjo soloist and composer who over the next decade designed several models (fig. 4-23, plates 4-18, 4-19). His first, patented in the late summer of 1888 but advertised by Thompson and Odell half a year earlier, offered a rim composed of two metal bands (inside and outside) with a third, of wood, sandwiched between them with its lip extending upward so that the skin head was stretched over it.[62] As Luscomb described his banjo, through its metal components this assembly provided the "necessary stiffness" to keep the rim from going out of shape, and because its parchment head was stretched over a band of wood, it offered "a resonant quality of tone" as well. In addition, in his patent Luscomb claimed a new method "to prevent the warping of the neck," strengthening it by placing crosspieces of wood into slots cut at different points on it. Endorsed by such leading banjoists as George L. Lansing, A. D. Grover, and L. H. Galeucia, members of the Boston Ideal Banjo Club, the Luscomb became a popular instrument.

In 1893 Luscomb refined this design on a banjo that became known as

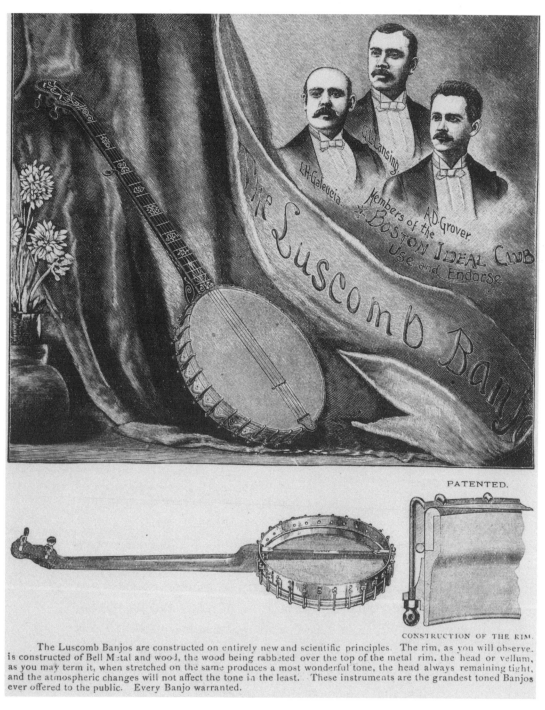

PATENTED.

CONSTRUCTION OF THE RIM.

The Luscomb Banjos are constructed on entirely new and scientific principles. The rim, as you will observe, is constructed of Bell Metal and wood, the wood being rabbeted over the top of the metal rim. the head or vellum, as you may term it, when stretched on the same produces a most wonderful tone, the head always remaining tight, and the atmospheric changes will not affect the tone in the least. These instruments are the grandest toned Banjos ever offered to the public. Every Banjo warranted.

Figure 4-23. Advertisement for Thompson and Odell's Luscomb banjo, named after a popular Boston performer and instructor, from a *Catalogue and Price List of Luscomb Banjos* (ca. 1897).

the Silver Chime.[63] A full-page advertisement in Gatcomb's journal shows a one-piece metal rim with a lip about a third of the way down on its outside, over which a wooden hoop was "rabbetted." Essentially a variation on the half-spun models that Fairbanks and Cole had made popular, like its predecessor this particular design allowed for the skin head to be stretched over wood, producing a "wonderful" tone. In addition, Thompson and Odell wrote, the head always remained tight, with changes in atmospheric conditions not affecting it in the least. "These instruments," they concluded, "are the grandest toned Banjos ever offered to the public."[64]

A few extant Luscombs were clearly presentation models, but the majority of this maker's instruments conform to standard catalog descriptions. The 1897 Thompson and Odell catalog, for example, lists the decade's standard round-back (or Neapolitan) mandolins, guitars, and sixteen different models of the firm's Artist banjos, ranging from $13.75 to $41.25. The firm sold the Luscomb in four grades, from $37.50 to $85, and offered as well three grades of banjeaurines ($42 to $60) and a piccolo with an eight-inch rim for $35.[65] Although never attaining the national and international renown of Fairbanks's and Cole's banjos, Thompson and Odell's instruments, particularly the Luscomb, were well made and justifiably popular in the last decade of the century (fig. 4-24, plates 4-20, 4-21, 4-22, 4-23).

William Nelson, the former head of the Vega Company (which at that date still had not attained prominence), reported that his company bought out Thompson and Odell in June of 1898, although both Odells continued to be highly visible in Boston's music scene through their important connections to the American Guild. In addition to editing *The Crescendo*, for example, and serving as an officer in the organization, the younger Odell remained in the music publishing business until at least 1918, operating at 165½ Tremont Street as H. F. Odell and Company.[66] The company he and his father ran for over twenty years, however, as well as their varied activities as promoters of the banjo at the beginning of a new era of its professionalization, made them an important part of Boston's banjo culture.

John C. Haynes (1825–1907), associated with the music business since the first days of minstrelsy, oversaw yet another of Boston's major banjo factories (fig. 4-25). As early as 1845 he had worked as an office boy for the Oliver Ditson Company, one of the city's largest music publishers. Oliver Ditson (1811–88) had begun to copyright and publish music as early as 1835, and by 1855 he had become "the leading American music house," as one historian puts it, eclipsing even the large New York music publishers and instrument wholesalers. During the next decade Ditson started branches of his business in other cities, most notably in Chicago in 1864, where his enterprise blossomed as Lyon and Healy. By 1867 he had invaded New York, establishing his son Charles in head-to-head competition with William Hall and Son as well as Firth, Son, and Company, both of whose catalogs and businesses the Ditsons finally acquired in the 1870s. In 1875 Ditson also marched on Philadelphia and secured the music and plates of the venerable firm of Lee and Walker four years later. In the 1880s, with outposts in so many of the nation's major cities, the Ditson firm was the country's most prominent music house, its Boston store the center of musical life in that city.[67]

Haynes grew with Ditson's enterprise. One of the firm's original two employees, in its first years he "opened and closed the shop, dusted, swept, washed windows, [and] made and stoked up the stove," besides which he "kept the stock in order, ran errands, carried bundles, and collected bills."[68] Ditson valued the young clerk's diligence and by 1852 gave him an interest in the mushrooming business. Haynes was made a codirector five years later, when the firm became Oliver Ditson and Company, and in 1865, a few years after Ditson had decided to add an instrument department, he installed Haynes over it (fig. 4-26).[69] A wholly separate operation at a different address, John C. Haynes and Company soon became one of the pre-

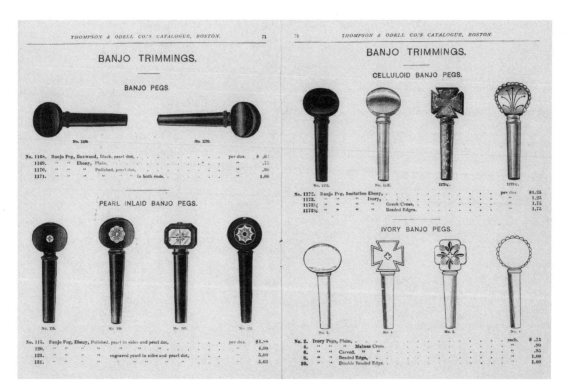

Figure 4-24. Advertisements for various "Banjo Trimmings" found in Thompson and Odell's catalog for 1897. These tuning pegs indicate how a player might customize any instrument purchased from large firms that carried a wide variety of musical paraphernalia.

mier wholesalers and, eventually, stringed instrument manufacturers in the city, making a half-million dollars annually by the century's end.[70] Indeed, Haynes himself was so highly regarded and indispensable that upon Oliver Ditson's death in 1888 he became president of that firm, a post he held until his own death in 1907.

Through the mid-1880s Haynes primarily acted as a wholesaler, making available in his retail building at 33 Court Street Henry C. Dobson's Silver Bell banjos, many of S. S. Stewart's models, and violins made by Andrew Hyde, and manufacturing William B. Tilton's patented Gold Medal guitars.[71] By 1885, however, he also had begun to market his own line of guitars and banjos, named the Excelsior. The guitars were made primarily by Pehr A. Anderberg, a Swedish-born luthier who learned his craft in Malmö before emigrating to New York City at the time of the Civil War, where he found work for the guitar wholesaler C. F. Bruno. About 1880 Anderberg settled in Somerville, Massachusetts, and began to work under contract for Haynes. Eventually, Haynes bought out his shop and hired him to oversee the firm's guitar works, which then employed about twenty-five craftsmen. Anderberg held that position until 1892, when he again went to work for himself (fig. 4-27, plates 4-24, 4-25).[72]

The Excelsior banjos were relatively unsophisticated instruments with

Figure 4-25. Portrait of John C. Haynes, from the back wrapper of the *Columbian Musical Gift and Keepsake Presented by John C. Haynes and Co.* (ca. 1889). Beginning his long career with the Oliver Ditson Company, by the 1890s Haynes was one of Boston's most highly regarded musical instrument makers.

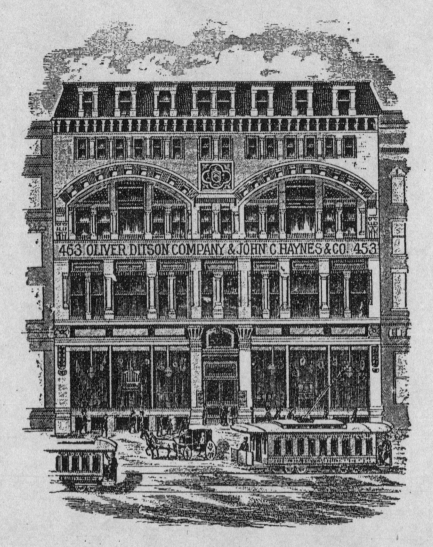

Figure 4-26. Engraving, from the same pamphlet cited in figure 4-25, of the Oliver Ditson Company's headquarters at 453–463 Washington Street, Boston, which contained a musical instrument department overseen by John C. Haynes.

Figure 4-27. Photograph, ca. 1895, of musician with a mandoline-banjo similar to those made for August Pollman by Pehr Anderberg, a Swedish-born luthier who at different times worked in the Haynes factory. Notice the shorter fifth string and the mandolin body, as well as the elegant inlay. Also see plate 4-24.

wooden rims, but no tone rings, and simple inlay patterns. By 1890, however, Haynes had established his Bay State line of stringed instruments, of which a new style of banjos formed a prominent part and with which he intended to compete against Boston's other prominent makers (fig. 4-28, plate 4-26). Bay State banjos featured full-spun German silver rims, streamlined necks, and new peg head shapes, based closely on S. S. Stewart's designs. Catalogs in the mid-1890s showed no fewer than eighteen Bay State models, priced from $15 to $112.50, and included several seven-inch piccolo banjos as well as twelve-and-a-half-inch banjeaurines. The most expensive regular style was the No. 354, with a floral-engraved rim and elaborately inlaid peg head and fingerboard. In addition to these models, Haynes made several extra-fancy presentation or "exhibition" grade instruments, including the No. 363 and No. 366 (fig. 4-29). This last was one of the most ornate banjos produced in the 1890s, featuring an inlaid rim, engraved both inside and out; a fingerboard of solid abalone inlaid with pearl designs; heel and neck carving extending to the peg head; real tortoise-shell veneers on the back strap; and the most elaborate ivory tuning pegs available. In terms of sheer decor, the No. 366 rivaled anything produced by Fairbanks, Cole, or Luscomb (plates 4-27, 4-28, 4-29, 4-30, 4-31).[73]

In addition, in the 1890s Haynes made the Lewis banjo, named after its designer, George E. Lewis. This novel instrument had an unusual one-piece metal rim construction, in which the brackets, hooks, nuts, and tailpiece hanger-bolt were affixed to a lip around the outer edge of the rim, obviating the need for bracket shoes or a tailpiece end-bolt. Advertisements for this instrument noted that the "continuous flange" around the rim "strengthen[ed]" and made "brilliant the bell-like quality of the tone." Further, it had "not the objection of other metal rim Banjos, as it [was] no heavier than the ordinary wood rim instrument." Featured in three grades—a very plain No. 1; a No. 2, with delicate vine inlay on the fingerboard; and a No. 3, an ornate model similar to the Bay State No. 354—the Lewis banjos display the continued technological experimentation by Boston's makers, but they never gained the popularity that the Bay State brand enjoyed.[74]

At the end of the century John C. Haynes and Company, with its close relationship to Oliver Ditson and Company, was Boston's largest stringed instrument manufactory—in terms of instruments produced as well as workers employed—but it still was a far cry from an immense operation like Chicago's Lyon and Healy, which by the late 1890s was distributing its George Washburn guitars, mandolins, and banjos in great numbers throughout the country (fig. 4-30). Instead, through his employment of

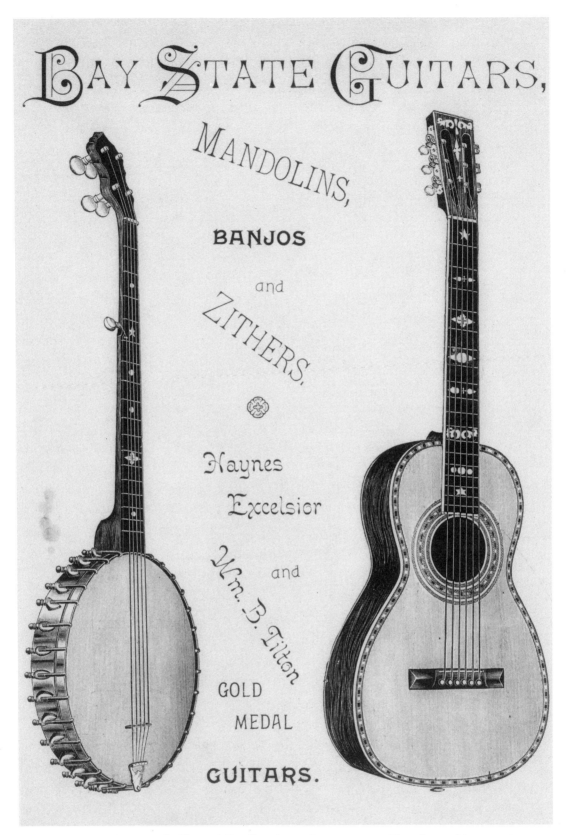

Figure 4-28. Advertisement for Haynes's Bay State instruments, ca. 1890. Note that at this time Haynes was selling guitars (a model originally patented by William Tilton) as well as mandolins and zithers.

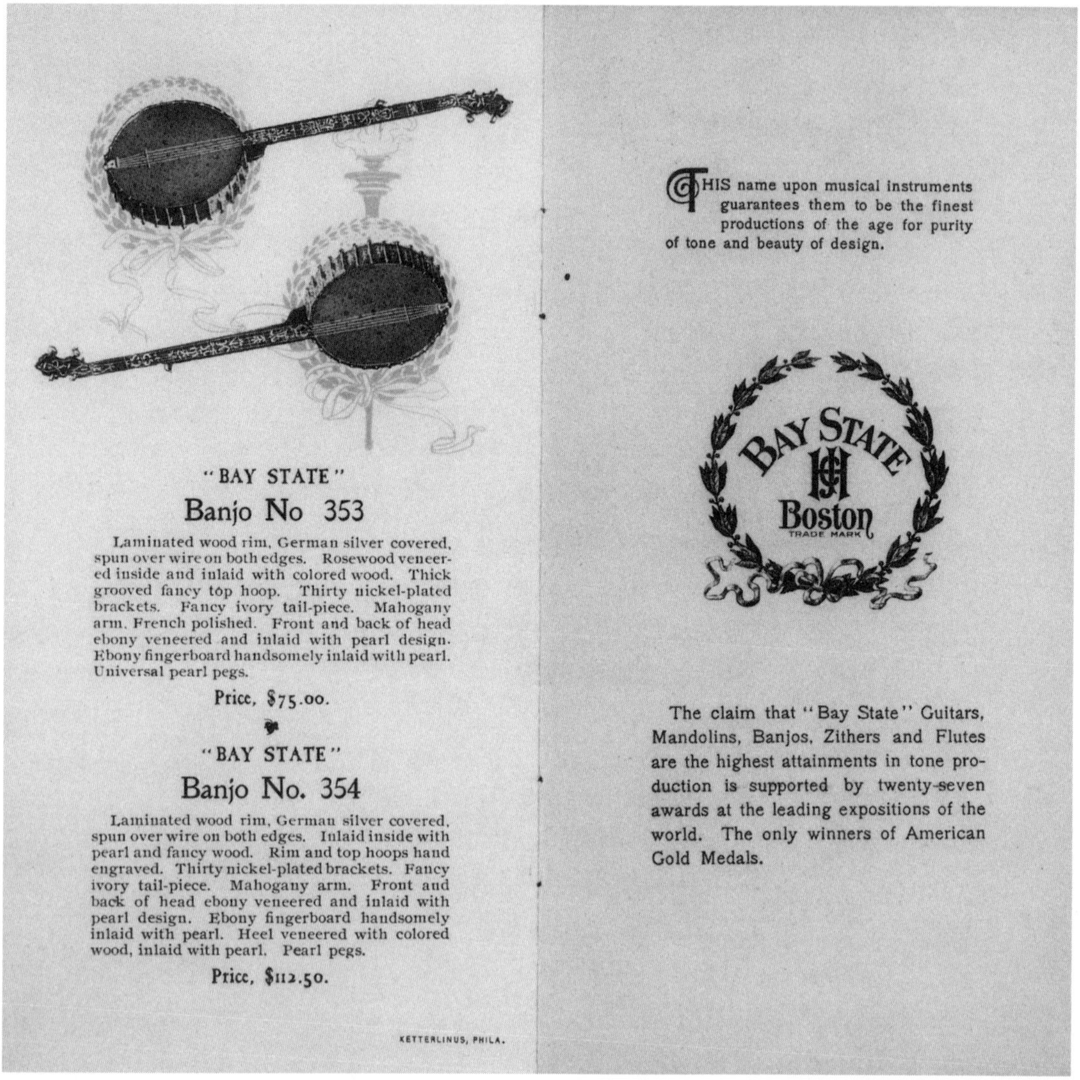
"BAY STATE"
Banjo No 353
Laminated wood rim, German silver covered, spun over wire on both edges. Rosewood veneered inside and inlaid with colored wood. Thick grooved fancy top hoop. Thirty nickel-plated brackets. Fancy ivory tail-piece. Mahogany arm. French polished. Front and back of head ebony veneered and inlaid with pearl design. Ebony fingerboard handsomely inlaid with pearl. Universal pearl pegs.
Price, $75.00.
"BAY STATE"
Banjo No. 354
Laminated wood rim, German silver covered, spun over wire on both edges. Inlaid inside with pearl and fancy wood. Rim and top hoops hand engraved. Thirty nickel-plated brackets. Fancy ivory tail-piece. Mahogany arm. Front and back of head ebony veneered and inlaid with pearl design. Ebony fingerboard handsomely inlaid with pearl. Heel veneered with colored wood, inlaid with pearl. Pearl pegs.
Price, $112.50.
KETTERLINUS, PHILA.
THIS name upon musical instruments guarantees them to be the finest productions of the age for purity of tone and beauty of design.
BAY STATE
Boston
TRADE MARK
The claim that "Bay State" Guitars, Mandolins, Banjos, Zithers and Flutes are the highest attainments in tone production is supported by twenty-seven awards at the leading expositions of the world. The only winners of American Gold Medals.

Figure 4-29. Advertisement, ca. 1889, for some of Haynes's higher-grade banjos, which rivaled those of Fairbanks and Cole in their beauty.

sophisticated craftsmen like Anderberg, Haynes offered the public the kinds of high-quality banjos, guitars, and mandolins that by the turn of the century had become the hallmark of the city's stringed instrument makers (plate 4-32). A mover and shaker in the larger world of American music—in the late 1870s, for example, he served as an officer of the Board of Music Trade, a national organization formed by major publishing houses to "adopt and sustain a fixed uniform price for all music published"—Haynes led Oliver Ditson and Company into the twentieth century without compromising his commitment to the production of fine stringed instruments.[75]

In the 1880s and 1890s several other makers produced banjos in Boston and its adjacent towns (plates 4-33, 4-34, 4-35). O. R. Chase, for example,

Plate 4-1.
Banjo made by A. C. Fairbanks, ca. 1879. 10½ × 24 in. Prior to his partnership with Cole, Fairbanks made a few hundred banjos. While most are fairly primitive aesthetically, this example, with Brazilian rosewood rim veneer, a carved ivory tailpiece, two-piece ball end nuts, and unusual but attractive rectangular pearl inlays in the fretless ebony fingerboard, anticipated the better grade Fairbanks and Cole instruments of the next decade.

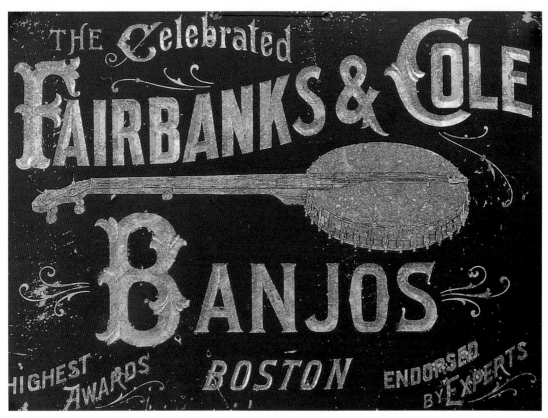

Plate 4-2. Rare embossed cardboard trade sign for Fairbanks and Cole, ca. late 1880s. During this period the firm's banjos equaled Stewart's for beauty and tone and made Boston one of the country's premier cities for banjo manufacture.

opposite
Plate 4-3. Banjo made by A. C. Fairbanks and Company, serial no. 14000, ca. 1896. 12 × 27 in. Of the six known "double griffin" peg head, presentation-grade Fairbanks banjos, this is the only example with "column" inlays, a lovely design found on a handful of custom pieces by this maker. Unfortunately, we know very little about the craftsmen who produced such elegant engraving.

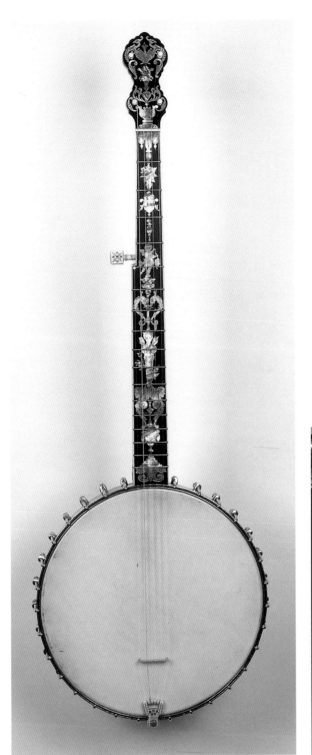

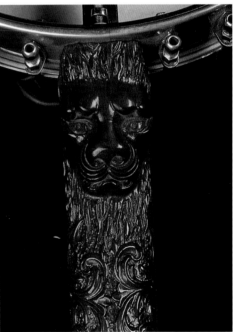

left
Plate 4-4. Banjo made by A. C. Fairbanks and Company, serial no. 15881, ca. 1896. 12 × 27 in. One of two presentation-grade Electrics known today with rosewood necks and lion's head carved heels, this example is one of the most ornate and desirable models of arguably the best banjo maker of the 1890s.

right
Plate 4-5. Detail of lion's head carved heel on Fairbanks banjo no. 15881.

Plate 4-6. Banjo made by A. C. Fairbanks and Company, serial no. 24567, ca. 1908. 12 × 28 in. A very rare example, because Electrics were relegated to second-class status with the introduction of the Whyte Laydie model in 1901, this high-grade instrument features a Deluxe dragon peg head inlay, No. 7–grade fingerboard inlays, and a silver-plated, engraved rim. It was probably a custom-ordered instrument.

Plate 4-7. Photograph of fretted instrument ensemble, ca. 1896. Lew Crouch, well-known Boston area teacher, performer, and composer, holds a guitar (probably manufactured by A. C. Fairbanks and Company) in the center of the back row. Also noteworthy is the custom-grade, lion's head carved heel, column-inlay Electric banjo pictured on the back row, right.

Plate 4-8. Rosewood jewelry box made by A. C. Fairbanks for his wife. Note the monogram "ETF." The pearl escutcheon plate around the key hole is actually a banjo inlay, and the wooden marquetry patterns on the top have nearly identical counterparts on some Fairbanks mandolin pick guards. Fairbanks instruments are marked by similar attention to detail.

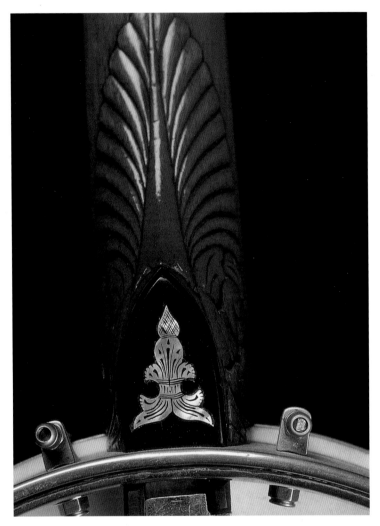

Plate 4-10. Detail of the heel carving on the Stetson presentation-grade banjo (plate 4-9).

opposite

Plate 4-9. Banjo made for J. F. Stetson, ca. 1894–96. 11 × 26 in. This is one of three known presentation models manufactured by A. C. Fairbanks and Company for Stetson, a brand name of J. W. Dyer and Brother of Minneapolis and St. Paul, Minnesota. A few lower-grade Fairbanks-made Stetson banjos and one presentation-grade Fairbanks (made for Stetson) guitar have been seen. The Fairbanks-made Stetson banjos all feature an unusual double-spun rim (that is, with metal inside and outside a wooden core).

Plate 4-11. Banjo made by William A. Cole, Eclipse, serial no. 998, ca. 1892. 11 × 25⅞ in. This is the earliest of four known examples of presentation-grade Cole banjos and the only one with inlay on the back of the peg head. Note the early-style saw-cut engraving (compare to the much more finely wrought work on the Stuber Cole, plate 4-14, with its intricately engraved pearl). Rim inlay, carved peg head edges, and gargoyle heel carving distinguish these banjos, among the most aesthetically satisfying instruments made in the 1890s.

Plate 4-12. Detail of the gargoyle-carved heel on Cole banjo no. 998 (plate 4-11).

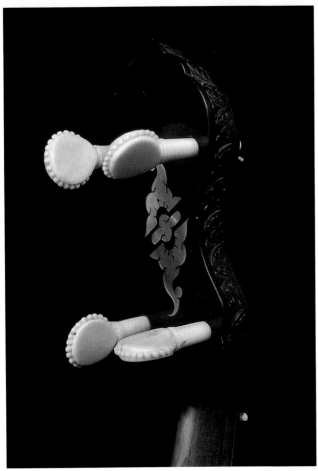

Plate 4-13. Detail of the back of the peg head on Cole banjo no. 998 (plate 4-11).

Plate 4-15. Gatcomb factory-issue poster, printed by George H. Walker and Company, ca. 1890s. This advertisement features a cut of a $100 Gatcomb presentation banjo with a rosewood neck and lion's head carved heel. Well-known Boston banjo composers George Lansing, A. A. Babb, Bert Shattuck, and E. M. Hall are pictured along with the firm's owner, Lincoln B. Gatcomb.

opposite

Plate 4-14. Banjo made by William A. Cole, serial no. 2203, ca. 1895. 10½ × 27 in. Plaque on the dowel of this presentation-grade banjo reads "Presented to Freddie Stuber by the Citizens of S. Bethlehem, Pa. W. A. Cole, Maker." Stuber was a child prodigy banjo player in the Philadelphia area whose early career had been shaped by S. S. Stewart and Thomas Armstrong.

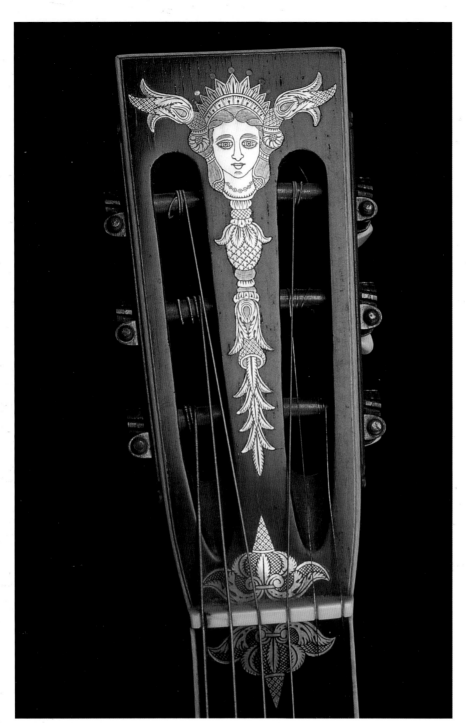

Plate 4-17.
Detail of the
peg head of
the unsigned
Boston guitar
in plate 4-16.

opposite
Plate 4-16. Unsigned Boston guitar, ca. 1895–1900. This lovely parlor guitar was decorated
by the same consummate craftsman who inlaid and engraved the Haynes banjo made for Stratton
(see plates 4-27 to 4-31). He probably decorated other instruments for Fairbanks, as well as for
other major Boston maker

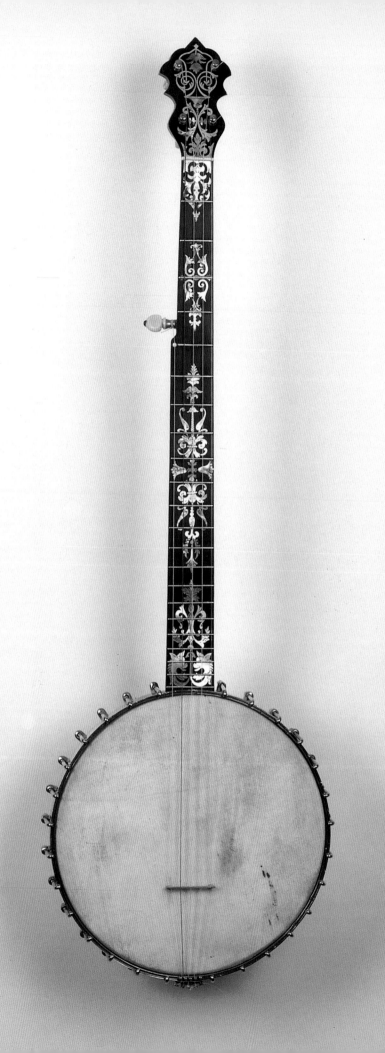

Plate 4-19. Detail of the dowel on the Luscomb-made banjo in plate 4-18, showing the owner's name inlaid in pearl script.

opposite
Plate 4-18. Unsigned Luscomb banjo, ca. 1896. 10⅝ × 27 in. The dowel stick of this instrument has the name "Maly Wales Matthews," most likely the name of the owner, inlaid in pearl script. The pearl in the fingerboard is nearly identical to the Haynes Bay State models 353 and 354, the highest grade regularly produced in that line. The identification of this instrument was made by examination of the heel and peg contours, dowel stick color and shape, style of hooks, nuts, and shoes, and, most important, the unique Luscomb two-screw neck adjuster. A similar banjo in the Bollman collection is also unsigned and features a carved heel.

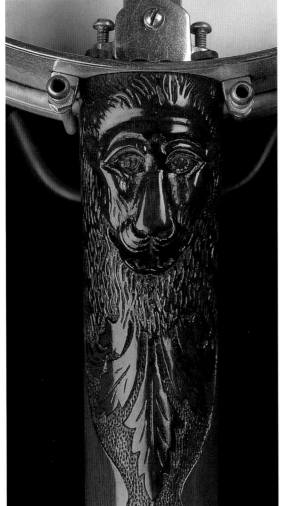

opposite
Plate 4-20. Unsigned Luscomb banjo, ca. 1897. 11½ × 26 in. This rare custom-grade banjo features an engraved rim, carved ivory pegs and tailpiece, rosewood neck, and lion's head carved heel. The beautifully engraved inlays are virtually duplicated on a Haynes Bay State presentation-grade instrument in the Bollman collection, indicating that some of the Boston makers shared the skilled craftsmen who carved and engraved their top-of-the-line instruments or subcontracted this work to those artists capable of this degree of sophistication.

top
Plate 4-21. Detail of the rim engraving on the Luscomb-made banjo in plate 4-20.

left
Plate 4-22. Detail of the lion's head heel carving on the Luscomb-made banjo in plate 4-20.

left
Plate 4-23. Unsigned banjorette, or "giraffe" banjo, by Luscomb, ca. 1895. 5 × 18¼ in. The small rim and relatively long neck on this banjo, an unusual form first promoted by S. S. Stewart, make it look out of proportion.

opposite
Plate 4-24. August Pollman mandoline-banjos. The Ultra Artist model on the left was manufactured under Haynes's Bay State label; the example on the right was perhaps manufactured, but certainly decorated, by the J. H. Buckbee Company. On 3 May 1887 Professor Antonio Bini of Brooklyn, New York, assigned his patent for this instrument to the August Pollman Company. Quite popular in the 1890s, only a handful of the top-of-the-line models survive. The Ultra Artist shows clear evidence of a connection to Haynes's Bay State line, for identical inlays and engravings are found on some of that firm's banjos. Probably Pehr Anderberg, a Swedish guitar maker connected to the Haynes Company for many years, constructed these instruments for Pollman. The instrument on the right shows the Buckbee influence with its simply engraved pearl and use of copper, pewter, and pearl inlay patterns. Also see figure 4-27.

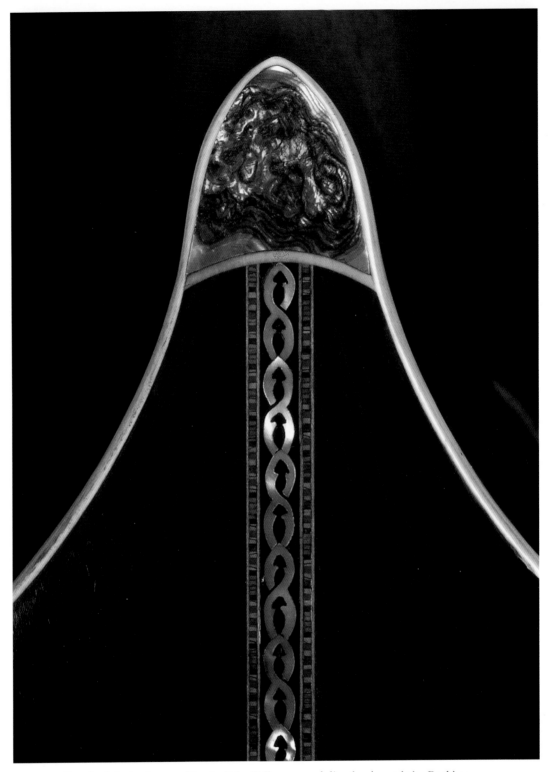

Plate 4-25. Detail of the heel cap and back of the Pollman mandoline-banjo made by Buckbee (see plate 4-24).

Plate 4-26. Cardboard embossed sign advertising Haynes's Bay State products. The high level of detail in this and other such signs allows us to identify the instruments pictured by comparing them to the company's catalogs from the same period. The banjo here is the Bay State model 333.

opposite
Plate 4-27. Banjo made by John C. Haynes, Bay State, ca. 1895. 10¾ × 26 in. This instrument was made for William E. Stratton, a well-known purveyor and teacher of fretted instruments in Lowell, Massachusetts. The banjo has remained in virtually mint condition, with all original hardware and beautifully engraved pearl inlay the full length of the fingerboard.

left
Plate 4-28. Detail of the pearl engraving on the Haynes banjo made for Stratton (plate 4-27), indicative of the finest work of the master craftsmen then working in this medium.

Plate 4-29. Detail of the neck of the Haynes banjo made for Stratton (plate 4-27), showing the carved ivory tuning peg as well as the detailed pearl engraving.

Plate 4-30. Detail of the back of the peg head of the Haynes banjo made for Stratton (plate 4-27).
Note the carved ivory tuning pegs and the carving on the peg head edge, which originates at the heel
and extends the full length of the fingerboard.

Plate 4-31. Detail of the carved gargoyle heel on the Haynes banjo made for Stratton (plate 4-27).

Plate 4-32. Paper lithographed store sign, ca. 1890s, for Haynes's Bay State instruments, picturing a top-of-the-line No. 5 mandolin.

opposite
Plate 4-33. Banjo made by
H. P. Kent, Providence, Rhode
Island, ca. 1885. 10 × 25 in.
Hexhum P. Kent was an
engraver in the bustling
Providence and Attleboro,
Massachusetts, jewelry trade.
It is possible that the two
extant Kent banjos were made
in England and sent to the
United States to be decorated
and sold by him. A similar
instrument in the Bollman
collection is signed "Daniels."
Joe Daniels was a well-known
English banjo personality in
the later nineteenth century.
In the towns surrounding
Boston other makers like
Kent, similarly known now
by only a few extant instru-
ments, tried to put a dent
in the business of the large
Boston firms.

top
Plate 4-34. Detail of the heel
on the Kent banjo (plate 4-33).

bottom
Plate 4-35. Detail of the
tail piece on the Kent banjo
(plate 4-33).

Plate 5-1. Unsigned fretless banjo, Appalachian "mountain" style, ca. 1880–1910. Difficult to date accurately, such instruments changed little even up to the mid-twentieth century. The marquetry devices and bone insert on the fingerboard set this example apart from most others, which are rarely decorated. Possible Civil War corps attribution in the fingerboard decoration suggests that the instrument was built by a veteran. The banjo was found recently in Pennsylvania but carried no known provenance.

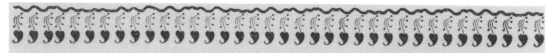

This engraving represents the famous factory of John C. Haynes & Co. Boston, Mass., the musical instrument department of the great Ditson houses where the celebrated **Bay State Guitars, Mandolins, Banjos and Zithers, and the Haynes Excelsior and Wm. B. Tilton Gold Medal Guitars** and other musical goods are manufactured.

A visit to this busy place will repay all people who are interested in the musical art, and who care to know how these wonderfully perfect goods are made.

Figure 4-30. Engraving, from advertisement, ca. 1889, of Haynes's Bay State instrument factory, the largest such enterprise in Boston during that period.

worked at 698 Washington Street, where he made the first Robinson banjos and secured two banjo-related patents in the early 1880s, one for a rather novel rim design that anticipated the Lewis banjo.[76] He used a one-piece cast bell-metal rim with its upper and lower edges turned inward and "tuned in harmony." He used no dowel stick but simply bolted the neck to the rim. Banjos by J. E. Quinlan, Harry Oakes, and A. F. Eibel (of Malden), resembling Fairbanks and Cole and early Fairbanks instruments, have also been found, and we have a reference to J. H. Stimpson (of Reading), and Albert A. Smith (of Cambridge).[77]

There were still other makers or wholesalers who were an integral part of the city's musical world but whose instruments were made elsewhere. We already have considered George C. Dobson, who from his headquarters at 290 Shawmut Avenue sold his Victor line of banjos, probably made by Buckbee of New York. Similarly, Elias Howe, who in 1860 had reestablished himself as a music publisher, also kept a large stock of stringed instruments. He sold low-grade banjos known as the Academy line, and finer ones, with German silver rims, called the Superbo line, some of which were manufactured by Cole. Howe was best known, however, for his stock of old-master violin-family instruments, which he boasted was the largest in the world.[78]

At the turn of the century, then, in terms of the quality of the instruments its craftsmen produced, Boston could rightly be called the center of the banjo trade in the United States. Marketing instruments with well-balanced tonal range and strong carrying properties, and of unmatched physical elegance, makers like Fairbanks, Cole, Gatcomb, Thompson and Odell, and Haynes brought the banjo to a pinnacle of sophistication. In large measure, they accomplished this by resisting the national trend toward more economical factory production. Like so many other businesses, of course, they invested in complex labor-saving machinery (in their case, to assist workers in preparing the wood and metal components of their instruments), but they continued to assemble and finish their instruments to the most exacting standards of handcraftsmanship.

In an advertisement in one of the early numbers of *Gatcomb's Banjo and Guitar Gazette*, Fairbanks and Cole briefly recapitulated the history of the nineteenth-century banjo.[79] They began by observing that "if there is any musical instrument which may be truly said to be essentially an American character[,] it is the banjo." "When first constructed," they continued, "as used by the Negroes of the South and even for some years after, as employed on the minstrel stage, its construction was crude and unsatisfactory." However, once the public discovered this instrument's true capacity

Figure 4-31. Photograph, ca. 1895, of a gentleman enjoying his banjo and his dogs. By the end of the nineteenth century this instrument had become as much a part of the Victorian parlor as these appreciative pets.

"for producing exquisite music, . . . experts undertook to make such improvements as would bring out clearer, better and purer tones" from it.

Clearly, Fairbanks and Cole believed that they were among such "experts," makers who devoted their time and money to finding better ways to produce a banjo that, by 1900, one enthusiast wrote, made its player "the boss of the hour."[80] In little more than a generation, such innovative entrepreneurs as the Dobsons, S. S. Stewart, A. C. Fairbanks, William Cole, and others had taken an instrument whose primary association had been with antebellum slavery and transformed it into a sophisticated musical machine whose music was appreciated by all ranks of society (fig. 4-31). As George C. Dobson noted when he published yet another of his banjo tutors, "No apology is deemed necessary for presenting to the music-loving public a new instruction book" for the instrument. For the banjo, he continued, "has already won its way to the hearts of people of all classes alike, and today its sweet, tender and idyllic music is heard on the public stage, [and] is the enjoyment of the home circle, and the fascination of refined and fashionable society."[81]

The banjo's very popularity, however, also made it attractive to those who fed the public's hunger by offering instruments quickly built of inferior materials, which as a consequence ill-served those who sought to play serious music on them. As Stewart himself had written, it was "a matter of some regret that so many musical instrument jobbers, without study and with but small concern for the interests or welfare of *the only Native American instrument, the Banjo*, have undertaken its manufacture."[82] By the turn of the century those seriously interested in stemming this tide of mediocrity finally banded together in the American Guild of Banjoists, Guitarists and Mandolinists, whose avowed purpose was to create "new interest and enthusiasm" for the instruments as well as to be "of direct benefit to the Profession and Trade."[83] Given the level to which the banjo had been brought in Boston in the 1890s, it was perfectly appropriate that the organization became based in that city, for it was indeed the workmanship characteristic of guilds that the Boston makers strove to preserve and promulgate. Among the Guild's first officers were George Lansing and the Odells, testament to the fact that the nation as a whole recognized the centrality of Boston to stringed instrument manufacture. In that city America's instrument reached its apogee of beauty and sophistication.

CONCLUSION

On the morning of 4 March 1904 fire swept through the A. C. Fairbanks factory, located in the Sherbourne Building on Washington Street in Boston. The firm was unwilling or unable to continue operations, and a few weeks later it was sold in its entirety for $925 to the Vega Company of 62 Sudbury Street, which since the 1880s had specialized in the manufacture of fine guitars and mandolins. One additional dollar bought the rights to the four patents granted to A. C. Fairbanks.[1]

The origins of the Vega Company lay in a cooperative venture begun in 1881 by several men who had worked for Pehr Anderberg's guitar works in Somerville.[2] In 1889 one of these individuals, Julius Nelson, a cabinet-maker before having turned to the stringed instrument trade, and his brother Carl bought out the interests of the original partners and formed a new company, named for a large star. Recognizing David L. Day's invaluable skills, the Nelsons retained him as their general manager and, alert to the name recognition of the Fairbanks Electrics and Whyte Laydies, continued to produce banjos nearly identical to the prefire models.[3] In the next decade Day's most important contribution to the Vega banjo line was his development of the Tubaphone (see Chapter 4), with its patented bracket band and unique brass tubular tone ring that improved the instrument's resonance.

Even as Vega assumed ownership of and continued to manufacture the most prestigious line of Boston banjos, however, other firms such as Lyon and Healy, with its George Washburn label of stringed instruments, contributed in their own ways to the banjo's improvement. But true to its history since the days of minstrelsy, the banjo continued to evolve in relation to changes in the nation's musical taste. Thus, by the 1920s five-string banjos accounted for only a minuscule portion of all banjos manufactured, for makers such as Vega and its competitors turned their attention to the large market for four-string tenor and plectrum models that better served the needs of musicians in the new Jazz Age.

This important shift in American music, which culminated in the emergence of jazz, began in the 1890s and again involved an appropriation from

African Americans, this time the kind of music known as ragtime. Essentially a "dance-based American vernacular music, featuring a syncopated melody against an even accompaniment," ragtime flourished in the first two decades of the new century, first in the immensely popular "coon" songs performed on the minstrel and variety hall stages, and then as instrumental music, usually played on the piano.[4] Based in African rhythms, and even by its earliest commentators linked to the preservation and adaptation of such music by African Americans, by the time of the World's Columbian Exhibition in 1892 this musical form appeared more and more frequently, particularly in the performances of black pianists from midwestern cities such as Chicago and St. Louis.

Until recently, however, historians of the genre have underemphasized the relationship between ragtime and the repertoire of nineteenth-century banjo tunes established from the 1850s on by musicians like Tom Briggs and Frank Converse. The musical notation of these tunes, for example, and the directions for the execution of the various rhythmic patterns in the stroke style contain the syncopation characteristic of such ragtime forms as the cakewalk.[5] Thus, late-nineteenth-century musicians familiar with minstrel and dance hall tunes might absorb rhythms that, when transferred to the piano, soon defined the genre. Nowhere was this linkage between the banjo and the piano made more explicit than by the popular writer Lafcadio Hearn. "Did you ever hear negroes play the piano by ear?" he asked a friend. "They use the piano," he explained, "exactly like a banjo." Although making the point at the expense of black piano players — "It is good banjo-playing," he concluded, "but no piano-playing" — Hearn's offhand remark was prescient.[6] If the musical idiom that now blossomed as ragtime had been kept alive anywhere in the transit from Africa to America, it was with the banjo.

Moreover, as Lowell Schreyer has pointed out, the great Scott Joplin himself, who for many people epitomizes ragtime, clearly was influenced by the banjo and its music (fig. 5-1).[7] Joplin was exposed to banjo music in his youth (his mother reportedly played the instrument), and as he began to compose in the new idiom of ragtime, he did not forget such roots. Thus, he "respectfully dedicated" one famous composition, "The Cascades," to "Kimball and Donovan, Banjoists," and perhaps his most well-known piece, "The Entertainer," was dedicated to "James Brown and His Mandolin Club," suggesting Joplin's familiarity with the world of late-nineteenth-century club music. Moreover, one of the pianists he met on a visit to the Columbian Exhibition was "Plunk" Henry, so named "for the banjo he had played earlier and from whom he had derived his piano rhythms."[8] Most tantalizing of all is the credit line to Joplin's first pub-

Figure 5-1. Carte-de-visite, ca. 1870–80, of a young African American banjoist. In the late nineteenth century the banjo was still played by African Americans in rural areas, who, with their white counterparts, kept alive tunes that dated to the antebellum period. The music known as ragtime emerged in large part among black pianists like Scott Joplin who were familiar with the distinctive syncopation of banjo music.

lished piece, "Original Rags," which reads "Picked by Scott Joplin" and "Arranged by Chas. N. Daniels." Although referring explicitly to the cover art, which depicts an African American rag picker putting another item in his sack, this locution could as easily describe banjo as piano playing.[9]

Through the compositions and performances of musicians such as Joplin, by the end of the century ragtime had become very popular, though, as one historian of the genre has pointed out, it was not received enthusiastically by all parties. Many devotees of classical music, for example, viewed it as an impediment to the further spread of the compositions of the European masters.[10] Interestingly, ragtime's critics (like those of the banjo two decades earlier) associated it with the low and vulgar in general, and with African Americans in particular, pointing to the derogatory lyrics of the "coon" songs as their prime evidence. Thus, as interest in the infectious new music spread, debate broke out in national periodicals about whether to encourage or eliminate it.

Indeed, S. S. Stewart, ever the champion of what he considered the highbrow in music, weighed in (as might be expected) against ragtime and, as he had done in his attempt to distance the banjo from its African American origins, once again denied the obvious, insisting, in a reply to a reader's request for a definition of ragtime, that such music had "no possible connection with a banjo, and was not originated with that instrument." Using the same language through which he had ridiculed George Dobson's simplified method, Stewart equated the enthusiasm for rags with poor taste and bad habits. "Everyone knows," he wrote, that it is "about 10 times as hard to get rid of a bad habit" as to acquire it. Likewise, "it is also much easier to acquire slang terms and a slovenly execution upon an instrument than it is to acquire a finished style of playing," that is, one presumably free of "ragged" rhythms.[11]

Ironically, Joplin's agenda to legitimize ragtime and win a wide audience to it bore much similarity to Stewart's effort to elevate the banjo, and ultimately it was much more successful. By the 1890s ragtime was everywhere, even in the music played by banjo clubs and orchestras, where banjos now frequently were linked, in repertoire as well as performance, to mandolins and guitars. Indeed, the five-string banjo was closely associated with ragtime, for by the late 1800s cakewalks, long a staple of minstrel shows, formed one of the most popular genres of composition—for the banjo as well as the piano—even by those whom Stewart thought should know better.[12] Further, this music was now widely available through the novel technology of Thomas Edison's wax sound cylinders, and those who first encountered ragtime through this medium were more likely to hear it played on the banjo by such virtuosos as Vess L. Ossman (1868–1923) and

Fred Van Eps (1878–1960) than on the piano, which before 1910 was rarely used for such recordings.[13] Precisely at this point, however, the banjo's history took another turn, one which made the five-string form of the instrument virtually obsolete.

The banjo's linkage to the mandolin precipitated this change, for in the first decade of the twentieth century some makers began to introduce new instruments—specifically, the banjo-mandolin or banjolin, and the tango or tenor banjo—whose string configuration derived from the mandolin, an instrument whose popularity had soared in the 1890s. As we have seen in Chapter 3, the banjo-mandolin had been anticipated in the 1880s by the Hartford maker John Farris and consisted of an eight-string mandolin neck grafted onto a small banjo rim. The tango or tenor instrument essentially was a shorter-necked (banjeaurine-length) banjo without the fifth string and also was tuned like a mandolin. Both of these instruments were used to accompany a new dance, the tango, that was very popular in the first decade of the century—hence, the name tango or tenor banjo. Musicians set up these instruments with steel strings, more readily available after the turn of the century, and played them with a plectrum, or pick, a style of performance particularly adapted to the fast rhythmic music of the new dances but not used previously on banjos.[14] Soon these new forms of the banjo were joined by another, the plectrum banjo, a full-sized instrument whose four strings were tuned in standard banjo tuning, but which again lacked the fifth string and was played, as the name suggests, with a pick.

While classic ragtime flourished, the finger-style playing of musicians like Ossman and Van Eps clearly was appropriate. But as musical forms evolved through the second decade of the century, particularly as musicians found their way to that most American of idioms, jazz, there was more call for the rapid chording and the strong rhythmic emphases that the plectrum instruments allowed. By the 1920s four-string banjos were the rage and supplanted the five-string instrument in the popular imagination. Though it evolved in part from Tin Pan Alley and vaudeville, where the five-string banjo still flourished, by 1920, when jazz came into its own, its rhythm sections all had large-rimmed banjos with heavy wooden resonators and only four strings. As a result, the five-string banjo became increasingly rare, with new firms like Gibson, Paramount, and Bacon and Day specializing primarily in tenor and plectrum models, and making only the occasional five-string.

This form of the instrument, however, did survive in a few places, especially in the rural South, where in the hands of African Americans as well as whites it remained central to the population's social music (fig. 5-2,

Figure 5-2. Photograph of rural family, ca. 1910, with father (center) and son (far right) with banjos. In the early twentieth century in Appalachia and other rural sections of the country, amateur musicians continued to play traditional and early "hillbilly" music on the five-string banjo, even as much of the nation was swept with enthusiasm for jazz.

opposite
Figure 5-3. Photograph of medicine show performers, ca. 1880–90. On vaudeville stages and in traveling medicine shows, musicians continued to perform tunes that had originated in the heyday of minstrelsy. Some of these performers, such as Uncle Dave Macon, eventually found their way to the Grand Ole Opry, where they contributed to the enthusiasm for "old-time" music.

plate 5-1). In Appalachia and the Piedmont Carolinas, tunes whose origins lay in the nineteenth century—and often with minstrelsy—remained vibrant reminders of a time when such music had been central to American culture.[15] During the 1920s and 1930s such "hillbilly" or "old-time" tunes and songs could be heard on another invention, the radio, with performers such as Uncle Dave Macon on the Grand Ole Opry continuing uninterrupted a line of showmanship that derived from the vaudeville and medicine show stages, and beyond that, from minstrelsy itself (fig. 5-3).[16] Amateur musicians, too, now able to buy 78 rpm records of their favorite performers, were central to the five-string banjo's survival. Playing on handmade instruments, or on those assembled in part from store-bought components, rural banjoists kept alive music and styles of playing that in

Figure 5-4. Photograph of Josh and Henry Reed of Glen Lyn, Virginia, ca. 1920. In the early twentieth century traditional musicians such as Henry Reed (on the right) still learned to play the five-string banjo, even though four-string, plectrum banjo playing was all the rage in the nation at large. Henry was a fiddler as well, whose vast and rare fiddle repertoire was eventually recorded by folklorists. Note that his brother still played the fiddle resting against the middle of his chest, as it might have been done in the eighteenth century. Courtesy of James H. Reed Jr.

the 1940s exploded into popularity with the rise of bluegrass music (fig. 5-4).[17] First in the hands of Earl Scruggs and later of Ralph Stanley, and in our own time in the immense popularity of commercial "country" music, America's instrument regained its prominence.[18]

Through the 1920s and 1930s there were many further changes in banjo design, most often in the tone ring and resonator, that marked Jazz Age instruments and then, as bluegrass emerged, the five-string models that companies again began to manufacture. Here the greatest success lay with the Orville Gibson Company, with its origins in the early twentieth century and its reputation established primarily by the fine instruments in its mandolin line, but other sophisticated makers—Paramount, Bacon and Day, and Weymann, to name a few—made equally strong and attractive banjos.[19]

But the stories of these companies and their instruments are fairly well known and, moreover, belong to the history of the new century. It has been the banjo's long journey from the southern plantation to the Victorian parlor and concert stage that has remained shrouded, in part because of the scarcity of source materials through which such a history could be assembled, and in part by some banjo enthusiasts' uncritical reliance on legend and misinformation. We hope that the narrative and illustrations we have presented will clear away some of this mist and moonshine so that once again people will appreciate, as they did in the nineteenth century, the clear, ringing tones of an instrument so deeply entwined with American culture as a whole. For as we have told the story of America's instrument, we believe that we have spoken to American history as well.

GLOSSARY

back strap: Veneer on back of peg head, and sometimes partially down the back of the neck, on high-grade banjos. Serves both a decorative function and to strengthen the neck.

bracket band: Associated with Fairbanks and Vega banjos, this metal ring around the outer edge of the rim obviates the need for holes through the rim for shoe bolts. Uses countersunk screws for shoe attachment. Also can be wooden, as in the case of Ashborn banjos.

bridge: A piece of hardwood or bone, usually with two or three feet (making the piece look like a bridge), with grooves on the top to position the instrument's strings. Transmits sound vibrations from the strings to the head.

dowel: The part of the neck that goes through the rim and then either abuts or goes through the rim's other end, and onto which the tailpiece is mounted. Sometimes called the *perchpole* or stick. Modern banjos often use metal coordinator rods in lieu of a dowel.

fifth-string tuner: The tuner, or *peg*, for the short string of the banjo (sometimes called the *chanterelle*), positioned on the left side of the neck when one looks at the instrument from the front. On older banjos it often was mounted vertically, but after the Civil War it most often went horizontally into the neck.

fingerboard: A thin wood strip, usually ebony or rosewood, glued to the top of the neck and into which the frets are set. Early fretless banjos often lacked a fingerboard.

flesh hoop: A thin wire hoop used to mount the skin head. The flesh hoop is pushed over the skin and rim, with the skin then tucked back. This provides a bead against which the tension hoop can be tightened.

fret: Mounted on the fingerboard or directly in the neck and made of metal (when raised above the fingerboard) or of bone, ivory, or wood (when mounted flush with the surface of the neck), frets are placed at precise intervals to allow one to press down a string at that point to sound a particular note. Although very early banjos were fretless, frets were being used by the 1850s and became common in the 1880s.

fretless: A banjo whose neck or fingerboard lacks frets.

head: A replaceable membrane, usually calfskin or goatskin, stretched over the rim, on which the bridge sits. The head amplifies the sound of a plucked string.

heel: The part of the banjo neck that abuts the rim. Fine banjos often had a carving and/or a *heel cap* covering the bottom of the heel that was made of fine wood like ebony or from metal, celluloid, or mother-of-pearl.

hooks: Also called the *bracket hooks*, these pieces of metal fit over the tension hoop and through holes in the shoes and are secured with nuts, thus allowing one to tighten the head of the banjo. Sometimes termed *strainers*.

neck: Sometimes called the *arm* or *handle*, this is the long wooden piece over which the strings are tightened and on which they are fretted to make different notes. On fine banjos necks are usually made of mahogany, maple, rosewood, or cherry, but they are found in other hard woods as well. The top of the neck through which the tuners are inserted is called the peg head, and the neck abuts the rim at the heel.

neck adjuster: Also called the *frog, cleat, or clamp*. Often a wooden wedge or U-shaped clamp affixed to the dowel to keep the neck tight against the rim.

nut: A piece of wood, bone, or ivory at the top of the neck or fingerboard through which the strings pass before being tightened with the tuners. The nut, like the bridge, allows for proper spacing of the strings. There also is a small fifth-string nut, usually cylindrical, attached to the fingerboard just below the fifth-string tuner to bear and guide the banjo's short string. Also refers to the piece of metal that attaches to the bracket hook and allows the tension hoop to tighten the head.

peg head: Sometimes called the *head stock*, this is the top of the banjo's neck through which the tuners are inserted. On later nineteenth-century banjos, the peg head often had a veneer and was further decorated with marquetry or mother-of-pearl. Each maker often had a readily identifiable design for the peg heads of his instruments. The *peg face* refers to the veneer often inlaid on the front of the peg head.

resonator: A circular piece of wood or metal (removable) that fits over the back or bottom of the rim and projects the sound forward. Beginning in the 1860s makers began to experiment with *closed-back* banjos, whose backs resemble resonators but were not as easily removed.

rim: A circular structure, sometimes called the *pot*, usually made of wood, metal, or a combination of the two, over which the head is tightened by means of the hooks, brackets, and nuts. A *full-spun* rim has a sheath of metal covering the outside of the rim; a *half-spun* rim has metal over only half of the outer part of the rim.

shoes: Pieces of metal that are attached to the rim with a small bolt and provide a bearing surface for the nuts, so that the tension hoop can be tightened over the head by the hooks, which pass through a hole in the shoes.

spun-over: A rim with an outer layer of metal, usually nickel silver, "spun" over it, to give a different sound to the banjo.

tack head: A banjo whose head is tacked around the circumference of the rim rather than being tightened by hooks. The earliest banjos were made in this way, and after the Civil War some inexpensive instruments were still so constructed.

tailpiece: Made of bone, wood, ivory, ivoroid, or metal, the tailpiece holds the strings at the bottom of the banjo. If the dowel protrudes through the rim, the tailpiece is secured around it with a string or wire; if the dowel abuts the inside of the rim, this part is attached either by an *end bolt* that itself goes through the rim into the dowel or by a *tailpiece hanger bolt* and *nut*.

tension hoop: Sometimes called a *stretcher band*, this circular piece of metal fits over the top of the rim and is pulled downward by the hooks, thus tightening the head of the banjo.

tone ring: A circular piece of metal mounted on the top of the rim, over which the head is drawn as it is tightened. Later nineteenth-century banjos are marked by a great variety of tone rings, designed to improve the sound of the instruments.

top-tension banjo: An instrument with a specially designed tension hoop that allows the head to be tightened from the top by screws. Top-tension banjos usually are *closed-back*; this system allows their heads to be adjusted without removing the back.

tuners: Also called the *pegs* or *tuning pegs*. Made of wood, bone, ivory, or ivoroid (an early synthetic material), these receive the strings at the peg head of the banjo. Most nineteenth-century banjos had simple one-piece friction tuners (like violin pegs) that tightened against the wood in the holes drilled for them, but some makers used a variant of metal geared tuners like those made for guitars. At the end of the century metal friction tuners were developed, allowing for more precise adjustment of the strings. These had bone, ivory, or ivoroid buttons on their ends.

NOTES

INTRODUCTION

1. See, for example, Russell Sanjek, *American Popular Music and Its Business: The First Four Hundred Years*, vol. 2, *From 1790 to 1909* (New York: Oxford University Press, 1988), 1–125; Gerald Boardman, *American Musical Theater* (New York: Oxford University Press, 1978); Robert C. Toll, *On with the Show: The First Century of Show Business in America* (New York: Oxford University Press, 1976); Nicholas Tawa, *Sweet Songs for Gentle Americans: The Parlor Song in America, 1790–1860* (Bowling Green, Ohio: Bowling Green University Press, 1980) and *A Music for the Millions: Antebellum Democratic Attitudes and the Birth of American Popular Music* (New York: Pendragon Press, 1984); W. Porter Ware and Thaddeus C. Lockard Jr., *P. T. Barnum Presents Jenny Lind: The American Tour of the Swedish Nightingale* (Baton Rouge: Louisiana State University Press, 1980); Ken Emerson, *Doo-dah!: Stephen Foster and the Rise of American Popular Culture* (New York: Simon and Schuster, 1997); and Vera Brodsky Lawrence, *Strong on Music: The New York Musical Scene in the Days of George Templeton Strong*, 2 vols. (Chicago: University of Chicago Press, 1987–95), esp. 2:36–81 on Lind's American visit.

2. But see, for example, Gary J. Kornblith, "The Craftsman as Industrialist: Jonas Chickering and the Transformation of American Piano Manufacturing," *Business History Review* 59 (1985): 349–69; Robert E. Eliason, "The Meachams, Musical Instrument Makers of Hartford and Albany," *Journal of the American Musical Instrument Society* 5–6 (1980): 54–73, and *Keyed Bugles in the United States* (Washington, D.C.: Smithsonian Institution Press, 1972); and Laurence Libin, *American Musical Instruments in the Metropolitan Museum of Art* (New York: W. W. Norton, 1985).

3. See Susan E. Hirsch, "From Artisan to Manufacturer: Industrialization and the Small Producer in Newark," in *Small Business in American Life*, ed. Stuart W. Bruchey (New York: Columbia University Press, 1980), 80–99; Kornblith, "The Craftsman as Industrialist"; and, more generally, Robert Higgs, *The Transformation of the American Economy, 1865–1914: An Essay in Interpretation* (New York: Wiley, 1971), and [Patrick] Glen Porter and Harold Livesay, *Merchants and Manufacturers: Studies in the Changing Structure of Nineteenth-Century Marketing* (Baltimore: Johns Hopkins University Press, 1971).

4. David L. Day, "The Banjo and Its Public," *The Music Trades*, 21 January 1905, p. 45.

5. Although not cited in standard dictionaries, the word "banjoist" was commonly used in the nineteenth century. As early as 1860, for example, it appeared in a *National Police Gazette* notice concerning the well-known musician Frank Converse (see Chapter 2), who had left one city without paying the rent for his concert hall. See vol. 15 (whole no. 764), 28 April 1860, p. 4.

Twenty-five years later the banjo maker S. S. Stewart noted that he was writing for the rising school of banjo players—"banjoists, notwithstanding the omission of the word from Webster's dictionary." See *The Banjo Philosophically: A Lecture* (Philadelphia: S. S. Stewart, 1886), 9.

6. On the popularity of brass bands, see Kenneth Kreitner, *Discoursing Sweet Music: Town Bands and Community Life in Turn-of-the-Century Pennsylvania* (Urbana: University of Illinois Press, 1990).

7. George C. Dobson, *Complete Instructor for the Banjo[,] with an Authentic History of the Instrument* (Boston: White, Smith, 1880), 4.

8. Another person, for example, claimed that the banjo was "the only 'native born' instrument, and the average American should be truly proud of it." "The Banjo," in *S. S. Stewart's Banjo and Guitar Journal* 15, no. 1 (April/May 1898): 4.

9. Karen Linn, *That Half-Barbaric Twang: The Banjo in American Popular Culture* (Urbana: University of Illinois Press, 1991). In his *The Banjo! A Dissertation* (Philadelphia: S. S. Stewart, 1888), S. S. Stewart claimed to provide a history "of the Banjo and its evolution and progress from the 'Plantation Banjo' of years ago, up to the high-class musical instrument of the present day," but in fact he paid little attention to the contribution of specific makers other than himself. See *S. S. Stewart's Banjo and Guitar Journal* 11, no. 1 (April/May 1894): 2.

10. In her indispensable study, "The Folk Banjo: A Documentary History" (*Ethnomusicology* 19 [September 1975]: 347–71), Dena Epstein observed that "the history of the folk banjo as distinct from the commercial instrument has hardly been attempted in any serious way," but we would argue that in fact neither has the history of the commercial instrument.

11. Z. Porter Wright, "Banjology," in *The Bacon and Day "Silver Bell" Banjo Family* (Groton, Conn.: Bacon Banjo Company, [ca. 1928]), 2.

12. Dobson, *Complete Instructor*, 3.

13. See, for example, "The Banjo" in *S. S. Stewart's Banjo and Guitar Journal* 15, no. 1 (April/May 1898): 4.

14. The whole question of when and by whom the shorter "fifth" string was added is vexing. One thing seems sure, however: *pace* the received wisdom, Joel W. Sweeney was not responsible for it. His claim was forwarded by Arthur Woodward in "Joel Sweeney and the First Banjo," *Los Angeles County Museum Quarterly* 7 (Spring 1949): 8. Jay Bailey reviews the evidence for this claim in his "Historical Origins and Stylistic Development of the Five-String Banjo," *Journal of American Folklore* 85 (1972): 58–65. S. S. Stewart, a fairly reliable historian if his own interests were not directly involved, noted the attribution to Sweeney but added that "whether this is true or not, I have no personal knowledge nor reliable information." He was sure, however, that "a Banjo today would not be a Banjo without its short fifth, or thumb string" (*The Banjo!*, 18). Even allowing for the fact that the extant Sweeney banjo cannot be positively dated, on some instruments the drone string seems to have been added much earlier than the 1830s. For example, a late-eighteenth-century watercolor (see Chapter 1) from the region around Charleston, South Carolina, clearly shows a banjo-like instrument with one shorter string.

15. See Robert F. Winans, "The Folk, the Stage, and the Five-String Banjo," *Journal of American Folklore* 89 (1976): 407–37, esp. 408, and Elias J. Kaufman, "Early American Banjo Methods, Part 1," *Five-Stringer*, no. 174 (Winter 1993–Spring 1994): 6–15, 23.

16. See Philip F. Gura, "Manufacturing Guitars for the American Parlor: James Ashborn's Wolcottville, Connecticut, Gui-

tar Factory, 1851–1856," *Proceedings of the American Antiquarian Society* 104, part 1 (April 1994): 117–55, for monographic treatment of Ashborn's factory.

17. What in the nineteenth century was called stroking or banjo style is similar to what contemporary musicians call the clawhammer style of playing. See, for example, *Frank Converse's Analytic Banjo Method* (New York: Gordon and Son, 1886), 14, where in "explaining the original, characteristic, . . . and effective style of execution on the banjo," Converse says that "the art of striking resembles the movement of a hammer." Compare to Miles Krassen, *Clawhammer Banjo* (New York: Oak Publications, 1974), 10–13.

18. Robert F. Winans and Elias J. Kaufman, "Minstrel and Classic Banjo: American and English Connections," *American Music* 12 (Spring 1994): 11–12, and Kaufman, "Early American Banjo Methods."

19. See "The Guitar," *S. S. Stewart's Banjo and Guitar Journal* 1, no. 9 (January 1883): 2, and ibid., no. 8 (December 1882): 2, where Stewart notes that the "guitar is more popular than ever" because "the banjo made it so." In the publisher's preface to *Briggs' Banjo Instructor* (Boston: Oliver Ditson, 1855), p. 4, Ditson notes that as a performer Thomas Briggs "elevated the banjo to the rank of the guitar."

20. Winans and Kaufman, "Minstrel and Classic Banjo," 14. The first, second, and fifth strings were wire and the remainder gut; a very bright, ringing sound resulted. Perhaps the most interesting feature of Cammeyer's design was the elimination of the fifth-string peg on the side of the neck; instead of attaching the fifth string in its usual place, he ran it up to the peg head through a tunnel between the fingerboard and the neck proper and attached it to a fifth peg there.

In this study we do not undertake to trace the development of the banjo in En-

gland. Anyone interested in the subject should turn first to Winans and Kaufman's admirable essay. Suffice it to say that minstrel troupes traveled across the Atlantic shortly after they emerged on the American stage, and comparable English groups and players soon took to the boards; see in particular Harry Reynolds, *Minstrel Memories: The Story of Burnt Cork Minstrelsy in Great Britain from 1836 to 1927* (London: Alston Rivers, 1928), and W.B., "Early Banjoism in England: A Retrospect," *The Major* 1, no. 3 (January 1899): 49, reprinted from an 1898 issue of an English periodical, *The Troubador*. In general the development of the banjo in England paralleled that in the United States, although in the 1860s and 1870s English makers frequently added more strings to their instruments—six or seven, most commonly—to enable them to be played in more keys. Without doubt, however, Cammeyer, who lived in England from the late 1880s, offered the most influential refinement. See Winans and Kaufman, "Minstrel and Classic Banjo," 10–15, and Alfred Cammeyer, *My Adventuresome Banjo* (London: Cammeyer, 1934).

21. See Linn, *Half-Barbaric Twang*, 5–39, for a discussion of the banjo's "elevation." The term, however, originates in the efforts of nineteenth-century proselytizers to make the instrument more respectable. In the 1880s, for example, Bert E. Shattuck, editor of one of the country's premier journals devoted to the banjo, observed that "probably no instrument has ever had to fight its way through such bitter antagonism as the BANJO." See *Gatcomb's Banjo and Guitar Gazette* 1, no. 1 (September 1887): 1.

22. See James F. Bollman, "The Banjomakers of Boston," in *Ring the Banjar!: The Banjo in America from Folklore to Factory*, ed. Robert Lloyd Webb (Cambridge, Mass.: MIT Museum, 1984), 37–54, for an earlier assessment of this group.

23. In our understanding of the significance of craft and invention in this period we have been particularly influenced by Miles Orvell, *The Real Thing: Imitation and Authenticity in American Culture, 1880–1940* (Chapel Hill: University of North Carolina Press, 1989).

24. See, for example, Winans, "The Folk, the Stage, and the Five-String Banjo," and his "Early Minstrel Show Music, 1843–1852," in *Musical Theatre in America*, ed. Glenn Loney (Westport, Conn.: Greenwood Press, 1984), 71–97; Winans and Kaufman, "Minstrel and Classic Banjo," 1–30; and Cecelia Conway, *African Banjo Echoes in Appalachia: A Study of Folk Traditions* (Knoxville: University of Tennessee Press, 1995), esp. 194–237.

25. See, for example, Eric Lott, *Love and Theft: Blackface Minstrelsy and the American Working Class* (New York: Oxford University Press, 1995); David Roediger, *The Wages of Whiteness: Race and the Making of the American Working Class* (London: Verso, 1991); Alexander Saxton, "Blackface Minstrelsy and Jacksonian Ideology," *American Quarterly* 27 (1975): 3–28; and, for a good overview, Annemarie Bean, James V. Hatch, and Brooks McNamara, eds., *Inside the Minstrel Mask: Readings in Nineteenth-Century Blackface Minstrelsy* (Hanover, N.H.: Wesleyan University Press, 1996).

CHAPTER ONE

1. George C. Dobson, *Complete Instructor for the Banjo[,] with an Authentic History of the Instrument* (Boston: White, Smith, 1880), 4. Dena Epstein writes that the basic elements of the African American banjo were "a body made from a gourd (or, in a few cases, from wood), covered with skin, and a wooden neck strung with gut or vine strings, varying in number from one to six"; see "The Folk Banjo: A Docu-

mentary History," *Ethnomusicology* 19 (September 1975): 349. Cecelia Conway notes that "the primary characteristics of the banjo are the rounded *sound chamber*, covered with the *head* (a vibrating membrane), and joined to the *neck*, with the *strings* extending across the surface of both the head and the neck"; see *African Banjo Echoes in Appalachia: A Study of Folk Traditions* (Knoxville: University of Tennessee Press, 1995), 166.

2. See Paul Oliver, *Savannah Syncopators: African Retentions in the Blues* (New York: Stein and Day, 1970), esp. 28–66; Michael Theodore Coolen, "Senegambian Archetypes for the American Folk Banjo," *Western Folklore* 43 (1984): 112–32; Epstein, "The Folk Banjo," 347–71; Conway, *African Banjo Echoes*, esp. 160–93; and Eric Charry, "Plucked Lutes in West Africa: An Historical Overview," *The Galpin Society Journal* 49 (1996): 3–37. Among the various possibilities, Coolen ("Senegambian Archetypes") suggests the *molo* and, more significantly, the *xalam* as the African progenitors of the banjo.

3. Epstein, "Folk Banjo." All subsequent researchers of the banjo in America are indebted to her listing of published sources for the instrument. Also see her *Sinful Tunes and Spirituals: Black Folk Music to the Civil War* (Urbana: University of Illinois Press, 1977), which covers African American music more inclusively.

4. Richard Jobson, *The Golden Trade; or, A Discovery of the River Gambra, and the Golden Trade of the Aethiopians* (London: N. Okes, 1623; reprint, London: Penguin Press, 1932), 105–8. The bandora is a plucked instrument of the late Renaissance period, about the size of a guitar. It was often played with the cittern. See Anthony Baines, *The Oxford Companion to Musical Instruments* (Oxford: Oxford University Press, 1992), 18–19.

5. Nieman's report is in Adam Jones,

German Sources for West African History, 1599–1699 (Wiesbaden, Germany: Steiner, 1983), 88.

6. Hans Sloane, A Voyage to the Islands of Madera, Barbados, Nieves, S. Christopher and Jamaica, with the Natural History of These Islands (London: privately printed, 1707), 1:lix, cited in Epstein, "The Folk Banjo," 352. For an interpretation of the significance of Sloane's observations, see Richard Cullen Rath, "African Music in Seventeenth-Century Jamaica: Cultural Transit and Transition," William and Mary Quarterly, 3d ser., 50 (1993): 700–726, and for more about Jamaican music, Astley Clerk, "Extract from the Music and Instruments of Jamaica," Jamaica Journal 9 (1975): 64–67.

7. Adrien Dessalles, Histoire Générale des Antilles (1678; reprint, Paris: Libraire-éditeur, 1847–48), 3:296–97, cited in Epstein, "The Folk Banjo," 351, with her free translation from the French.

8. John Oldmixon, The British Empire in America Containing the History of the Discovery[,] Settlement[,] Progress and Present State of All the British Colonies on the Continent and Islands of America (London: J. Nicholson, 1708), 1:123, cited in Epstein, "The Folk Banjo," 352.

9. The Importance of Jamaica to Great Britain Consider'd . . . in a Letter to a Gentleman (London: A. Dodd, [1740?]), 18, cited in Epstein, "The Folk Banjo," 352.

10. Thomas Grainger, The Sugar-Cane. A Poem. In Four Books (ca. 1763), reprinted in The Works of the English Poets, from Chaucer to Cowper, ed. Alexander Chalmers (London: J. Johnson, 1810), 14:12, line 584 and note, cited in Epstein, "The Folk Banjo," 352. Edward Long, The History of Jamaica (London: T. Lowndes, 1774), 423, cited in ibid., 353.

11. Thomas Masterman Winterbottom, An Account of the Native Africans in the Neighborhood of Sierra Leone (1803; reprint, London: F. Cass, 1969), 1:113, quoting from

Bryan Edwards's History, Civil and Commercial, of the British Colonies in the West Indies (London: J. Stockdale, 1793).

12. South Carolina Council records, cited by Philip D. Morgan, Slave Counterpoint: Black Culture in the Eighteenth-Century Chesapeake and Low Country (Chapel Hill: University of North Carolina Press, 1998), 474.

13. Pennsylvania Gazette, 7 July 1749, 2 November 1749, and 17 November 1757.

14. South Carolina and American General Gazette, 12 December 1766.

15. James Barclay, The Voyages and Travels of James Barclay, Containing Many Surprising Adventures and Interesting Narratives ([London?]: privately printed, 1777), 27.

16. John Bernard, Retrospections of North America, 1781–1811, ed. Mrs. Bayle Bernard (New York: Harper and Brothers, 1887), 206.

17. Maryland Journal, 10 October 1778 and 8 January 1782.

18. Maryland Gazette, 3 March 1768.

19. Thomas C. Cornell, Adam and Anne Mott: Their Ancestors and Descendants (Poughkeepsie, N.Y.: Haight, 1890), 26.

20. Rath, "African Music," 704, notes this juxtaposition of the instruments for comparison.

21. Epstein, "The Folk Banjo," 354; but Coolen ("Senegambian Archetypes," 123, n. 11) argues that the tuning pegs and bridge as they are illustrated in the painting are atypical of the molo. For a detailed discussion of this painting and its provenance, see American Folk Paintings and Drawings Other than Portraits from the Abby Aldrich Rockefeller Folk Art Center (Boston: Little, Brown, 1988), 121–23. We also note a now untraceable engraving, "Musical Instruments of African Negroes," dated London, 1791, that unquestionably shows a banjo-like instrument with a shorter string on its side; see Banjo-Mandolin-Guitar 62 (December 1964): 100. Finally, one banjo-

like instrument, in the Rijksmuseum voor Volkenkunde in Leiden, Netherlands, supposedly collected in Dutch Guiana in the 1770s by John Gabriel Stedman, has a gourd body, a sheepskin head, and four strings, one of them short. For a picture of this instrument see Conway, *African Banjo Echoes*, 163. Also see Stedman's *Narrative of a Five Years' Expedition Against the Revolted Negroes of Surinam, in Guiana, on the Wild Coast of South America, from the Year 1772 to 1777*, 2 vols. (London: J. Johnson, 1796), 2:286, where he describes such a "Creole-bania."

22. Epstein, *Sinful Tunes and Spirituals*, 35.

23. *The Journals of Benjamin Henry Latrobe, 1799–1820: From Philadelphia to New Orleans*, ed. Edward C. Carter II, John C. Van Horne, and Lee Formwalt (New Haven: Yale University Press, 1980), 203.

24. Cynric R. Williams, *A Tour through the Island of Jamaica, from the Western to the Eastern End, in the Year 1823* (London: Hunt and Clarke, 1826), facing p. 100.

25. Nicholas Creswell, *Journal of Nicholas Creswell, 1774–1777* (New York: The Dial Press, 1924), 18–19.

26. Jonathan Boucher, *Boucher's Glossary of Archaic Words* (London: Black, Young and Young, 1832), xlix.

27. D. C. Johnston, *Scraps (no. 4) For the Year 1833, in which is included Trollopiana* (Boston, 1833), sketch 15. Peter Randolph, *Sketches of Slave Life; or, Illustrations of the "Peculiar Institution," by Peter Randolph, An Emancipated Slave*, 2d ed. enlarged (Boston: privately printed, 1855), 68.

28. Alfred Mercier, *L'Habitation Saint-Ybars; ou, Maîtres et Esclaves en Louisiane* (Nouvelle-Orléans: Imprimerie Franco-Américane, 1881), 51.

29. John Allan Wyeth, *With Sabre and Scalpel: The Autobiography of a Soldier and a Surgeon* (New York: Harper and Brothers, 1914), 61–62.

30. William Ferguson Goldie, *Sunshine and Shadow of Slave Life, Reminiscences as told by Isaac D. Williams to "Tege"* (East Saginaw, Mich.: Evening News Printing and Binding House, 1885), 62.

31. See, for example, Carl F. Wittke, *Tambo and Bones: A History of the American Minstrel Stage* (Durham, N.C.: Duke University Press, 1930); Robert C. Toll, *Blacking Up: The Minstrel Show in Nineteenth-Century America* (New York: Oxford University Press, 1974); and Hans Nathan, *Dan Emmett and the Rise of Early Negro Minstrelsy* (Norman: University of Oklahoma Press, 1962).

32. See Alexander Saxton, *The Rise and Fall of the White Republic: Class and Politics in Nineteenth-Century America* (London: Verso, 1990), 165–82 (166 for the quotations here). Also see David A. Roediger, *The Wages of Whiteness: Race and the Making of the American Working Class* (London: Verso, 1991), 115–32, and Eric Lott, *Love and Theft: Blackface Minstrelsy and the American Working Class* (New York: Oxford University Press, 1995).

33. See, for example, Nathan, *Dan Emmett*, 62–66; William J. Mahar, "'Backside Albany' and Early Blackface Minstrelsy," *American Music* 6, no. 1 (1988): 1–27; and Dale Cockrell, *Demons of Disorder: The Early Blackface Minstrels and Their World* (New York: Cambridge University Press, 1997).

34. Nathan, *Dan Emmett*, 62.

35. Wittke, *Tambo and Bones*, 58; broadsheet for a performance at the "Bowery Theater, Thursday Evening, March 18, 1841" (collections of the American Antiquarian Society, Worcester, Mass.).

36. Wittke, *Tambo and Bones*, 58.

37. See Robert F. Winans and Elias J. Kaufman, "Minstrel and Classic Banjo: American and English Connections," *American Music* 12 (Spring 1994): 1–9.

38. Robert F. Winans, "Early Minstrel

Show Music, 1843–1852," in *Musical Theatre in America*, ed. Glenn Loney (Westport, Conn.: Greenwood Press, 1984), 71, 78. As early as 1845 the banjo was so indelibly inscribed in popular culture that the fiction writer J. H. Ingraham named one of his African American characters "Banjo." See "Trout-Fishing: Or, Who Is the Captain[?]," in *Henry Howard; or, two Noes Make One Yes* (Boston: Henry L. Williams, 1845). We thank Ronald and Mary Zboray for this reference.

39. *New York Mirror*, 3 July 1897.

40. *Briggs' Banjo Instructor* (Boston: Oliver Ditson, 1855), publisher's preface.

41. George Inge to J. E. Henning, 16 July 1890, *The Elite Banjoist* 1, no. 1 (October/November 1890): 3.

42. *New York Clipper*, 13 April 1878. On Sweeney see Arthur Woodward, "Joel Sweeney and the First Banjo," *Los Angeles County Museum Quarterly* 7, no. 3 (1949): 7–11, and also a letter from the banjo maker Fred Mather in *Gatcomb's Banjo and Guitar Gazette* (2, no. 2 [November/December 1888]: 2), in which he recalls meeting Sweeney in 1850. Mather notes that because Sweeney "only played in what is now technically called 'banjo style,' (i.e. with thumb and first finger) . . . he passed out of the profession as the banjo improved in compass."

43. See, for example, Saxton, *Rise and Fall of the White Republic*, 171.

44. A. Baur, "Reminiscences of a Banjo Player," *S. S. Stewart's Banjo and Guitar Journal* 9, no. 6 (February/March 1893): 7–8. For a vivid re-creation of such encounters between the races in the antebellum period, see Wesley Brown's novel, *Darktown Strutters* (New York: Cane Hill Press, 1994).

45. Andy Cahan, "Manly Reece and the Dawn of North Carolina Banjo," in booklet accompanying the compact disc, *The North Carolina Banjo Collection*, CD 0439/40 (Cambridge, Mass.: Rounder, 1998), [1–7] ([5] and [6] for cited letters).

46. *New York Clipper*, 20 June 1874. Also see Howard L. Sacks and Judith Rose Sacks, *Way Up North in Dixie: A Black Family's Claim to the Confederate Anthem* (Washington, D.C.: Smithsonian Institution Press, 1993), for more information on where Emmett acquired his music.

47. "Early Days of the Banjo, By An Old Timer," *The Cadenza* 1, no. 2 (November/December 1894): 5, also cited in Z. Porter Wright, "Banjology," *The Bacon and Day "Silver Bell" Banjo Family* (Groton, Conn.: Bacon Banjo Company, [ca. 1928]), 2.

48. Frank Converse, "Banjo Reminiscences," *The Cadenza* 7, no. 11 (July 1901): 2–4, and 8, no. 8 (April 1902): 3–4. It is worth noting that when William Sidney Mount, the mid-nineteenth-century genre painter and fiddler from Long Island, sought someone to make a violin on a new design he had developed, he depended on local craftsmen—a worker at the local piano factory, another at a carriage factory, another known primarily as a carpenter. His biographer writes: "Mount's statement that certain violins of his were put together by piano makers at odd moments reflects the amateurish tinker's world from which these instruments came." See Alfred Frankenstein, *William Sidney Mount* (New York: Abrams, 1975), 79–80.

49. "H. C. Dobson, Banjo Instructor, Dead," *The Cadenza* 15, no. 1 (July 1908): 15.

50. George H. Coes, "The Origin of the Banjo," *Gatcomb's Banjo and Guitar Gazette* 2, no. 2 (November/December 1888): 1. For another early reminiscence see Ralph Keeler, "Three Years as a Negro Minstrel," *Atlantic Monthly* 24 (July 1869): 71–85. Recalling his first experience of a minstrel show, at age twelve, Keeler noted that he could "convey no idea of the pleasurable thrill" he felt "at the banjo solo and the

plantation jig," and he thereupon bought himself a banjo "and had pennies screwed on the heels of [his] boots to practice 'Juba'" (71). Keeler's reminiscences of the minstrel stage are also found in his *Vagabond Adventures* (Boston: Fields, Osgood, 1870), 101–223.

51. Robert Soutar, ed., *A Jubilee of the Dramatic Life and Incident of Joseph A. Cave: Author, Manager, Actor, Vocalist* (London: Thomas Vernon, [1894]), 69–74; and Winans and Kaufman, "Minstrel and Classic Banjo," 2–8, for the banjo's early history in England.

52. For biographies see Edward LeRoy Rice, *Monarchs of Minstrelsy: From "Daddy" Rice to Date* (New York: Kenney Publishing Company, 1911), 12, 18, 22, 46. The last four players are the banjoists mentioned by "Ziska," the pen name of a New Yorker who, in a letter to the *Boston Daily Evening Voice* ("Our New York Letter," 20 October 1866, reprinted in *Banjo Newsletter* 4, no. 7 [May 1977]: 20–21), cited these along with Briggs as the earliest popularizers of the banjo. For their biographies see Rice, *Monarchs of Minstrelsy*, 59, 119, 51, 92.

53. One of the earliest banjo contests occurred in July 1857 at the Old Chinese Assembly Room at 539 Broadway, when Charles Plummer beat Picayune Butler and won a banjo worth $100. See "The First Banjo Tournament in America," *S. S. Stewart's Banjo and Guitar Journal* 7, no. 2 (June/July 1890): 1–2. The broadside in plate 1-6 announces another such contest just a few months later.

54. On Howe's career see Patrick Sky, *Mel Bay Presents Ryan's Mammoth Collection* (Pacific, Mo.: Mel Bay Publishing, 1995), 10–21.

55. [Elias Howe], *The Complete Preceptor for the Banjo . . . by Gumbo Chaff, A. M. A. First Banjo Player to the King of the Congo, and Author of the Ethiopian Glee Book* (Boston: Elias Howe, [1848]), unique copy at the American Antiquarian Society. Also see Elias J. Kaufman, "Early American Banjo Methods, Part 1," *Five-Stringer*, no. 174 (Winter 1993–Spring 1994): 6–15, 23, who cites an 1851 edition of the *Preceptor* published by Oliver Ditson and Company as the first. The contents of the 1851 edition, however, are the same as that issued by Howe in 1848. While Howe's tutor provides no information about how the banjo was played, it is significant for its indication of what tuning (C-F-C-E-G) was used on the minstrel stage in the 1840s.

56. In the 1890s Albert Baur claimed that Briggs's tutor was actually prepared by Frank Converse, who after 1860 published several other methods himself. See A. Baur, "Reminiscences of a Banjo Player," *S. S. Stewart's Banjo and Guitar Journal* 8, no. 5 (December 1891/January 1892): 7; *Briggs' Banjo Instructor*, publisher's preface; and *New York Musical World* 14, no. 262 (5 April 1856): 168. The poignant report of Briggs's death included in the preface to his tutor evidently was written by one George Wilkes; see "Ziska," "Our New York Letter."

57. [Elias Howe], *Howe's New American Banjo School* (Boston: Henry Tolman, 1857); *Phil. Rice's Correct Method for the Banjo: With or Without a Master* (Boston: Oliver Ditson, 1858; reprint, Bremo Bluff, Va.: Tuckahoe Music, 1998); and James Buckley, *Buckley's New Banjo Book* (Boston: Oliver Ditson, 1860; reprint, Bremo Bluff, Va.: Tuckahoe Music, 1996). Joe Ayers has suggested that Buckley is the central figure in this group, for he well may have had a hand in the compilation and publication of Briggs's and Rice's tutors. Moreover, Ayers believes that Buckley was the first to use European-style music notation to capture the uniqueness of African American banjo tunes. See "The Banjo in 1858: The Early Jazz of Phil Rice," *Tuckahoe Review* 1, no. 2 (Spring 1997): 4, 12–14, and "Banjo

Style: European Methodology Applied to African-American Technique" (paper read at the Conference on Antebellum Culture and the Banjo, Charlottesville, Va., 22 March 1997). Also see Chapter 2.

58. Nancy Groce, *Musical Instrument Makers of New York: A Directory of Eighteenth- and Nineteenth-Century Urban Craftsmen*, Annotated Reference Works in Music, no. 4 (Stuyvesant, N.Y.: Pendragon Press, 1991), 151, citing the *New York Business Directory for 1844*; also see pp. 93, 130. As further proof that by this period the banjo had become a commodity, a lithographed sheet-music cover showing William Hall and Son's music emporium in 1849 distinctly depicts banjos with guitars in the display windows; see George M. Warren, *Broadway Waltzes* (New York: William Hall and Son, 1849). Charles H. Kaufman, *Music in New Jersey, 1655–1860: A Study of Musical Activity in New Jersey from Its First Settlement to the Civil War* (Rutherford, N.J.: Fairleigh Dickinson University Press, 1981), 262. *Catalogue of the Eighteenth Exhibition of American Manufactures, Held in the City of Philadelphia. 1848* (Philadelphia: William S. Young, 1848), 5; *Catalogue of the Nineteenth Exhibition of American Manufactures* (Philadelphia: Young, 1849), 19; *Catalogue of the Twentieth Exhibition of American Manufactures* (Philadelphia: Young, 1850), 19.

59. *Reports of the First Exhibition of the Worcester County Mechanics Association* (Worcester, Mass.: Howland, 1848), 37; *Reports of the Second Exhibition of the Worcester County Mechanics Association* (Worcester, Mass.: Tyler and Hamilton, 184), 13.

60. Groce, *Musical Instrument Makers*, 82, 99, 32, 134, 88; *Transactions of the American Institute of the City of New-York, for the Year 1851* (Albany: Van Benthuysen, 1852), 642. *Official Catalogue of the New-York Exhibition of the Industry of All Nations* (New York: George P. Putnam, 1853), 95. *Transactions of the American Institute of the City of New-York, for the Years 1859–60* (Albany: Van Benthuysen, 1860), 76. Kaufman, *Music in New Jersey*, 262, 265, 267.

61. *Exhibition of the Metropolitan Mechanics' Institute* (Washington, D.C., 1853), 12–13, 24–25; *Report on the 26th Exhibition of American Manufactures Held in the City of Philadelphia . . . 1858 . . . by the Franklin Institute* (Philadelphia: Young, 1858), 9; *Reports of the Third Exhibition of the Worcester County Mechanics Association* (Worcester, Mass.: Webb, 1851), 56.

62. *The Seventh Exhibition of the Mass. Charitable Mechanic Association* (B. Damrell and Moore, and George Coolidge, 1853), 97; *The Ninth Exhibition of the Massachuetts Charitable Mechanic Association* (Boston: Rand and Avery, 1860), 119. Arey continued to exhibit through the 1860s, both in Boston and in Lowell, Massachusetts. See *The Tenth Exhibition of the Massachusetts Charitable Mechanic Association* (Boston: Wright and Potter, 1865), 132, and *The Third Exhibition of the Middlesex Mechanics' Association . . . in 1867* (Lowell, Mass.: Stone and Hue, 1868), 118. *Annual Report of the Board of Managers of the Maryland Institute for the Promotion of the Mechanic Arts* (Baltimore: Mills, 1851), 47, 68, 74; *The Book of the Exhibition: Ninth Annual Exhibition of the Maryland Institute for the Promotion of the Mechanic Arts* (Baltimore: Mills, 1856), 85, 185; *Twelfth Annual Report of the Board of Managers and Treasurer of the Maryland Institute for the Promotion of the Mechanic Arts* (Baltimore: Mills, 1860), 92, 183–84. Boucher also entered both a banjo and a guitar in the 1853 Crystal Palace Exhibition, the only banjo maker from outside New York to do so; see *Official Catalogue*, 95.

63. *LeCount and Strong's San Francisco Directory for the Year 1854* (San Francisco: Herald Office, 1854), 7, 48 (of advertising supplement); *New York Musical World* 17, no. 318 (2 May 1857): 282; and Henry G.

Langley, comp., *San Francisco Directory for 1859* (San Francisco: Valentine, 1859), 206, 323.

64. Groce, *Musical Instrument Makers*, 155, 112, 131; Rice, *Monarchs of Minstrelsy*, 142; *S. S. Stewart's Banjo and Guitar Journal* 2, no. 4 (August 1883): 2.

65. George Inge to J. E. Henning; R. B. Pore to J. E. Henning, 25 July 1890, *The Elite Banjoist* 1, no. 1 (October/November 1890): 3.

66. Soutar, *Jubilee*, 73.

67. A. Baur, "Reminiscences of a Banjo Player," *S. S. Stewart's Banjo and Guitar Journal* 5, no. 2 (June/July 1888): 12.

68. Thomas J. Armstrong, "The Banjo and Its Makers," *The Crescendo* 7, no. 2 (August 1914): 20–21.

69. Baur, "Reminiscences," 12.

70. One reference occurs in the minstrel song "Picayune Butler's Come to Town." A verse notes that "about some twenty years ago, / Old Butler reigned wid his old Banjo, / Ah, ah, / Twas a gourd, three-string'd, and an old pine stick. . . ." See *Rice's Correct Method*, 33.

71. *The Book of the Exhibition: Fifth Annual Exhibition of the Maryland Institute for the Promotion of the Mechanic Arts* (Baltimore: Mills, 1852), 65. Oddly, the judges were unable to evaluate this banjo for a premium because "the Banjo was in a locked case, the key of which was not at hand" when they came to examine the instrument (117).

72. *Rice's Correct Method*, 8.

73. *George C. Dobson's New Banjo School* (Boston: White, Smith, [1877]), 23; *Buckley's New Banjo Book*, 6. But Dobson warned against skin that appeared transparent, for that was a sure sign that it had been treated in some way. Also see Jackson S. Schultz, *The Leather Manufacture in the United States: A Dissertation on the Methods and Economies of Tanning* (New York: Shoe and Leather Reporter Office, 1876), which, for all its thoroughness, unfortunately does not speak specifically to the issue of drum or banjo heads.

74. The graphic art produced to accompany sheet music was not strictly representational. Much of it partook either of the delineator's shorthand—after all, these were artists producing advertising copy rather than draftsmen preparing blueprints—or of the racial stereotyping common in that period.

75. *Rice's Correct Method*, 8, 12. The generally received opinion has been that frets were not regularly added to banjos until the 1870s, but given the fact that some makers (such as Ashborn) also produced guitars, to find frets or flush position markers on antebellum instruments should not be surprising. The early banjo maker Fred Mather, in a reminiscence of Joel Sweeney, recalled that "in Sweeney's time no player went below the fifth fret," thus obviating the need for position markers. See *Gatcomb's Banjo and Guitar Gazette* 2, no. 2 (November/December 1888): 2. But another banjo player recalled a fretted banjo that he saw in Boston "in the fall of 1847," owned by the minstrel W. W. Newcomb. "I also know," he added, "that W. W. Newcomb owned the banjo up to the time of his death in 1874." See "Early Days of the Banjo," *The Cadenza* 1, no. 2 (November/December 1894): 5.

76. *S. S. Stewart's Banjo and Guitar Journal* 9, no. 4 (October/November 1892): 5.

77. On Boucher see Laurence Libin, *American Musical Instruments in the Metropolitan Museum of Art* (New York: W. W. Norton, 1985), 109, and Lloyd P. Farrar, "Under the Crown and Eagle," *Newsletter of the American Musical Instrument Society* 16, no. 3 (October 1987): 8–9. Boucher's drum making is discussed in G. Craig Caba, *United States Military Drums, 1845–1865: A Pictorial Survey* (Harrisburg, Pa.: Civil War Antiquities, 1977), 80–81, and is

significant because it indicates that Boucher already would have known how to bend wood into a circular shape—the same process, in other words, necessary to make banjo rims.

78. See *Matchett's Baltimore Directory for 1849–50* (Baltimore: R. J. Matchett, 1849) for the first separate listing of the younger Boucher.

79. *Ninth Annual Exhibition*, 185, 190; *Twelfth Annual Report*, 184, 186.

80. Document in the possession of Boucher's descendants, photocopy provided to the authors by Laurence Libin.

81. The report of one mechanics' exhibition noted that Boucher entered "a very large Bass drum" whose "improvement consist[ed] of round brass hooks, placed at regular intervals around the brace hoops, instead of the old-fashioned perforations in the hoops themselves, for securing the bracing cords" (*Ninth Annual Exhibition*, 185). Because of the mention of cords, this system thus does not appear to be the sort of hook-and-nut assembly that he used on his banjos but does indicate that in general he was trying to improve his tensioning devices. See note 83 below for discussion of the one extant Boucher banjo without hooks.

82. Robert F. Winans has speculated that these indentations are position markers, indicating the octave (twelfth-fret) position on the fingerboard, if the bridge is located in the center of the head, as it should be to produce the best sound from such banjos. Communication to the authors.

83. In *American Musical Instruments* (108) Libin includes a photograph of the Metropolitan Museum of Art's Boucher banjo, which has a typical neck that appears to have been wedded at a later date to a gourd body with a tack head. Given the sophistication of all other extant Bouchers, it seems unlikely that he produced such a gourd instrument.

84. Farrar, "Under the Crown and Eagle," 9.

85. On C. F. Martin and his company, see Mike Longworth, *Martin Guitars: A History*, 3d ed. (Nazareth, Pa.: Longworth, 1988); Walter Carter, *The Martin Book* (San Francisco: GPI Books, 1995); and Jim Washburn and Richard Johnson, *Martin Guitars* (Emmaus, Pa.: Rodale Press, 1997).

86. Libin, *American Musical Instruments*, 74–75; and "The Eisenbrandt Family Pedigree," in Friedemann Hellwig, ed., *Studia Organologica: Festschrift für John Henry van der Meer zu seinem fünfundsechzigsten Geburtstag* (Tutzing: Schneider, 1987), 335–42.

87. Farrar, "Under the Crown and Eagle," 8–9, and *Baltimore Business Directory* (Baltimore: Murphy, 1845), 56, for an advertisement for "William Boucher's Music Store," where, among other things, "Lessons on the Accordeon" were offered.

88. See Carter, *Martin Book*, 9, and Washburn and Johnson, *Martin Guitars*, 18–23.

89. Ashborn's journal is owned by Philip F. Gura, who has published a monograph on the guitar factory; see "Manufacturing Guitars for the American Parlor: James Ashborn's Wolcottville, Connecticut, Guitar Factory, 1851–1856," *Proceedings of the American Antiquarian Society* 104, part 1 (April 1994): 117–55. Ashborn might have kept a separate account for his banjo making, but the extant document shows him repairing other kinds of instruments and performing other, related labor as well.

The logical assumption about the lack of mention of any banjos—that he might not have begun to make them before 1856—is undercut by the fact that the patent he filed in 1852 for a "guitar key" shows four of his novel tuning pegs in what unmistakably is a banjo, not a guitar, head stock, of the same trapezoidal shape as his extant banjos. On the other hand, William Hall's advertisement of 1858 for a "new" banjo that the firm planned to make "a leading article" among their goods, strongly suggests that date for Ashborn's instrument. Hall mentioned "the improvement of the head, the screws, and in every part of the instrument," which certainly could describe the Ashborn. Moreover, the firm believed that this new model "will be the means of introducing it into every parlor," so that thereafter the banjo would not be used "only in Negro Minstrelsy, but will be found in the hands of every musical lady" (see *New York Musical World* 19, no. 20 [15 May 1858]: 316). To complicate matters, though, Ashborn's extant banjos have the stamps of either William Hall and Son, which operated throughout the 1850s and 1860s, or William Pond and Company, which commenced in 1864. Ashborn went out of business in the mid-1860s.

90. Full documentation of this section on Ashborn and his factory is found in Gura, "Manufacturing Guitars."

91. For an important discussion of the mechanic class in this period, see Sean Wilentz, *Chants Democratic: New York City and the Rise of the American Working Class, 1788–1850* (New York: Oxford University Press, 1984).

92. Stuart M. Blumin notes that cabinetmaking was one of the first industrialized trades of the antebellum period, evolving "rather quickly after the introduction around 1840 of circular saws for cutting veneers, from the traditional collection of small, independent, handworking, custom shops of the preindustrial era, to a more complicated arrangement of interdependent factories, dealers, auction houses, sawmills, and specialized small workshops" (*The Emergence of the Middle Class: Social Experience and the American City, 1760–1900* [Cambridge: Cambridge University

Press, 1989], 69). Ashborn's operation typifies this very transformation.

93. Jonathan Prude notes that the investment needed in the small factories like Ashborn's was not too great, and that frequently artisans themselves eventually turned into the entrepreneurs who "orchestrat[ed] industrialization." See "Capitalism, Industrialization, and the Factory in Post-Revolutionary America," in *Wages of Independence: Capitalism in the Early Republic*, ed. Paul Gilje (Madison, Wis.: Madison House, 1997), 89–93.

94. Peter Danaa, "Guitar," *New Grove Dictionary of American Music*, 4 vols. (New York: Grove Dictionaries of Music, 1986), 2:297, citing the United States census of 1860.

95. William Sidney Mount based his redesign of the violin, which he patented 1 June 1852, on similar time- and labor-saving principles. As one historian puts it, the impetus for Mount's violin "was the appearance, in the 1840s, of an urban-based mass market." He continues, "Mount himself advertised the commercial benefit of his violin's design—it was composed of a mere twenty-eight or thirty mass-produceable parts, rather than the fifty-six characteristic of a hand-crafted instrument." See Peter G. Buckley, "'The Place to Make an Artist Work': Micah Hawkins and William Sidney Mount in New York City," in *Catching the Tune: Music and William Sidney Mount*, ed. Janice Gray Armstrong (Stony Brook: The Museums at Stony Brook, 1984), 22. Also see Frankenstein, *Mount*, 79–94.

96. Particularly in rural manufacturing of the kind represented by Ashborn's works, division of labor rather than outright mechanization "was at the heart of the industrial revolution." See Richard Stott, "Artisans and Capitalist Development," in Gilje, *Wages of Independence*, 104. Prude concurs. "Early industrialization,"

he writes, "not only embraced both mechanized and unmechanized work operations" but also a "division of labor" that "could be accomplished by doling out subsidiary processes to networks of employees in decentralized workplaces, including the workers' own homes." "Early factories," he concludes, "were about organization as much as the length of work rosters or the roar of intricate machines." See "Capitalism, Industrialization, and the Factory," 86–87.

97. For initial information about Ashborn's patents we are indebted to Edmund Britt of Wakefield, Massachusetts, who has generously shared information about early banjos.

98. U.S. patents no. 7,279, 16 April 1850, and no. 9,268, 21 September 1852.

CHAPTER TWO

1. Patrick Sky, *Mel Bay Presents Ryan's Mammoth Collection* (Pacific, Mo.: Mel Bay Publishing, 1995), 11.

2. Elias Howe, *Howe's New American Banjo School* (Boston: Henry Tolman, 1857), 3. In 1859 Howe published an *Abridged Edition of Howe's New American Banjo School* (Boston: Russell and Tolman, 1859), which incorporates the same introductory material. See Elias J. Kaufman, "Early American Banjo Methods, Part 2," *Five-Stringer*, no. 176 (Winter 1994–Spring 1995): 6.

3. L. M. Gottschalk, *The Banjo: An American Sketch* (New York: William Hall and Son, 1855), written two years earlier. Other, similar compositions are W. K. Batchelder's *Imitation of the Banjo* (1850); T. Frank Bassford's *Banjo Dance* (1853), dedicated to Gottschalk; and H. C. Harris's *The Banjo: An Imitation of the Inimitable Instrument* (1863). On Gottschalk's interest in the banjo in the 1850s see S. Frederick Starr, *Bamboula!: The Life and Times of Louis Moreau Gottschalk* (New York: Oxford University Press, 1995), 146–48. Starr notes that in the 1850s Gottschalk wrote a newspaper review of an appearance of Buckley's Serenaders (147) and that one contemporary critic claimed that *The Banjo* was the composer's tribute to Thomas Vaughan, banjoist for Christy and Woods' Minstrels (148). Also see Paul Ely Smith, "Gottschalk's 'The Banjo,' op. 15, and the Banjo in the Nineteenth Century," *Current Musicology* 50 (1992): 47–61. Walt Whitman, *Notebooks and Unpublished Prose Manuscripts*, ed. Edward F. Grier, 6 vols. (New York: New York University Press, 1984), 1:152.

4. *Frank B. Converse's New and Complete Method for the Banjo with or without a Master* (New York: S. T. Gordon, 1865; reprint, Bremo Bluff, Va.: Tuckahoe Music, 1993).

5. Joseph W. Ayers, "Banjo in 1858: The Early Jazz of Phil Rice," *Tuckahoe Review* 1, no. 2 (Spring 1997), esp. pp. 6–10. S. S. Stewart noted that Buckley "was one of the first who added the guitar style frets to his banjo," although Stewart "believed that he played almost entirely 'banjo' or 'stroke' style," making many doubt his "wisdom" in using them. See S. S. Stewart, *The Banjo Philosophically: A Lecture* (Philadelphia: S. S. Stewart, 1886), 1.

In their study of the banjo in England, Robert F. Winans and Elias J. Kaufman note that the first sophisticated English tutor, E. W. Mackney's *Mackney's Banjo Tutor* (London: Music Publishing Company [1863]), derived from both Briggs's and Buckley's works. See their "Minstrel and Classic Banjo: American and English Connections," *American Music* 12, no. 1 (Spring 1994): 7, and notes 26 and 27. One other early English publication worth our notice is Edward Panormo's *Banjo Tutor for 5, 6, or 7 Strings* (London: Panormo, [1864]). The nephew of an important guitar maker, Panormo here documents that by this early date banjos with more than five strings were evidently available in England. See Introduction, note 20, above.

6. James Buckley, *Buckley's New Banjo Guide* (New York: C. H. Ditson, 1868), 2, where the editor notes that the book has been "carefully put together by Mr. James Buckley (father of 'Buckley's Serenaders') who has had twenty-six years experience as a teacher and player, and has improved the banjo by applying screws, and in other ways." Precisely what this "improvement" was is unknown, but it probably had to do with a tensioning mechanism for the head. It also is significant that from an early date Buckley evidently used a fretted instrument, the better to play the notes demanded by the new repertoire. In this same *Banjo Guide*, for example, he included a section on "How to Fret the Banjo." As he described it (4), "the frets are to be put the entire width of the fingerboard, with the exception of the 2nd, which only crosses the 2nd, 3rd and 4th strings." "On the first string," he continued, "you must have a small fret an eighth of an inch nearer the first fret." Note the resemblance of this description to the Ashborn banjo owned by Peter Szego (plate 1-30).

7. James Buckley, *Buckley's New Banjo Book* (New York: Oliver Ditson, 1860), 3.

8. *Briggs' Banjo Instructor* (Boston: Oliver Ditson, 1855), [4]. John S. Adams, *Adams' New Musical Dictionary* (New York: S. T. Gordon, 1865), 27. Adams also noted that the banjo "has five strings, played with the fingers and hand, its body in the form of a hoop, over which parchment is stretched, as over a drum."

9. Van Hagen was listed in city directories as a piano tuner (1857–60) and Kilbourne (without the final "e" on his name) as a drum maker (from 1857 through at least 1876). After 1863, however, Kilbourne operated a restaurant, with his brother William continuing drum and banjo manu-

facture. In the 1866 city directory William's advertisement included "Bass and Snare Drums" and tambourines and also noted him as "manufacturer of the Patent Guitar Banjo." The accompanying woodcut illustrates the same kind of instrument that is in the patent drawing. See *The Albany Directory for the Year 1866* (Albany: Sampson, Davenport, 1866), 239.

10. Biographical information on Converse is available in Edward LeRoy Rice, *Monarchs of Minstrelsy: From "Daddy" Rice to Date* (New York: Kenney Publishing Company, 1911), 119; Joseph Ayers's reprint of *Frank B. Converse's New and Complete Method for the Banjo with or without a Master* (Bremo Bluff, Va.: Tuckahoe Music, 1993), 1; and Frank Converse, "Banjo Reminiscences," *The Cadenza* 7, no. 11 (July 1901): 4, and 7, no. 10 (June 1901): 2–4.

11. *Frank Converse's "Old Cremona" Songster* (New York: Dick and Fitzgerald, 1863). By this period Converse had acquired a good deal of notoriety. An issue of the *National Police Gazette*, for example, reported that in April 1860 "Frank Converse the banjoist, his beautiful wife, and a young gentleman from Richmond, said to be smitten by the latter's charms, skipped away from Petersburg, Va., by the Southern train, leaving the 'Converse Opera Troupe' to fulfill the engagement at Mechanics' Hall as best they could." Evidently, Converse had left Richmond without paying for the rental of his hall and had gotten word that a writ soon would be served by the aggrieved parties. The article went on to remind readers that Converse was "the hero of a romantic marriage in Elmira, N.Y." and his wife "the possessor of a handsome fortune of $100,000, acquired by a previous marriage, Converse being her third husband." The report concluded: "Converse has proven himself unworthy of the public confidence, and should be posted as such, wherever there is

any probability of his imposing himself." See *National Police Gazette* 15 (whole no. 764), 28 April 1860, p. 4.

12. He uses this phrase in the preface to *Frank B. Converse's Banjo Instructor without a Master* (New York: Dick and Fitzgerald, 1865), iii.

13. Converse later published another important method, *The Banjo and How To Play It* (New York: Dick and Fitzgerald, 1872), similar in format to his *Banjo Instructor without a Master* and issued by the same publisher. It was, however, an entirely new book.

14. *Converse's Banjo with or without a Master*, 39.

15. Winans and Kaufman agree that the "physical structure" of the banjo was changing during this time, "becoming less rudimentary and better adapted to playing more elaborate music, though whether," they continue, "the better banjos 'allowed' for improvements in playing style or the style changes themselves created a demand for better instruments would be hard to say." "Clearly, however," they conclude, "a critical interplay between technological and musical developments was occurring." See "Minstrel and Classic Banjo," 9–10.

16. We should note, however, that the wood-bodied mandoline-banjo developed in the 1880s by August Pollman (see fig. 4-27, plate 4-24, and Chapter 4, note 72, below) incorporates some of Brown's ideas. But Pollman's instrument had a cut-out sound hole on its top and is not circular in shape.

17. Christopher F. Burrowes, U.S. patent no. 224,512, 17 February 1880.

18. Nancy Groce, *Musical Instrument Makers of New York: A Directory of Eighteenth- and Nineteenth-Century Urban Craftsmen*, Annotated Reference Works in Music, no. 4 (Stuyvesant, N.Y.: Pendragon Press, 1991), 72.

19. Ibid., 157. [C. Bruno and Son], *Descriptive Price List . . . C. Bruno and Son . . . Importers and Wholesalers in Musical Instruments* (New York: Wynkoop and Hallenbeck, 1874), 16.

20. Groce, *Musical Instrument Makers*, 11; *New York Clipper*, 8 March 1873, p. 8, and 5 April 1873, p. 8; and a four-page advertising brochure, "John J. Bogan, Manufacturer of Silver Rim, Stage and Parlor Banjos, and Dealer in All Kinds of Musical Instruments and Strings" (New York, ca. 1870).

21. S. S. Stewart, *The Banjo! A Dissertation* (Philadelphia: S. S. Stewart, 1888), 24. Overall, however, Stewart was deeply critical of Dobson's various "improvements." As early as 1882 he had observed that "the closed-back banjo seems to be going down hill fast," and he blamed the 1867 closed-back model on Dobson's misguided "idea of supplying the demand for a Banjo that was not a Banjo, but was an attempt at something else—purely a miscarriage of ideas." Admittedly, the instrument was loud, Stewart continued, "but the loudness was caused rather by compound and conflicting vibrations than by increased musical power of tone, and therefore had a certain lack of musical quality." *S. S. Stewart's Banjo and Guitar Journal* 1, no. 8 (December 1882): 2, and Stewart, *The Banjo!*, 24.

22. *New York Clipper*, 5 April 1873, p. 8. "Ziska," "Our New York Letter," *Boston Daily Evening Voice*, 20 October 1866; reprinted in *Banjo Newsletter* 4, no. 7 (May 1977): 20–21. The author of this piece must have known Dobson closely (or perhaps was Dobson himself), for although this article was published before the banjo was patented the author was privy to much detailed information about it. He noted, for example, "that a new patent banjo has just been completed, and will soon be on the market at a lower price than any other instrument. It does away with screws on the side, which flay the dresses of lady per-

formers, and has a back of wood with perforations for the sound to escape."

23. By the late 1880s the L. B. Gatcomb Company of Boston was touted because "every part of a banjo is made in their own shop." "Consequently," one writer continued, "every part is interchangeable," manufactured by machines "which have been constructed at great expense" and which could not be found "in any other establishment." The result "so reduced the cost of time and labor that a beautiful instrument can be sold at a price which others cannot rival" (*Gatcomb's Banjo and Guitar Gazette* 2, no. 4 [March/April 1889]: 2).

24. Stiles also noted that, depending on how "metallic" one liked the tone, his banjo could be strung with either gut or metal strings, one of the earliest references to using the latter on the banjo.

25. Philip Scranton makes this distinction in his recent study of early American manufacturing; see his *Endless Novelty: Specialty Production and American Industrialization, 1865–1925* (Princeton: Princeton University Press, 1997), 10–12. In batch production instruments are made in small lots of various sizes, often on the basis of aggregated advance orders. In bulk production the manufacturer makes much larger numbers of goods based on what he perceives as the potential size of the market for them. In the late 1880s Albert Baur recalled that the "factory banjo" had first made its appearance "during the war" ("Reminiscences of a Banjo Player," *S. S. Stewart's Banjo and Guitar Journal* 5, no. 2 [June/July 1888]: 12); he may well have had in mind Ashborn's Connecticut factory (see Chapter 1). We also should keep in mind, however, that during this period small workshops continued to turn out instruments. In 1870, for example, the New York maker Theodore Lohr manufactured banjos with the help of just one "workman" and "two boys" yet had in stock "150 dozen

banjos"; see Groce, *Musical Instrument Makers*, 99.

26. [Bruno and Son], *Descriptive Price List*, 15.

27. Herman Sonntag, *Illustrated Catalogue of Musical Instruments, Strings, &c.* (New York, [ca. 1877]), 20–21.

28. Baur, "Reminiscences," 12, draws this distinction between "factory" and "legitimate" banjos and notes that "there is as much difference between the factory-made banjo and one constructed by a man who knows his business, as there is between a well-made custom shoe and a prison-made brogan." "Store tubs" is S. S. Stewart's phrase, used (among other places) in his *Banjo Philosophically*, 3. Like Baur's letter, Stewart's lecture contains important information about these factories.

29. Groce, *Musical Instrument Makers*, 24.

30. Baur, "Reminiscences," 12. The remainder of our discussion of these factories is drawn either from this article, pp. 12–13, or from Stewart, *Banjo Philosophically*, 3–4.

31. In 1833, for example, from another firm Buckbee ordered twenty-five dozen 11-inch banjo "hoops," along with many more dozen larger sizes for drums, specifying that the banjo parts be of "straight grained maple." He also complained that some from the firm's last shipment were "very rough" and "thinner by 1/16 in." than he wanted and asked them "to please look after these points and make them right" (letter from J. H. Buckbee to H. B. Smith and Son, 3 September 1883; courtesy of David Fridy). In Baur's comment we find an early indication of the distinction between "authentic" instruments and those of lower quality, mere "imitations," that would become so important to banjo makers in the 1890s. For an illuminating discussion of Victorian America's concern with the authentic, see Miles Orvell, *The*

Real Thing: Imitation and Authenticity in American Culture, 1880–1940 (Chapel Hill: University of North Carolina Press, 1989).

32. Such agreements between banjoists, manufacturers, and wholesalers were often complex and occasionally rancorous. In the late 1880s, for example, Converse sued John F. Stratton and Company, claiming that they had not lived up to their agreement in the manufacture of the "Frank B. Converse Banjo." Evidently Stratton had sold other banjos (presumably inferior instruments) with Converse's name, in violation of their contract, had marketed the Converse model without his trademark for their own profit, and had neglected to keep accurate accounts of those sold under his name. A New York judge ruled in Converse's favor, rescinding the contract, delivering the trademark to him, and appointing a "referee" to ascertain the royalties due. See *Gatcomb's Banjo and Guitar Gazette* 1, no. 5 (May/June 1888): supplement.

33. *Norton's Daily True Whig*, 28 March 1853, cited in Howard L. Sacks and Judith Rose Sacks, *Way Up North in Dixie: A Black Family's Claim to the Confederate Anthem* (Washington, D.C.: Smithsonian Institution Press, 1993), 229, n. 87. *Root and Cady's Illustrated Catalogue and Price List* (Chicago: Root and Cady, [ca. 1870]), 66. Also see *J. Howard Foote's Descriptive Catalogue of Musical Instruments, Strings, &c.* ([New York and Chicago, 1868]), 47–48. Foote had music stores in both New York and Chicago and in this catalog offered banjos "for boys" as cheaply as $1.50, with full-size instruments only twenty-five cents more. And as early as 1854 one A. Morris published *The Virginia Merchants Purchasing Memorandum Book, and Pocket Companion* (Richmond: A. Morris, 1854), "designed to Facilitate in making a correct list of Wants, before leaving home," and "Prepared Expressly for the Use of Country Merchants." On page 2 he called himself an "Importer of Musical Instruments" who had in stock "Guitars, Violins, Accordeons, Flutes, Banjos and Strings," and among the items for the country merchant to consider he listed an even wider range of musical instruments.

34. Stewart used the term "rage" to describe the country's infatuation with the banjo. See *The Banjo!*, 106. One homemade banjo from the 1870s in Philip F. Gura's collection has a very unsophisticated neck and rim, with only its guitar-style tuners and its hooks, nuts, and bracket shoes coming from a factory.

35. In 1866 "Ziska," in "Our New York Letter," noted that "the manufactory of the Dobsons is situated in the upper part of the city, and turns out from fifty to one hundred banjos a day."

36. Alvin F. Harlow, *Old Bowery Days: Chronicles of a Famous Street* (New York: Appleton, 1931), 272. "Ziska" ("Our New York Letter") also reported that "when a boy, Henry frequently 'went his six-pence' in Charles White's old Ethiopian Opera House, and there imbibed a passion for the banjo which pervaded his soul like the dream of a maniac."

37. *S. S. Stewart's Banjo and Guitar Journal* 15, no. 1 (April/May 1898): 4; "Ziska," "Our New York Letter."

38. See Groce, *Musical Instrument Makers*, 41–43, for biographical information about these brothers; unless otherwise noted, our facts come from this source. Unfortunately, Groce does not provide vital statistics for Frank Dobson. Also, for Henry C. Dobson, see "H. C. Dobson, Banjo Instructor, Dead," *The Cadenza* 15, no. 1 (July 1908): 15.

39. In this period *The American Musical Directory* (New York: T. Hutchinson, 1861), 116, listed only two banjo teachers in New York City: George C. Dobson and James Buckley. Providing information for his father's obituary, Henry's son George (not to

be confused with Henry's brother George C. Dobson) noted that his father "opened his first teaching class in 1853 at Broadway and Amity Street." "He set himself," his son wrote, "to combat the prejudice that the banjo was an instrument exclusively for negroes, and so well succeeded that he introduced the instrument to the attention of the wealthy residents of New York." See "H. C. Dobson, Banjo Instructor, Dead," 15.

40. "Ziska," "Our New York Letter." The information about Henry Dobson in the following two paragraphs derives from this article.

41. A. Baur, "Reminiscences of a Banjo Player," *S. S. Stewart's Banjo and Guitar Journal* 4, no. 8 (February/March 1888): 2.

42. "Ziska," "Our New York Letter," in which the writer comments on their tutoring Thalberg, who became "proficient on the instrument" and introduced it "in his performances before the crowned heads of Europe."

43. Ibid., and *New York Clipper*, 29 November 1873, p. 8.

44. "Henry C. Dobson's Great Parlor, Stage and Solo Banjos" ([New York, ca. 1884]).

45. Information on the banjo is available from the patent and also in the advertising brochure mentioned in note 44. Three years later (U.S. patent no. 294,451) Dobson reworked this same design. Instead of the flange he used a hollow brass tube with holes cut at intervals to allow the sound to escape, an arrangement that enhanced the instrument's "bell-like reverberation." Although Dobson acknowledged that other makers recently had experimented with various kinds of tone rings, he was not aware "that any banjo has ever yet been made or patented the ring or rim of which consists of an annular metal tube." He probably had in mind the patents of Christopher Burrowes (see note 17 above) and James Morrison (U.S. patent no. 264,893,

26 September 1882), both of which had experimental tone rings.

46. *New York Clipper*, 26 March 1881, p. 6. With his usual animus against competitors, however, S. S. Stewart severely criticized all of Dobson's improvements. After Dobson's closed-back models had been "tabooed by the Banjo-playing public and remitted to pawnbrokers' establishments," Stewart wrote, Dobson "lost no time in placing upon the market a 'patent open-back' banjo, constructed upon another principle, but equally crude and fallacious." See *The Banjo!*, 25.

47. "Ziska," "Our New York Letter."

48. Christine Merrick Ayars, *Contributions to the Art of Music in America by the Music Industries of Boston, 1640–1936* (New York: H. W. Wilson, 1937), 275. Also see F. O. Jones, *A Handbook of American Music and Musicians, Containing Biographies of American Musicians and Histories of the Principal Musical Institutions, Firms, and Societies* (Canaseraga, N.Y.: privately printed, 1886), 49.

49. *Geo. C. Dobson's Simplified Method and Thorough School for the Banjo: Two Books in One* (Boston: John F. Perry, 1874), 2. In speaking of George's brothers Henry and C. Edgar, however, "Ziska" noted in 1866 that they "invented notes and published a note book," suggesting that the new method had been developed as much by the family as by any one brother. "Ziska," "Our New York Letter."

50. *Dobson's Simplified Method*, 3. During this period banjo makers and players continued to debate the question of whether to use frets. See, for example, S. S. Stewart's "The Subject of Frets" (*S. S. Stewart's Banjo and Guitar Gazette* 3, no. 9 [April/May 1886]: 2–3), in which he claims that "one of the greatest objections" he has to the use of frets is that "it becomes impossible to alter the situation or position of the bridge after the banjo has been fretted." "With a smooth

fingerboard," he continued, "a good player can, by changing the position of the bridge upon his instrument, alter the pitch a half tone or even a full tone either way, in a second of time."

51. *Dobson's Simplified Method*, 8–9.

52. In an extensive catalog of sheet music that the well-known White, Smith and Company published in 1871, three of the four banjo tutors for sale were by the Dobsons: "Dobson's Brothers Modern Method" at $1; "George C. Dobson's New School for the Banjo" at seventy-five cents; and "Star Method for the Banjo—Dobson" at twenty-five cents. (The last was "Shay's Method New and Easy" at seventy-five cents paper, $1 in boards.) Of the five pieces of separately issued banjo music then available through the company, all were written by George C. Dobson. *Catalogue of the Sheet Music and Musical Works Published by the White, Smith and Co.* (Boston: White, Smith, [1877]), 238, 227.

53. Stewart, *The Banjo!*, 30–31; "The Idiot's Delight," *S. S. Stewart's Banjo and Guitar Journal* 2, no. 3 (July 1883): 4; and ibid. 2, no. 9 (April/May 1884): 2.

54. *S. S. Stewart's Banjo and Guitar Journal* 2, no. 3 (July 1883): 4, and Stewart, *The Banjo!*, 31. Stewart's allusion to others making money off this system probably refers to businesses like the Dime Banjo Music Company, located at 203 and 205 Fulton Street, Brooklyn, which in the mid-1880s circulated a broadsheet entitled "BANJO TAUGHT BY MAIL" (see fig. 2-39). "Only Three Characters" were used, and one could buy any of 3,000 tunes, at ten cents each. "Every Tune," the advertisement continued, was "fully explained by printed directions on the back, and the most unmusical person [was] guaranteed to learn" from it. The system was identical to Dobson's. Frank Batchelder, of Woodburn, Indiana, had firsthand experience with it. He wrote Stewart that when he had progressed on the banjo far enough to want "a little larger collection" of tunes he "entered negotiation with a concern calling it the Dime Banjo Music Company and got a large lot of simplified music." However, he found the method "a grand humbug" that did him "no good." *S. S. Stewart's Banjo and Guitar Journal* 1, no. 10 (February 1883): 2.

55. *George C. Dobson's Victor Banjos* (Boston: Farwell, 1885), 1–2. In an extant fragment of an article on Dobson from *The Folio* (ca. 1885), one writer noted that Dobson's Victor banjos had become "so justly famous that great numbers" were exported to Europe "on nearly every steamer, mostly for the English market." The writer also noted that "an entire factory is kept constantly at work manufacturing them" but did not mention where it was, thus allowing the possibility that (as Baur suggested) at least some parts of the Dobsons' instruments were made in New York City. In any event, as Stewart suggested, Dobson probably did not himself operate the factory but, rather, "supervised" the construction of instruments made to his specifications by other workmen.

56. See, for example, *Geo. C. Dobson's Star Instructor and Simplified Tunes for the Banjo* (Boston: White, Smith, 1879), which gave "Full Directions How to Play the Instrument Without Study or Learning Notes," and his *Complete Instructor for the Banjo* (Boston: White, Smith, 1880). The quotation is from the latter's preface.

57. "Ziska," "Our New York Letter." Again, we remind readers of the possibility that one of the Dobsons might have written this piece; see note 22 above.

58. Groce, *Musical Instrument Makers*, 42.

59. *Briggs' Banjo Instructor*, 4. *Price List of S. S. Stewart's Parlor[,] Concert[,] and Orchestra Banjos* ([Philadelphia: S. S. Stewart], 1887).

60. Groce, *Musical Instrument Makers*, 41–42.

61. *American Musical Directory of the United States and Provinces, 1885* (Syracuse: Central Publishing House, 1885), 203; Groce, *Musical Instrument Makers*, 42. From 1884 to 1892 this Dobson lived in London, where he kept a teaching studio. See W. W. Brewer, "The Banjo in America," *Banjo-Mandolin-Guitar* 49 (August 1952): 266.

62. "Ziska," "Our New York Letter."

63. Ibid.

CHAPTER THREE

1. H. P. Wayne, "A Brief Sketch of the Life of S. S. Stewart, Maker of the Celebrated Banjos," in S. S. Stewart, *The Minstrel Banjoist. Containing The Rudiments of Music and A Course of Instruction for the Banjo: Together with a Choice Collection of Jigs, Reels, Schottisches, etc.* (Philadelphia: S. S. Stewart, 1881), 49–52; and "What Is Said About S. S. Stewart," *S. S. Stewart's Banjo and Guitar Journal* 6, no. 3 (October/November 1889): 5, a column reprinted from the *Daily Hotel Reporter*. Unless otherwise noted, biographical material on the early part of Stewart's life is drawn from these two sources.

2. For information on Simmons, see Edward LeRoy Rice, *Monarchs of Minstrelsy: From "Daddy" Rice to Date* (New York: Kenney Publishing Company, 1911), 126.

3. In our use of the term "middle-class" throughout this work we have been guided by Stuart M. Blumin's important study, *The Emergence of the Middle Class: Social Experience in the American City, 1760–1900* (Cambridge and New York: Cambridge University Press, 1989), esp. chaps. 5–8.

4. Karen Linn's chapter, "The 'Elevation' of the Banjo in the Late Nineteenth Century," in *That Half-Barbaric Twang: The Banjo in American Popular Culture* (Ur-

bana: University of Illinois Press, 1991), offers an important discussion of this topic. By the 1880s the phrase was in fairly common usage. When the minstrel Billy Snow published a tutor in 1883, for example, he told the public that he hoped that his "little work" would "assist in elevating the instrument" in the public's eye. *Billy Snow's Banjo and Cornet Instructor* (New York: New York Popular Publishing Company, 1883), 7.

5. Over the course of his career Stewart filed only two patents, one (U.S. patent no. 355,896, 11 January 1887) for a metal supporting rod for the banjo neck and another (U.S. patent no. 413,579, 22 October 1889) for a banjo "thimble," that is, a thin piece of metal to cover the tip of one's finger so that one could pluck the strings more firmly and loudly. Stewart also suggested that one could use a thin piece of tortoise shell that simulated more accurately the fingernail.

6. *S. S. Stewart's Banjo and Guitar Journal* 6, no. 3 (October/November 1889): 4, quoting the *New York Clipper* article. Elias J. Kaufman (in "S. S. Stewart Banjos," *Mugwumps* 2, no. 3 [May 1973]: 3) notes that Stewart "ballyhooed his merchandise in a way that would cause P. T. Barnum to blush for shame." Also see Kaufman's subsequent articles on Stewart in ibid., no. 4 (July 1973): 15–16, no. 5 (September 1973): 3–5, and no. 6 (November 1973): 3–6; and F. Hickinbottom, "S. S. Stewart and His Banjos," *Banjo-Mandolin-Guitar* 66 (September 1969): 360–1, and 67 (October 1969): 7–8.

7. After Stewart's death in 1898 the journal was continued by his associate Charles Morris and, in its final year, by Stewart's sons Fred and Lemuel.

8. The best account of Swaim's Panacea is given in James Harvey Young, *The Toadstool Millionaires: A Social History of Patent Medicines in America before Federal Regulation* (Princeton, N.J.: Princeton University

Press, 1961), 58–74. For an example of Swaim's advertising, see William Swaim, *Cases of Cures Performed by the Use of Swaim's Panacea* (Philadelphia: Clark and Raser, 1827). The details of how the business was operated come from *The Will of Dr. James Swaim, who died in Paris, 13th March, 1870* (Philadelphia: Jas. B. Rodger, [1870]), 11. In the arrangement codified therein, Franklin Stewart was to receive an annual stipend of $2,500 for conducting the business for the benefit of James Swaim's son, William, as he had done for the testator. We are indebted to James Green of the Library Company of Philadelphia for information regarding the Swaim and Stewart families.

9. In the 1880s John Davis, a prominent music teacher in Springfield, Massachusetts, recalled that when he began playing the banjo (ca. 1870), he used to be "dreadfully ashamed of it" because it was "considered a low kind of instrument, only fit for drumming plantation jigs." Thus, when he took it out of doors he "covered it up" as well as he could and "slipped along the back streets" where he would be "least seen." Davis also remembered that when he began on the instrument "there were not more than two or three persons in the city who played the banjo at all, and those were colored men." See *Gatcomb's Banjo and Guitar Gazette* 2, no. 2 (November/December 1888): 2.

10. S. S. Stewart, *Complete American Banjo School. Complete in Two Parts* (Philadelphia: S. S. Stewart, [1883]). This was Stewart's most popular tutor and supposedly went through over thirty editions.

11. "Plain Facts! Matter of Vital Importance to All Banjoists," [1]. This is an eight-page promotional brochure whose testimonials all date from the late 1870s or early 1880; hence, we date it ca. 1880, a supposition also supported by the address on the materials, No. 429 North Eighth Street, which was Stewart's location at this point in his career. Also see "All About the Banjo, By S. S. Stewart" ([Philadelphia, ca. 1880]) for more invective against the Dobson method.

12. "Plain Facts!," [1].

13. See the promotional broadsheet, "A Few Plain Facts for Banjo Players, and Those Interested in the Instrument, by S. S. Stewart, the Artistic Banjoist" ([Philadelphia]: Johnson, [ca. 1880]).

14. In the early 1880s, at his American Banjo School and Instruction Rooms, Stewart offered students instruction in both "comic and Artistic Banjo playing, for the professional or for their own amusement." He charged $15 for one quarter's tuition (twenty-four lessons). See *S. S. Stewart's Banjo and Guitar Journal* 2, no. 4 (August 1883): 4.

15. Stewart, *The Minstrel Banjoist*, 3–5.

16. "A Few Plain Facts for Banjo Players"; "Plain Facts!," [2], [4]. Both the Dime Banjo Music Company (see Chapter 2) and the Keystone Banjo Music Company of Philadelphia offered to teach pupils the banjo by mail. See *S. S. Stewart's Banjo and Guitar Journal* 2, no. 6 (November 1883): 6.

17. "All About the Banjo," and *S. S. Stewart's Banjo and Guitar Journal* 4, no. 3 (April 1887): 2. As we shall see, similar sentiments occur everywhere in Stewart's writings through the 1880s. In a four-page flyer from 1879, "How to Order Banjos and Other Goods," for fifty cents Stewart offered to arrange for the banjo any published "piano song." A "piano march" cost $1.

18. The scholarly literature on this topic is immense, but the reader should consider especially James D. Norris, *Advertising and the Transformation of American Society, 1865–1920*, Contributions in Economics and Economic History, no. 110 (Westport, Conn.: Greenwood Press, 1990), esp. 1–46, 71–94, and Jackson Lears, *Fables*

of Abundance: A Cultural History of Advertising in America (New York: Basic Books, 1994), esp. 137–96, and, as well, Robert Higgs, The Transformation of the American Economy, 1865–1914: An Essay in Interpretation (New York: Wiley, 1971); Daniel Horowitz, The Morality of Spending: Attitudes toward the Consumer Society in America, 1875–1940 (Baltimore: Johns Hopkins University Press, 1985); and [Patrick] Glen Porter and Harold Livesay, Merchants and Manufacturers: Studies in the Changing Structure of Nineteenth-Century Marketing (Baltimore: Johns Hopkins University Press, 1971). Also, by the later 1880s Stewart's understanding of the importance of advertising was shared by others in the music business. See, for example, Margaret Downie Banks and James W. Jordan, "C. G. Conn: The Man (1844–1931) and His Company (1874–1915)," Journal of the American Musical Instrument Society 14 (1988): 89–93, for a discussion of similar advertising techniques by the premier maker of brass instruments.

19. A. Baur, "Reminiscences of a Banjo Player (Ninth Letter)," S. S. Stewart's Banjo and Guitar Journal 9, no. 2 (June/July 1892): 5; and ibid. 4, no. 7 (December 1887/January 1888): 3. Baur recalled getting only a few numbers of Converse and DeGroot's journal, and also that in 1872 he got a copy of "The Banjoist," into which the earlier effort "had been merged." We have not located any copy of a journal edited by any of the Dobsons.

20. S. S. Stewart's Banjo and Guitar Journal 3, no. 9 (April/May 1886): 2.

21. Ibid. 1, no. 5 (September 1, 1882): 1. "We want," Stewart wrote in this issue, "a few hundred more teachers to act as agents for the Journal and other publications."

22. Ibid. 2, no. 9 (April/May 1884): 1.

23. Ibid. 4, no. 7 (December 1887/January 1888): 2. Gatcomb's Banjo and Guitar Gazette first appeared in October 1887 and continued through 1899. The Banjo Herald was published by Walter C. Bryant, who allowed it to be absorbed by Gatcomb's periodical when he discovered that it took too much time from his work as a banjo instructor; see Gatcomb's Banjo and Guitar Gazette 1, no. 2 (November 1887): 1. Clearly modeled on Stewart's journal, Gatcomb's venture lacked Stewart's vitriol against other makers. As one correspondent put it, Gatcomb's journal "is always a pleasure to read," for it "contains none of the petty jealousy and spiteful allusions which form such a feature of another American periodical we wot of" (ibid. 7, no. 11 [August 1894]: 40).

24. New York Clipper, 25 April 1891.

25. S. S. Stewart's Banjo and Guitar Journal 3, no. 12 (October/November 1886): 3.

26. This weekly exchange of challenge and vituperation is found in the New York Clipper between 4 December 1880 and 22 January 1881.

27. For biographical information on these players, see Rice, Monarchs of Minstrelsy, 46, 183, 186–87, 152, and 215. On Weston, also see Elias J. Kaufman, "Horace Weston," The Five-Stringer, no. 115 (Fall 1974), and on Baur see S. S. Stewart's Banjo and Guitar Journal 18, no. 2 (January 1901): 19.

28. S. S. Stewart's Banjo and Guitar Journal 1, no. 5 (September 1, 1882): 4. It is interesting to note that in this period Fairbanks and Cole did not chase endorsements as Stewart did; their ads, while well-written and witty, did not include lists of players.

29. Price List of S. S. Stewart's Parlor[,] Concert[,] and Orchestra Banjos ([Philadelphia: S. S. Stewart, ca. 1887]), which, in addition to Huntley's, has full-page woodcuts of and endorsements by such other well-known players as J. E. Henning, John H. Lee, and Horace Weston; New York Clipper, 25 April 1891.

30. S. S. Stewart, The Banjo! A Disserta-

tion, 3d ed. (Philadelphia, S. S. Stewart, 1894), 116.

31. In his *Old Slack's Reminiscence and Pocket History of the Colored Profession* (1892; reprint, Bowling Green, Ohio: Popular Press, 1974), the African American "Banjo Comique" Ike Simond lists by name over a dozen other black banjoists in the minstrel profession; see pp. 24–25. Two particularly important ones were the Bohee Brothers, James (1844–97) and George (1857–1930), who like Weston were instrumental in extending interest in the banjo. Associated first with Haverly's Colored Minstrels, by the 1890s they had settled in England, where they were lionized as performers and instructors. See Robert F. Winans and Elias J. Kaufman, "Minstrel and Classic Banjo: American and English Connections," *American Music* 12, no. 1 (Spring 1994): 13–14.

32. Clarence L. Partee, "Thirty Years of the Banjo in America, 1879–1909," *Banjo-Mandolin-Guitar* 7 (February 1910): 77.

33. "Plain Facts!," 3; *S. S. Stewart's Banjo and Guitar Journal* 1, no. 9 (January 1, 1883): 4.

34. [S. S. Stewart], *The Black Hercules; or, The Adventures of a Banjo Player* ([Philadelphia: S. S. Stewart], 1884). This ephemeral item has twenty-six double-column pages, with several woodcuts of Weston, Stewart, and others prominent in the banjo world.

35. *S. S. Stewart's Banjo and Guitar Journal* 7, no. 2 (June/July 1890): 1–2, reprinted in *Tuckahoe Review* 1, no. 2 (Spring 1997): 2–3, 13, 15. This is a letter sent to Stewart by the San Francisco banjoist and maker, Charles Morrell, who reports in some detail on what the contestants were asked to play and how the contest was judged. The competition was won by Charles Plummer, who edged out the well-known Picayune Butler. For a very early notice of such a contest, see plate 1-6.

36. *S. S. Stewart's Banjo and Guitar Journal* 2, no. 1 (May 1883): 2.

37. Ibid., no. 2 (June 1883): 2.

38. S. S. Stewart, *The Banjo! A Dissertation* (Philadelphia: S. S. Stewart, 1888), 83–84.

39. S. S. Stewart, *The Banjo Philosophically: A Lecture* (Philadelphia: S. S. Stewart, 1886), 1, 9. Subsequent references to this work in this section are given parenthetically in the text.

40. *S. S. Stewart's Banjo and Guitar Journal* 5, no. 4 (October/November 1888): 2.

41. Stewart, *The Banjo!*, 6.

42. According to Stewart (*Banjo Philosophically*, 5), German silver was an alloy composed of copper, nickel, and zinc "in various proportions, according to what it is intended to be used for." In other words, one had to know what kind of German silver to procure specifically for banjo rims. Sometimes called "white silver," he added, or "argentan," it took a fine polish and "may be nickel-plated, so as to retain a high finish for years."

43. See, for example, *The Troy Directory for the Year 1873* (Troy, N.Y.: Sampson, Davenport, 1873), 59, 242.

44. See Rice, *Monarchs of Minstrelsy*, 142, for a biographical notice of Clarke.

45. *New York Clipper*, 25 April 1891.

46. Stewart, *The Banjo!*, 10. Subsequent references to this work in this section are given parenthetically in the text.

47. *S. S. Stewart's Banjo and Guitar Journal* 5, no. 4 (October/November 1888): advertisement, inside front cover.

48. Ibid., 14.

49. In "What the Four Million Bought: Cheap Oil Paintings of the 1880s" (*American Quarterly* 48, no. 1 [March 1996]: 77–109), Saul E. Zalesch observes that in this period "objects of physical property" became "vital status markers." "Correct materialism," he continues, "was central to middle-class existence," for "Victorians

climbed the ladders of social mobility by purchasing appropriate symbols of gentility" (80–81).

50. On the relationship of gentility to consumer culture during this period, see especially John F. Kasson, *Rudeness and Civility: Manners in Nineteenth-Century America* (New York: Hill and Wang, 1990), esp. 41–43 and 257–60.

51. *S. S. Stewart's Banjo and Guitar Journal* 1, no. 9 (January 1, 1883): 2, and 3, no. 10 (August/September 1886): 8.

52. Ibid. 4, no. 4 (June/July 1887): 2. See *Gatcomb's Banjo and Guitar Gazette* 1, no. 2 (November 1887) for a briefer description of another such factory operation, in Boston.

53. *S. S. Stewart's Banjo and Guitar Journal* 4, no. 7 (December 1887/January 1888): 4; and 5, no. 6 (February/March 1889): back cover.

54. Ibid. 14, no. 5 (December 1897/January 1898) for his merger with Bauer. This new business arrangement may have been instigated by the increasing success of the Lyon and Healy Company of Chicago, which by the 1890s was manufacturing an extensive line of guitars and mandolins as well as banjos. For a history of this company, see John Teagle, *Washburn: Over One Hundred Years of Fine Stringed Instruments* (New York: Music Sales Corp., 1996). For a late advertisement for Stewart banjos, see *The Cadenza* 13, no. 9 (May 1907): 52, where potential customers are asked to consider "the Standard of the World," the "Original S. S. Stewart Banjo," issued by Bauer's company.

55. *New York Clipper*, 25 April 1891.

56. See "A Great Instrument Factory," *S. S. Stewart's Banjo, Guitar, and Mandolin Journal* 16, no. 3 (August/September 1899): 7–9.

57. *S. S. Stewart's Banjo and Guitar Journal* 2, no. 6 (November 1883): 7. The cuts were used again in *Catalogue and Price List of S. S. Stewart's Celebrated Banjos* (Philadelphia: S. S. Stewart, [1885]).

58. "A Great Instrument Factory," 7. The following discussion of the factory is taken from this article, which very likely was written by Stewart himself.

59. See, for example, Alfred D. Chandler, *The Managerial Revolution in American Business* (Cambridge, Mass.: Harvard University Press, 1977), 247–49, and also David A. Hounsell, *From the American System to Mass Production, 1800–1932: The Development of Manufacturing Technology in the United States* (Baltimore: Johns Hopkins University Press, 1984), 125–52, who uses the example of the Singer Sewing Machine Company to challenge some of Chandler's conclusions. If we understand the term "machinery" in the way the author of "A Great Instrument Factory" uses it, we see that the chief difference between Stewart's factory and a much larger operation like Buckbee's or Benary's lay not in the degree of mechanization in each (for the technology was basically the same) but in who moved the raw materials through the various steps of the manufacturing process and how quickly they did so.

60. The hiring and retention of quality craftsmen evidently was a matter of some pride in the banjo trade. One of Stewart's Boston competitors, L. B. Gatcomb, for example, announced in his trade journal that he had "recently engaged the services of Mr. Geo. F. Palmer, one of Boston's finest banjo makers." The addition of this man to his "already large corps of finished workmen," he continued, made his "facilities for turning out high grade work most complete" (*Gatcomb's Banjo and Guitar Gazette* 2, no. 2 [November/December 1888]: 4).

61. See, for example, "All About the Banjo" for descriptions of Stewart's early instruments. His mention of his curing the skin heads is tantalizing, for it suggests that some banjo makers bought the raw

skins from slaughterhouses or tanneries and then finished them in their own shops. Unfortunately, we have unearthed no further information on this subject.

62. "Plain Facts!," [5]; "How to Order Banjos," [2].

63. By neck length Stewart meant the distance from the nut at the top of the instrument to where the neck met the rim. Thus, it is not the same as the fret "scale" (double the distance from the nut to the twelfth-fret [i.e., the octave] position), now the more common way of calculating neck length.

64. Price List, [5]. See the illustrations in Akira Tsumura, Banjos: The Tsumura Collection (New York and Tokyo: Kodansha International, 1984), 94–99, for illustrations of some of these instruments, and, as well, Akira Tsumura, 1001 Banjos (New York and Tokyo: Kodansha International, 1993), 163–226.

65. See S. S. Stewart's Extra Fine Banjos ([Philadelphia: S. S. Stewart, 1896]) for the descriptions of his full line of banjos. These included the eight-inch Pony Concert (with a twelve-inch neck), the nine-inch Lady Stewart, and the ten-inch American Princess, in addition to other of the sizes mentioned below. Some of this information is summarized in Kaufman's article on Stewart banjos in Mugwumps 2, no. 4 (July 1973): 15–16.

66. See Tsumura, 1001 Banjos, 172–85, for examples of Stewart's presentation-grade fretless banjos.

67. Price List, [6].

68. See, for example, [C. Bruno and Son], Descriptive Price List . . . C. Bruno and Son . . . Importers and Wholesalers in Musical Instruments (New York: Wynkoop and Hallenbeck, 1874), 15, and Herman Sonntag, Catalogue of Musical Instruments (New York: Root, Anthony, 1872), 34.

69. Catalogue and Price-List [of] S. S. Stewart's Celebrated Banjos (Philadelphia: S. S. Stewart, [1894]), 16, where Stewart notes that readers of his Banjo and Guitar Journal and the New York Clipper would know that it was first advertised in 1886 and that he introduced it "long before that time at the NOVELTIES EXHIBITION of the Franklin Institute, Philadelphia." Further, in Stewart's Extra Fine Banjos, 12, Stewart noted that he "first introduced and named" the banjeaurine in 1885.

70. Stewart, Banjo Philosophically, 7.

71. Thomas J. Armstrong, "Banjo, Mandolin and Guitar Orchestras," S. S. Stewart's Banjo and Guitar Journal 12, no. 3 (August/September 1895): 24. Also see Gatcomb's Banjo and Guitar Gazette 4, no. 4 (March/April 1891): 2, where the editor provides instructions on how to organize a banjo club.

72. S. S. Stewart's Banjo and Guitar Journal 4, no. 7 (December 1887/January 1888): 2.

73. Catalogue and Price-List, [11], and Stewart, Banjo Philosophically, 7. At p. 15 of the Catalogue Stewart listed a similar banjeaurine, though with an eleven-and-a-half-inch rim, for "ladies' use."

74. Stewart's Extra Fine Banjos, 12.

75. Ibid., 20–21, for a complete description of these unusual banjos.

76. Armstrong, "Banjo Orchestras," 24. Often these groups included mandolins and guitars. In his article Armstrong took it upon himself to provide more "accurate and methodical rules for forming these organizations," indicating how many of each kind of banjo and how many mandolins and guitars one should have to play duets, trios, quartets, quintets, sextets, septets, and octets. A sextet, for example, could consist of two banjeaurines, one first banjo, two guitars, and one second banjo, or two banjeaurines, one first banjo, one piccolo banjo, and two guitars.

77. This is not to say, however, that the banjo was ever fully accepted by those for

whom European opera and symphony, performed with traditional instrumentation, still defined "high" culture. See Lawrence Levine, *Highbrow/Lowbrow: The Emergence of Cultural Hierarchy in America* (Cambridge, Mass.: Harvard University Press, 1988), for an illuminating discussion.

78. See Teagle, *Washburn*, esp. 16–20, 25. Teagle notes (95–97) that Lyon and Healy were slow in adding the banjo to their line, at first serving as agents for the Dobson Silver Bell instruments and offering lower-grade instruments of their own for as little as $2 (for a wooden rim, tackhead instrument). In the early 1890s, however, they developed their Professional line, which rivaled Stewart's banjos in beauty and sophistication.

79. *Stewart's Extra Fine Banjos*, 3.

80. U.S. patent no. 264,893, 26 September 1882.

81. U.S. patent no. 269,178, 19 December 1882.

82. U.S. patent no. 210,906, 20 January 1885. Other patents were equally bizarre. See, for example, that of Hercules McCord of St. Louis, U.S. patent no. 283,352, 14 August 1883, discussed in Chapter 4.

83. U.S. patent no. 262,564, 15 August 1882.

84. U.S. patent no. 315,135, 7 April 1885.

CHAPTER FOUR

1. Carter (b. 1834) is unusual among the early minstrels in having come from the Deep South; he was born in St. Bernard Parish, Louisiana, in 1834. See Edward LeRoy Rice, *Monarchs of Minstrelsy: From "Daddy" Rice to Date* (New York: Kenney Publishing Company, 1911), 94. Also see *Billy Carter's Great Banjo Solo Songster* (New York: A. T. Fisher, 1873), with a lithographed cover of Carter in blackface. An-

other banjoist and maker associated with Boston but whose father "was in the antebellum days a plantation owner in the South" was George Florence (1836–95). After "business reverses swept away" his father's property, the family moved to New York City, where young George learned "thimble-style playing." See *Gatcomb's Banjo and Guitar Gazette* 7, no. 2 (October 1893): 2.

2. "The Banjo Craze," *Gatcomb's Banjo and Guitar Gazette* 1, no. 3 (January 1888): 2, reprinting an article from a local newspaper, the *Boston Herald*.

3. Biographical facts about Gatcomb can be gleaned from "L. B. Gatcomb," *The Cadenza* 2, no. 1 (September/October 1895): 2; Christine Merrick Ayars, *Contributions to the Art of Music in America by the Music Industries of Boston, 1640–1936* (New York: H. W. Wilson, 1937), 74, 83, 228, 276; and James F. Bollman, "The Banjomakers of Boston," in *Ring the Banjar! The Banjo in America from Folklore to Factory*, ed. Robert Lloyd Webb (Cambridge, Mass.: MIT Museum, 1984), 44–45. See *Gatcomb's Banjo and Guitar Gazette* 1, no. 2 (November 1887): 1, for a notice about his purchase of Bryant's journal. Gatcomb's periodical ran from September 1887 at least through October 1899, the last issue that we have seen. In 1894 he changed its name to *Gatcomb's Musical Gazette*. In 1890 J. E. Henning, a Chicago maker, issued a few numbers of another journal, *Henning's Elite Banjo, Guitar, and Mandolin News*. Gatcomb commented that he looked "in vain for any news in it," though, for its columns were "pretty much made up of articles covering their new banjos"; see *Gatcomb's Banjo and Guitar Gazette* 4, no. 2 (November/December 1890): 3.

4. See Chapter 3.

5. In an article in his journal entitled "The Banjo Boom," Stewart pointed out this noticeable rise in the popularity of all

stringed instruments. Just as "all intelligent and cultivated people know that banjo is the fashionable and popular instrument of the present and rising generation," so, too, there was renewed interest in the guitar. "The banjo has made it so," he continued, for "one instrument helps along the other, and hand in hand they go, like brother and sister" (*S. S. Stewart's Banjo and Guitar Journal* 1, no. 8 [December 1, 1882]: 1).

6. Although during his lifetime Stewart's rivalry with other makers was intense and sometimes heated, after his unexpected death there came acknowledgment of his immense significance to banjo culture. See, for example, Stewart's obituary by the music publisher C. L. Partee ("Death of S. S. Stewart," *The Cadenza* 4, no. 5 [May/June 1898]: 11), who observed that Stewart "did great work in the interests of the banjo and always devoted the best efforts of which he was capable to the advancement of the instrument."

7. Beginning in February 1900, in *S. S. Stewart's Banjo and Guitar Journal*, Morris presented his plan for such an organization for teachers, players, and manufacturers of stringed instruments, and in the issue for June 1 he printed a draft constitution for all interested parties to discuss. The October issue carried a formal announcement of the formation of the American Guild and a "contract" for prospective members. See vol. 17, no. 3 (February 1900); 17, no. 7 (June 1900); and 18, no. 2 (October 1900). The quotation comes from the preamble to the draft constitution.

8. In a 1914 article in *The Crescendo*, the official journal of the American Guild, the eminent banjoist Thomas J. Armstrong listed those whom he considered to be the most prominent contemporary makers. In addition to firms in Boston, New York, and Philadelphia, he noted makers in Brooklyn, Chicago, Milwaukee, Portland (Maine),

and several other places. See *The Crescendo* 7, no. 2 (August 1914): 20.

9. See Chapter 1 for notice of the earliest makers associated with Boston. *The Boston Directory, Embracing the City Record, General Directory of Citizens, and a Business Directory for 1869* (Boston: Sampson, Davenport, 1869), 816; *The Boston Directory . . . for 1872* (Boston: Sampson, Davenport, 1872), 854; and *The Boston Directory . . . for 1876* (Boston: Sampson, Davenport, 1876), 1054.

10. "Early Days of the Banjo, by An Old Timer," *The Cadenza* 1, no. 2 (November/December 1894): 5.

11. Fairbanks's biography can be pieced together from an obituary in *The Cadenza* 26, no. 3 (November 1919): 28; Ayars, *Contributions*, 275; Bollman, "Banjomakers," 37–42; Elias J. Kaufman, "The Fairbanks and Vega Companies," *Mugwumps* 6, no. 2 (Spring 1978): 18–20; and James F. Bollman, Dick Kimmel, Doug Unger, "Vega/Fairbanks Banjos: A History," *Pickin'* 5, no. 5 (June 1978): 26–38.

12. See Cole's obituary in *The Cadenza* 15, no. 12 (August 1909): 25; Walter Vreeland, "William A. Cole," *The Crescendo* 2, no. 2 (August 1909): 12–13; Ayars, *Contributions*, 192, 228, 275; and Bollman, "Banjomakers," 37, 42–44.

13. The controversy is found in the *New York Clipper* between 4 December 1880 and 22 January 1881; no week passed without one or the other answering the previous week's provocation.

14. *S. S. Stewart's Banjo and Guitar Journal* 5, no. 1 (April/May 1888): 2. In this same issue (p. 13) Stewart also inveighed against his Boston competitors for their claim to have originated certain metal attachments that braced the dowel against the rim. Complete with cuts of his own similar hardware, Stewart made his case sound convincing.

15. U.S. patent no. 306,731, 21 October

1884, for a "case for banjos and other instruments." U.S. patent no. 322,054, 14 July 1885, for a "peg supporting device for banjos."

16. U.S. patent no. 327,779, 6 October 1885.

17. As early as 1882, for example, Oliver Chase of Boston offered a rim made of a single piece of metal, which he thought would "increase the sonorousness and resonance" of the banjo's tone (U.S. patent no. 269,178, 19 December 1882). And Thomas Williams of Brooklyn made a banjo with a dome-shaped rim and a removable wooden back (U.S. patent no. 288,905, 20 November 1883). Like many other instruments in this decade of experimentation, neither of these banjos caught the public's attention.

18. See Edmund A. Bowles, "Nineteenth-Century Innovations in the Use and Construction of Tympani," *Journal of the American Musical Instrument Society* 5–6 (1980): 74–143. U.S. patent no. 283,352, 14 August 1883; U.S. patent no. 296,596, 8 April 1884. See the discussion of McCord banjos in Laurence Libin, *American Musical Instruments in the Metropolitan Museum of Art* (New York: Norton, 1985), 114–16, with pictures of these unusual instruments at p. 115.

19. U.S. patent no. 312,457, 17 February 1885.

20. U.S. patent no. 360,005, 29 March 1887. We should recall that as early as the 1860s James Ashborn had devised a way to obviate drilling through the rim to secure the hooks, in his case having them go through a bracket band that was glued to the outer middle of the rim. Fairbanks would late revisit such a design in his assembly of the Whyte Laydie banjo.

21. In this section we quote from [Fairbanks and Cole], *Le Grande Imperial Banjos, and the Acme Banjos and Banjorines* (Boston: Fairbanks and Cole, [1889]), a twenty-four-page catalog illustrating their full line of instruments.

22. Fairbanks and Cole did not claim that the fingerboard extension per se was their "invention," for it has been used "from time immemorial" on violins, guitars, and other stringed instruments. Of course, Stewart had put such an extension on his banjeaurines, but Fairbanks and Cole were technically correct in claiming that it was new "as applied to the banjo by us." Some Dobson instruments had a metal plate at the base of the neck that extended over the rim a bit. Fairbanks and Cole claimed that such construction was more an "obstruction" than an improvement, for it caused "a loss of clear notes in the higher register." See *Le Grande Imperial Banjos*, [12].

23. U.S. patent no. 349,308, 21 September 1886.

24. See, for example, *The Artists' Prize Collection. No. 1. Fairbanks and Cole's First Grand Prize Banjo Music Competition* (Boston: Fairbanks and Cole, [1885]).

25. See Bollman, "Banjomakers of Boston," 38–40. Fairbanks family tradition points to a personal falling out between the two men over a family heirloom (a pewter charger linked to the *Mayflower*) that Fairbanks had taken to the shop for repair and that was stolen. Lucy Toohey, interview by James F. Bollman, Quincy, Massachusetts, September 1990.

26. U.S. patent no. 443,510, 30 December 1890. See Michael I. Holmes, "Vega Banjo Tone Rings," *Mugwumps* 6, no. 1 (Winter 1977): 20.

27. The banjo did not use electricity but was so named because electricity was one of the defining inventions—and metaphors—of the age.

28. *Gatcomb's Musical Gazette* 8, no. 3 (December 1894): 4. With this notice, Fairbanks began to advertise regularly in Gatcomb's publication. He had not done so previously, nor had Fairbanks and Cole.

29. The designations of the Fairbanks models, however, were even more complex.

Many early Electrics were simply marked Electric and sometimes stamped twice. They were mostly fairly plain banjos with full-spun rims. The first Curtis Electric was serial no. 872, and all of these models had full-spun rims. The first Imperial Electrics were serial nos. 1376 and 1741, and both were very fancy custom models with half-spun rims. Further, all half-spun pots we have seen have upside-down scalloped tone rings, but we have also found full-spun pots with the rings in that position as well as right side up. The first Special Electric designation came fairly late, serial no. 15942. Finally, to complicate matters more, both Imperial and Special Electrics have been seen with both types of tone rings, as have Whyte Laydies, but the upside-down rings generally are on very early models.

30. Several other Boston makers, whom we discuss below, issued comparably decorated presentation-grade banjos. This suggests that there was a small cadre of pearl engravers who worked among the major companies in that city. Rarely is such engraving found on Stewart's instruments, nor on those made by the various companies in New York City, and never with the execution of the Boston makers.

31. It is unclear if these rims were made by Fairbanks, but they may be variations of a design he patented in 1893 (U.S. patent no. 489,470, 10 January 1893), in which the inside and outside were spun, with the "trusses" that marked the Electric now part of the interior of the rim. Also, some of the hooks, nuts, and shoes were the same as those used on Fairbanks products.

32. See *J. W. Pepper's Illustrated Catalogue and Price List of Musical Instruments* (Philadelphia: J. W. Pepper, 1893), 110, and Bollman, "Banjomakers of Boston," 40–41.

33. U.S. patent no. 928,948, 27 July 1909. This suggests that Day was in fact the one who had developed this novel man-ner of mounting the shoes. We should also recall, however, that since the mid-1880s Fairbanks had focused on different ways to hang the hooks, including one in his patent of 1887, mentioned above. Also, in light of Fairbanks's neglect of patent protection, we note that shortly after he began to ship the Whyte Laydie to England, the prominent English maker Clifford Essex began to make his own version of it, which, except for rim hardware, was remarkably like the American original, down to the tone ring and bracket band.

34. After a long career with Vega, in 1922 Day joined Fred Bacon, another banjo designer and maker with ties to Fairbanks, to form the company of Bacon and Day. On Day see *The Cadenza* 29, no. 2 (October 1922): 24–5, and Akira Tsumura, *Banjos: The Tsumura Collection* (Tokyo: Kodansha International, 1984), 16.

35. *Fairbanks Banjos, Mandolins, Guitars, Strings and Sundries* (Boston: Vega Company, [1906]), [5–6].

36. Beginning with volume 8 (1901–2), for several years virtually every issue of *The Cadenza* carried on its back cover a prominent advertisement for the Whyte Laydie. This important periodical was started in Kansas City, Missouri, in 1894 (vol. 1, no. 1 is the September/October issue) by Clarence L. Partee, who in 1900 moved the operations to New York City. In May 1908 the journal was bought by the Boston publisher Walter Jacobs, and beginning with the July number in that year it was issued from Boston until its last number, in 1924. Jacobs claimed to have printed 10,000 copies for his first issue and then had to raise it to 17,500.

37. [C. L. Partee], "The Trade Department," *The Cadenza* 8, no. 12 (August 1902): 42.

38. This unusual name may derive from the great excitement caused by a total solar eclipse on 1 January 1889, an astro-

nomical event that attracted much attention, both popular and scientific. Further, another astronomical reference, the shooting star and crescent moon on one model's peg head, may have originated in the sighting of a highly visible comet in 1893, about the time that Cole patented his tone ring. See, for example, Henry Smith Pritchett, *The Total Eclipse of the Sun, January 1, 1889: . . . A Report of the Observations Made by the Washington University Eclipse Party, at Norman, California* (Cambridge, Mass.: J. Wilson and Son, 1891).

39. U.S. patent no. 513,761, 30 January 1894. Cole initially applied for the patent on 30 March of the previous year. Many Eclipse models from the early 1890s carry the stamp "pat. appl'd for" on the dowel stick beside William A. Cole's name as "Maker." Frank Cole also patented his design for the Imperial mandolin (U.S. patent no. 452,465, 19 May 1891), which featured an improved way to connect the ribs of the instrument without using paper or tape for reinforcement. Cole claimed that with his new method one could use thinner wood for the ribs and thus improve the resonance of the instrument.

40. See, for example, *The Cadenza* 1, no. 2 (November/December 1894): 12.

41. *The Cadenza* 7, no. 10 (June 1901): inside cover.

42. On this wood "dryer," see Cole's ad on the inside cover of *The Cadenza* 7, no. 8 (April 1906).

43. See *Music-Dealers' Guide Book, Being a Comprehensive Catalog of Musical Merchandise for the Trade Only* (Boston: Oliver Ditson, [1906]), 173–77.

44. See Bollman, "Banjomakers of Boston," 43; these attributions are through instruments we have seen with these labels but which obviously were manufactured by Cole.

45. C. L. Partee, "Trade Department," *The Cadenza* 9, no. 1 (September 1902): 42.

46. Ayars, *Contributions*, 275, for the sale of the firm to Nokes and Nicolai, and 272, on that firm's drum making.

47. Frank Cole's obituary is in *The Cadenza* 29, no. 1 (September 1922): 32. In the early twentieth century Cole touted a new bridge arrangement, which carried two of these five-footed bridges, developed and patented by the Boston music instructor P. H. Foley (U.S. patent no. 752,664, 23 February 1904). The two bridges were supposed to divide the strain and pressure, yielding longer vibrations and a clear, firmer tone. They were marketed at twenty-five cents a pair. See *The Cadenza* 9, no. 2 (October 1902): inside cover, where Cole advertises "Two Cole Bridges on a Banjo" and indicates that the company is "indebted" to Foley for the idea.

48. See *Gatcomb's Banjo and Guitar Gazette* 2, no. 6 (July/August 1889): 1, for Gatcomb's description of his new factory. He noted that prior to their move, "there have been times when we could not supply the demand, but this removal leaves a greatly enlarged space." With such "increased facilities" he was confident that he could "keep up with the call."

49. See the article on the Boston Ideal Banjo, Mandolin and Guitar Club in *Gatcomb's Banjo and Guitar Gazette* 1, no. 1 (September 1887): 4.

50. *Gatcomb's Banjo and Guitar Gazette* 2, no. 5 (May/June 1889): 4.

51. H.W.P., "What A Contributor Says of the Banjo," *Gatcomb's Banjo and Guitar Gazette* 1, no. 2 (November 1887): 1; and "Grace Notes," ibid. 2, no. 4 (March/April 1889): 2.

52. See the advertisement in *Gatcomb's Musical Gazette* 11, no. 10 (June 1897), and *Net Price List . . . The Gatcomb Banjo . . . The Lansing Banjo . . . The Gatcomb Mandolin* (Boston: L. B. Gatcomb, [1894]).

53. U.S. patent no. 476,083, 31 May 1892.

54. U.S. patent no. 448,674, 24 March 1891. We also note that Fairbanks made Robinson's banjos between about 1901 and 1904. These instruments had superb engraving, equal to that of the Fairbanks instruments around serial no. 22,000, the banjos considered by some to be the most elegant of that firm's creations.

55. *Gatcomb's Musical Gazette* 5, no. 4 (December 1891): 3; U.S. patent no. 448,674, 24 March 1891.

56. *Gatcomb's Musical Gazette* 11, no. 2 (October 1897): back cover; Ayars, *Contributions*, 276. Ayars erroneously writes that Gatcomb did not make instruments after 1895 but rather concentrated on his music publishing. Again, through at least the fall of 1897 he still was doing both.

57. Notice from *The Metronome*, in *Gatcomb's Musical Gazette* 9, no. 5 (January 1895): 3, and another, from the *Washington Press*, reprinted in *Gatcomb's Banjo and Guitar Gazette* 3, no. 1 (September/October 1889): 2.

58. *The Boston Directory, Embracing the City Record, General Directory of Citizens, and a Business Directory for 1874* (Boston: Sampson, Davenport, 1874), 1078; *The Boston Directory . . . for 1875* (Boston: Sampson, Davenport, 1875), 1054.

59. On Thompson and Odell, see Ayars, *Contributions*, 22, 27. Also see *The Cadenza* 8, no. 6 (February 1902): 21, and *The Crescendo* 2, no. 3 (September 1909): 10–11, both articles devoted to Odell. Odell assumed the presidency of the American Guild in 1902. Very little is known about Thompson. On the younger Odell, see *The Cadenza* 8, no. 7 (March 1902): 14; *S. S. Stewart's Banjo and Guitar Journal* 18, no. 3 (February 1901): 15; and his obituary, *The Crescendo* 27, no. 10 (April 1926): 24–25. Herbert had been trained as a pianist at the New England Conservatory and the Tremont School of Music and also had studied violin and voice. From 1890 on he directed

the Euterpe Mandolin and Banjo Club, a highly regarded group that toured Europe in 1895, and was an accomplished mandolin soloist. In the early twentieth century he composed many numbers for the mandolin and also wrote studies for the instrument.

60. See, for example, the advertisement in *Gatcomb's Banjo and Guitar Gazette* 1, no. 5 (May/June 1888): supplement, 3.

61. U.S. patent no. 301,832, 8 July 1884.

62. U.S. patent no. 388,781, 28 August 1888. Thompson and Odell had advertised this banjo as early as March in *Gatcomb's Musical Gazette* 1, no. 4 (March 1888).

63. U.S. patent no. 504,810, 12 September 1893.

64. *Gatcomb's Musical Gazette* 10, no. 10 (June 1897): 16.

65. *Catalogue and Price List of Luscomb Banjos . . . Manufactured by Thompson and Odell* (Boston: Thompson and Odell, 1897).

66. Bollman, "Banjomakers of Boston," 50. During this time Odell also published a number of tutors for mandolin; see, for example, his *Method for the Mandolin*, 4 vols. in 2 (Boston: Oliver Ditson, 1906–8), and *The Mandolin Orchestra: A Book for Directors, Managers, Teachers and Players* (Boston: H. F. Odell, [1913]).

67. See Ayars, *Contributions*, 28–35; Russell Sanjek, *American Popular Music and Its Business: The First Four Hundred Years*, vol. 2, *From 1790 to 1909* (New York: Oxford University Press, 1988), 107–11; and William Arms Fisher, *Notes on Music in Old Boston* (Boston: Oliver Ditson, 1918). It was Ditson, we recall, who bought out his rival, Elias Howe Jr., in 1850 (see Chapter 2).

68. See Sanjek, *American Popular Music*, 2:109.

69. Ayars, *Contributions*, 30, 265.

70. Sanjek, *American Popular Music*, 2:376; Fisher, *Music in Old Boston*, 40, 73–74, 77; and Michael I. Holmes, "John C.

Haynes Company," *Mugwumps* 4, no. 2 (1975): 16–18.

71. See, for example, *Gatcomb's Banjo and Guitar Gazette* 2, no. 2 (November/December 1888): 8. Hyde (b. 1842) made fine violins in Northampton, Massachusetts; see Karel Jalovec, *Encyclopedia of Violin Makers*, 2 vols. (London: Paul Hamlyn, 1968), 1:423.

72. Bollman, "Banjomakers of Boston," 46, information based on an interview with Ernest A. Anderberg, Pehr's son, cited in Ayars, *Contributions*, 274–75. Anderberg trained many prominent guitar makers, including C. A. Sundberg and John Swenson, two early principals of the Vega Company. After he left Haynes, from his shop in Chelsea, Massachusetts, Anderberg made instruments for August Pollman and Son of New York, who marketed a unique mandoline-banjo, which had a five-string banjo neck mounted on a tear-drop shaped, flat-back mandolin body. When he lost his shop in a large fire, Anderberg moved to Philadelphia to work for Stewart and Bauer; following Stewart's death he returned to Boston, where Haynes again employed him, this time as chief repairman.

73. See, for example, *The Banjo Player's Problem* [Boston: John C. Haynes, 1897] and *Columbian Musical Gift and Keepsake Presented by John C. Haynes and Co.* [Boston: John C. Haynes, ca. 1889], both of which contain cuts of the entire Bay State line.

74. *John C. Haynes and Co.* ([Boston: Oliver Ditson], 1895), 18. Advertisement also illustrated in Bollman, "Banjomakers of Boston," 47.

75. Sanjek, *American Popular Music*, 2:370–71.

76. U.S. patents no. 269,178, 19 December 1882, for the novel rim design, and no. 305,148, 16 September 1884, for improvements relating to the tension hoop. Also see Bollman, "Banjomakers of Boston," 42.

77. Bollman, "Banjomakers of Boston," 53.

78. Ibid., 47–48.

79. *Gatcomb's Banjo and Guitar Gazette* 1, no. 2 (November 1887): 3.

80. Ibid. 1, no. 3 (January 1888): 2. This writer also noted that "the star strummers among the men are in demand at the smartest parties, and have the choosing of the society of the most charming girls."

81. George C. Dobson, *Complete Instructor for the Banjo* (Boston: White, Smith, 1880), 3.

82. *S. S. Stewart's Extra Fine Banjos* ([Philadelphia: S. S. Stewart, 1896]), 4.

83. *The Crescendo* 1, no. 1 (July 1908): 1.

CONCLUSION

1. See James F. Bollman, "The Banjomakers of Boston," in *Ring the Banjar!: The Banjo in America from Folklore to Factory*, ed. Robert Lloyd Webb (Cambridge, Mass.: MIT Museum, 1984), 52; Christine Merrick Ayars, *Contributions to the Art of Music in America by the Music Industries of Boston* (New York: H. W. Wilson, 1937), 275.

2. See Bollman, "Banjomakers of Boston," 52–53, and Ayars, *Contributions*, 229–30.

3. Until 1910 Vega continued to use the Fairbanks Company's metal plates (tacked to the dowel) to mark the instruments, but after 1910 they stamped them "FAIRBANKS BANJO BY THE VEGA COMPANY." After 1923 they dropped the Fairbanks name altogether. See Bollman, "Banjomakers of Boston," 52.

4. We have derived our understanding of the history of ragtime primarily from Edward A. Berlin's *Ragtime: A Musical and Cultural History* (Berkeley and Los Angeles: University of California Press, 1980), and John Edward Hasse, ed., *Ragtime: Its History, Composers, Music* (New

York: Schirmer Books, 1985). The quotation here is from Hasse, "Ragtime from the Top," in ibid., 2.

5. Here we are indebted to the seminal essay by Lowell H. Schreyer, "The Banjo in Ragtime," in Hasse, *Ragtime*, 54–69. Also see Hans Nathan, *Dan Emmett and the Rise of Early Negro Minstrelsy* (Norman: University of Oklahoma Press, 1962), 195–213, who also points out similarities between early banjo music and ragtime.

6. Lafcadio Hearn to H. E. Kriebel, 1881, in Elizabeth Bisland, *The Life and Letters of Lafcadio Hearn*, 2 vols. (Boston and New York: Houghton Mifflin, 1906), 1:232.

7. Unless otherwise noted, the information in this paragraph is gleaned from Schreyer, "Banjo in Ragtime," 58.

8. Rudi Blesh and Harriet Janis, *They All Played Ragtime*, 3d ed., rev. (New York: Oak Publications, 1966), 41. Also see Rudi Blesh, "Scott Joplin: Black-American Classicist," in *Scott Joplin: Collected Piano Works*, ed. Vera Brodsky Lawrence (New York: New York Public Library, 1971), xiii–xl, for a good introduction to Joplin.

9. See the reproduction of this cover art in Lawrence, *Scott Joplin*, 19.

10. See Berlin, "The Ragtime Debate," in Hasse, *Ragtime*, 32–60.

11. *S. S. Stewart's Banjo and Guitar Journal* 14, no. 6 (February/March 1891): 5.

12. Stewart's endorser William Huntley, for example, published "Darkie's Cake Walk" in 1896, and C. L. Partee, the publisher of *The Cadenza*, frequently wrote such music; see Schreyer, "Banjo in Ragtime," 61.

13. See David A. Jasen, *Recorded Ragtime, 1897–1958* (Hampden, Conn.: Archon Books, 1973), 9. Evidently, early sound engineers could more easily record banjo music than they could music from the piano.

14. See Robert Lloyd Webb, "Confidence and Admiration: The Enduring Ringing of the Banjo," in Webb, *Ring the Banjar!*, 24.

15. See, for example, Cecelia Conway, *African Banjo Echoes in Appalachia: A Study of Folk Traditions* (Knoxville: University of Tennessee Press, 1995); Art Rosenbaum, *Old-Time Mountain Banjo* (New York: Oak Publications, 1968); and Cherill P. Heaton, "The Five-String Banjo in North Carolina," *Southern Folklore Quarterly* 35, no. 1 (1971): 62–82.

16. See Bill Malone, *Country Music, U.S.A.: A Fifty-Year History* (Austin: University of Texas Press, 1968), 3–78.

17. Neil V. Rosenberg, *Bluegrass: A History* (Urbana: University of Illinois Press, 1985); Robert C. Cantwell, *Bluegrass Breakdown: The Making of the Old Southern Sound* (Urbana: University of Illinois Press, 1984).

18. See Malone, *Country Music, U.S.A.*, and *Southern Music, American Music* (Lexington: University of Kentucky Press, 1979).

19. For brief descriptions of these and other companies and elegant photographs of their various models, see Akira Tsumura, "Banjos of the Jazz Age," in *Banjos: The Tsumura Collection* (Tokyo and New York: Kodansha International, 1984), 11–82, and *1001 Banjos* (Tokyo and New York: Kodansha International, 1993).

SELECTED BIBLIOGRAPHY

Adler, Thomas. "The Physical Development of the Banjo." *New York Folklore Quarterly* 28 (September 1972): 187–208.

Ayars, Christine Merrick. *Contributions to the Art of Music in America by the Music Industries of Boston, 1640–1936.* New York: H. W. Wilson, 1937.

Ayers, Joseph W. "The Banjo in 1858: The Early Jazz of Phil Rice." *Tuckahoe Review* 1, no. 2 (Spring 1997): 4, 12–14.

Bailey, Jay. "Historical Origins and Stylistic Development of the Five-String Banjo." *Journal of American Folklore* 85 (1972): 58–65.

Bean, Annemarie, James V. Hatch, and Brooks McNamara, eds. *Inside the Minstrel Mask: Readings in Nineteenth-Century Blackface Minstrelsy.* Hanover, N.H.: Wesleyan University Press, 1996.

Bollman, James F. "The Banjomakers of Boston." In *Ring the Banjar!: The Banjo in America from Folklore to Factory*, edited by Robert Lloyd Webb, 37–54. Cambridge, Mass.: MIT Museum, 1984.

Bollman, James F., Dick Kimmel, and Doug Unger. "Vega/Fairbanks Banjos: A History." *Pickin'* 5, no. 5 (June 1978): 26–38.

Buckley, James. *Buckley's New Banjo Book.* Boston: Oliver Ditson, 1860. Reprint, Bremo Bluff, Va.: Tuckahoe Music, 1996.

———. *Buckley's New Banjo Guide.* New York: C. H. Ditson, 1868.

The Cadenza. Kansas City, 1894–1900; New York, 1900–1908; and Boston, 1908–24.

Cockrell, Dale. *Demons of Disorder: The Early Blackface Minstrels and Their World.* New York: Cambridge University Press, 1997.

Converse, Frank B. *The Banjo and How to Play It.* New York: Dick and Fitzgerald, 1872.

———. *Frank B. Converse's Banjo Instructor without a Master.* New York: Dick and Fitzgerald, 1865.

———. *Frank B. Converse's New and Complete Method for the Banjo with or without a Master.* New York: S. T. Gordon, 1865. Reprint, Bremo Bluff, Va: Tuckahoe Music, 1993.

Conway, Cecelia. *African Banjo Echoes in Appalachia: A Study of Folk Traditions.* Knoxville: University of Tennessee Press, 1995.

Coolen, Michael Theodore. "Senegambian Archetypes of the American Folk Banjo." *Western Folklore* 43 (1984): 112–32.

Dobson, George C. *Complete Instructor for Banjo[,] with an Authentic History of the Instrument.* Boston: White, Smith, 1880.

———. *George C. Dobson's Simplified Method and Thorough School for the Banjo: Two Books in One.* Boston: John F. Perry, 1874.

Epstein, Dena. "The Folk Banjo:
A Documentary History." *Ethnomusicology* 19 (September 1975):
347–71.

———. *Sinful Tunes and Spirituals: Black
Folk Music to the Civil War.* Urbana:
University of Illinois Press, 1977.

Fisher, William Arms. *Notes on Music
in Old Boston.* Boston: Oliver Ditson,
1918.

Gatcomb's Banjo and Guitar Gazette.
Boston, 1887–99.

Groce, Nancy. *Musical Instrument Makers of
New York: A Dictionary of Eighteenth-
and Nineteenth-Century Urban Craftsmen.*
Annotated Reference Works in Music,
no. 4. Stuyvesant, N.Y.: Pendragon
Press, 1991.

Gura, Philip F. "Manufacturing Guitars
for the American Parlor: James
Ashborn's Wolcottville, Connecticut,
Guitar Factory, 1851–1856."
*Proceedings of the American Antiquarian
Society* 104, part 1 (April 1994):
117–55.

Kaufman, Elias J. "The Fairbanks and
Vega Companies." *Mugwumps* 6, no. 2
(Spring 1978): 18–20.

———. "S. S. Stewart Banjos." *Mugwumps*
2, no. 3 (May 1973): 3–4; no. 4 (July
1973): 15–16; no. 5 (September 1973):
3–5; and no. 6 (November 1973): 3–6.

Keeler, Ralph. *Vagabond Adventures.*
Boston: Ticknor and Fields, 1877.

Lhamon, W. T. *Raising Cain: Blackface
Performance from Jim Crow to Hip Hop.*
Cambridge, Mass.: Harvard University
Press, 1998.

Libin, Laurence. *American Musical
Instruments in the Metropolitan Museum
of Art.* New York: W. W. Norton,
1985.

Linn, Karen S. *That Half-Barbaric Twang:
The Banjo in American Popular Culture.*
Urbana: University of Illinois Press,
1991.

Lott, Eric. *Love and Theft: Blackface
Minstrelsy and the American Working
Class.* New York: Oxford University
Press, 1995.

Nathan, Hans. *Dan Emmett and the Rise
of Early Negro Minstrelsy.* Norman:
University of Oklahoma Press, 1962.

Rice, Edward LeRoy. *Monarchs of
Minstrelsy: From "Daddy" Rice to Date.*
New York: Kenney Publishing,
1911.

Rice, Phil. *Phil. Rice's Correct Method for
the Banjo: With or Without a Master.*
Boston: Oliver Ditson, 1858. Reprint,
Bremo Bluff, Va.: Tuckahoe Music,
1998.

Sacks, Howard L., and Judith Rose Sacks.
*Way Up North in Dixie: A Black Family's
Claim to the Confederate Anthem.*
Washington, D.C.: Smithsonian
Institution Press, 1993.

Sanjek, Russell. *American Popular Music
and Its Business: The First Four Hundred
Years.* 3 vols. New York: Oxford
University Press, 1988.

Schreyer, Lowell H. "The Banjo in
Ragtime." In *Ragtime: Its History,
Composers, Music,* edited by John
Edward Hasse, 54–69. New York:
Schirmer Books, 1985.

Soutar, Robert, ed. *A Jubilee of the
Dramatic Life and Incident of Joseph A.
Cave: Manager, Actor, Vocalist.* London:
Thomas Vernon, [1894].

S. S. Stewart's Banjo and Guitar Journal.
Philadelphia, 1882–1902. (After 1898
the name changed to *S. S. Stewart's
Banjo, Guitar, and Mandolin Journal,*
with the last issues published in New
York City.)

Stewart, S[amuel] S[waim]. *The Banjo! A
Dissertation.* Philadelphia: S. S. Stewart,
1888.

———. *The Banjo Philosophically: A
Lecture.* Philadelphia: S. S. Stewart,
1886.

Teagle, John. *Washburn: One Hundred Years of Fine Stringed Instruments.* New York: Music Sales, 1996.

Toll, Robert C. *Blacking Up: The Minstrel Show in Nineteenth-Century America.* New York: Oxford University Press, 1974.

Tsumura, Akira. *Banjos: The Tsumura Collection.* New York and Tokyo: Kodansha International, 1984.

———. *1001 Banjos.* New York and Tokyo: Kodansha International, 1993.

Webb, Robert Lloyd. "Confidence and Admiration: The Enduring Ringing of the Banjo." In *Ring the Banjar!: The Banjo in America from Folklore to Factory,* edited by Robert Lloyd Webb, 1–36. Cambridge, Mass.: MIT Museum, 1984.

———, ed. *Ring the Banjar!: The Banjo in America from Folklore to Factory.* Cambridge, Mass.: MIT Museum, 1984.

Winans, Robert F. "The Folk, the Stage, and the Five-String Banjo." *Journal of American Folklore* 89 (1976): 407–37.

Winans, Robert F., and Elias J. Kaufman. "Minstrel and Classic Banjo: American and English Connections." *American Music* 12 (Spring 1994): 1–30.

Wittke, Carl F. *Tambo and Bones: A History of the American Minstrel Stage.* Durham, N.C.: Duke University Press, 1930.

Woodward, Arthur. "Joel Sweeney and the First Banjo." *Los Angeles County Museum Quarterly* 7, no. 3 (1949): 7–11.

INDEX

References to illustrations are given in *italics*. Books and banjo tutors are indexed by title. Instrument model names are indexed under maker.

Buckley, James, 39, 84, 266
(n. 57), 272 (n. 6); tutor book
by, 38–39, 70, 71, 76, 81–82,
86; and efforts to elevate banjo,
81–82, 85; as banjo instructor,
81–82, 110, 275 (n. 39); innovations of, 271 (n. 5)
Buckley, R. Bishop, 20
Buckley's Minstrels, 153
Buckley's New Banjo Book, 38–39,
70, 71, 76, 81–82
Buckley's Serenaders, 271 (n. 3)
Burrowes, Christopher, 92, 276
(n. 45)

Cabinetmaking, 64, 270 (n. 92).
See also Banjo—makers: cabi-
netmakers as
The Cadenza (periodical), 9, 220,
287 (n. 36)
California, 38, 48
Cammeyer, Alfred: as banjo
maker, 261 (n. 20); zither-banjo
designed by, 6
Carciutto, Carlo, 194
Caribbean, 4, 12–13, 15
Carter, Billy, 191, 284 (n. 1)
Cave, Joseph, 34–37, 36, 49
Chase, Oliver R., 215, 230, 242,
286 (n. 17); patent designs by,
181, 186–87
Chicago, Ill., 107, 139, 183, 192,
233, 238, 246, 285 (n. 8)
Christy's Minstrels. *See* E. P.
Christy's Minstrels
Cincinnati Circus Company, 29
Civil War, 2, 4, 26, 28, 30, 31, 48,
70, 108, 134
Clark, Edmund, 144, 145
Clarke, James W., 48, 162
Clocks: and banjos, *pl. 3-11*
Coes, George H., 31, 34
Cohen, Jacob, 43
Cole, Frank, 220, 227, 288 (n. 47);
and patent for Eclipse banjo
tone ring, 220, 222, 223; as-
sumes control of brother's business, 225; as musician, 225;
innovations by, 225, 288 (n. 47);
and patent design for Imperial
mandolin, 288 (n. 39)
Cole, William A., 8, 139, 192–93;
resists large-scale maunfacture,
192; biography of, 194; tutored
by Dobson, 194; as instructor,
194, 199; and Imperial Quartet
(Mexican Serenaders), 194,
195; as composer, 208; business
locations of, 220, 225; on
improvements to banjo, 222,
224; competes with Fairbanks,
224; as banjo maker for other
companies, 224–25, 242; and
artistry of production, 225,
242; and elevation of banjo,

243; patent designs by, 288
(nn. 38, 39)
—banjo designs, 229–30, 238,
pl. 4-14; Eclipse line, 8, 220,
222, 223, 224–25, 227, 287
(n. 38), 288 (n. 39), *pl. 4-11*,
pl. 4-12, *pl. 4-13*
See also Fairbanks and Cole
Cole Children, 225
Columbian Exhibition. *See*
World's Columbian Exhibition
Complete American Banjo School
(Stewart), 140
Complete Preceptor for the Banjo
(Howe), 38
Connecticut, 5, 39, 43, 65–66, 101
Converse, Frank B., 31, 38, 85, 86,
108, 109, 129, 246, 259 (n. 5),
266 (n. 56), 272 (n. 11), 275
(n. 32); tutor books by, 81,
84–87, 273 (n. 13); biography
of, 84–85; as composer and
arranger, 85; and efforts to ele-
vate banjos, 85; as minstrel, 85;
advocates guitar style, 88; and
banjos made by Buckbee, 107;
creates early banjo magazine,
144
Corbett, Horatio N., 42
Cotton, Ben, 25
Country music, 253
The Crescendo (periodical), 231,
233, 285 (n. 8)
Crouch, Lew, *pl. 4-7*
Crystal Palace Exhibition, 43, 64,
267 (n. 62)

Day, David L., 1, 245, 287
(nn. 33, 34); joins A. C. Fairbanks Company, 212; and
patent for Electric tone ring,
214; patent designs of, 219.
See also Bacon and Day
Devere, Sam, 152
Diamond, John, 18, *pl. 1-3*
Dime Banjo Music Company, 127,
277 (n. 54), 279 (n. 16)
Ditson, Charles, 234
Ditson, Oliver, 233–34, 289
(n. 67); and consolidation of
banjo trade, 234. *See also* Oliver
Ditson and Company; Lyon
and Healy
"Dixey's Land Galop" (song), 20
Dobson, Charles Edgar, 109, 131,
134; criticized by Baur, 107;
and Egyptian banjo, 107; as
player, 110, 116, 130, 154–55;
as instructor, 111, 115; forms
Dobson and Brother, 129–30;
as dealer, 130; patent designs
by, 130, 132
Dobson, Edward Clarendon, 109,
133; criticized by Baur, 107; as
instructor, 109, 130; as player,

130, 155; and Silver Chime
banjos, *pl. 2-12*
Dobson, Frank Prescott, 109,
154; patent designs by, 129; and
debate over technique, 129–30;
forms Dobson and Brother,
129–30; and Harp banjo, 154
Dobson, George Clifton, 3, 6–7,
109, 117, 126, 129, 268 (n. 73);
on African origins of banjo,
11–12; criticized by Baur, 107;
and Victor banjo, 107, 116, 118,
126, 242, 277 (n. 55); patent
designs of, 115; as innovator,
116; as player, 116; as instructor, 116, 126, 275 (n. 39); "simplified method" of, 116–19, 121,
123–24, 126, 140, 248, 277
(n. 54); tutor books by, 116–19,
243; business locations of, 126,
137, 193, 242; and Stewart,
137–38; on history of banjo,
243–44
Dobson, Henry Clay, 6, 101, 109,
109, 129, 134; patent designs
of, 100, 101, 110–15, 111, 113,
114, 276 (n. 45); criticized by
Baur, 108; as instructor, 109;
learns to play from African
Americans in the North, 109;
biography of, 109–10; as player,
110; and guitar style; as innovator, 110, 115; business locations of, 112; and Silver Bell
banjos, 115, 235, 284 (n. 78);
joins brother in business, 130;
and advertising, 144; and Cole,
194
—banjo designs and models,
95, 98, 100, 102, 104, *pl. 2-7*,
pl. 2-8, *pl. 2-9*, *pl. 2-10*, *pl. 2-11*
Dobson and Brother, 129–30
"Dobson's Banjo Magazine," 144
Duncklee, George O., 43
*Duncombe's Ethiopian Songster and
Mississippi Screamer*, 36
Dyer, J. W. *See* J. W. Dyer and
Brother

Eckland, Frank, 154
Edison, Thomas, 248
Eibel, A. F., 242
Eisenbrandt, Heinrich Christian,
64–65
Eleventh Street Opera House, 138
Emerson, Billy, 152
Emmett, Dan, 20, 29–31
England. *See* Banjo: in England
E. P. Christy's Minstrels, 31, 33,
43, 271 (n. 3)
Epiphone, 3
Ethiopian Opera House, 108, 275
(n. 36)
Ethiopian Serenaders, 26